Discovering Medieval Ferns, County Wexford

Discovering Medieval Ferns, County Wexford

Stephen Mandal, Michael Potterton
& Denis Shine

EDITORS

FOUR COURTS PRESS

Typeset in 10.5pt on 13.5pt AdobeGaramondPro by
Carrigboy Typesetting Services for
FOUR COURTS PRESS LTD
7 Malpas Street, Dublin 8, Ireland
www.fourcourtspress.ie
and in North America for
FOUR COURTS PRESS
c/o IPG, 814 N Franklin St., Chicago, IL 60610.

A catalogue record for this title is available from the British Library.

ISBN 978-1-80151-021-9

SPECIAL ACKNOWLEDGMENT

This volume is the result of a partnership between Wexford County Council, the Irish Archaeology Field School and Rediscovering Ancient Connections – The Saints (Ancient Connections), the latter of whom have generously funded this publication through the EU ERDF Ireland–Wales Cross-border Co-operation Programme (2017–2020). Ancient Connections is a cross-border arts, heritage and tourism project linking north Pembrokeshire and north Wexford. The project aims to revive the ancient links between communities in Wexford and Pembrokeshire and hopes to motivate both communities to rediscover their shared heritage while trading knowledge, experience and skills.

Printed in Poland
by L&C Printing Group Kraków

Contents

Illustrations

FIGURES

TABLES

APPENDICES

Abbreviations

ACAS	Aisling Collins Archaeology Services
AD	Anno Domini
AFM	Annals of the Four Masters
AI	Annals of Inisfallen
AMS	accelerator mass spectrometry
aOD	above Ordnance Datum
ATig.	Annals of Tigernach
AU	Annals of Ulster
BC	before Christ
BH	Ballyhoge Formation
BP	before present
bp	bishop
BY	Ballylane Shale Formation
C14	radiocarbon (Carbon 14)
CA	Caradoc Age
CAfv	Caradoc Age felsic volcanics
CAiv	Caradoc Age intermediate volcanics
cal.	calibrated
CCCP	Clone Church Conservation Project
Chron. Scot.	*Chronicon Scotorum*
CIFA	Chartered Institute for Archaeologists
cm	centimetre(s)
D.	diameter
E	excavation
ed.	editor/edited by
EM	electromagnetic (waves)
ESRI	Economic and Social Research Institute
FHP	Ferns Heritage Project
GPR	ground-penetrating radar
GPS	global positioning system
H.	height
ha	hectare(s)
IA	Irish Antiquities (division, NMI)
IAC	Irish Archaeological Consultancy
IAFS	Irish Archaeology Field School
IGAS	Irish Geophysical and Archaeological Services

IRC	Irish Research Council
ISAP	Irish Stone Axe Project
ITM	Irish Transverse Mercator
km	kilometre(s)
L.	length
LCW	Leinster Cooking Ware
m	metre(s)
MA	Master of Arts degree
MFE	Medieval Ferns Experience
MHz	megahertz
MU	Maynooth University
no.	number
NGR	national grid reference
NMI	National Museum of Ireland
NMS	National Monuments Service, OPW
NMS www	NMS online database: https://maps.archaeology.ie/HistoricEnvironment
OA	Oaklands Formation
OD	ordnance datum
OPW	Office of Public Works
OSI	Ordnance Survey Ireland
pers. comm.	personal communication
PhD	doctoral degree
RDO	Research Development Office
repr.	reprint/ed
ser.	series
SMR	Sites and Monuments Record
Th.	thickness
TII	Transport Infrastructure Ireland
trans.	translator/translated by
TVAS	Thames Valley Archaeological Services
UBA	Queens University Belfast (radiocarbon prefix)
UCC	University College Cork
UCD	University College Dublin
UoCD	University of Colorado, Denver
W.	width
WCC	Wexford County Council
WCM	Wexford County Museum
WX	Wexford county

Contributors

SAMUEL S. CHEN is a post-baccalaureate researcher in the Department of Physics at the University of Colorado, Denver, specializing in displaying laser-scanning data via a web browser.

KATE COLBERT is a research fellow who specializes in monasticism and carved stone in the south-east of Ireland, in the University of Galway.

CHRISTIAAN CORLETT is an archaeologist with the National Monuments Service who has published widely on the archaeology and history of Ireland.

GER DOWLING is an independent geophysical surveyor and archaeologist with over twenty years of experience in the design, implementation and management of geophysical survey projects.

IAN DOYLE is an archaeologist and is Head of Conversation at the Heritage Council.

IAN ELLIOTT is an archaeo-geophysical survey and heritage consultant, and a director of Irish Geophysical and Archaeological Surveys.

LAUREN GOODALL-BYRNE is a staff archaeologist with the Irish Archaeology Field School who has been involved in several excavations in Ferns and its environs.

BARRY LACEY is a staff archaeologist with Irish Archaeological Consultancy who specializes in the history and archaeology of Ferns.

ANNE-JULIE LAFAYE is an archaeologist with the National Monuments Service who specializes in religious orders in medieval Europe, especially the mendicant orders in Ireland.

LINDA LYNCH is an archaeologist with the National Monuments Service, having previously worked for over twenty-five years as an independent osteoarchaeologist and archaeologist.

STEPHEN MANDAL is a director of the Irish Archaeology Field School/Irish Heritage School and a founding partner of the Discovering St Aidan's Monastery Project.

CLARE McCUTCHEON is a medieval pottery specialist. She has spent over thirty years analysing pottery from Anglo-Norman excavations in Ireland.

DAVID McILREAVY is a site director with the Irish Archaeological Consultancy.

CATHERINE MacPARTLIN is a member of Ferns Heritage Project, a sub-group of Ferns Community Development Association, who have been instrumental in guiding heritage experiences locally.

TADHG O'KEEFFE is a lecturer, and former head of School, in the School of Archaeology at University College Dublin. He has published widely on the archaeology and history of medieval Ireland.

DANIEL O'MEARA is a freelance archaeologist and photographer who has worked around the world, but most extensively in Ireland and the Orkneys. Dan joined the Irish Archaeology Field School in 2021.

MICHAEL POTTERTON is a lecturer in the Department of History at Maynooth University. He has published widely on the archaeology and history of medieval Ireland.

MICHAEL 'BODHI' ROGERS is chair of the Physics Department at the University of Colorado, Denver. He is a registered professional archaeologist who has led several 3D scanning projects in Ireland.

DENIS SHINE is a director of the Irish Archaeology Field School/Irish Heritage School and a founding partner of the Discovering St Aidan's Monastery Project.

KATE TAYLOR is a Company Director of TVAS Ireland and has excavated extensively across the UK and Ireland for over twenty years. She has published widely on a variety of excavations.

KIMBERLEY TEALE is a Programme Manager with DigVentures. She has much experience as a geophysical surveyor and archaeologist across a range of projects in the UK.

Foreword

> The Romanesque and Gothic architecture of the ecclesiastical ruins, the Celtic crosses, the holy well of its first bishop, the carved and lichened stone of the abbey and the noble remnant of the Anglo-Norman castle all point to the important position that Ferns occupied in the past, and remind us that this ancient site was for many centuries the abode when living, and the resting place when dead, of the ecclesiastic and the soldier.

So wrote Philip Herbert Hore in volume 6 of his *History of the town and county of Wexford* published in 1911.

It is not just Hore's fine prose that is of interest, it is also that he understood Ferns as an ancient power centre in terms of its secular and religious past. The association with the Uí Chennselaig ruling elite seems to be the key process that shaped Ferns from the early Middle Ages onwards and into the later medieval period. During the twelfth-century religious reforms the church most closely aligned with this ruling dynasty was selected as the basis of the new diocese, thereby giving existence to the medieval and modern-day diocese of Ferns. For many it is associated with the figure of Diarmait Mac Murchada who was instrumental in introducing the Anglo-Normans to Ireland. It is a moot point now, but even if the complex power play of the twelfth century had never happened, it was inevitable that Ireland would be drawn more closely to England as its monarchy strengthened through the thirteenth century.

As set out in this volume, there is now a new association that is strong and positive. Previously, the archaeological remains of Ferns received scant reference in scholarly research, but recent work by a new generation, from both archaeological and historical disciplines, has addressed this major gap, and this volume represents a detailed opening statement on the potential of Ferns as a royal and ritual landscape. Irish archaeology has benefited in recent times from research and fieldwork that has given a much-improved understanding of ecclesiastical settlements, their role in past economies and their operation as centres of power and patronage. Through this volume, Ferns is now rightly taking its place in that body of work.

What is equally heartening is that this has been done in partnership with the local community, as evidenced so engagingly by the final chapter below. The degree of collaboration and cooperation in this book shows the power of modern heritage practice to contribute to local communities and to bring people together.

IAN DOYLE
Head of Conservation
The Heritage Council
1 August 2023

Preface

INTRODUCTION

This volume is a key outcome of a four-year partnership between the Irish Archaeology Field School (IAFS), the local community of Ferns, the Ancient Connections[1] project and Wexford County Council. The project, entitled Discovering St Aidan's Monastery, represents a commitment to bring the heritage of St Mary's Abbey and Ferns to life and to afford Irish and international students and visitors, and – equally importantly – the local community, a deeper and more meaningful understanding of what happened here across a 1,500-year period. In so doing, the partnership aims to draw on best-practice archaeological research to highlight the wider heritage story of Ferns in a creative and sustainable manner, thus providing added economic, educational and amenity value to the local community.

Prior to their Ferns research, the IAFS commenced the Digging the Lost Town of Carrig Project in 2018, focused on the excavation of the first recorded Anglo-Norman fortification in Ireland in the Irish National Heritage Park, Ferrycarrig, Co. Wexford (Shine et al. 2019). Ferns was a key fieldtrip location for this project, helping participating students to understand the politics and landscape of Ireland leading up to the arrival of the Anglo-Normans. In the summer of 2019 Ferns Castle was chosen as one of the hosts of a lecture series commemorating 850 years since the arrival in Ireland of the Anglo-Normans. That summer, the IAFS also commenced field research in the town when we collaborated with Michael 'Bodhi' Rogers to document Ferns Castle, St Edan's Cathedral and St Mary's Abbey using 3D laser scanners (ch. 8). That was the start of four years of highly rewarding research and community engagement at Ferns.

The cornerstone of the work of the IAFS in Ferns were the archaeological excavations at St Mary's. As with all IAFS projects, this one was based on an inclusive, partnership model, the underlying ethos of which is that for a project to be successful it must be of clear value to the local community. The involvement of international third-level archaeology students was key to the success of the project, since they provided the main labour and funding pool. Local volunteer participation was also an integral part of each season of excavation and, together with a very active programme of public events, community excavations (including at Clone, a second excavation close to Ferns; ch. 12), archaeology camps and events for children, online courses,

1 Ancient Connections is a heritage, tourism and arts project, funded by the European Union's Ireland–Wales Cross-border Cooperation Programme (2017–20), via the European Regional Development Fund. The cross-border programme links Co. Wexford in Ireland with north Pembrokeshire in Wales, specifically the ancient towns of Ferns and St Davids. The aim is to support rural communities and the local economy, improving cultural offerings and attracting more overseas tourists to both regions.

schools workshops and open days, this ensured fantastic support from the vibrant community of Ferns, in particular from the *Ferns Heritage Project* (FHP) (a sub-group of *Ferns Community Development Association*) and the *Clone Church Conservation Project* (a sub-group of the Ferns Heritage Archive Group).

FERNS

The landscape around Ferns is rich and versatile and there is archaeological evidence for Neolithic, Bronze Age and Iron Age activity in the area (ch. 1). Tradition has it that St Máedóc founded a church there in the late sixth or early seventh century (ch. 2). The local Uí Chennselaig dynasty rose to prominence as the most powerful and influential family in southern Leinster and Ferns was the main residence of the Meic Murchada kings of Leinster during the eleventh and twelfth centuries. Churchmen and other rulers of Ferns appear regularly in the early historical sources – annals, martyrologies, triads and others – usually as a result of the death of a prominent ecclesiastic or secular ruler, battles, massacres, pestilence, raids and attacks by the Vikings. Three versions of the Life of Máedóc survive, while the significance and scale of the early church are reflected, for instance, in the extent of the area enclosed by the surrounding ditches rediscovered in recent years. In 1111, Ferns was selected as one of the five dioceses of Leinster, and fifty years later King Diarmait Mac Murchada established a community of Augustinian canons regular beside the cathedral (ch. 3).

Ferns was MacMurchada's command centre and there he had a castle. He and Ferns both feature prominently in the story of the coming of the Anglo-Normans to Ireland and the demesne and diocese both became exceptionally wealthy. Ferns is a key location in the Irish works of Gerald of Wales (Giraldus Cambrensis) and the Norman-French epic poem known as 'The song of Dermot and the earl'. Notable individuals associated with Ferns in the later Middle Ages include Strongbow, William Marshal, Albin O'Mulloy, John St John, William and Aymer de Valence, Art MacMurrough Kavanagh, John Talbot, Leonard Grey, Thomas Masterson and Fiach MacHugh O'Byrne. Several bishops of Ferns were educated at Oxford and other great universities, and some progressed to very high secular offices. The wealth of the settlement is reflected in the surviving architectural remains and a variety of archaeological discoveries. There are some good examples of Romanesque and Gothic stone carving and the castle chapel is arguably the most impressive in the country. Items imported from overseas – notably western England and south-western France – include building stone, floor tiles, pottery, silk and coins. Among the medieval 'stray' finds (that is to say, those discovered accidentally and outside the context of an archaeological excavation) are a fine example of a rowel spur of thirteenth-century date, a decorated book clasp and a rare type of glazed floor tile. As much as the evidence indicates wealth and prosperity in the late twelfth and thirteenth centuries, the tide clearly turned in the fourteenth. Now the sources refer to unpaid debts, property disputes, prison-breaks, perjury and other crimes. Ferns was captured during the Bruce Wars in 1317 and repeatedly by the Gaelic Irish thereafter. On the one hand, it was key to Anglo-Norman resistance against the Mac Murchada revival while, on the other, it was a primary target for the resurgent Irish. The Black Death left its mark on Ferns too, and in the winter of 1348 its bishop became the latest victim of the plague.

Canons and prebendaries of Ferns were increasingly absent (usually in England) and clerics left behind found themselves embroiled in all sorts of accusations and allegations – several were said to be 'notorious fornicators' and 'open concubinaries'. In due course the bishop transferred the episcopal residence south to Fethard Castle. The sixteenth-century Dissolution of the Monasteries dealt one final knock-out blow to a struggling religious community at Ferns, bringing another chapter to a close. Towards the end of the sixteenth century, Ferns was labelled 'an ancient ruined town' and, a thousand years after the church was founded, the see of Ferns was united with the see of Leighlin. Ferns was not walled, was not on a major river, was not close to the sea and had few of the attributes enjoyed by Wexford town, which would ultimately become the county capital.

The rise and fall of medieval Ferns were part of a precarious rollercoaster ride experienced over the course of a millennium and more. In many respects, Ferns provides a microcosm of Ireland's medieval history and archaeology and, as such, it lends itself well to a case study such as this.

EXCAVATIONS & SURVEYS

Central to field research in the town in the last four years have been the projects coordinated by the IAFS and supported by Ancient Connections. In 2019, the IAFS partnered with the Clone Church Conservation Project to investigate potential enclosures identified at Clone Church, 2.25km south of Ferns, by drone survey during the drought of 2018. The investigations, which comprised geophysical surveys by Ian Elliott followed by targeted community excavations in 2019 and 2021, provided valuable evidence for the form, date and function of the enclosures (ch. 12). Three sets of enclosing ditches measuring *c.*200m, 130m and >45m in diameter respectively were identified, as well as ancillary features such as furrows, post-holes, hearths and pits. At least one of these features, the outermost ditch, continued in use from the early to the later medieval period with the available dating evidence (from pottery and radiocarbon readings) indicating it was finally backfilled in the twelfth century. This differs from dates returned from both the inner ditch of the outer enclosure and the inner enclosure itself, which were backfilled much earlier, sometime between the seventh and ninth centuries. The smallest oval enclosure appears to be even earlier, having been backfilled in the fifth or sixth century, which raises intriguing questions about Clone's antiquity and its relationship with St Aidan's primary monastery at Ferns, founded around the turn of the seventh century.

Development-led archaeological excavations directed by Kate Taylor in 2019 revealed elements of a timber watermill within the ecclesiastical core at Ferns (ch. 11). A major programme of geophysical survey was undertaken in 2021 (across six areas in the town totalling 10 hectares), predominantly to investigate the boundaries of St Aidan's monastery (ch. 8). The surveys were undertaken by Ger Dowling on behalf of the University of Colorado, Denver, in collaboration with the IAFS and local archaeologist Barry Lacey. Coupled with evidence from previous research, including geophysical survey by Dowling for the Monastic Ireland project and excavations by Catherine McLoughlin, these surveys have shed valuable light on the scale, form and extent of the monastic enclosures around Ferns. Further geophysical survey was undertaken by DigVentures in the grounds of St Mary's Abbey, and this provided valuable guidance in determining the locations of excavation cuttings (ch. 10).

The IAFS, with the generous permission of the landowner Patrick Cousins, undertook research excavations over three seasons from 2021 to 2023 at Ferns Demesne townland adjacent to St Mary's Abbey, a recorded monument (WX015-003004-) that forms part of a significant multi-period complex. The excavations were conducted under Ministerial Consent, with a total of six cuttings opened. The purpose of these cuttings was to assess both the early medieval monastery of St Aidan and the later medieval church of St Mary's, specifically investigating if St Mary's had an attached claustral court. While the final season of excavations had not commenced at the time of writing, and post-excavation analysis was on-going, the preliminary findings have already cast new and intriguing light on the two distinct phases of monasticism, the early medieval monastery and, more extensively, the twelfth-century abbey (ch. 8). Radiocarbon dating of the outer enclosure of St Aidan's suggests a seventh- to eighth-century date for the backfilling of this feature. The inner enclosure was most likely constructed in the early medieval period but apparently not backfilled until around the time St Mary's Augustinian abbey was built (1160s). The presence of a claustral court at St Mary's was confirmed, including the likely existence of a northern range and a single wall where a western range would typically stand. The eastern range was examined in the greatest detail and was confirmed as being 5m wide internally, defined by two large 1.25m-wide walls and containing several internal features, including a rough floor surface, burnt deposits and a fire-pit. The east range was laid out after a period of burial in this area of the site, with one of the range walls cutting through a confirmed burial and apparently cutting two more unexcavated graves, raising interesting questions as to the phasing of the church, the burials and the claustral court. The cloistral arcade or ambulatory was not definitively dated, so this will be explored again in subsequent excavations. Based on available artefactual and dating evidence, the ranges are thought to date to the twelfth to fourteenth centuries. A double-aisled structure was also found to have been built over the outer ditch – seemingly in the twelfth to fourteenth century, based on the recovery of datable pottery and a thirteenth-century coin. The double-aisled structure and claustral court appear to have been constructed over the outer and inner early medieval enclosures respectively.

CONCLUSIONS

The research carried out at Ferns and outlined below has generated an impressive array of data, throwing important new light on the history of Ferns and its place in medieval Leinster and Ireland. The new data begs new questions too, and it highlights the need for further research. Through extensive geophysical survey (sometimes followed by targeted excavation), we now have a significant outline of possible sub-surface archaeological activity around both St Mary's Abbey and the town at large, revealing a wealth of anomalies and possible monuments that could repay archaeological investigation in the future. It would be beneficial to extend the surveys into lands that have not been accessible to date, and to conduct additional research in already surveyed areas with alternative methods of geophysical prospection (for example, earth resistance), as this would undoubtedly yield further information. While excavations at St Mary's have answered most of the project's key questions, tantalizing new queries have arisen regarding the scale, form and complexity of the abbey and its relationship with the early monastic enclosures. Furthermore, we know from the geophysical surveys that this field contains a great wealth of multi-period features, which would benefit from a major programme of additional research. Survey and excavation at nearby Clone also addressed many questions while posing a variety of new ones and suggesting future avenues of archaeological enquiry. For example, what was the relationship between Clone and St Aidan's in Ferns? Did Clone have a specific function, related to the main monastery? Was it used as a pilgrimage site? And, as if to remind us that St Aidan ventured into a landscape that had already been inhabited for millennia, the return of a Neolithic date from Clone, together with the presence of one of the only known pieces of passage-tomb art in Wexford, raises captivating questions about Clone's prehistoric significance.

Finally, it is imperative to note that research outlined in this volume focused primarily on excavations and surveys of only three sites – St Mary's, St Aidan's and Clone Church. Notwithstanding their significance, a plethora of other known and potential monuments within Ferns and its hinterland would benefit significantly from similar investigations. The work outlined in this volume highlights how invested the local community is in its heritage, and how motivated they are to preserve and further understand it, while making it accessible to the community and visitors. For example, the programme of lidar survey could be adapted and utilized to benefit the community in telling the story of their town. Whatever future research avenues might be pursued, they should continue in the spirt of cooperation and partnership that has characterized the last four years of archaeological investigations in Ferns. Ultimately, working with the local community will also help give any archaeological research project the best possible chance of a sustainable and long-term future.

ACKNOWLEDGMENTS

The various contributors to the current volume would like to thank the people who helped with their research and fieldwork, and those who provided assistance, information and illustrations for the essays below. Research by the IAFS at Ferns would not be possible without the support of several statutory bodies and universities – as well as partner institutions/organizations and the numerous students who attend every year: thank you for your hard work and good humour! The students have been supervised by wonderful staff (and interns), to whom we offer many thanks for their continued professionalism and enthusiasm. The excavations are actively supported by Ancient Connections and Wexford County Council (WCC). The IAFS gratefully acknowledges the support of these partners in providing partial funding, notably for our community excavations, community outreach and project publications. A special word of thanks is due to Eoghan Greene, manager of the Ancient Connections project in WCC, for his constant encouragement; he has consistently gone 'above and beyond' in his support of this project. The IAFS would also like to acknowledge the support of the National Monuments Service (NMS) and National Museum of Ireland (NMI) in processing efficiently our Ministerial Consent and Licence applications. Many specialists are already contributing to the analyses of the Ferns collections – including Fiona Beglane (faunal remains), Clare McCutcheon (medieval ceramics), Lorna O'Donnell (wood identification), Brendan O'Neill (metal slag), Ger Dowling (survey support) and Dermot Moore (lithics analysis). Phil Parkes, Jane Henderson and Susannah Kelly provide continued archaeological conservation support. Sincere thanks are also due to the numerous other specialists and professionals (too many to mention) who have provided advice in advance of (or during) each excavation season. Most importantly, to our host community in Ferns who have steadfastly supported the excavation since its inception, with advice, logistical support, volunteer hours and friendship – your support is one of the reasons the project is so special. In particular, thank you to the Cousins and Breen families for letting us excavate on your lands (and come down repeatedly for 'one last survey'!) and to Dean Mooney and Phil Murphy for the generous use of St Edan's Cathedral and Mogue's Cottage. Thanks also to the many other landowners who permitted access for the 2021 programme of geophysical surveys. We are keen to acknowledge Colm Morris, Catherine McPartlin and Barry Lacey on the ground in Ferns. Barry has been instrumental in many projects and helped coordinate a superb 'home setting' together with our other fantastic homestay coordinator Tara Sinnott.

The research coordinated by the IAFS at Clone would also not be possible without the support of the many volunteers, across two seasons, who gave of their time freely and enthusiastically. Several professionals also assisted on the dig, with surveys or in post excavation; namely, Aisling Lacey, Taylor Walk, Liza Kavanagh, Cele Wolman and Sean Lacey – the latter for backfilling the cuttings in his 'spare time'. Many thanks are also due to the OPW for access to facilities in the first season. Thanks to all specialists and experts who provided services and/or advice including Stephen Hoper, Catherine McLoughlin, Crannóg Media and Christiaan Corlett. Special thanks are due to Richard Clutterbuck for his generous help in preparing the base maps for the illustrations in chapter 1.

In particular, Christiaan Corlett (chs 5, 7) is grateful to Pauline Gleeson, Michael Moore, Flora O'Mahony and Mairtín D'Alton for their help and support in recording the remains at Clone, Colm Morris of Ferns for invaluable assistance, and Michael Potterton, Denis Shine, Stephen Mandal and Máirtín D'Alton for on-site discussions and insights. DigVentures (ch. 10) would like to thank Ancient Connections for inviting them to take part in their project and to carry out a series of geophysical surveys across Wexford and Pembrokeshire. They would also like to thank Ursula and Pat Cousins for their assistance with accessing the grounds of St Mary's Abbey and for their support with the survey, Susan Ovenden and Rose Geophysics for their assistance with the Depth Slices and data processing, and Jodie Hannis for collaborating on the project.

Michael Potterton (ch. 2) would like to thank Edel Bhreathnach for extremely valuable feedback on an earlier draft of his essay, some of which will certainly have saved his blushes. He is also grateful to his colleagues in the Department of History at Maynooth University and in Special Collections at MU Library, as well as staff at the Royal Irish Academy, the Royal Society of Antiquaries of Ireland and the Image Library of the National Museum of Ireland – notably Clare McNamara. For assistance and advice, Michael would also like to thank the following: Michael Ann Bevivino; David Collins; Christiaan Corlett; Anthony Corns, Ger Dowling; Ian Doyle; Anne-Julie Lafaye; Barry Lewis; Megan McAuley; Margaret Murphy; Sara Nylund; Colmán Ó Clabaigh; Karen Potterton; Matt Seaver, Robert Shaw and David Sweetman.

Kate Taylor (ch. 11) is grateful to project funders Wexford County Council as well as the engineers and archaeologists from TII and Tramore House RDO who managed it. Thanks are due to Bernice Kelly, James Eogan, Tim Murphy, Donal McLoughlin and Sean Dobbs. The testing, excavation and post-excavation involved a team of archaeologists: Gordana Baljkas, Niamh Barry, Dylan Duane Roche, Graham Hull, Katherine Hurley, Roisin Hurley, Byron Jones, Jake Justice, Damien McCarthy, Yohann Paci, Orlagh Walsh and Yvonne Whitty. Specialist reports and videography were prepared by Conor Brady, David Brown, Garry Byrne, CHRONO Centre, Steve Davis, Natasiu Duhau, Alfie Hollingsworth, Kevin Kearney, Susannah Kelly, Susan Lyons, Mags Mannion, Clare McCutcheon, Cathy Moore, John Nicholl, Brendan O'Neill, Paul Rondelez, Orla Scully and Paul Stevens. The local community in Ferns supported the archaeological work, and particular thanks go to Pat Cousins and Ursula Cousins, Catherine McPartlin, Colm Morris and Bryanna Young. The assistance of the following was also much appreciated: Tracy Collins, Christiaan Corlett, Ger Dowling, Catherine McLoughlin, Nessa O'Connor, Martin Reid, Denis Shine, Mushroom Civil and Priority Geotechnical.

In relation to her essay below (ch. 13), Clare McCutcheon notes that every effort was made to contact the licence-holders of each excavation for permission to reference their rushlight holder. She thanks the following for permission to access, measure and discuss their rushlight holders: National Museum of Ireland Matt Seaver; Denis Shine; Liam Hackett; Cathy Sheehan; Orla Scully; Yvonne Whitty; and especially Sara Nylund for her fine illustrations. Regarding the essay (ch. 14), Michael Rogers and Samuel Chen would like to acknowledge that the project to scan Ferns Castle was funded in part by the University of Colorado at Denver, and Ithaca College in Ithaca, New York. Thanks are in order for the excellent fieldwork done by the research students Christina Cuzzi, Andrew Polcari, Wyatt Vigilante and Sam Weeks.

The following institutions are thanked for their permission to reproduce illustrations: Climate, Heritage and Environment of Reefs, Islands and Headlands (CHERISH) Project; Discovery Programme; Economic and Social Research Institute; Geological Survey of Ireland; Government of Ireland; Irish Geophysical and Archaeological Services; Laois County Council; Medieval Ferns Experience; Monastic Ireland; National Monuments Service; National Library of Ireland; National Museum of Ireland; OpenStreetMap; Ordnance Survey Ireland; Royal Irish Academy; Royal Society of Antiquaries of Ireland; Teagasc; The National Archives (UK); Thames Valley Archaeological Services. The staff in each of those institutions were efficient and helpful with our requests for all images and maps. Additionally, these individuals kindly provided illustrations: John Bradley; Richard Clutterbuck, Christiaan Corlett; Ger Dowling; Michael Freeman; Catherine McLoughlin; John Nicholl; Sara Nylund; Alan Owens; Robert Shaw; Keith Smith.

The editors would like to thank each of the contributors for their work in researching and preparing their chapters. As ever, the team at Four Courts Press, especially Martin Fanning, Martin Healy and Anthony Tierney, have been exceptionally supportive and helpful. We are delighted that Ian Doyle agreed to write the foreword and we thank Michael Ann Bevivino for compiling the index. Finally, the editors would like to thank their families for allowing us the time to complete this book. Each of us has day jobs meaning publications like these eat away at time with our partners and children. Thank you for your support, patience and understanding.

BIBLIOGRAPHY

Shine, D., Potterton, M., Mandal, S. and McLoughlin, C. (eds), 2019. *Carrick, County Wexford: Ireland's first Anglo-Norman stronghold*. Dublin.

THE EDITORS
17 August 2023

CHAPTER ONE

Setting the scene: the formation of the Ferns landscape and life before St Aidan

STEPHEN MANDAL, MICHAEL POTTERTON & DENIS SHINE

INTRODUCTION

Ferns today is a small county town with a population of just over 1,400, situated in north Co. Wexford, *c.*86km south of Dublin and *c.*28km north of Wexford (fig. 1.1). The main urban focus is at the meeting point of three townlands: Ferns Upper, Castleland and Coolbaun. Although the town boasts many splendid upstanding archaeological and built-heritage remains (including the ruins of Ferns Castle and St Mary's Church), much of the former splendour and importance of the town over many centuries lies in historical records and buried beneath the surface. Medieval Ferns was one of south-eastern Ireland's most important settlements. It played a key role in local, regional and national history from its foundation by St Aidan in *c.*598, especially when serving as Diarmait Mac Murchada's royal seat and the capital of an influential medieval diocese (ch. 2).

The landscape into which St Aidan first set foot at the very end of the sixth century, when he chose this place as the site for a new monastery, was formed through a long and complex sequence of geological and glacial processes and subsequently shaped by several millennia of human settlement. The history of Ferns is inextricably linked to the natural landscape, the underlying bedrock, glacial sediments and soils, which not only influenced the selection of the site, but also provided the raw material with which successive settlements were built. Knowing about these processes and human interactions is an important part of understanding the story of Ferns and sets the stage for the arrival of St Aidan and the subsequent rise of the town as a royal seat in the twelfth century.

TOPOGRAPHY

The site of Aidan's monastery, and indeed of Mac Murchada's Augustinian community founded some six centuries later, is in open pasture on a gentle east/north-east-facing slope at between 45m and 35m above sea level (fig. 1.2). The topography is controlled by a north-west/south-east-running watercourse, known locally as Barney's Stream, that flows approximately 200m north of the current ruins of St Mary's Church, and

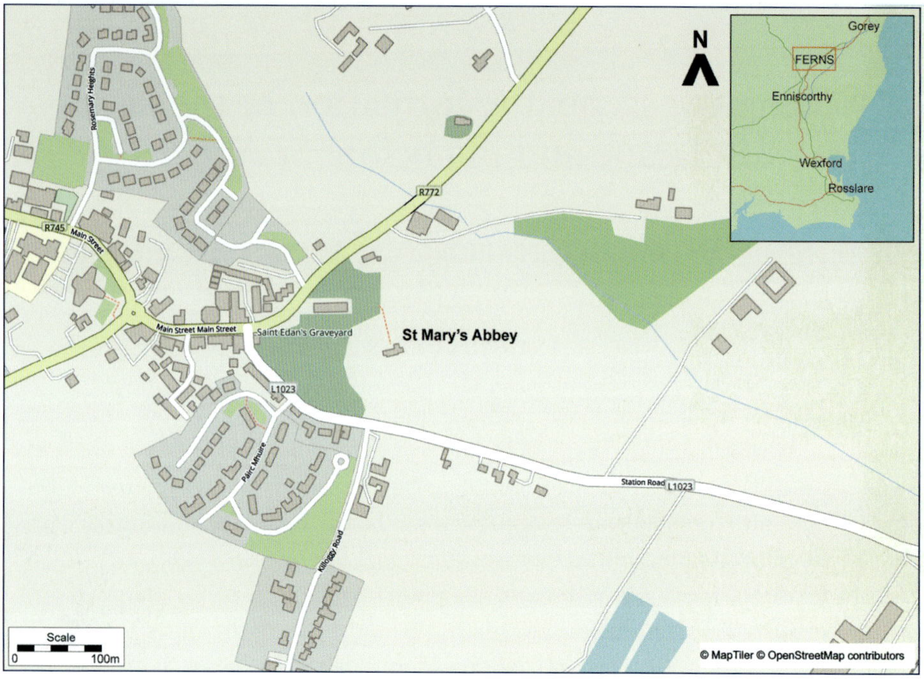

1.1 Ferns: map showing location of St Mary's Abbey

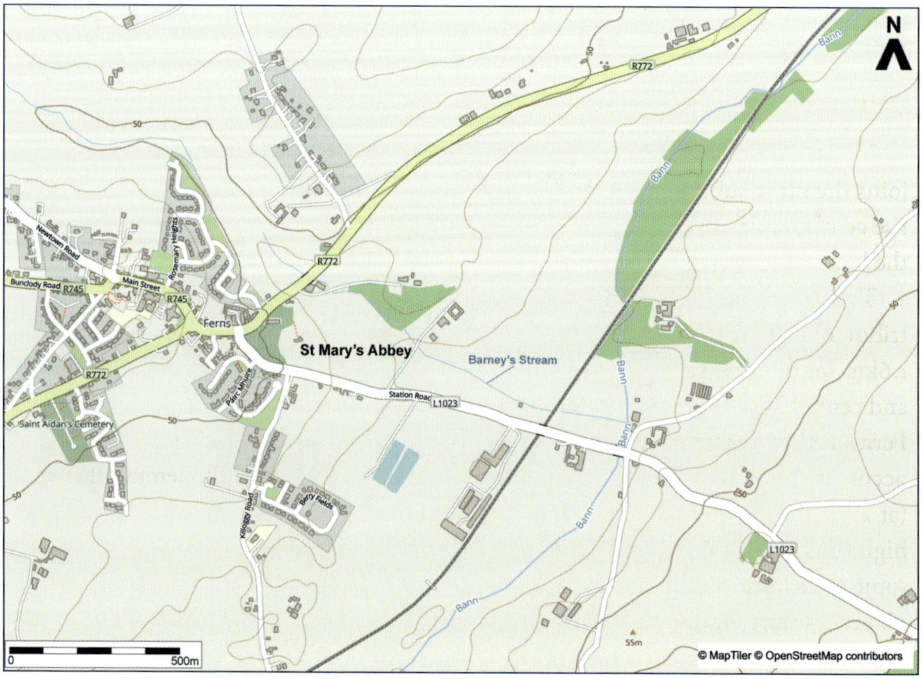

1.2 Ferns: map of local topography showing location of St Mary's Abbey

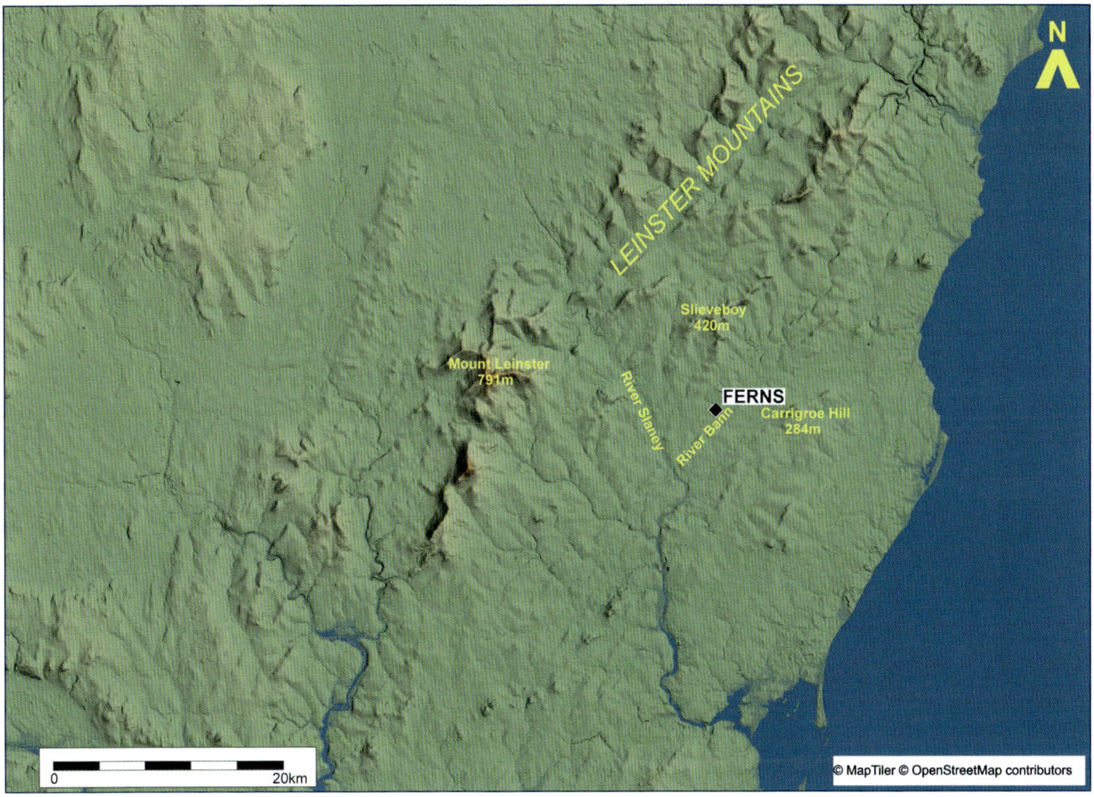

1.3 Ferns: regional topography

joins the more substantial River Bann some 900m to the east/south-east. The lands rise gently on the opposite side of the stream and the river to the east, while to the west the land reaches *c.*65m above sea level at Ferns Castle.

The wider landscape comprises a series of low-lying gentle hills separated by tributaries of the Bann, which itself is a tributary of the River Slaney, which it joins *c.*6km south of Ferns (fig. 1.3). The Slaney, which dominates the landscape of north and central Wexford, flows from north/north-west to south/south-east, to the west of Ferns, *c.*5km distant at its closest point. The highest ground in the wider landscape occurs at Carrigroe Hill (at 284m above sea level, *c.*7km to the east), Slieveboy (at 420m, *c.*7km north) and Mount Leinster (at 794m, *c.*19km west). These areas of high land represent the southern extent of the Leinster Mountains. While there are some areas of relatively high ground to the south, for example at Forth Mountain (at 289m, *c.*31km south), in general the land drops from the Leinster Mountains to the south-east coast. Ferns is *c.*19km from the Irish Sea, due east at Donaghmore.

1.4 Ferns: regional geology (source: Geological Survey of Ireland)

SOLID GEOLOGY, GLACIAL AND SOILS

The bedrock underlying Ferns broadly consists of sediments laid down during the Ordovician Period (*c.*485 to 440 million years ago; fig. 1.4), into which volcanics were erupted (see Tietzsch-Tyler and Sleeman 1994). These represent a time when the Iapetus Ocean, which once separated the north-west of Ireland from the south-east, was closing, with the subduction of plates and the generation of volcanoes and earthquakes. Mountains were formed to the north, and there was an increase in sediment being carried by rivers into the closing ocean. Today, these rocks form a north-east to south-west-trending band of sediments and volcanics that extends through the south-east of Ireland. The rocks are generally youngest in the north-west and progressively older towards the south-east.

The bedrock at the site consists of felsic volcanics (CAfv), which represent a member of the Campile Formation of rhyolitic volcanics, grey and brown siltstone (CA – Caradoc Age); these make up the bedrock to the south-east and north-west. The Campile Formation also includes intermediate volcanics (CAiv). Some 250m to the north-west occur green, red-purple and buff-coloured slate and siltstone belonging

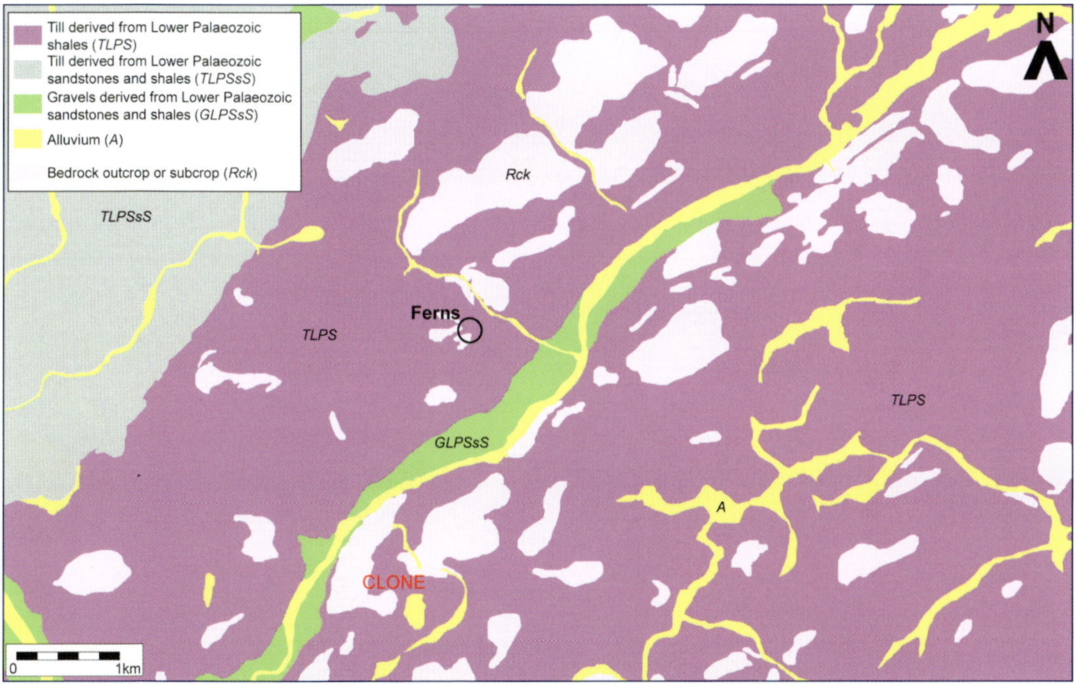

1.5 Ferns: regional glacial deposits (source: Geological Survey of Ireland)

to the underlying Oaklands Formation (OA – Arenig Age). These are underlain by green and grey slates with thin siltstones of the Ballylane Shale Formation (BY – Tremadoc-Arenig Age), which occur to the west of the site. The oldest rocks in the area actually occur *c.*6km to the south-east, separated by a south-west to north-east-trending major fault. These rocks consist of dark grey slates with siltstone laminae belonging to the Ballyhoge Formation (BH – Tremadoc Age).

Bedrock is generally not exposed in Ferns and the surrounding area, although it is close to the surface in pockets in the wider area (fig. 1.5). The area is widely covered with glacial sediments laid down during the Quaternary Period, starting some 1.7 million years ago. During this time, a series of glacial events formed Ireland's landscape. In reality, although this period is often referred to as the Ice Age, there were numerous ice ages throughout this time, interspersed by periods when the climate was warmer and the ice sheets retreated completely.

The last ice age in Ireland began *c.*37,000 years ago and at its peak it covered even the highest mountains and extended westwards to the Atlantic shelf break, eastwards into the Irish Sea Basin and southwards to the Celtic Sea shelf edge. By *c.*20,000 years ago, the ice sheets appear to have retreated to the current coastline or thereabouts, retreating faster in the south-east, although there were several fresh advances after this date when the climate cooled again. It is believed that the climate warmed rapidly

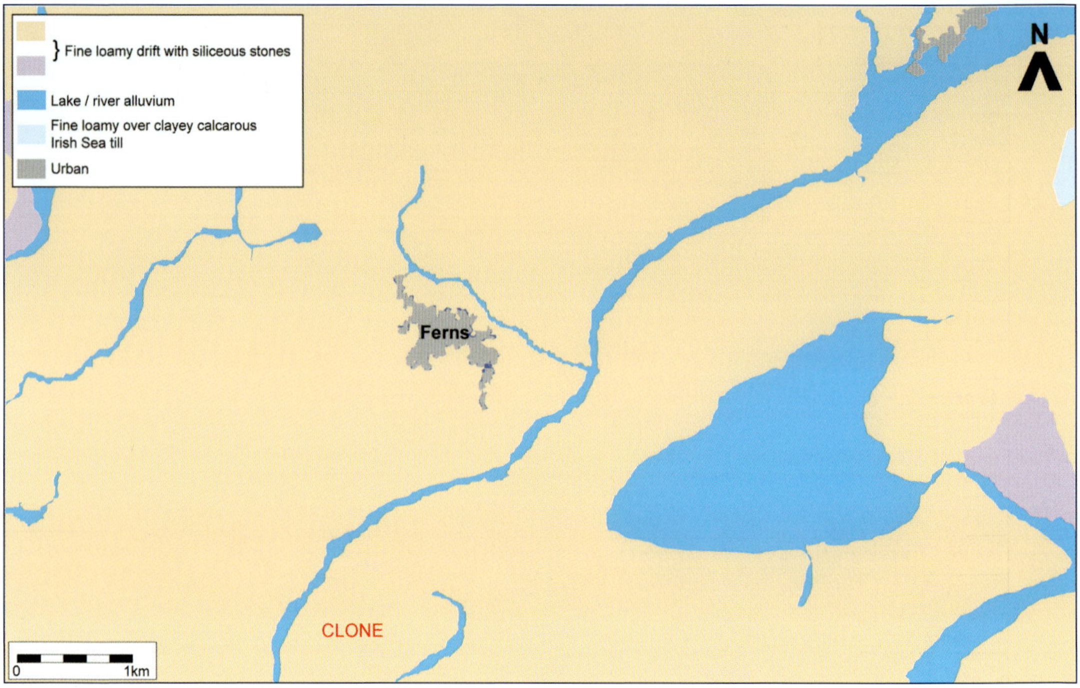

1.6 Ferns: regional soils (source: Geological Survey of Ireland)

*c.*15,000 years ago, and this caused the complete melting of ice in low-lying areas. Even then there were periods during which the climate cooled again and small glaciers returned to some mountainous areas, notably during the Nahangan stadial (*c.*12,900–11,700 cal. BP) (Ó Cofaigh and Ballantyne 2017).

It is hard to envisage the depth and power of the ice sheets across the country, but their impact can be seen in the glacial landforms that remain throughout the island. Ice-sculpted mountains, glaciated valleys, corrie lakes, eskers, drumlins and moraines dominate the Irish topographical landscape (Mitchell and Ryan 1987). In the south-east, the impact of the ice sheets was to mould the hilly landscape and deposit layers of glacial tills and gravels, which broadly represent the underlying geology (fig. 1.5). The predominant glacial sediment in the area consists of tills derived from Lower Palaeozoic shales. Within this are pockets of higher ground where there are little or no tills, where bedrock is at or near to the surface. To the north-west and west occur similar tills that also contain sandstones. Alluvial sediments appear along the rivers (in particular the Bann). Also along the Bann occur gravels, similarly derived from Lower Palaeozoic sandstones and shales. The topography carved through and over the bedrock by the ice sheets is, more or less, the same today as it was when the first people arrived into this area. The agricultural landscape, however, with fields in open pasture,

Table 1.1 Prehistoric archaeological sites and monuments in the region

	Distance from Ferns		
Site Type	**2.5km**	**5km**	**10km**
Neolithic			
Passage-tomb art	1	1	1
Linkardstown burial	-	-	1
Pit – Neolithic	-	-	1
Cairn	-	-	3
Cremation pit	-	-	1
Bronze Age			
Flat cemetery	1	3	4
Barrow	-	-	3
Cist	-	-	4
Pit – Bronze Age	1	1	6
Hut site	1	1	1
Standing stone	-	-	4
Fulachta fiadh	-	13	38
Burnt mound/spread	3	11	25
Bronze/Iron Age			
Ring-ditch	5	6	22
Totals	**12**	**36**	**114**
Total SMRs	77	144	457
Prehistoric	16%	25%	25%

enclosed by stone walls and hedgerows, is completely different, down to the soils that overly the glacial sediments.

As the ice sheets retreated due to increasing global temperatures and we entered the Holocene (*c.*12,000 years ago), the sea level rose and the environment changed dramatically. It should be noted, however, that due to the effects of isostatic rebound, there were times when the sea level fell relative to the Irish landmass (e.g., Brooks 2008). This process is recorded by the raised beaches common along the Wexford coast, for example at Fethard and Cullenstown (Meehan et al. 2018, 23).

In terms of soil geomorphology, soils started to develop as the landscape became more stable *c.*13,000 years ago, though the abovementioned Nahangan stadial saw a return of ice and permafrost and the destruction of interstadial soils. By *c.*10,000 years ago there was limited periglacial activity restricted to upland areas, and soils developed. Over this period, Ireland went from open ground to low scrub and heathland to open grassland, reverting to tundra and low Alpine scrub during the Nahangan stadial, before recovering to open scrub, open woodland and ultimately, by *c.*9,500 years ago, woodland (Mitchell and Ryan 1987, 84). Over the next few thousand years, coinciding with a marked increase in the human population in Ireland, vast woodlands grew throughout the country. Juniper, willow and birch developed first, followed by hazel, pine, oak, elm, alder and ash (ibid., 112).

Today, the soils of the area consist of fine loamy drift containing siliceous stones (derived from the overlying tills) (fig. 1.6). Lake and river alluvium occurs along rivers and streams, and in lowland areas. The archaeological excavations at the site of St Aidan's and St Mary's monastic settlements, described in detail in Chapter 9 (see also Shine et al. 2021), have indicated that topsoil at the site comprises a sod (depth 15 to 40cm) of mid-greyish brown colour with occasional small angular stone inclusions, overlying a heavily ploughed agricultural layer (average depth 15cm) of mid-greyish brown silty sand/clay with small to medium angular and subangular stone inclusions. This in turn overlays a moderately compact mid-greyish brown clayey sand and/or sandy silt (depth 11cm to 35cm), which in Cutting 2 (downslope of Cutting 1) had frequent large angular and subangular stone inclusions.

PREHISTORIC FERNS

Ferns town, and St Aidan's monastery in particular, have an extensive history reflected in historical sources, built heritage and sub-surface archaeology. These have been described previously (e.g., Bhreathnach and Dowling 2021; Corlett 2012; O'Keeffe and Bates 2016) and the medieval history of Ferns is discussed in detail in the chapters below. In this chapter, the focus is on life before St Aidan or, more broadly, life in prehistory, prior to the arrival of Christianity in the region. Of the seventy-seven recorded monuments within *c.*2.5km of Ferns, twelve (16%) are prehistoric; this rises to 36 (25%) of 144 within *c.*5km and 114 (25%) of 457 within *c.*10km (table 1.1; fig. 1.7) (NMS www). The rise in percentage of known prehistoric monuments as we move away from Ferns is probably best explained by two factors: first, Ferns has a wealth of medieval monuments relative to the more rural landscape away from the town and, secondly, urban development over the centuries undoubtedly impacted on earlier sites.

We know that Ireland was widely settled by Mesolithic hunter gatherers by *c.*10,000 years ago (Woodman 1978, Warren 2022); however, there is evidence of humans in Ireland since at least the Late Upper Palaeolithic, in the form of a butchered bear patella found in Alice and Gwendoline Cave in Co. Clare, which has been dated to *c.*10,750 cal. BC (Dowd and Carden 2016). It is thus surprising that in the south-east corner of Ireland, probably the first part of Ireland to be free of ice, there is relatively little evidence of hunter-gatherer activity, other than lithic assemblages interpreted as Mesolithic, such as the one from Coolnaveagh, on a plateau overlooking the River

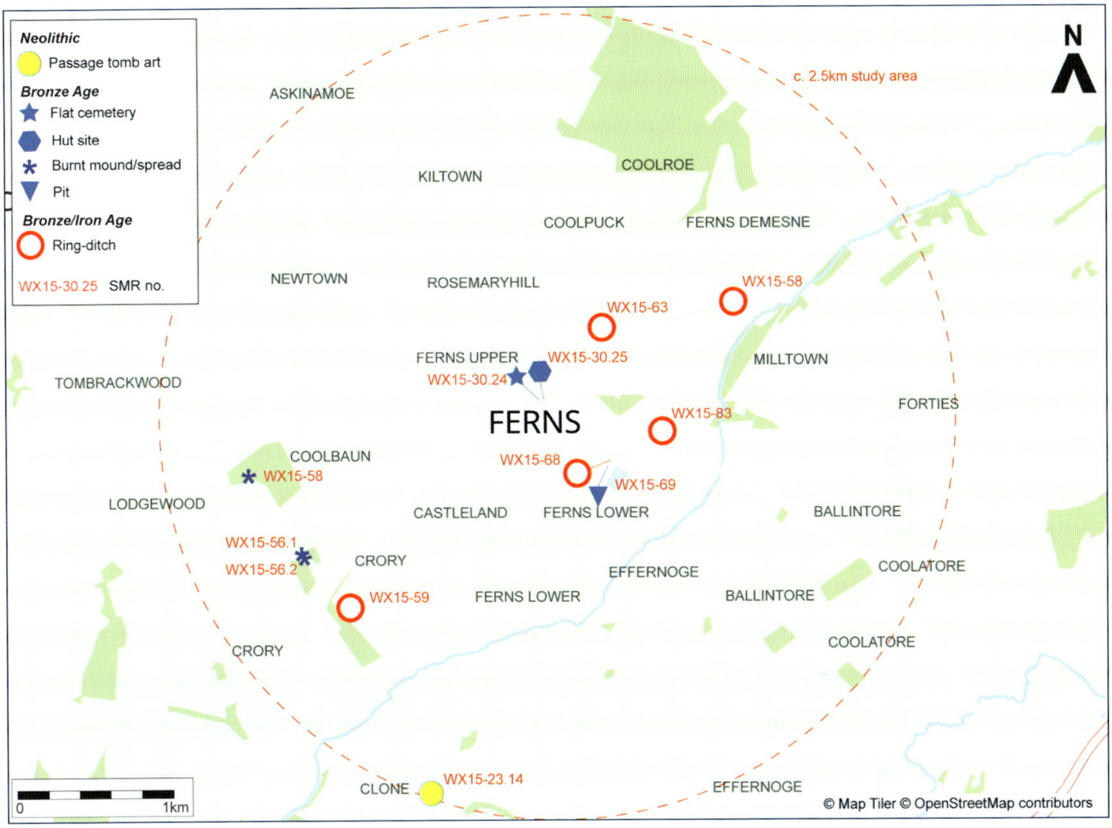

1.7 Ferns: recorded prehistoric archaeological sites and monuments in the vicinity (source: http://archaeology.ie)

Banoge (Moore 2008), Camolin, Carnsore and Kilmichael Point (Stout 1987, 3), and along the banks of the River Barrow in Wexford and Waterford (Green and Zvelebil 1990).

The Neolithic, defined by the arrival of farming in Ireland about 6,000 years ago, brought a sea-change in the use of the landscape; for example, the clearing of woodland for farming and to acquire resources, more permanent and substantial settlements, and the building of megalithic structures (e.g., Cooney 2000, 22). As with the preceding Mesolithic, the evidence of Neolithic activity in Wexford is relatively sparce. Nonetheless, seven megalithic tombs have been identified in the county (although one is known from historical records only). These comprise two portal tombs (at Ballybrittas and Newbawn), four unclassified tombs and one megalithic structure (NMS www). The closest recorded Neolithic site to Ferns is at Clone, *c.*2.5km to the south, in the form of passage-tomb art (SMR WX015-0230014-; fig. 1.7). It is currently located within the graveyard (SMR WX015-023002-) close to the Romanesque doorway of Clone parish church (SMR WX015-023001-) and

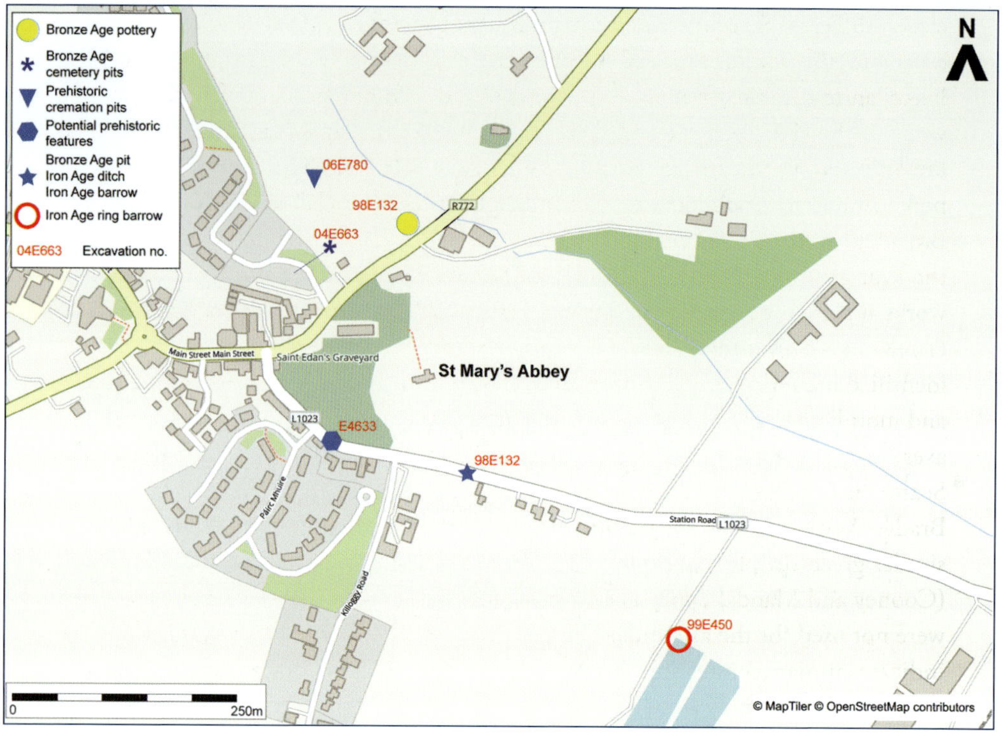

1.8 Ferns: recorded prehistoric archaeological excavations in the vicinity (source: http://excavations.ie)

appears to be a grave-marker with a rough point on top. The east face of the stone has a lightly pecked curvilinear design, covering most of the stone. The design, which has been interpreted as passage-tomb art (anon. 1889), is most likely evidence of Neolithic activity in the area. Interestingly, excavations on the outer enclosure at Clone (also associated with St Aidan), *c*.2km from Ferns, have also returned a Neolithic date from charcoal retrieved within the ditch basal fills (Shine et al. 2020; ch. 12).

Perhaps the most telling evidence of human habitation in the area in the Neolithic comes from the material culture and, in particular, artefacts found on excavations and as stray finds. The single-most numerous artefact type surviving from prehistory in Ireland are stone axeheads, long regarded as one of the characteristic objects of the Mesolithic and Neolithic (e.g., Cooney and Mandal 1998; Woodman 1978; 1987; Cooney and Grogan 1994). To date, the Irish Stone Axe Project (ISAP) has recorded thirty-seven stone axeheads from Wexford (a significant increase from the sixteen recorded to 1998 (Cooney and Mandal 1998, 31)). Interestingly, the range of rock types utilized is broad, from locally available material such as shale and sandstone, to lithologies that are not available, either in bedrock or in glacial tills. The most striking are the six porcellanite and four green-tuff axeheads. Of the porcellanite examples, the closest to Ferns was one found during ploughing at Tobergal (Registration WCM10), *c.*6km to the south-east, and another from Enniscorthy (Registration WCM7). Porcellanite accounts for over 50 per cent of the total number identified through the work of the ISAP (Cooney and Mandal 1998, 63). A significant number are also known from Britain (Sheridan et al. 1992, 410). There are two known locations of porcellanite axe production, at Tievebulliagh near Cushendall in Co. Antrim, and at Brockley on Rathlin (Knowles 1903; 1906; Mandal 1997). Even more interesting are the four green-tuff axeheads, the closest to Ferns being found during construction works at Killisk, *c.*14km to the south of Ferns (NMI IA/151/65). Cooney and Mandal (1998, 111–73), using thin-section and x-ray diffraction analysis of Irish tuff axes, identified more than 120 examples from findspots in Ireland that are petrographically and morphologically consistent with the numerically most important British group of axes, namely Group VI epidotized intermediate tuff, from sources in and around the Scafel Pike and Great Langdale areas of Cumbria (see Clough and Cummins 1988; Bradley and Edmonds 1993). Interestingly, although there are sources in Ireland of similar green tuff, for example in and around the Lough Gur area of Co. Limerick (Cooney and Mandal 1998, 118–19), the petrographical evidence suggests that these were not used for the axeheads. The significance of these stone axeheads is that they indicate human connection / trade from the north to the south of the island of Ireland, and from north-east to south-west from Great Langdale to Wexford.

Evidence of Neolithic activity in Ferns has been identified on the archaeological excavations, comprising worked flint and chert, along with pottery of that period (chs 11, 12). A sherd of Neolithic pottery and a number of worked flints were found during excavations of a Bronze Age pit and Iron Age ring-ditch in Ferns Lower (Ryan 2012, 273–89; see below).

The Bronze Age (from *c.*4,500 BP) saw the introduction of metalworking technologies. The earliest evidence of mining for metals in Ireland (or indeed north-west Europe) is from Ross Island, Co. Kerry, where copper ore was extracted from seams in the Carboniferous Age bedrock. Extraction of copper started at the end of the Neolithic, and by *c.*4,000 BP tin was being added to produce the alloy bronze (O'Brien 1995; 2004). Although tin occurs in ore in Ireland, Budd at al. (1994, 522–3) concluded that it was not extractable during the Bronze Age and tin was probably sourced in Cornwall in the south-west of England. Perhaps due to its proximity to the Copper Coast of the south of Ireland and to the tin sources in the south of England, there is a marked increase in the footprint of human habitation in Wexford in the Bronze Age (see table 1.1 and fig. 1.8).

Six cremation pits (and some domestic features) forming part of a Bronze Age flat cemetery were excavated on the western side of the R772 road, *c.*90m north-west of St Edan's Cathedral (Kavanagh 2007; licence 04E0663; SMR WX015-003024; see fig. 1.8). A hut-site (SMR WX015-003025) was identified *c.*15m to the west of this cemetery. The site consisted of a semi-circle of post-holes (*c.*7.5m in diameter) associated with traces of a slot-trench and burnt daub. Although several pits in the vicinity produced sherds of medieval pottery, it was concluded that the site was probably related to and contemporary with the adjacent flat cemetery (Doyle 2016; Kavanagh 2007; Sheehan 2006). A Bronze Age pit was excavated in advance of sewerage works in Ferns Lower, *c.*450m south-east of Edan's Cathedral. No artefacts were recovered, but a sample of oak yielded a Middle Bronze Age date (Doyle 2016; Ryan 2000; Ryan and Henry 2000).

Three burnt mounds from the townland of Coolbaun, *c.*1.5km to the west of Ferns, were exposed by ploughing. Burnt mounds, often termed *fulachta fiadh* are the most common surviving archaeological site from the Bronze Age (they date predominantly to the Bronze Age but date ranges from the Mesolithic to the medieval period have been returned: Waddell 2000). *Fulachta fiadh* have been interpreted in various ways, mainly as cooking troughs but other interpretations see them as places for washing, ritual initiations, bathing, tanning and even brewing (Burnt offerings 2001; Buckley 1990; Ó Drisceoil 1988; O'Kelly 1954; Quinn and Moore 2009).

Five ring-ditches have been recorded from the area. Four were identified as crop-marks (SMR nos WX015-058; 59; 63; 83; see fig. 1.8), ranging from *c.*8m to 10m in diameter. The term 'ring-ditch' is used to describe a circular or near circular fosse, usually less than 20m in diameter (NMS www). They are a widely distributed site type belonging to the barrow tradition (Newman 1997, 196; see also Woodward 2000). Ring-ditches are distinguished by the absence of an external bank or internal mound and are generally considered to have had a funerary role, though some may have had a ceremonial rather than a sepulchral role (Corlett 2005). An Iron Age ring-ditch was uncovered in Ferns Lower, *c.*20m to the north of the above-mentioned Bronze Age pit (licence 99E450). This excavation produced the skeletal remains of a minimum of four burials and the cremated remains of seven individuals. Three of the burials were rich in grave goods including a variety of glass beads, an amber bead, copper-alloy and iron objects, a sherd of Neolithic pottery and several worked flints (as noted above). Radiometric dates indicate Iron Age activity, with a lifespan of approximately the fourth century BC to the first century AD (Doyle 2016, 52: Ryan 2000; 2012, 283). Doyle noted, however, that the assemblage of artefacts uncovered and the potential association with the nearby Bronze Age pit suggest a far longer timespan for the site, from the Neolithic and through the Bronze Age (ibid.). It is worth noting that excavations in 1998, as part of the Ferns Sewerage Scheme, revealed a ditch at the junction of Clone road and Station road that has since been interpreted as part of the early medieval monastic enclosure (Doyle 2016, 54). The ditch, measuring *c.*2.6m wide at road level and extending 1.7m below the surface hardcore, contained a tertiary fill of charcoal-rich brown soil, overlying a horizontal band of charcoal containing slag and what was described as a 'furnace bottom' (Ryan 2000, 8). A sample of alder charcoal from the ditch returned a date of cal. AD384–535; that is, at the cusp of the Iron Age and the early medieval period.

WHY HERE?

The siting of St Aidan's monastery in 598, by means of a grant of land in the territory of the Uí Chennselaig, is unlikely to have been a coincidence. An assessment of the topographical map of the region gives an indication of the potential of Ferns as an attractive area for settlement (see fig. 1.4). The Bann river valley runs north-east to south-west between Slieveboy at the southern extent of the Leinster Mountains, and Carrigroe Hill, providing access by water to the Irish Sea south of Gorey. To the south-west, the Bann flows into the Slaney, which itself is a major river and valley running from north to south, entering the Irish Sea at Wexford.

It is likely that St Aidan's early monastic site was deliberately placed at this location due to its favourable landscape and the fact that it had an established prehistoric significance – as has been observed at several other monastic sites throughout the county (e.g., O'Sullivan et al. 2018). This hypothesis is supported by the results of excavations conducted at the north-western limits of the field containing St Mary's Abbey. This excavation revealed a small cluster of features, namely a pit tentatively identified as prehistoric. A single sherd of possible prehistoric pottery and a struck flint were also recovered (Taylor and Hurley 2021; ch. 11). Several prehistoric lithics have also being recovered ex situ from the excavations of the Irish Archaeology Field School at St Mary's Abbey.

While the evidence of occupation is limited, the known burial sites indicate that a significant axis of prehistoric settlement is present from Ferns town centre to the River Bann, crossing through the field containing St Mary's. This conjecture seems to be confirmed when recent geophysical surveys are considered, especially those conducted in 2021, which indicate that a major multi-period complex of features surrounds the excavation site (chs 6, 7, 8, 9).

Whatever the reasons for choosing this site, the founding of a monastic settlement by St Aidan changed Ferns forever and was the start of a long, complex and intriguing story of religion and politics.

BIBLIOGRAPHY

Anon. 1889. 'Proceedings'. *Journal of the Royal Society of Antiquaries of Ireland*, 19, 1–19.

Bhreathnach, E. and Dowling, G. 2021. 'Forming an episcopal see and an Augustinian foundation in medieval Ireland: the case of Ferns, Co. Wexford'. *Proceedings of the Royal Irish Academy*, 121C, 191–226.

Bradley, R. and Edmonds, M. 1993. *Interpreting the axe trade.* Cambridge.

Brooks, A.J., Bradley, S.L., Edwards, R.J., Milne, G.A., Horton, B.P. and Shennan, I. 2008. 'Post-glacial relative sea-level observations from Ireland and their role in glacial rebound modelling'. *Journal of Quaternary Science*, 23:2, 175–92.

Buckley, V.M. (ed.). 1990. *Burnt offerings: international contributions to burnt mounds in archaeology.* Dublin.

Budd, P., Gale, D., Ixer, R. and Thomas, R. 1994. 'Tin sources for prehistoric bronze production in Ireland'. *Antiquity*, 68:260, 518–24.

Burnt Offerings Conference, 2001. The Botanical Gardens, Glasnevin, Dublin.

Clough, T.H.McK. and Cummins, W.A. (eds). 1988. *Stone axe studies II.* London.

Cooney, G. and Grogan, E. 1994. *Irish prehistory: a social perspective.* Dublin.

Cooney, G. and Mandal, S. 1998. *Irish Stone Axe Project, monograph I.* Dublin.

Cooney, G. 2000. *Landscapes of Neolithic Ireland.* London.

Corlett, C. 2005. 'Ring-barrows: a circular argument with a ring of truth?' In Condit, T. and Corlett, C. (eds), *Above and beyond: essays in memory of Leo Swan*, 63–71. Dublin.

Corlett, C. 2012. 'Ferns, Co. Wexford'. *Archaeology Ireland*, Heritage Guide 59. Dublin.

Dowd, M. and Carden R. 2016. 'First evidence of a Late Upper Palaeolithic human presence in Ireland'. *Quaternary Science Reviews*, 139, 158–63.

Doyle, I. 2016. 'Telling the dancer from the dance: the archaeology of early medieval Wexford'. In Doyle, I. and Browne, B. (eds), *Medieval Wexford: essays in memory of Billy Colfer*, 35–61. Dublin.

Green, S.W. and Zvelebil, M. 1990. 'The Mesolithic colonization and agricultural transition of south-east Ireland'. *Proceedings of the Prehistoric Society*, 56, 57–88.

Kavanagh, J. 2007. 'Ferns Upper, Ferns. Multi-period'. In Bennett, I. (ed.), *Excavations 2004: summary accounts of archaeological excavations in Ireland*, 466–7, no. 1806. Dublin.

Knowles, W.J. 1903. 'Stone axe factories near Cushendall, Co. Antrim'. *Journal of the Royal Anthropological Institute*, 33, 360–6.

Knowles, W.J. 1906. 'Stone axe factories near Cushendall'. *Journal of the Royal Society of Antiquaries of Ireland*, 36, 383–94.

Mandal, S. 1997. 'Striking the balance: the roles of petrography and geochemistry in stone axe studies in Ireland'. *Archaeometry*, 39, 289–308.

Meehan, R., Hennessy, R. Parkes, and Gatley, S. 2018. *The geological heritage of Wexford: an audit of county geological sites in Wexford.* Geological Survey of Ireland online publications (www.gsi.ie/en-ie/publications/Pages/The-Geological-Heritage-of-Wexford.aspx).

Mitchell, F. and Ryan, M. 1987. *Reading the Irish landscape.* Dublin.

Moore, E. 2008. 'N11 Gorey to Arklow link: archaeological resolution. Preliminary report. E3486. Site 21–22, Coolnaveagh, Co. Wexford'. Unpublished report for V.J. Keeley Ltd.

Newman, C. 1997. *Tara: an archaeological survey.* Dublin.

Ó Cofaigh, C. and Ballantyne, C.K. 2017. 'The last Irish ice sheet: extent and chronology'. In Coxon, P., McCarron, S. and Mitchell, F. (eds). *Advances in Irish Quaternary Studies*, 1.

O'Keeffe, T. and Carey Bates, R. 2016. 'The abbey and cathedral of Ferns, 1111–1253'. In Doyle, I. and Browne, B. (eds), *Medieval Wexford: essays in memory of Billy Colfer*, 73–96. Dublin.

O'Drisceoil, D.A, 1988. 'Burnt mounds: cooking or bathing?' *Antiquity*, 62, 672.

O'Brien, W. 1995. 'Ross Island: the beginning'. *Archaeology Ireland*, 9:1, 24–7.

O'Brien, W. 2004. 'Ross Island: mining, metal and society in early Ireland'. *Bronze Age Studies*, 6.

O'Kelly, M.J. 1954. 'Excavations and experiments in ancient Irish cooking places'. *Journal of the Royal Society of Antiquaries of Ireland*, 84, 105–55.

O'Sullivan, M., Rodgers, M., Shine, D. and Mandal, S. 2018. 'Seir Kieran: place, pilgrimage and tradition in the monastic midlands'. *Offaly Heritage*, 10, 21–42.

Quinn, B. and Moore, D. 2009. '*Fulachta fiadh* and the beer experiment'. In Stanley, M., Danaher E. and Eogan, J. (eds), *Dining and dwelling: proceedings of a public seminar on archaeological discoveries on national road schemes, August 2008*, 43–53. Dublin.

Ryan, F. and Henry, M. 2000. 'Ferns sewerage scheme: multi-period'. In Bennett, I. (ed.), *Excavations 1999: summary accounts of archaeological excavations in Ireland*, 300–2 no. 875. Bray.

Ryan, F. 2000. 'Archaeological findings from monitoring of Phase 1 of Ferns sewerage scheme, Co. Wexford'. Unpublished report for Mary Henry Archaeological Services.

Ryan, F. 2012. 'Excavation of a late Iron Age ring-ditch at Ferns Lower, Co. Wexford'. In Corlett, C. and Potterton, M. (eds), *Life and death in Iron Age Ireland in the light of recent archaeological excavations*, 273–90. Dublin.

Sheehan, C. 2006. 'Ferns Upper, Ferns: medieval'. In Bennett, I. (ed.), *Excavations 2003: summary accounts of archaeological excavations in Ireland*, 532, no. 2018. Dublin.

Sheridan, J.A., Cooney, G. and Grogan, E. 1992. 'Stone axe studies in Ireland'. *Proceedings of the Prehistoric Society*, 58, 389–416.

Shine, D., Lacey, B., Corlett, C., Elliott, I. and Mandal, S. 2020. 'Clone, Ferns: a meadow of St Aidan?' *Archaeology Ireland*, 34:4, 24–9.

Shine, D., Lynch, L., Mandal, S. and O'Meara, D. 2021. 'Discovering St Aidan's monastery: preliminary archaeological excavation report (December 2021)'. Unpublished technical report produced for the National Monuments Service.

Stout, G. 1987. 'Wexford in prehistory, 5000BC to 300AD'. In Whelan K., and Nolan, W. (eds), *Wexford, history and society: interdisciplinary essays on the history of an Irish county*, 1–39. Dublin.

Taylor, K. and Hurley, K. 2021. 'R772 Ferns village pavement scheme Phase 2, Ferns, Co. Wexford'. Unpublished technical report for Wexford County Council.

Tietzsch-Tyler, D. and Sleeman, A.G. 1994. *Geology of Carlow–Wexford: a geological description to accompany the Bedrock Geology 1:100,000 scale Map Series, Sheet 19, Carlow–Wexford*. Sligo.

Waddell, J. 2000. *The prehistoric archaeology of Ireland*. 2nd ed. Galway.

Warren, G. 2022. *Hunter-gatherer Ireland making connections in an island world*. Oxford.

Woodman, P.C. 1978. *The Mesolithic in Ireland*. Oxford.

Woodman, P.C. 1987. 'The impact of resource availability on lithic industrial traditions in prehistoric Ireland'. In Rowley-Conwy, P., Zvelebil, M. and Blankholm, H.P. (eds), *Mesolithic north-west Europe: recent trends*, 138–46. Sheffield.

Woodward, A. 2000. *British barrows: a matter of life and death*. Stroud.

CHAPTER TWO

From caput to caput: the rise and fall of medieval Ferns, *c.*600–*c.*1600

MICHAEL POTTERTON

EARLY MEDIEVAL FERNS: A POTTED HISTORY

Situated close to the River Bann, a small and meandering tributary of the Slaney, Ferns, perhaps related to the Irish word *fern* 'an alder tree', is one of the oldest towns in Wexford (fig. 2.1). It was the main residence of the Uí Chennselaig dynasty from the tenth century and of the Meic Murchada kings of Leinster during the eleventh and twelfth centuries. Tradition has it that St Máedóc (d. *c.*625: AU; ATig.; AFM; CS; AClon.) founded a church there in the early seventh century (Ó Riain 2011, 432–6). The founder's name was originally *Áed* or *Áedán* (anglicized Aidan), *Máedóc* being the hypocoristic form 'Mo Áed-óc' (anglicized Mogue) (Kenney 1997, 448). Máedóc was the founder of many churches and is said to have been succeeded (though not directly) at Ferns by St Moling Luachra (d. 696/7), who had previously established a church at St Mullins, Co. Carlow, and was himself a disciple of Máedóc's (Plummer 1922, vol. ii, 183, 267; de Paor 2001, 123–4). The holy well just 60m to the north-east of Ferns Cathedral (fig. 2.2) may have been dedicated by Moling to Máedóc (Plummer 1922, vol. i, 211; Grattan Flood 1916, ix).

The Uí Chennselaig rose to prominence as the most powerful and influential family in southern Leinster from the tenth century onwards. For most of the early medieval period, Ferns was administered by a discard branch of the Uí Chennselaig, the Uí Laidgnéin, a hereditary family variously described as *ab* (abbot), *airchennach* (head of church lands), *comarba* (hereditary head of a church) and *princeps* (superior) of the church (Bhreathnach and Dowling 2021). It seems that the role was passed from father to son or from brother to brother. The names of more than forty abbots and bishops of Ferns are recorded in the various sets of annals before the arrival of the Anglo-Normans *c.*1170 (see table 2.1). The earliest identifiable contemporary reference to Ferns dates to 654 and records the death that year of 'Do-Chua of Luachair, abbot of Ferna' (AU; ATig.; AFM).

There appears to have been some considerable infighting among the Uí Chennselaig in the mid-eighth century. Áed Menn ('stammering') mac Colgan (d. 738) of the splinter group Síl Cormaic gained control of Ferns *c.*734, from which time his sept dominated Leinster until the battle of Ferns in 769. Áed's brother Bresal's

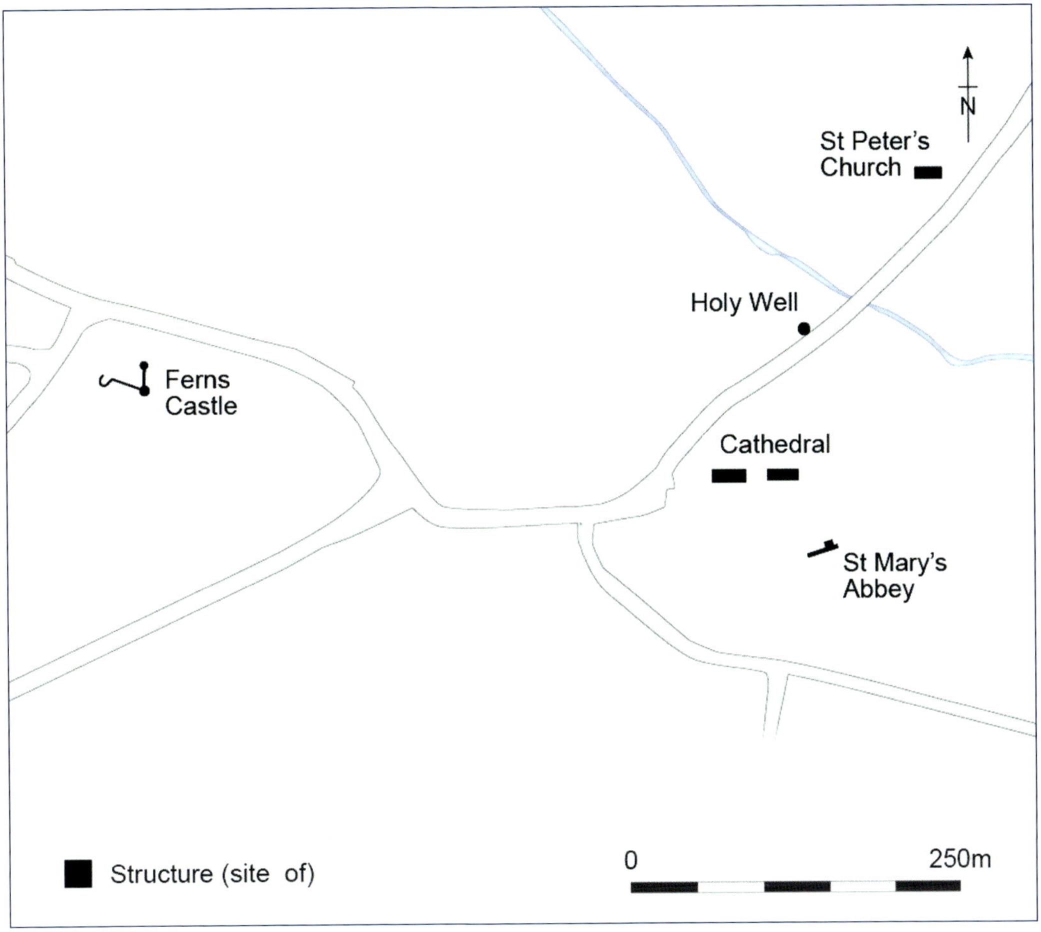

2.1 Ferns: town plan showing key medieval upstanding remains (after Bradley and King 1990; redrawn by Sara Nylund)

obit is recorded in the annals for 749 (AU; ATig.; AFM). Bresal had been abbot of Ferns from 741 (McGettigan and Mac Shamhráin 2009). Annalists report that Dub Calgaid mac Laidgnéin was defeated and killed by Cennselach mac Brain (d. 770) of the southern Síl Máeluidir sept, and Cennselach succeeded Dub Calgaid (AU; AFM, *s.a.* 764; Mac Niocaill 1972, 130). A further battle took place at Ferns in 783, this time between the abbot Cathal and Fiannachtach the steward/bursar (*economus*) (AU; Ó Corráin 1972, 86). The latter may have been victorious as his death is recorded sixteen years later in 799 (AU; AFM), while we hear no more of Cathal.

The Síl Máeluidir held power in southern Uí Chennselaig from 809, but Ferns remained in the hands of the Síl Cormaic (Colfer 2002, 12). This situation resulted in a bloody battle in 817 in which Ferns came under renewed attack from Cathal mac Dúnlainge, the Síl Máeluidir king of Uí Chennselaig, reinforced by the community of

2.2 Ferns: cathedral and chapter house from the south-east (photograph courtesy of Christiaan Corlett)

Tech Munnu (Taghmon, the church of St Munna), 35km south of Ferns. According to reports, some four hundred people were slain and Ferns was defeated (AU); Abbot Cilléne died that year too, although it is not clear if he died in the battle. In any case, when Cathal mac Dúnlainge's death was reported two years later, he was recorded as king of Uí Chennselaig *and* prior/vice-abbot (*secnap – secundus abbas*) of Ferns (AU, *s.a.* 819). Kathleen Hughes surmised that the monastic family at Ferns was forced into his appointment on foot of his victory in battle (Hughes 1966, 190–1, 212), and this appears likely. Cathal was succeeded by his sons Cú-chongelt (d. 821) and then Cairpre (d. 844) (Mac Shamhráin 2009). The Ferns-versus-Taghmon battle is typical of the inter-monastic warfare depicted in the annals at this time.

In the early medieval Irish text known as *Félire Óengusso* ('The martyrology of Óengus'), the author refers to 'a lamp lucid (and) beautiful is Ferns the mighty, good-great' (*Lóichet laindrech lígach / Fernae fortrén eobail*) (Stokes 1905, 25). This text has been dated by Pádraig Ó Riain to *c.*830 (2006, 97–8). Ferns is also mentioned in another ninth-century collection, the miscellany known as *The Triads of Ireland* (Meyer 1906; Kelly 2004). Among these eclectic three-part proverbs and pearls of wisdom, Ferns is referred to as the 'The House of Wages [or 'Hire'] of Ireland' (https://celt.ucc.ie/published/T103006.html, ¶13). While it is not known what exactly is meant by this description, it is clear that Ferns was prominent enough in the ninth century to merit inclusion.

The wealth or status of Ferns was also sufficient by the 830s to entice the Vikings to attack (835, 839: AU; AFM; CS), and further raids are noted in the tenth century (917, 919: AFM). The annals revert to more mundane death notices for Ferns for the remainder of the ninth century (table 2.1). Diarmait (d. 870) was possibly the first abbot of Ferns from another branch of the Uí Chennselaig, the Síl nOnchon, ancestors of the house of Diarmait Mac Murchada (Flanagan 2005, 89–90; FA; AFM). In 906, when Áed mac Dubgilla, tánaiste of the Uí Chennselaig, was slain by the Uí Bairrche, the annalists referred incidentally to 'the land of peaceful Fearna ... great Fearna of the thousand noble graces' (AFM; see also FA). Prosaic obits resume for most of the tenth century, the first of whom (Laighnen, d. 937: AFM) is the earliest to be listed as *comarba* 'head' of the church, perhaps attesting the further rise to prominence of Ferns at this time (Flanagan 2005, 90).

It was not unusual during the early medieval period for the head of the church of Ferns to also be in charge of another religious community. Such pluralism of ecclesiastical office is evident, for instance, in 875 when Lachtnán mac Mochtigern was bishop of *Cell Dara* (Kildare) *and* superior of Ferns (AU; AFM). When Laignén died in 937, he was *comarba* of Ferns and Tallaght (AFM), while Cairbre mac Laidgnéin (d. 965) was abbot of Ferns and St Mullins (AFM).

Internecine rivalry is evident once again at Ferns in the early years of the eleventh century. In 1003, for instance, Áed mac Echthigern, an Uí Chennselaig royal heir, was treacherously killed by Máel-na-mBó, king of Uí Chennselaig, in St Máedóc's oratory or prayer-house at Ferns (AU; ATig.; AI). When Ferns was burned by an alliance of Donnchad mac Briain (Bóruma), king of Munster, and Murchad mac Dúnlainge, king of Leinster, in 1042, Diarmait mac Máel-na-mBó took revenge by burning *Glenn Uissen* (Killeshin, Co. Laois), tearing down its oratory, killing a hundred people, and taking several hundred hostages (AU; ATig.; AFM; ALC; CS). The following year, Cairpre (AU) or Conchobhar (AFM) Ua Laidgnéin, *airchinnech* (= *erenagh* 'head of church lands') of Ferns and Tech Moling, died. The ecclesiastical head of Ferns in at least 965 and 1043 was at the same time head of St Mullins and it may be that this situation was the motivation behind later authors claiming St Moling's succession at Ferns in the seventh century (Mac Shamhráin 1996, 9; Sharpe 1991, 359–60). It must surely also be related to the fact that St Mullins was linked with the Síl Cormaic, 'a demoted segment of the Uí Chennselaig' (Mac Shamhráin 1996, 42n7).

It is hard to know why the Uí Laidgnéin appear to have been side-lined in the mid-eleventh century, but Diarmait Ua Rodacháin, bishop (d. 1050: AFM), and Conaing Ua Fairchellaig, abbot (d. 1059), are recorded at Ferns at that time (AU, ATig., AFM). The Uí Laidgnéin returned briefly (e.g., Murchad Ua Laidgnéin, *airchinnech* of Ferns (d. 1062: AFM)), but after the death of Úgaire son of Ua Laidgnéin in 1085 they are not heard of at Ferns again (AU; AFM). Pestilence hit Ireland in 1095 and Cairbre Ua Ceithernaig, abbot of Ferns, was among those to succumb (AU; AI). The names of other church heads of Ferns are recorded in the second half of the eleventh century (table 2.1).

Through these centuries, Ferns developed as a wealthy and populous focal point for commerce, politics and religion. The Mac Murchada dynasty emerged as kings of Uí Chennselaig in the eleventh century. In 1111, Ferns took its place as one of the five cathedral sees of Leinster, giving its name to one of the principal dioceses of the eastern province (McErlean 1914, 11, 16, 23; Gwynn and Hadcock 1970, 78–9; Doyle 2016, 51–5). It appears that the extent of the new diocese was roughly equivalent to the territory of Uí Chennselaig, which included, for instance, part of south-east modern Co. Wicklow (Colfer 2002, 4) and part of eastern Carlow. A new cathedral may have been built at Ferns – or an old church remodelled – to mark its new status but, either way, nothing visible remains above ground of that building. It is likely to have been on the same site as the present cathedral and, judging by the location of the surviving granite crosses, earlier incarnations of the ecclesiastical core of Ferns were located here too. There is also an early medieval cross-slab (Corlett 2011) and fragments of at least two decorated crosses (Kelly and Corlett 2020). The significance of the early medieval church site and the scale of the complex are echoed in the extent of the area enclosed by the surrounding ditches identified in recent years through archaeological excavation and survey (Kavanagh 2006; 2007; Doyle 2016, 53–5; McLoughlin and Stafford 2020; McLoughlin 2020; Bhreathnach and Dowling 2021; ch. 8). The enclosures have impacted the landscape around Ferns, emanating from the centre like ripples in a pond. Modern field boundaries, property plots and roadways more than one kilometre from the centre of the enclosure may reflect the medieval arrangement and organization of the landscape and the effect of the earliest enclosure on the subsequent development of its hinterland.

Aubrey Gwynn and R.N. Hadcock surmised that Bishop Cellach Ua Colmán, who died in 1117 (AU; AFM), was present at the 1111 Synod of Ráith Bressail when Ferns was given diocesan status (1970, 79). Máeleoin Ua Dunagáin, who died in 1125 (AFM; Lynch 1944), was referred to as 'bishop of Uí Chennselaig', a title sometimes used interchangeably with 'bishop of Ferns' (Gwynn and Hadcock 1970, 79; Etchingham 2011, 34). In 1129 Mac Muirgheasa, *fer léigind* of Ferns, passed away (AFM). The term *fer léigind* was commonly used in the annals in the eleventh and twelfth centuries to refer to a head of a school, lector, chief scholar or head of Latin learning (Simms 1998, 248, 254n18). Whatever Mac Muirgheasa's exact job description, the reference gives an impression of the multifunctional nature of the church complex at Ferns at this time.

According to a detailed charter preserved in a seventeenth-century transcript, Diarmait Mac Murchada established a community of Augustinian canons regular at Ferns in 1160X2 (Flanagan 2005; 1998, 114–15; Caley et al. 1817–30, vol. ii, 1040). The foundation was dedicated to St Mary – it was 'the Abbey of Saint Mary the Queen, the Glorious Lady and Virgin' (Mullally 2002, 162–5). St Mary's may have been a new foundation, but it is perhaps more likely that Mac Murchada introduced the Augustinian (perhaps Arrouasian) rule and possibly even some of its practitioners to an existing monastery (Flanagan 1998, 114). Mac Murchada was a remarkable church founder, reformer and patron, and the introduction of Augustinian canons to Ferns was part of a wider picture of church transformation in twelfth-century Ireland. Indeed, what occurred at Ferns reflected a pattern replicated elsewhere, involving a secular patron, colocation of royal seat, cathedral and abbey or priory, and all situated at an ancient church site (Bhreathnach 2019, 10–11). Comparable examples can be found at Louth, Tuam (Galway) and possibly Clonard (Meath). Other sites – such as Glendalough – can be compared with Ferns in several of these categories. At Ferns, Mac Murchada bestowed upon St Mary's income from certain of his lands, as well as ale or mead from his town (*villa*) of Ferns and his chapel/chaplaincy (*capellania mea*), but it is not entirely clear if the canons serviced the cathedral chapter. Marie Therese Flanagan has identified a handful of Irish ecclesiastical sites colocated with secular royal residences at which such a brewing-render may have existed in the twelfth century (Flanagan 1999, 167).

Ferns had daughter 'cells', including Kilmakilloge (Clonattin Upper) and possibly Clone (O'Keeffe 1997, 54; chs 5, 12), while a church and lands associated with Abbot Finach (d. 956) were also said to be granted by Mac Murchada to the Augustinians (Hore 1900–11, vol. vi, 180). Could this have been on the site later occupied by St Peter's (fig. 2.1)? In the early 1540s, the services and rents due to the abbey of Ferns included half an ox carcass, twelve gallons of beer, a sheep, a pig, a hen, four plough-days, three hook-days, three weeding days and six cart-days (White 1943, 371–3). These specifications are likely to have changed little from those set out in the original grant almost four hundred years earlier.

Three versions of the Life of St Máedóc survive, and it is probable that the earliest one dates to the late twelfth century (Kenney 1997, 448–9; Plummer 1922, passim; Doherty 1986; 2002; Sharpe 1991, 223–7, 295–6). It has something of an Augustinian bias (Ó Riain 2011, 432–6), just possibly related to the fact that the canons were ensconced at Ferns from the early 1160s. One of the recurring themes in the Life of Máedóc is the burial at Ferns of generations of Uí Chennselaig kings, including Brandub, who was interred at Ferns, 'where his seed and descendants are

2.3 The *Breac Máedóc* (photograph courtesy of National Museum of Ireland)

buried from that time forth, and the kings of Leinster with their full complement' (Plummer 1922, vol. i, 232 (no. 143); vol. ii, 225 (no. 143); Sharpe 1991, 357–60). The *bachall* or 'staff' of Brandub was left to Ferns as a highly symbolic relic (ch. 4). It is possible that Mac Murchada wished to mark the royal sepulchral tradition of Ferns with the construction of a state-of-the-art Romanesque church (St Mary's) not far to the south-east of the cathedral (chs 3, 6–9). All that survive above ground at St Mary's are the north side of the bicameral church, a possible sacristy (chs 6, 7), an unusual west-end belfry and a vaulted chancel, all of which could date to the decades just before 1160. When the opportunity arose, Mac Murchada established an Augustinian community there, and perhaps also commissioned them to formalize the written Life of St Máedóc. The fact that the monastic complex at St Mary's was not developed by the Augustinians *ab initio* would explain why the traces of a cloister there seem not to align perfectly with the church (chs 6, 7). If St Mary's began as a royal chapel, its status may have been elevated to that of a royal *mortuary* chapel after Mac Murchada's burial there in 1171 (Bhreathnach and Dowling 2021, 199, 203; Kelly and Corlett 2020, 40;

AU; AFM; ALC; MIA; Scott and Martin 1978, 74–5). A fragment of a decorated high cross in the cathedral graveyard is said locally to mark Mac Murchada's grave (Grattan Flood 1916, 28), but this is unlikely to be the case (even though it was probably originally 'a truly monumental cross': Kelly and Corlett 2020, 42).

Mac Murchada's brother-in-law was the church-reformer and archbishop of Glendalough (1153–62) Lorcán Ua Tuathail, who clearly exerted considerable influence over the Leinster king. Architectural similarities between St Mary's in Ferns and St Saviour's Augustinian house at Glendalough (O'Keeffe 1997; chs 6, 7) are unlikely to be coincidental. Ua Tuathail also installed an Augustinian community at Christ Church Cathedral in Dublin around the same time Mac Murchada established St Mary's, the charter for which was witnessed by Ua Tuathail among others.

The Irish-language version of Máedóc's Life contains details about his relics (https://celt.ucc.ie/published/T201000G/text012.html). We are told that he left his staff, bell and reliquary to Ferns, Drumlane and Rossinver, respectively. The staff is now missing, but the reliquary (the *Breac Máedóc*, fig. 2.3) can be found at the National Museum of Ireland (P1021; P1022), while the bell is in Armagh Public Library (Crawford 1923; Laing 2006; Lucas 1986; O'Toole 2013; Moss 2014; Murray 2005). Given what was to unfold later (see below), it is perhaps ironic that the growth in the cult of Máedóc of Ferns may be associated with the rise to power of the Uí Ruairc in Bréifne (Doherty 2002, 269).

In addition to being an ecclesiastical centre, Ferns developed as a secular political hub and became the primary royal residence of the Meic Murchada (Colfer 2013, 60–9; see also O'Keeffe 2015, 196, fig. 89). When the young Mac Murchada became king of Leinster in 1132, he made Ferns his caput. There can be little doubt that he invested heavily in Ferns over the following decades, making it a fitting reflection of his undoubted aspirations. Numismatist Michael Dolley has suggested that bracteate coins were minted in Ferns in the middle of the twelfth century (1987, 817–18). This would fit well with Mac Murchada's reign and would make Ferns, along with Clonmacnoise, one of the very rare sources of Gaelic Irish coinage in pre-Anglo-Norman Ireland.

With a view to extending his kingdom, Mac Murchada launched a raid on Bréifne in 1152. He rustled thousands of cattle from its king Tigernán Ua Ruairc but, more significantly, he also allegedly abducted Ua Ruairc's queen, Derbforgaill, and took her back to Ferns (Mullally 2002, l. 110; MIA). Years later, in revenge, Ua Ruairc, aided by Diarmait Ua Máelsechlainn and the 'Foreigners of Dublin', raided Ferns in 1166, burning Mac Murchada's camp (*longphort*), taking hostages and demolishing his 'stone house' (*caisteóil/caistiall*) (ATig.; AFM; AI; MIA). On the strength of this reference, Ferns is thought by many to be one of the few places in Ireland (and the *only* one outside Connacht) to have had a castle before the coming of the Anglo-Normans (Graham 1988; Flanagan 1996; Barry 2007; Valante 2015). The exact location of the castle is not known, and while it may have been on the site now occupied by Ferns

2.4 Ferns: castle viewed from the south

Castle (fig. 2.4), it is possible that it was closer to the early church site. Indeed, Edel Bhreathnach and Ger Dowling suggest that a rectangular anomaly identified underground through geophysical survey in the field to the south-east of St Mary's represents the remains of Mac Murchada's royal residence (2021, 214, 216–17, 219–24). Although the dating evidence revealed through excavations in 2021 and 2022 does not contradict this interpretation, the function of the building could not be determined (ch. 9).

Several unnamed 'bishops' are mentioned in various sources during the twelfth century (Leslie 1936, 1), but very little is known about most of them, partly because there is no dedicated set of annals for Leinster for that period. The names of some others are known, but little else (table 2.1). Ioseph Ua hÁeda (d. 1183: AFM; Lynch 1944) may have been bishop from as early as 1155 (Cotton 1848, vol. ii, 331), and was certainly in office by the late 1170s (Leslie 1936, 1). He may have been one of the two bishops who negotiated the surrender of the Hiberno-Norse town of Wexford to Diarmait Mac Murchada and Robert Fitz Stephen in 1169 (Colfer 2002, 210–11).

Table 2.1 Names of ecclesiastical heads of Ferns, *c.*600–*c.*1600

Name	Role	Died	Source(s)
Máedóc	bishop	625	AU; ATig.; AFM; CS; AClon.
Do-Chua of Luachair	abbot	654	AU; ATig.; AFM; AClon.
Máedóc		659	ATig.; CS
Tu-Enóc mac Finntan	abbot	663	AU; ATig.; FA; AFM; AClon.
Maol Dogar	bishop	678	ATig.; AFM [676]
Comán	bishop	678	AU
Dirath	bishop	693	AU; ATig.; CS; AFM; AClon.
Moling	bishop	696/7	Plummer 1922, vol. ii, 183, 267; de Paor 2001, 123–4
Cilléne	bishop/abbot	714	AU; ATig.; AFM; AClon.
Aireachtach mac Cuanu	superior	741	AU; AI; ATig.; AFM
Bresal mac Colgan	abbot	749	AU; ATig.; AFM; AClon.
Reothaide	abbot	763	AU; ATig.; AFM
Duibhinnreacht mac Fergus	abbot	776	AU; AFM; AClon.
Crónán		787	AFM
Fiannachtach		799	AU; AFM
Cilléne	abbot	817	AU; AFM
Cathal mac Dúnlainge	prior	819	AU
Cú-chongelt mac Dúnlainge		821	DIB
Cairpre mac Dúnlainge		844	DIB
Finnchellach	abbot	862	FA; AFM
Diarmait	abbot	870	FA; AFM; AClon.
Lachtnán mac Mochtigern	superior	875	AU; AFM
Ferghil	abbot	880	AFM
Lachtnán	abbot	905	AU; AFM
Laidgnén	*comarba*	937	AFM
Flathghus	abbot	944	AFM
Finnachta mac Laidgnéin	*erenach*	956	AU; AFM
Lachtnán	*airchinneach*	958	AU; AFM
Cairbre mac Laidgnéin	abbot	965	AFM
Cathan	abbot	975	AFM
Conn Ua Laidgnéin	abbot	996	AFM
Áed mac Echthigern		1003	AU; AI; ATig.; AFM

Table 2.1 Names of ecclesiastical heads of Ferns, *c.*600–*c.*1600 *(continued)*

Name	Role	Died	Source(s)
Cairpre Conchobhar Ua Laidgnéin	*airchinneach*	1043	AU; AFM
Diarmait Ua Rodacháin	bishop	1050	AFM
Conaing Ua Fairchellaig		1059	AU; ATig.; AFM
Murchadh Ua Laidhgnen	*airchinneach*	1062	AFM
Flan O'Corboy[1]			Harris and Ware 1764, i, 438; Cotton 1848, vol. ii, 331
Fogdath O'Haurecain[1]			Harris and Ware 1764, i, 438; Cotton 1848, vol. ii, 331
Nelan McDonegan[1]			Harris and Ware 1764, i, 438; Cotton 1848, vol. ii, 331
Úgaire son of Ua Laidgnéin	superior	1085	AU; AFM
Cairbre Ua Ceithernaig	abbot	1095	AI; Cotton 1848, vol. ii, 331
Cellach Ua Colmán	bishop	1117	AU; AFM
Carthagus O Malgebry		?	Lynch 1944; Cotton 1848, vol. ii, 331
Máeleoin Ua Dunagáin	bishop	1125	AFM; Lynch 1944
Mac Muirgheasa	lector	1129	AFM
Máelísa Ua Catháin		1135	AFM; Lynch 1944
Rodericus (Rory) Ó Trassy		?	Lynch 1944; Cotton 1848, vol. ii, 331
Brigdenus/Brighdéin Ua Catháin		1172	AFM; ATig.; Lynch 1944
Ioseph Ua hÁeda	bishop	1183	AFM; Lynch 1944
Ailbe Ua Máel Muaid	bishop	1223	AClon.
John St John	bishop	1243	Leslie 1936, 2
Geoffrey St John	bishop	1258	Leslie 1936, 2
Hugh de Lamport	bishop	1282	Leslie 1936, 2; Sweetman 1875–86, vol. ii, 96, no. 587
Richard of Northampton	bishop	1304	Leslie 1936, 2; Anon. 1893, 34, 38
Simon (Hernesby) of Evesham	bishop	1304	Cotton 1848, ii, 332
Robert Walrand	bishop	1311	Mills 1914
Adam of Northampton	bishop	1346	Cotton 1848, ii, 332

1 Henry Cotton noted that 'the times of these prelates' incumbency are not ascertained': Cotton 1848, vol. ii, 331.

Table 2.1 Names of ecclesiastical heads of Ferns, *c.*600–*c.*1600 *(continued)*

Name	Role	Died	Source(s)
Hugh de Saltu/Leixlip	bishop	1347	Cotton 1848, ii, 332–3
Geoffrey Grandfield/ Groseld	bishop	1348	Cotton 1848, ii, 333
John Esmond	bishop	*fl.* 1349	Cotton 1848, ii, 333
William Charnels	bishop	1362	Cotton 1848, ii, 333
Thomas Denne	bishop	1400	Cotton 1848, ii, 333
Patrick Barrett	bishop	1415	Cotton 1848, ii, 333–4
Tadgh O'Beirne/Thady O'Byrne	bishop	*fl.* 1451	
Robert Whitty	bishop	1458	Twemlow 1906, 45, 90; Cotton 1848, ii, 334
John Purcell I	bishop	1479	Twemlow 1921, 193; Cotton 1848, ii, 334
Laurence Neville	bishop	1503	Cotton 1848, ii, 334
Edmund Comerford	bishop	1509	Cotton 1848, ii, 334
Nicholas Comyn	bishop	*fl.* 1519	Cotton 1848, ii, 334
John Purcell II	bishop	1539	Cotton 1848, ii, 334
Bernard Ó Dónaill	bishop	1541	
Gabriel de S. Serio	bishop	1542	
Alexander Devereux	bishop	1566	Morrin 1861, 50; Leslie 1936, 5–6; Cotton 1848, ii, 334–5
John Devereux	bishop	1578	Morrin 1861, 497; Leslie 1936, 6; Cotton 1848, ii, 335
Hugh Allen	bishop	1597	Cotton 1848, ii, 335
Abbots of St Mary's			
Thomas O'Druffin	abbot	1438–60	Grattan Flood 1916, 32; Twemlow 1933, 109
Donald O'Murphy	abbot	1460+	Grattan Flood 1916, 32
Nicholas O'Druffin	abbot	1460s?	Twemlow 1933, 110
Patrick O'Murphy	abbot	1460s?	Twemlow 1933, 278
Dermot O'Druffin	abbot	1477+	Grattan Flood 1916, 32
Owen Doyle	abbot	1488+	Grattan Flood 1916, 32
William Lacy	abbot	1507+	Grattan Flood 1916, 32
William Doyle	abbot	<1539	Grattan Flood 1916, 32

FERNS UNDER THE ANGLO-NORMANS

Control of Uí Chennselaig was divided between the Meic Gilla Pátraic of Osraige and Murchadh Mac Murchada. Diarmait Mac Murchada was banished to England but, before he left, he burned Ferns so that it would not come into the hands of his enemies (AFM). He returned within a year (Mullally 2002, 402–3), however, and embedded himself at Ferns in anticipation of the arrival of a party of foreign mercenaries. In May 1169 Robert Fitz Stephen with 390 fighting men and Maurice Fitz Gerald with about 140 soldiers arrived at Bannow Bay from south Wales. The main Anglo-Norman forces disembarked the following year, led by Richard Fitz Gilbert de Clare, earl of Pembroke, now better known as Strongbow. Following Strongbow's arrival, Mac Murchada's position strengthened considerably and he was restored as king of Leinster.

According to Gerald of Wales, Mac Murchada had offered Strongbow his daughter Aífe's hand in marriage, along with succession to the kingship of Leinster after his death (Scott and Martin 1978, 28–9; Flanagan 2009). Their marriage was celebrated in Christ Church Cathedral at Waterford on 23 August 1170 and Strongbow became heir to Mac Murchada. Mac Murchada died suddenly 'of an insufferable and unknown disease' in May 1171 at Ferns, where he was buried (AU; AFM; ALC; MIA; Scott and Martin 1978, 74–5; Mullally 2002, l. 1731).

As anticipated, Strongbow was acknowledged as the new king of Leinster. He spent more than a week at Ferns in early 1172, and returned soon afterwards to give his daughter Basilia's hand in marriage to Robert de Quency (Mullally 2002, ll 2157–9, 2741–6), whom he had appointed constable of Leinster. Strongbow cultivated some loyal supporters among the Gaelic Irish of the region, among whom was Domnall Mac Murchada Cáemánach (Kavanagh) who the earl ordered to execute Murchad Ua Briain (who had seemingly deserted Strongbow's father-in-law in his hour of need) and his son (Mullally 2002, ll 2177–80; Scott and Martin 1978, 287n8, 294n32, 309n132). The men were hunted down, captured, brought to Ferns and publicly decapitated. Their bodies were fed to dogs. The lands thus seized from Ua Briain were then granted by Strongbow to his son-in-law de Quency. Strongbow was clearly consolidating control in the region and this included the town, which was quite evidently the centre of his operations here. In *c.*1175 he granted to the Knights Hospitaller one burgage at Ferns, as well as ten carucates (*c.*1,215ha) on the manor (Anon. 1891, 11–12; Colfer 2013, 25, 27). In 1212 William Marshal was arbiter in a dispute between the Hospitallers and the bishop of Ferns over several churches; these may have formed part of Strongbow's original grant. The 1175 reference to a burgage at Ferns confirms its borough status, and it may have been Strongbow who issued its first charter (although none is known to survive).

Strongbow clearly recognized the historical, political and strategic importance of Ferns and the richness of its hinterland and so he chose to retain it as demesne

2.5 Glascarrig, Co. Wexford: motte overlooking the Irish Sea (photograph courtesy of the Discovery Programme, Robert Shaw and the Climate, Heritage and Environment of Reefs, Islands and Headlands (CHERISH) Project)

('belonging to a lord') land. As a diocesan seat, Strongbow could not allow the bishop of Ferns to be a puppet of his own supporters or, worse still, the Meic Murchada. The mensal estate of Ferns, which soon became a key seignorial manor of the new settlers, was roughly equivalent in extent to the large medieval parish of the same name, which, in turn, was essentially the *trícha cét* of Fearna.[2] Similarly, the liberty of Wexford as created by the lords of Leinster, the territory of the Uí Chennselaig and the diocese of Ferns were all approximately coterminous with each other. It is possible that Glascarrig (fig. 2.5) operated as the port for Ferns (Colfer 2002, 11, 42), but it may still have been the challenge of accessing Ferns from the sea that made Strongbow select Wexford as his caput in Ireland rather than the traditional Uí Chennselaig capital (Orpen 1968, vol. i, 373).

2 A *trícha cét* – literally 'thirty hundred' – was a unit of landholding in eleventh- and twelfth-century Ireland.

Strongbow died in 1176 and, due to the minority of his daughter and heir Isabel, his lands passed into the hand of Henry II. The king appointed loyal courtier William Fitz Audelin as Isabel's ward and deputy over Strongbow's properties in Ireland. The following year Fitz Audelin allocated Ferns to Maurice Fitz Gerald's sons (William, Gerald and Alexander), possibly in exchange for Wicklow Castle (Leland 1773, vol. i, 136–7). The Fitz Geralds built a castle at Ferns, even though (or perhaps *because*) it was surrounded by enemies (Scott and Martin 1978, 170–3; Butler 1849, 13; Orpen 1968, vol. ii, 7; vol. iii, 54–6). The castle, which was almost certainly a motte or a ringwork, was soon destroyed by Fitz Audelin's nephew Walter 'the German', governor of Wexford, on the orders of Muirchertach Mac Murchada. Muirchertach was a nephew of Diarmait and had been permitted to remain in Ferns having come to terms with Strongbow (Orpen 1968, vol. i, 390). Gerald of Wales recounted the tale of *Fantasticus*, a young member of the Fitz Gerald household, who plundered the church and Ferns, went mad and then predicted repeatedly that the castle would be destroyed and 'our men slain' (O'Meara 1982, 87–8, no. 76; Busby 2017, 209).

In August 1189 Isabel de Clare married William Marshal and once she was old enough the couple were allocated their Irish lands including Ferns. In due course, their estates passed first to their eldest son William II and then, on his death in 1231, to their second son Richard. The Ferns grant was not straightforward, as it was made up of two separate manors, the larger of which was granted in 1232 by Richard Marshal to his sister-in-law Eleanor, countess of Pembroke, as part of her dower (Sweetman 1875–86, vol. i, 289, no. 1950). In 1245 the Marshal manor was valued at £81 15*s*. (Hore 1900–11, vol. vi, 6, 9; Sweetman 1875–86, vol. iv, no. 306), making it the most profitable demesne in the county (Colfer 2013, 60–1). The second, smaller, manor, which was held by the bishop of Ferns, extended to some 12,500 statute acres and was another of the principal estates in medieval Wexford (MacDonnell 1904, 61; Colfer 2002, 212–15). In 1280 the episcopal manor was worth more than £11 10*s*. per year, £2 of which came from the burgesses of Ferns (Hore 1900–11, vol. vi, 190–1). Except for Dublin, Ferns was the wealthiest diocese in the whole of the country according to the papal taxation of 1303–6 (Whelan 2018, 28). At the time of the Civil Survey in the mid-seventeenth century, the bishop of Ferns still held the townlands of Lower Ferns, Kilboro, Kilthomas and Bolinaspick (Colfer 2002, 215; Simington 1953, 266). The place-name 'Bolinaspick' (*buaile an easpaig* 'cattle-fold' or 'summer-pasture' of the bishop: www.logainm.ie) to the north-east of the town must surely reflect the practice of booleying/transhumance and episcopal ownership in the Middle Ages. In general terms, the land around Ferns is agriculturally rich and versatile, being situated in the Clonroche Soil Series, which are among the most productive and easily tilled in the south-east of Ireland (Colfer 1987, 93; ch. 1).

Formerly abbot of the Cistercian house at Baltinglass (Gwynn and Hadcock 1970, 79), Ailbe Ua Máel Muaid (Albin O'Mulloy) was elected bishop of Ferns in 1186 and was the last Gaelic Irishman to hold that office (Leslie 1936, 1–2). He is said to have been present at the coronation of King Richard I ('the Lionheart') at Westminster Abbey in 1189 (Mac Geoghegan 1844, 278), was at Nottingham with John in 1192 and dedicated a chapel at Waverley Abbey in Surrey in 1201. He was papal judge delegate in Irish affairs and in 1215 he attended the Fourth Lateran Council in Rome (Sweetman 1875–86, vol. i, 101, no. 658). It has been tentatively suggested that the first compilation of Latin Lives of Irish saints was collected and edited by Ua Máel Muaid (Sharpe 1991, 362–3) during his tenure at Ferns. According to himself, Gerald of Wales was offered the bishopric of Ferns (Gwynn and Hadcock 1970, 79; Liebermann and Pauli 1885, vol. ii, 13), but he turned it down as it was his ambition to become bishop of St David's in south Wales.

The unusual 'double' manor of Ferns inevitably resulted in disputes between the secular and ecclesiastical lords (Orpen 1968, vol. iii, 29–31). In 1218, for instance, William Marshal I became engaged in a dispute with Bishop Ua Máel Muaid concerning ownership of certain lands. The bishop was in possession of a letter from Pope Innocent III requiring the earl to return these crosslands, under threat of excommunication (Anon. 1864, 138–9; Orpen 1968, vol. i, 295–6; Dunning 1961, 106–7). The matter was not resolved, however, and appears to have rumbled on for years. Some believed a bishop's curse was the cause of the end of the Marshal line (Luard 1872–84, vol. iv, 491–3; Hanmer 1633, 352; Keating 1908, 359; Cox 1689, 58; Mac Geoghegan 1844, 301). A misunderstanding – or opportunism – in relation to the 'double' manor of Ferns may have been behind an occurrence in 1280 after which William de Valence secured a royal pardon (from his nephew, King Edward I) for the trespass of his seneschal (Walter de Raddesham) in granting pardons for homicide in the lands of the bishop of Ferns (Sweetman 1875–86, vol. ii, 348, no. 1690; Hand 1967, 12). In 1299, Philip de Barry, constable of Ferns Castle, was charged along with more than twenty-five other men by Bishop Richard of Northampton with entering the crosslands of Ferns and taking cattle and goods from the Irish betaghs (*hibernici*) of the bishop, to the value of £40 (Mills 1905, 254–5; Colfer 2002, 217–18). The cattle and goods were returned. In 1306, Johanna de Valence was caught up in a dispute with Roger de la Hide, sergeant of the crosslands of Ferns, who was involved in releasing prisoners from Wexford Castle, which was outside his jurisdiction (Mills 1914, 239, 283, 310; Colfer 2002, 82).

The reference to the bishop's betaghs at Ferns in 1299 is interesting in terms of understanding the nature of agricultural labour in the town's hinterland. Betagh (*biatach*) tenure was a medieval system whereby a person held land from his lord in return for carrying out certain manual tasks, mostly agricultural work, on the demesne lands of the manor (Curtis 1936, 62–76; Mills 1892; Price 1966; Mac Niocaill 1966; Hand 1966, 99–102). These tenants, or betaghs, were almost exclusively Gaelic Irish, and had a status roughly equivalent to that of the villein in England (Potterton 2005,

2.6 Ferns: late medieval iron plough coulter (photograph courtesy of Catherine McLoughlin)

125–8; Murphy and Potterton 2010, 184–9). Although they were not exactly slaves, betaghs were unfree, had no property rights, and could be sold or given away with their property. The work they did for their lord did not exempt them from land rent, and they normally paid the same amount as the other classes of tenant on the manor. Betaghs constituted a socially cohesive and distinctive section of society, albeit at the bottom of the social scale.

Bishop Ua Máel Muaid died in 1223 (AFM; ALC; AI; AClon.) having overseen some hagiographical compilation at Ferns that may have been motivated by his contretemps with the Marshal (Mac Shamhráin 2013, 336–7). Ua Máel Muaid was succeeded by the diocese's first Anglo-Norman bishop, John St John (d. 1243; Sweetman 1875–86, vol. i, 167, nos 1099, 1101; 171, no. 1122). St John had been treasurer of Limerick from 1212, and was later a justice itinerant (Leslie 1936, 2). One of a number of medieval bishops of Ferns involved in significant secular administration, he was also treasurer of the exchequer at Dublin from 1226 to 1232 (table 2.4). The growth of central administration with its detailed written records and complex financial operations required competent, literate and numerate officials. The higher ranks of clergy – many of whom came from knightly families – proved to be a rich source of such men in Ireland as in other parts of medieval Europe (Turner 1988).

James Ware recorded that St John was a benefactor of the see and may have erected or endowed a deanery in Ferns (Harris and Ware 1764, i, 440). In 1226 St John was given the right to hold a market each Sunday at Ferns as well as an annual eight-day June fair (Sweetman 1875–86, vol. i, 216, no. 1429). Close to Rosslare at the south-eastern tip of Wexford, Mayglass became an episcopal manor of the bishop of Ferns (Hore 1900–11, vol. vi, 190) and it may have been St John who founded the borough there (Bradley and King 1990, 94). He certainly seems to have been a dynamic and versatile individual, and he was clearly held in high regard by the crown. In 1234 he was granted safe conduct for his trip to England to speak with the king (Anon. 1906a, 46). St John held the right to hold a weekly market and annual fair at Enniscorthy (Sweetman, 1875–86, vol. i, no. 1429) but he elected to swap his holdings at Enniscorthy with the Prendergasts in return for lands more convenient elsewhere in

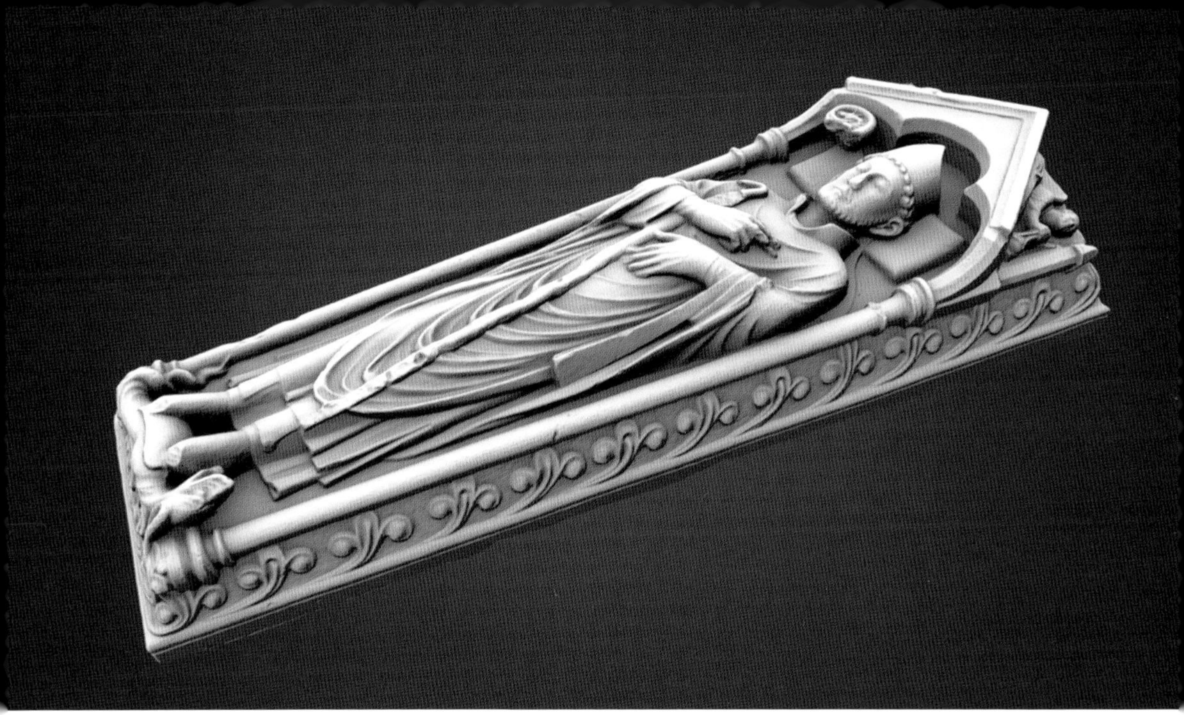

2.7 Ferns: effigial tomb in the cathedral (image courtesy of the Discovery Programme and Robert Shaw)

the diocese (Gwynn and Hadcock 1970, 175; Hore, 1900–11, vol. vi, 343; Moore 1996, no. 1436). It has been suggested that St John was also responsible for introducing the practice of manorial agriculture at Ferns, which would tie in well with the documented presence of 'betaghs of the bishop' on the manor, and perhaps the discovery by Catherine McLoughlin of a large medieval iron plough coulter at Castleland in 2018 (McLoughlin and Stafford 2020, 92–4, 98–9; fig. 2.6). The latter find is all-the-more interesting considering the earliest known reference to a plough coulter in Ireland appears in the Life of Máedóc of Ferns (Monk 2018, 49).

It is likely that the present cathedral was begun during St John's episcopacy (O'Keeffe and Carey Bates 2016, 84–92; Gwynn and Hadcock 1970, 78–80; Hore 1900–11, vol. vi, 185; Moore 1996, no. 1445). The fine 2.3m mid-thirteenth-century effigial tomb of a bishop in the south wall of the cathedral (fig. 2.7) is likely to commemorate St John (d. 1243) (Hunt 1974, vol. i, cat. 262, pp 237–8; vol. ii, pl. 65; Rae 1987, 760–1). He wears a mitre and carries a crozier, while a dragon can be seen at his feet. It has also been suggested that the tomb commemorates not John St John but Adam of Northampton or Geoffrey St John or even St Máedóc (Hore 1910, 297–300). If it *is* a Northampton, it seems more likely to be Richard than Adam, as Richard is known to have been buried at Ferns Cathedral in 1304 (Leslie 1936, 2; Cotton 1848, ii, 332).

While the *later* medieval bishopric of Ferns was not dominated by a small group of families to the same extent as it had been in the *early* Middle Ages, a handful of surnames do crop up repeatedly (both within ecclesiastical offices and across other administrative roles). John St John was succeeded as bishop by his namesake Geoffrey – although perhaps not directly. Geoffrey had been a clerk of John as early as 1224

2.8 Ferns: window tracery reused in St Peter's Church (photograph courtesy of Christiaan Corlett)

(Sweetman 1875–86, vol. i, 185, no. 1215; vol. ii, 52, no. 337) and later held the offices of treasurer of Limerick and escheator of Ireland before being elected bishop of Ferns in 1254 (Leslie 1936, 2). It is possible but not proven that Geoffrey and John were brothers (Harris and Ware 1764, i, 441), and it is probable that the other St John church officials in Ferns were kinsmen (see below, p. 40).

Annalists noted 'a very severe pestilence' in various parts of Ireland in 1204 and St Mary's Abbey in Ferns was among the houses to suffer (AI). Such events were exceptional, however, and, as was the case with large parts of the country, Ferns thrived through most of the thirteenth century (Potterton 2019). The medieval borough was almost certainly located along the main street between the castle and the cathedral. While the borough appears to have been unwalled (Thomas 1992, vol. i, 162), its success is indicated by the fact that by about 1280 the population had reached some two hundred burgesses (Hore 1900–11, vol. vi, 190–1; Bradley and King 1990, 49). The Norman-French epic poem called by some 'The song of Dermot and the earl' refers to certain lodgings at Ferns as '*osteus*' (Mullally 2002, l. 818), but it is not clear what form these took. Various crafts and occupations are attested in the archaeological record, while the thirteenth-century Dublin guild merchant roll lists a tanner from Ferns (Connolly and Martin 1992, 51). In the early fourteenth century, the lords of the town were able to derive some income from the ovens there as well as from honey produced in the surrounding woods. It appears that pannage was also practised (the right to allow livestock (especially pigs) to feed on fallen acorns and other nuts in a forest) (Hore 1900–11, vol. vi, 9).

Despite the presence of imported wares, archaeological excavations at Ferns Castle and elsewhere in the town have demonstrated that most of the pottery in medieval Ferns was made locally (Sweetman 1979, 225–32, 241). The modern Church of Ireland cathedral (St Edan's) was built in 1817 and renovated in 1901–3 (Grattan

2.9a Ferns: Romanesque masonry at St Peter's Church (photograph courtesy of Christiaan Corlett)

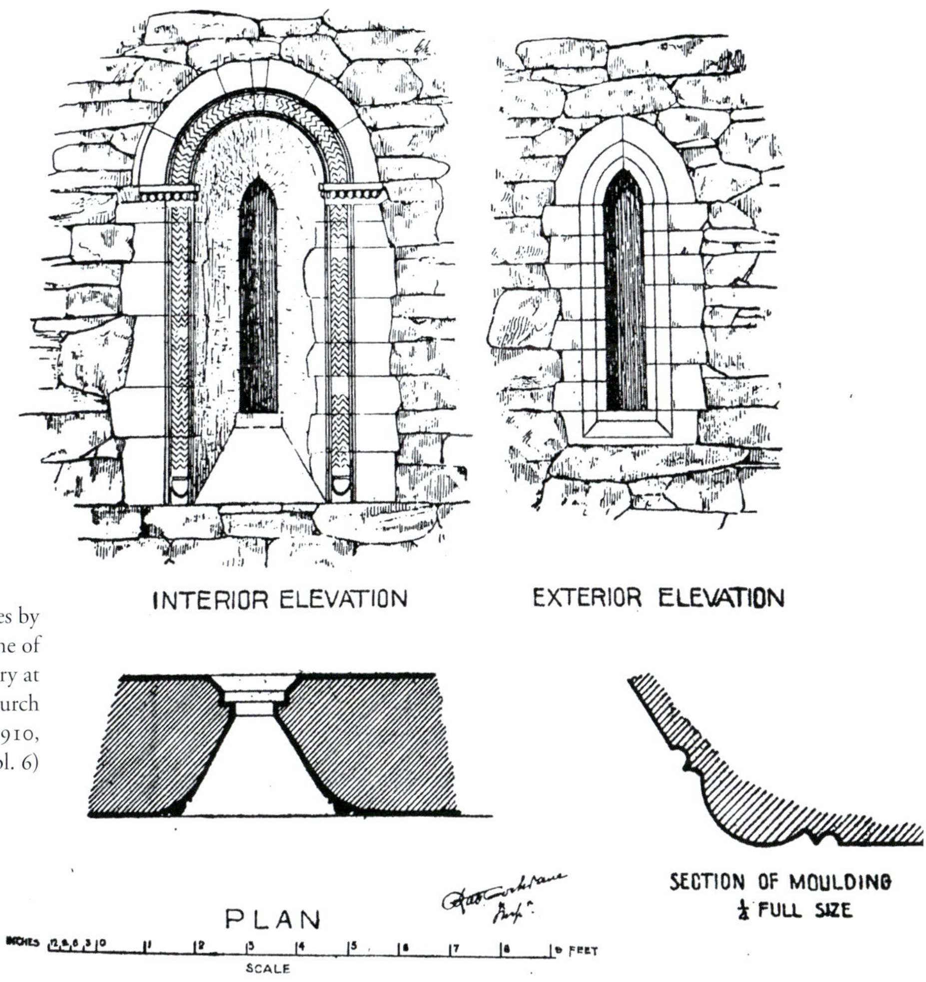

2.9b Ferns: sketches by Robert Cochrane of Romanesque masonry at St Peter's Church (after Cochrane 1910, 57, pl. 6)

2.10 Ferns: sketch of tile depicting deer with arrow through its neck (after Eames and Fanning 1988, 106 (T66))

Flood 1916, 32), but it incorporates parts of a thirteenth-century forerunner, notably the north and south walls of the chancel. It is possible that some of the thirteenth-century window tracery reused in the later St Peter's Church (fig. 2.8) nearby came from the cathedral (and some Romanesque masonry at St Peter's was probably taken from St Mary's; ch. 5; fig. 2.9). Several fine medieval floor tiles were found at the west end of the cathedral during works in 1956, including a unique fragmentary example depicting a bird or a stag with an arrow through its neck (Eames and Fanning 1988, 74, 81, 82, 84–5, 106 (T66), 109 (T121), 115 (T204), 117 (T236); fig. 2.10). In 2016 part of an inlaid and glazed thirteenth-century floor tile was found near the cathedral (Corlett 2018; Byrne 2018; NMI 2018:90; fig. 2.11). The tile displays the upper portion of a mounted knight. Roof tiles were excavated at Ferns Castle in the 1970s (Sweetman 1979, 232–3), while features carved from Dundry stone can also be seen at Ferns. In 1931 John Doyle found an enamelled bronze book clasp decorated with millefiori near St Mary's Abbey (*Irish Times*, 8 Sept. 1931; Mahr and Raftery 1932–41, vol. i, 41; pl. 41:4; Bradley and King 1990, 61; NMI 1931:315; fig. 2.12). The discovery of a fine iron rowel spur of possible thirteenth-century date in the graveyard reflects the wealth of the population (Bradley and King 1990, 61; fig. 2.13).[3] The general picture is of a place well-connected internationally at this time.

Indications are that things were relatively secure in the early to mid-thirteenth century, and resources were available to keep it that way. In May 1251, for instance, royal letters 'of unlimited protection for the abbot and convent of St Mary's of Ferns' were issued (Anon. 1908, 97; Sweetman 1875–86, vol. i, 468, no. 3149), while during vacancies the bishopric typically would be guarded by 'horse soldiers' (*servientes equites*)

3 The rowel spur is on display in the National Museum of Ireland (Wk108/7913W5).

2.11 Ferns: tile fragment depicting mounted knight (photograph courtesy of Christiaan Corlett)

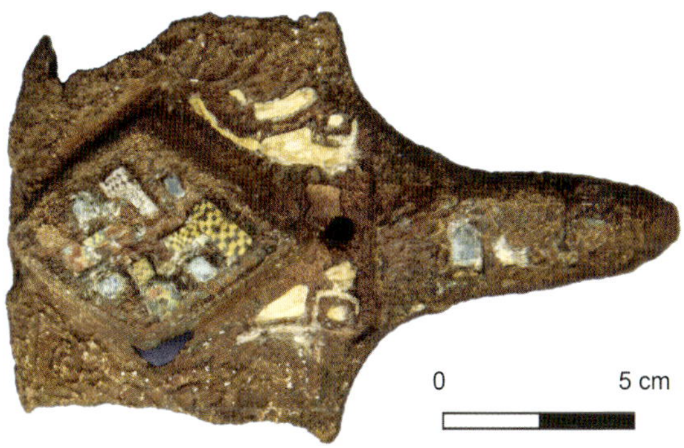

2.12 Ferns: fragment of bronze book clasp (photograph courtesy of National Museum of Ireland)

2.13 Ferns: iron rowel spur with sixteen spikes (photograph courtesy of National Museum of Ireland)

(e.g., 1266: Sweetman 1875–86, vol. ii, 129–30, no. 807). In 1253, the bishop of Ferns is recorded as having at his caput a park (possibly called 'John's Park') containing wild cattle (Sweetman 1875–86, vol. ii, 45, no. 297; Beglane 2015, 25, 52, 56, 186, 191). The remains of fallow deer have been recovered at Ferns Castle (Whelan 1979; Beglane 2015, 51, 56). Zooarchaeologist Fiona Beglane estimates that 'St Edan's and Ferns Demesne are likely to cover the site of the original park held by the bishop of Ferns' (2015, 186). In this context, it is interesting that Elizabeth Eames and Thomas Fanning suggested that the (probable mid-thirteenth-century) tile picked up at Ferns Cathedral in 1956, seemingly depicting a deer (or a bird?) with an arrow piercing its neck (fig. 2.10), was perhaps part of a hunting scene (Eames and Fanning 1988, 74, 81, 106 (T66)).

The cathedral staff included a precentor, an archdeacon and canons (table 2.2). The office of dean of Ferns was created in 1255 (Gwynn and Hadcock 1970, 80; Sweetman 1875–86, vol. ii, 95, no. 579; 151–2, no. 891; Connolly 1995, 140–1; Mills 1914, 48–9, 155; Sheehy 1962–5, vol. ii, 174, 234). The unusual building to the east of the cathedral appears to date to around this time and it might have been a diocesan chapter house. There were also a treasurer, a chancellor, a clerk and ten prebendaries. On 10 June 1281 Richard of Northampton, dean of the chapter of Ferns, notified the king of the death of Hugh, their late bishop, and sent Philip de Braybrook and Hamo de Wexford, 'purveyors' (*iconomi*: officials in charge of the finances of a church) of their church, to request a licence to elect a successor (Sweetman 1875–86, vol. ii, 439, no. 1932; 443, no. 1940; Anon. 1893, 30). Dean Richard, 'a man provident and discreet', was elected unanimously (Sweetman 1875–86, vol. ii, 443, no. 1943; 446, no. 1962; 453–4, no. 1985; Anon. 1893, 34, 38).

Several canons of Ferns are named (table 2.3). One Richard 'the chancellor' of Ferns, who also served as canon in 1252–3, had studied in Paris and was awarded an MA (Hayes Somers 1997, 159; Theiner 1864, 56). Like several other canons, Robert Walrand eventually became bishop (and he died at Ferns in 1311 (Harris and Ware 1764, i, 442; Anon. 1894, 415)). In 1414 Richard Montayne, clerk and prebendary of Ferns, was given licence to absent himself from Ireland for three years and to receive all issues and profits of his prebend, notwithstanding any statute, while studying at Oxford or Cambridge (Crooks, PR 2 Henry V, no. 220; see also Anon. 1907, 440). The licence was extended in 1417, for half his absence only (Crooks, PR 5 Henry V, no. 45). William Furlong, a priest from Ferns, studied canon law at Oxford between 1419 and 1427. He received a canonry of Ferns before becoming rector of Tintern (Hayes Somers 1997, 166; CPL 7:168, 482). The John Ingram listed as a canon of Ferns in the early fourteenth century (Sweetman 1875–86, vol. v, 101, no. 297; Connolly 1995, 140; Leslie 1936, 2–3) is likely to be the same John Ingram commemorated in a Latin inscription (*Hic jacet Dom. Joãẽs Ingram quodã Rector istius Ecclesiæ, cujus anima tu dõne miserere Deus*) on a stone grave cover with an incised

Table 2.2 Officers of the cathedral of Ferns

Name	Office	Year(s)	Source(s)
Nicholas	archdeacon	1285	Connolly 1987, 94; Gilbert 1884, vol. ii, lxxxiv–lxxxv
G. de Eswell	precentor	1262	McNeill 1950, 95
Hugh de Lamport	treasurer	1250s	Sweetman 1875–86, vol. ii, 96, no. 586; Leslie 1936, 2
Richard of Northampton	dean of chapter	1281	Sweetman 1875–86, vol. ii, 439, no. 1932; 443, no. 1940; Anon. 1893, 30
Nicholas le Botiller	chancellor	1304	Sweetman 1875–86, vol. v, 125, no. 373; Connolly 1995, 141
William de Braybrook	clerk	1304	Sweetman 1875–86, vol. v, 125, no. 373; Connolly 1995, 141
Nicholas de Sandford	dean	1309	
Thomas Walshe	clerk		McNeill 1950, 269; Brewer and Brodie (eds) 1920
Philip de Braybrook Hamo de Wexford	purveyors		Sweetman 1875–86, vol. ii, 439, no. 1932; 443, no. 1940; Anon. 1893, 30
Robert Sotlewell[4]	chancellor	1331	Gilbert 1884, vol. i, 528
Galfridus[4]	treasurer	1331	Gilbert 1884, vol. i, 528
Richard le Latimer[4]	precentor	1331	Gilbert 1884, vol. i, 528
Nicholas Moncel[4]	dean	1331	Gilbert 1884, vol. i, 528
Nicholas[4]	archdeacon	1331	Gilbert 1884, vol. i, 528
Roche	dean	1479	Leslie 1936, 5
Thomas Hay	dean	1536	Morrin 1861, 22, 26, 28
William Phillips	archdeacon	1552	Morrin 1861, 278
Reginald	archdeacon		*CSMA*, vol. ii, 170–2
Peter de Currache	archdeacon	1363	Anon. 1912, 343, 349
Robert Collyn	archdeacon	1393	Twemlow 1902, 449
Robert Done/Denne	archdeacon	1393	Twemlow 1902, 449
Gerald Sutton	precentor	1398	Twemlow 1904a, 101
Nicholas Brown (d. 1412)	treasurer	1409, 1412	Crooks, PR 10 Henry IV, no. 165; Twemlow 1904, 242, 370–1
Augustine MacBradaich	treasurer	1412	Twemlow 1904, 370–1
Nicholas Alhart	treasurer		Twemlow 1904, 118, 120, 370
Thomas Wogan	clerk	1411	Twemlow 1904, 243
Elias Borlagh	treasurer	1415–16	Crooks, PR 3 Henry V, no. 68; PR 3 Henry V, no. 105
Laurence Boscher	archdeacon	1437	Twemlow 1909, 660
John Laffran	clerk	1453	Twemlow 1915, 626
Thomas Petit (d. *c.*1461)	dean	1437, 1461	Twemlow 1909, 650–1; 1933, 111
Laurence Hobme/Neville	archdeacon	1462	Twemlow 1933, 156
Nicholas Kethyn (d. 1470)	dean	1461, 1470	Twemlow 1933, 111, 780
Henry Roche	dean	1470	Twemlow 1933, 780
Roche	dean	1479	Leslie 1936, 5
Thomas Purcell	clerk	1483	Crooks, PR 22 Edward IV, no. 13
Thomas Hay	dean	1536	Morrin 1861, 22, 26, 28
William Phillips	archdeacon	1552	Morrin 1861, 278

4 These officials were signatories to an agreement between the bishop of Ferns and the abbot of Dunbrody in the year that the bishop transferred his seat from Ferns to Fethard (1331), but it is not clear if the officials had yet moved south.

floriated cross in the chancel of St Catherine's Church, Tacumshin, where Ingram was once rector (Moore 1996, no. 1218).

The process by which church officials were appointed is not entirely clear, but it is likely that the bishop was responsible for most of them. During the episcopacy of John St John, we find H. St John as his treasurer, G. St John as his chancellor, W. St John as his precentor and N. St John as his archdeacon (Gilbert 1884, vol. i, 82; vol. ii, 170–2). Archdeacon Nicholas St John was still in office in 1284, even though he was by then 'blind and infirm' (Sweetman 1875–86, vol. ii, 564, no. 2361; vol. iii, 21, no. 35; 27–8, no. 49; 48, no. 149).

The dean and two canons of Ferns (acting as the bishop's commissaries) were severely reprimanded in November 1263 by the priors of Newtown Trim (in Meath) and Colp (in Louth); they were called out for their effrontery, audacity and malignity and for disturbing and trying to impede the jurisdiction of the priors in question in relation to a land dispute in the diocese of Dublin involving the Hospitallers (McNeill 1950, 96, 97, 100–1; see also Virtuani 2016, 201–2). The Hospitallers appear to have been especially suspicious of the representatives from Ferns, while the prior of Colp wished 'that they were discreet and wise' and wondered why they sought to 'set their teeth' into him and his colleague. In general, however, Ferns clerical staff seem to have been well regarded and an apprenticeship at Ferns was, for many, a ticket to high office (table 2.4). Nicholas Fleming took his MA at Oxford and was a canon of Ferns. In 1385 he was appointed prebend of St Patrick's Cathedral, Dublin. Fleming was chancellor of Dublin until 1404, when he was appointed archbishop of Armagh, a position he held until his death in 1416 (Hayes Somers 1997, 166). Fleming was succeeded (in 1418, after a vacancy) by John Swayne, who had also been a canon and prebendary of Ferns.

Through his marriage to William Marshal's grand-daughter Joan de Munchensi, French nobleman William de Valence (half-brother of King Henry III) became lord of Wexford *c.*1250. He was succeeded in this role in 1296 by his son Aymer (d. 1324). The de Valences were generally not present in Ireland and appointed constables in their place. Their absence meant that even major restoration and reinforcement of their key castle were unlikely to stem the Gaelic revival that was gathering momentum in north Wexford. Upgrades at Ferns Castle in the mid-to-late thirteenth century can probably be attributed to the de Valences and are likely – in part at least – to be a response to increasing threats from the Gaelic Irish (Colfer 2013, 62–5). Tadhg O'Keeffe and Margaret Coughlan consider that Ferns Castle was built in its *entirety* by the de Valences after they took over the lands in the mid-thirteenth century; the current edifice is all that survives of a castle built in the 1270s or 1280s (2003, 147; see also O'Keeffe 2021, 159–61). In this case, references to the castle of Ferns in the 1220s and 1230s likely relate to a Marshal construction that was either on a different site or, more probably, demolished to make way for the de Valence fortification.

Table 2.3 Canons of the cathedral of Ferns

Name	Year(s)	Source(s)
G. de Valle		*CSMA*, vol. ii, 170–2
I. de Tantun		*CSMA*, vol. ii, 170–2
Richard 'the chancellor'	1252–3	Hayes Somers 1997, 159; Theiner 1864, 56
John the chaplain	1253	Anon. 1908, 248
John de Banewe	1263	McNeill 1950, 97, 100–1
John Fitz Thomas		
John O'Flanagan		Twemlow 1960, 228
Simon de Capella	1263	McNeill 1950, 97, 100–1
Philip de Braybrook	1282	Leslie 1936, 2
Hamo de Wexford	1282	Leslie 1936, 2
Robert Walrand d. 1311	1305	Harris and Ware 1764, i, 442; Anon. 1894, 415; Mills 1914, 48–9
T. Barath		*CSMA*, vol. ii, 170–2
Thomas Cantok	1305	Mills 1914, 48–9
William Denne		Twemlow 1904, 243
John Ingram	Early 14C	Sweetman 1875–86, vol. v, 101, no. 297; Connolly 1995, 140; Leslie 1936, 2–3
Stephen de Carlioun	1311	Leslie 1936, 3
Nicholas Whitty	1347	Anon. 1905, 526
Nicholas Fleming	*c.*1380	Hayes Somers 1997, 166
Robert Marchal	1385	Anon. 1900, 282
Robert Huntyngden	1386	Crooks, PR 9 Richard II, no. 168
John de Keton	1388	Anon. 1900, 282, 431, 435; Crooks, PR 12 Richard II, no. 56; CR 12 Richard II, no. 1
Richard Montayne	1414	Crooks, PR 2 Henry V, no. 220; Crooks, PR 5 Henry V, no. 45; Anon. 1907, 440; Davis 2000, 154–5
John Swayne	*c.*1415	Crooks, PR 7 Henry IV, no. 160, PR 10 Henry IV, no. 160; Twemlow 1904, 349, 374; Twemlow 1904a, 614–15
William Furlong	*c.*1428	Hayes Somers 1997, 166; CPL 7:168, 482
David O'Druffin	1447–8	Twemlow 1915, 400, 413
John Whitty	1450, 1453	Crooks, PR 28 Henry VI, no. 13; Twemlow 1915, 667–8
John Purcell	1457	Twemlow 1921, 193, 324, 329, 338; Leslie 1936, 5
Thomas O'Fergal	1461	Twemlow 1933, 109
Patrick O'Byrne	1467	Twemlow 1933, 278
Laurence Neville	1478	Leslie 1936, 5
Thomas Purcell	1483	Crooks, PR 22 Edward IV, no. 13
John Faelan	1487	Twemlow 1960, 208

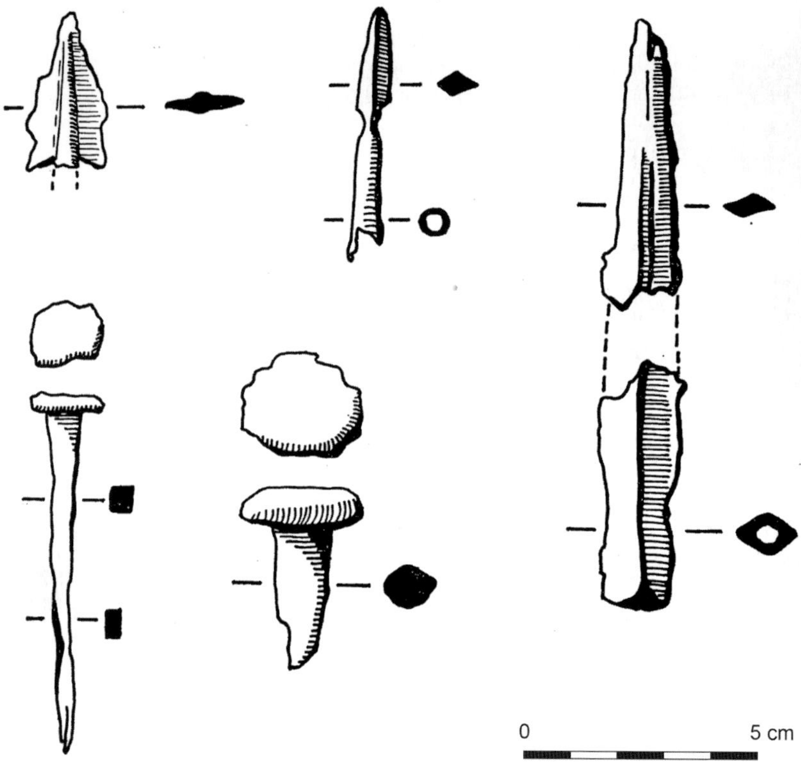

2.14 Ferns: arrowheads recovered during excavations at Ferns Castle (drawing courtesy of David Sweetman)

Owing to its strategic importance and the presence of a strong castle, Ferns was key to Anglo-Norman resistance against the Mac Murchada revival. According to the financial accounts of John Sandford, archbishop of Dublin and justiciar of Ireland, the itinerary of an extensive journey around Ireland undertaken by the justiciar in the summer of 1290 ended on 17 August at Ferns (Frame 2022, 172–3; Sweetman 1875–86, vol. iii, 274–6, no. 559), where perhaps he stayed at the castle. Sandford had previously served as treasurer of Ferns (Watt 1961, 161), so he may have wished to end his nine-week visitation in familiar surroundings. In 1294 Alexander Talemy, bailiff of William de Valence, in consultation with Seneschal Maurice de Caunteton and his council, arranged for provisions to be stock-piled at Ferns Castle in anticipation of a rising by the Meic Murchada (Mills 1905, 148–9; Lydon 1987, 260; Colfer 2013, 75). Among the arrowheads recovered during excavations at Ferns Castle were several armour-piercing examples of late thirteenth-/early fourteenth-century type (fig. 2.14), as well as part of a dagger and a leather scabbard (Sweetman 1979, 237–9); it is

2.15 Ferns: castle chapel with fine rib vaulting

Table 2.4 Officeholders in Ferns Cathedral who also held high office elsewhere in Ireland

Name	Ferns office	Later office(s)	Sources
Reginald	archdeacon	abbot of Mellifont	Gilbert 1884, vol. ii, 20, 170–2
Nicholas	archdeacon	prior of St Mary's (Dublin)	Gilbert 1884, vol. i, 259, 335, 528; vol. ii, lxxiv
Thomas Cantok	canon	bishop of Emly; chancellor of Ireland	Gilbert 1884, vol. ii, 291; Brand 2009
John Garvey	dean	archbishop of Armagh	Clavin and Barry 2009b; Harris and Ware 1764, i, 231
John Esmond	archdeacon	bishop of Emly	Anon. 1909a, 367
Nicholas Fleming	canon	chancellor of Dublin; archbishop of Armagh	Hayes Somers 1997, 166; Cotton 1848, vol. ii, 188; Crooks, CR 4 Richard II, no. 115, 9 Rd II, no. 63; Anon. 1914, 349
John St John	bishop	treasurer of Ireland	Colfer 2002, 218
John Sandford	treasurer	archbishop of Dublin; justiciar of Ireland	Watt 1961, 161; Frame 2022, 172–3; Sweetman 1875–86, vol. iii, 274–6, no. 559
William Charnels	bishop	treasurer of Ireland	Connolly 1998, 504, 508; Anon. 1911, 551
John Swayne	canon, prebendary	archbishop of Armagh	Crooks, PR 7 Henry IV, no. 160, PR 10 Henry IV, no. 160; Twemlow 1904, 349, 374; Twemlow 1904a, 614–15
Patrick Barrett	bishop	lord high chancellor (1410)	Anon. 1909b, 172, 282
John Laffran	clerk	notary public (1453)	Twemlow 1915, 626

tempting to see these weapons as part of the seneschal's arsenal. David Sweetman's excavations showed that horses were stabled at Ferns Castle 'for a fairly long period of time at the end of the thirteenth and the beginning of the fourteenth century' (1979, 241), probably during the constableship of Philip de Barry (Sweetman 1979, 218; Mills 1905, 254–5).

There was clearly a great deal worth protecting in Ferns at this time. High status and wealth are reflected in the architecture of Ferns Castle itself, which houses the 'most remarkable Anglo-Norman castle chapel in Ireland' (O'Keeffe 2015, 178; O'Keeffe and Coughlan 2003, 138–42; see also Stalley 1971, 26–7; fig. 2.15). Archaeologists recovered several fragments of silk, 'probably imported from France or England', in late thirteenth-/early fourteenth-century deposits at the castle (Sweetman 1979, 239, 241), while the discovery of polychrome pottery indicates contact with southern France in the late thirteenth century (Sweetman 1979, 225, 240–1). Saintonge wares, from the wine-rich region of Bordeaux, also turned up (Sweetman 1979, 225), as well as Ham Green Ware from the kilns outside Bristol (Sweetman 1979, 226).

The 1280 population of two hundred burgages was probably a peak, and all the indications are that decline soon set in. Contraction is reflected, for instance, in the paucity of moated sites in the area and the relatively small number of townland names suffixed -town (compared with the south of the county: Colfer 2002, 125, 245), while the fact that the manor of Ferns was coterminous with one large parish suggests that little development took place there or that it was abandoned at an early stage. When Richard of Northampton was appointed bishop of Ferns in 1282 (Anon. 1893, 34, 38), he was consecrated in Ireland 'to save his expenses in repairing to England, his see being much wasted and impaired by the Irish rebels' (Leslie 1936, 2). It may also have been due to the volatile situation in the region that a case being heard at the episcopal court in Ferns in 1284/5 was transferred south to Waterford the following year (Coleman 2016, 192). By the time of William de Valence's death in 1296 there were almost fifty abandoned burgages in Ferns (Hore 1900–11, vol. v, 100; vol. vi, 192), and by 1307 the value of the Marshal manor had dropped by more than half to just over £38 16*s.* per year (Hore 1900–11, vol. vi, 6, 9; Sweetman 1875–86, vol. iv, no. 306). In 1298 Bishop Richard paid 20*s.* 'to have again the liberty of bread and ale at Ferns' (Sweetman 1875–86, vol. iv, 247, no. 550). A mill on the River Bann continued to function and in 1307 it generated an income of 56*s.* 8*d.* (Hore 1900–11, vol. vi, 9; ch. 10).

GAELIC RESURGENCE

As the ancestral caput of the Uí Chennselaig and the Meic Murchada, in addition to being an important administrative, economic, military and religious centre, Ferns was a primary target for the resurgent Irish. It was an increasingly dangerous place in the early years of the fourteenth century. Four prominent members of the Mac Murchada family were massacred at Ferns in 1305. Witnesses stated that Henry was killed, stripped and robbed; Muirchertach Mór took refuge in the church of St Mary's Abbey but was dragged out and murdered; while Murchadh and Domhnall Óg Mac Murchada were simply 'feloniously slain' in a house in which they had taken shelter (Mills 1914, 466–7; O'Byrne 2003, 64). An enquiry later that year found that the four had travelled to Ferns under a promise of safe conduct from the justiciar, John Wogan, but that certain Englishmen there had taken the law into their own hands to settle an old score. Naturally, this event strengthened Irish resolve and united otherwise disparate groups (O'Byrne 2003, 64–5). There are repeated indications of the loss of control by the settlers; for instance, in 1309 Constable Nicholas de Sandford was fined by the treasurer of Ireland for allowing two prisoners to escape from Ferns Castle (Hore 1900–11, vol. vi, 9). Other Irish prisoners had been released in error in 1302 (Mills 1905, 391). There are also signs of internal pressure among the religious community at Ferns; at Easter in 1306, for example, Chaplain William de Braybrook was involved in a legal case against the dean and chapter of Ferns over an unpaid debt (Mills 1914, 250, 284, 314). In 1375 Gilbert Sutton, precentor of the cathedral, was outlawed and then pardoned for not settling a debt owed to John Broun, archdeacon of Ferns (Crooks, PR 49 Edward III, no. 134). Between the death of Bishop Walrand in 1311 and the appointment of Adam of Northampton in 1312, it appears that William de Rudyard was '*custos* of the vacant bishopric of Ferns' (Gallagher 2009). Such interruptions are likely to have been particularly disruptive during these already fractious times.

Perhaps surprisingly, there appear to have been no military tenants on the manor of Ferns (Colfer 2002, 81). For safety, the bishop chose to transfer his episcopal residence south to New Ross (Gwynn and Hadcock 1970, 101) and, sure enough, Ferns was captured during the Bruce Wars in 1317 and again by the Leinster Irish in the years that followed (Hore 1900–11, vol. vi, 195–6; Gwynn and Hadcock 1970, 175). Adam of Northampton, bishop of Ferns, is said to have supplied the Bruces with men, money and provisions and so an order was issued for his arrest for treason (Leslie 1936, 3). Northampton may have been arrested but he retained the bishopric and died in office almost three decades later in 1346. Ferns was in the hands of Aymer de Valence at the time of the Bruces' interventions in Ireland and it is perhaps unsurprising that Ferns came under direct attack from the Bruces, given that they had been engaged in battle against de Valence on several occasions in 1306–7 while he served as a military commander in Scotland (Traquair 1998, 137, 146).

An enquiry carried out after the death of de Valence in 1324 found that the mill at Ferns had been ruined, the hundred court had ceased to operate, the castle had been destroyed and the entire manor was worthless, for it had been 'totally wasted by Irish felons' (Sharp and Stamp 1910, 326; Hore 1900–11, vol. vi, 9; Otway-Ruthven 1968, 252). At that time, 160 burgages in Ferns belonged to the castle and, in better times, these had returned an annual rent of £8 4*d*., payable half yearly at Easter and at Michaelmas. The castle was taken into the king's hand due to neglect by its absentee owners (Hore 1900–11, vol. vi, 10). It was raided and burnt by the Irish (Ó Tuathail) of Leinster in 1331 (Butler 1849, 22; Gilbert 1884, vol. ii, 376; Hore 1900–11, vol. vi, 196), in consequence of which the bishop moved south to the relative security of Fethard (Gilbert 1884, vol. i, 526; Colfer 2002, 218; fig. 2.16).[5] By this time, much of northern Wexford had been retaken by the Gaelic Irish and, like the manorial

5 The shift south to Fethard was particularly apposite, given that the early church there had been founded by St Máedóc (Bradley and King 1990, 73; Colfer 2002a, 211; 2004, 51; 2013, 46; Moore 1996, nos 1447, 1449; Hore 1900–11, vol. iv, 308–10).

2.16 Fethard, Co. Wexford: multi-period castle

tenants themselves, the frontier moved steadily southwards. 'Proximity to Irish strongholds, challenging terrain and distance from secure ports made it impossible for the remaining colonists to survive and by the end of the [fourteenth] century the north of the county was fully under the control of the Gaelic Irish' (Colfer 2002, 226).

A certain Richard Whitty was constable of Ferns Castle in 1334–5, when he was paid by the exchequer at the rate of twenty marks annually (Crooks, CR 8 Edward III, no. 38; one mark was two-thirds of a pound, or 13*s.* 4*d.*). In about 1346 Sir William Fitz Eustace de la Rupe (also known as Roche) was appointed constable of Ferns Castle (Colfer 2013, 65–6; Hore 1900–11, vol. vi, 11), but this did not prevent a siege and occupation by the Irish (Connolly 1998, 421; Hore 1900–11, vol. vi, 11). Ralph Meyler was sent with his force by the deputy justiciar to relieve de la Rupe. Meyler forcibly recaptured the castle, occupied it and repaired it, for which he was remunerated to the tune of £20 (Connolly 1998, 421).

There was some confusion over the election of Bishop Adam of Northampton's successor. Hugh de Saltu/Leixlip was erroneously appointed without royal licence or assent in 1347 and, while he was initially pardoned, fined and allowed to remain in office, he was subsequently replaced by the legitimately elevated Augustinian Geoffrey Groseld (aka Grandfield/Cranfield) (Anon. 1905a, 25–6; Anon. 1903, 265). The Black Death of the mid-fourteenth century exacerbated already challenging times at Ferns and in October 1348 Bishop Geoffrey succumbed to the plague (Hore 1900–11, vol. vi, 197; Colfer 2002, 219). Groseld's successor, the 'high-spirited' Bishop John Esmond (Harris and Ware 1764, i, 443), seems to have fared little better and was deposed by Pope Clement VI in 1349, at which time he took refuge in Ferns Castle, supported by almost thirty of the 'leading men of Wexford', including ten other Esmonds. He was finally removed, and Dominican William Charnels was appointed in his stead (Twemlow 1921, xxx; Leslie 1936, 3; Colfer 2013, 66). In consolation, Esmond was granted by the pope the canonry and prebend of Taghmon in 1352 (Twemlow 1921, xxxi) and then appointed bishop of Emly in 1356 (Anon. 1909a, 367). The repercussions of the Esmond debacle appear to have rumbled on for years, and as late as 1382 the bishop of Ferns petitioned the government regarding a property dispute between 'outlawed' John Esmond and another tenant of Ferns (Crooks, PR 5 Richard II, no. 82). Esmond was neither the first nor the last bishop of Ferns to stay at Ferns Castle, and it has even been suggested that the castle functioned as a form of episcopal palace at various times in the Middle Ages (O'Keeffe and Coughlan 2003, 146; Grattan Flood 1916, 33; Collins 2018, 239). This might help to explain the remarkably fine chapel.

No fewer than five bishops served in Ferns across a period of just four years between 1346 and 1350, and this is reflective of the turbulent times politically, socially and economically. There was still a resident population at Ferns, however, and in 1350 Bishop Charnels paid 40*s*. for the right to hold fairs and markets there (Hore 1900–11, vol. vi, 200). Charnels was also paid fees as keeper of Ferns Castle in 1354–5 (at £20 per year), while Brother Richard of Northampton, also keeper of Ferns Castle, was paid at the same rate the following year (Connolly 1998, 459, 467). The Irish had clearly relinquished the castle at this time, but they soon recaptured it, 'held it against the king for a long time and threw down its walls and bridge' (Connolly 1998, 482–3). Charnels was paid £20 in 1358 after he 'recovered it with a large number of armed men at his own expense and stayed in the castle until the walls and bridge had been suitably repaired, on which he spent more than £100 to preserve the king's honour'. Charnels, who had received a Masters in Theology at Paris (Hayes Somers 1997, 159), was clearly a crown favourite and in the early 1360s we find him in the role of treasurer of the exchequer of Ireland (table 2.4). It was perhaps while Charnels' attention was elsewhere that the Meic Murchada recaptured Ferns Castle, after it had been repaired (Hore 1900–11, vol. vi, 13; Bradley and King 1990, 50; Sweetman 1979; Moore 1996, no. 1440; Colfer 2002, 219; Anon. 1906, 42). There may even have been a sixth, short-term, bishop of Ferns in this narrow window, as the patent rolls of Edward III for November 1347 record that one 'Richard, bishop of Ferns', was in England at this time, having appointed attorneys in his place in Ireland (Anon. 1903, 419).

Bishop Thomas Denne, 'a man of ancient and illustrious family' (Cotton 1848, vol. ii, 333), petitioned the king's council in 1375, complaining that he, his men and his tenants at Ferns 'were gravely disturbed by certain persons taking their goods and chattels against their will and without payment' (Crooks, PR 49 Edward III, no. 176). The king confirmed the provision of 'special protection and defence' for the bishop and his charges, but such protection was not as effective on the ground as it appeared on parchment. The crown also levied 9 marks on the crosslands of Ferns (Crooks: PR 49 Edward III, no. 269; Colfer 2002, 218), which must have added to the challenges being experienced by the episcopacy. Ultimately, the unstable situation in north Co. Wexford forced the bishop to flee the diocesan capital at Ferns, and the high-status late fourteenth-century castle at Fethard became an episcopal residence. Fethard Castle may have been built for Bishop Denne in about 1375 (Colfer 2002, 219–20). Son of a former seneschal of Co. Wexford (1319–20) and grandson of the builder of Dennes' Castle, Thomas was born at the castle of Kayer and educated at Oxford University (Theiner 1864, 322; Leslie 1936, 4; Colfer 2013, 106). He was a chaplain at Carrick and then archdeacon of Ferns (1356; Anon. 1912, 349) before being elected in 1363 to the bishopric, which he held for some thirty-seven years. Denne made several sojourns to England (he had been ordained at Chelmsford in Essex in 1362: Davis 2000, 156; Anon. 1897, 230; Anon. 1912, 350), during one of which he was feared dead. One of the episcopal funerary effigies at Fethard (now in the graveyard but formerly in the church) has an Anglo-Norman French inscription and is likely to commemorate Bishop Denne (Cloney 1989, 95–6; Potterton 2019, 45–6, fig. 2.25). An inventory of Denne's household goods and chattels, taken on his death in 1403, provides a very interesting glimpse of the sorts of belongings a person of his rank owned at that time. Among the items listed are silver goblets and cutlery, brass pots and ewers, pewter platters and dishes, furred robes and other vestments, various napkins and towels, four yards of English cloth, as well as one horse, six oxen and one hundred sheep (Hore 1900–11, vi, 211). Robert Denne was archdeacon of Ferns in 1388, when he was permitted to be absent from Ireland for three years to study at the University of Oxford (Crooks, PR 12 Richard II, no. 125; Hayes Somers 1997, 163). It is not clear in what way Robert and Thomas were related, if at all.

By 1385 Ferns was still worth nothing because it had been 'devastated by the Irish' (Dawes et al. 1974). The following year, William St John, dean of Ferns, was given royal licence to remain in England for three years and to receive the fruits of his benefice while overseas (Crooks, CR 19 Richard II, no. 11). Canons and prebendaries of Ferns Cathedral were increasingly absent (usually in England) from the second half of the fourteenth century (e.g., Anon. 1905, 266, 333, 470; Anon. 1911, 438; Anon. 1907, 440). In 1395 Art MacMurrough Kavanagh formally submitted to Richard II, but north Wexford continued to be extremely unstable. In 1398 the abbot of Ferns was outlawed for favouring Mac Murchada, but he was pardoned in 1403 (Grattan Flood 1916, 32). Archaeological excavations in the early 1970s revealed little evidence for occupation at the castle after the fourteenth century, and Sweetman surmised that 'the Irish resurgence of the middle of the fourteenth century probably [...] terminated any attempt by the Normans to hold such outposts as Ferns' (1979, 240).

Pressure continued to mount, and warfare was rife in north Wexford. Bishop of Ferns Patrick Barrett was engaged to interact with the Gaelic magnates of Leinster, and then to treat with the king's enemies in Wexford and elsewhere in 1403 (Beresford 2009). The following year he was appointed as a justice of the peace for the county and crosslands of Wexford. The Gaelic revival continued relentlessly in the Ferns region, however, and in 1409 Barrett was given permission to move his residence from the diocesan capital at Ferns south to a castle he built at Mountgarrett overlooking the River Barrow just north of New Ross (Gwynn and Hadcock 1970, 101; Colfer 2002, 219–20). Barrett, who had been appointed lord high chancellor in 1410 (Anon. 1909b, 172, 282), died in 1415, at which time John Walsh, chancellor, and Elias Borlagh, treasurer of Ferns, received a licence to elect Barrett's successor (Butler 1849, 28; Crooks, PR 3 Henry V, no. 68). In the meantime, custody of the temporalities of the bishopric of Ferns were granted to Richard Talbot, brother of John Talbot, lieutenant of Ireland (Crooks, PR 3 Henry V, no. 95). The dean and chapter duly elected Robert Whitty, former precentor of Ferns (Leslie 1936, 4; Cotton 1848, vol. ii, 333–4). Whitty held the position until his retirement in 1457. He had been bedridden for almost ten years and died at the age of 87 in 1458.

It is not clear if there was a family connection, but in 1450 a £20 fine was paid by John Whitty, canon of Ferns, for an offence committed at the parliament of Drogheda that year (Crooks, PR 28 Henry VI, no. 13). Canon Whitty was later (1453) said to have 'publicly kept a kinswoman as his concubine, committed incest and perjury, and dilapidated and alienated and uselessly consumed a number of the possessions of his canonry of Ferns ... and laid violent hands on a priest' (Twemlow 1915, 667–8).

Agents employed to collect taxes on behalf of the papacy operated across Ireland in the Middle Ages. In 1447 Henry Hertman was sub-collector of the papal camera in the city and diocese of Ferns (Twemlow 1915, 400–1) but by 1469 Rory MacConmara was the sole collector in Ferns (Twemlow 1933, 658). The papal letters and registers in the Vatican Archives are also replete with references to cases of adultery, fornication, concubinage and other illicit activities among the clergy of Ferns in the fifteenth century. There are accusations and allegations, claims and counter-claims. A snapshot is provided here because it highlights the challenges facing the ordinary running of the church in Ferns and the degree to which it had broken down. In July 1437, for instance, the pope was informed by Premonstratensian canon Thomas O'Druffin of Annaghdown that Abbot Patrick of St Mary's, Ferns, had 'dilapidated goods thereof, is a notorious fornicator, and is involved in divers other crimes' (Twemlow 1909, 654). Thomas, the son of an Augustinian abbot and an unnamed unmarried woman, stood to replace Patrick as abbot if the allegations were shown to be true by three named men including the bishop of Ferns. Also in July 1437, in a suspiciously similar letter, Patrick MacAluard, clerk of Ferns, informed the papacy that Thomas Petit, dean of Ferns, had 'dilapidated goods of the deanery, and been guilty of perjury and other excesses and crimes' (Twemlow 1909, 650–1). If the allegations were found to be true, Thomas was to be deprived of his position, and replaced by Patrick, 'son of a priest and an unmarried woman'. Abbot Thomas wrote back to the pope *c.*1439 to complain that former abbot Patrick (now canon) had 'dilapidated the goods [of St Mary's], been a notorious fornicator and had been accused of divers other crimes' (Twemlow 1915, 306). In 1444 MacAluard, by now a canon of St Mary's Priory, Roscommon, notified the pope that Thomas O'Druffin, now abbot of St Mary's, Ferns, had 'dilapidated goods thereof and committed perjury and on account of these and divers other crimes is defamed in those parts' (Twemlow 1912, 434–5; Gwynn and Hadcock 1970, 175; Grattan Flood 1916, 32). If this was shown to be true, the pope ordered that Patrick should be elevated in Thomas's stead.

In 1438 Thady O'Byrne, a secular clerk, was said to have 'detained [the priory of Glascarrig] for more than two years without any canonical title' (Twemlow 1912, 30). By 1444 he was still in possession of the priory (Twemlow 1912, 420–1) and even when removed he appealed the decision to the apostolic see. In 1448 O'Byrne was accused of publicly keeping a concubine, dilapidating the possessions of the priory of Glascarrig and committing simony (Twemlow 1915, 413–14). In May 1453 it was found that O'Byrne, seemingly still prior of Glascarrig, had written to the pope to inform him that Bishop Robert Whitty of Ferns had died (Twemlow 1915, 163, 244–5, 329). The pope gave permission for O'Byrne to replace Bishop Robert only to find that O'Byrne had fabricated the story and depositions and Robert was still alive, albeit bedridden (see above).

In August 1461 it was alleged by Donald O'Murphy that Thomas O'Druffin, abbot of Ferns, who had been excommunicated,

> had celebrated or rather profaned, more than once, masses and other divine offices in contempt of the Keys, and taken part therein, incurring irregularity; that he has dilapidated etc. the goods of the monastery and consumed them for evil and unlawful uses; that he has expelled the canons, neglected to supply them with the necessaries of life, and allowed them to wander, so that some have died without the monastery through penury and poverty and want of the necessities of life and his negligence, and so that not one religious is at present in the

> monastery on account of the said Thomas, who neglects divine worship therein and goes elsewhere for the celebration of masses, and in other ways destroys the monastery in spirituals and temporals; and that he has committed perjury, about which and divers other crimes he is defamed in those parts (Twemlow 1933, 109–10).

Donald himself was said to be the illegitimate son of a priest and an unmarried woman, but if the allegations he made about Abbot Thomas were found to be true, Donald was to be made abbot in his place.

It appears that Thomas O'Druffin remained at the abbey, however, because in 1467 we find that Patrick O'Byrne, clerk of Ferns, applied for permission to enter the Augustinian monastery of Ferns, claiming that the excommunicated Abbot Thomas (O'Druffin) had committed perjury and was still celebrating masses and other divine offices there. O'Byrne also complained that the illegitimate Donald O'Murphy, on the strength of some invalid letters, retained possession of St Mary's, and that O'Byrne could not safely meet them within the city or diocese of Ferns (Twemlow 1933, 278). Pope Paul II agreed to O'Byrne becoming a canon and abbot of St Mary's if his allegations and fitness were proved to a named panel of three from Leighlin diocese.

In 1488 Eugene MacDowell, a canon of St Columba's, Inistioge, claimed to have been elected abbot by the convent of St Mary's, Ferns, although he was 'perhaps born of parents related in the double fourth degree of kindred' (Twemlow 1960, 222–3). In any case, MacDowell held the abbacy for three to four years, despite the fact that its fruits were insufficient for his maintenance.

If the late fifteenth century was difficult for the community at St Mary's Abbey, it was equally challenging for the dean and chapter of the cathedral. In September 1461, Dermot O'Druffin, clerk of Ferns, informed Pope Pius II that his colleague Philip Nogul, priest and chancellor of Ferns, was 'an open concubinary' and 'a public and notorious fornicator, … so ignorant of letters that he cannot speak Latin properly and does not intelligibly speak or understand the language of the place' (Twemlow 1921, 430, 596–7). Dermot, who was apparently 'illegitimate', feared Philip's power and felt he had 'no hope of obtaining justice in the city and diocese of Ferns'. The pope wrote to the bishop, dean and a canon of Leighlin, asking them to intervene and possibly to assign the chancellorship of Ferns ('a non-major, non-elective dignity with cure') to Dermot in place of Philip, notwithstanding Dermot's said 'defect'.

The dire state of the church in Ferns at this time is made clear again when in the same year (1461), it was claimed that Nicholas Kethyn, a priest of the diocese of Ferns, had for more than a year after the death of Dean Thomas Petit held the deanery of Ferns under false pretences and, fearing the power of Nicholas, Dermot O'Kirwan claimed he had 'no hope in obtaining justice in the city and diocese of Ferns' (Twemlow 1933, 111). Dermot was to be made dean in his place.

2.17 Edmund Comerford's seal as prior of St John's in Kilkenny, *c.*1507 (image courtesy of John Bradley)

A former canon of Ferns, John Purcell was elevated to the bishopric when Robert Whitty retired in 1457 (Twemlow 1921, 193, 324, 329, 338; Leslie 1936, 5). Similarly, Purcell's successor, Laurence Neville, had served as a canon before he became bishop in 1478 (Leslie 1936, 5). Neville was exempted from attendance in England to take his oath on account of 'the dangers of travel'. He would have been glad of the promotion, given that it had earlier been found that 'the income from the archdeaconry and annexed prebend was insufficient to allow Laurence to "live becomingly"' (Twemlow 1933, 156). Like Lamport, Esmond, Denne and Whitty before him, Neville was a member of a prominent Wexford Anglo-Norman family (Colfer 2002, 212). In this, as in many other ways, the later medieval Anglo-Norman bishops of Ferns were much like their early medieval Gaelic counterparts.

From time to time the government attempted to regain control of Ferns, in one way or another. According to an indenture sealed at Naas in November 1446, for instance, Donough Mac Murchada was requested to hand over Ferns Castle to the lieutenant John Talbot (Dryburgh and Smyth 2005, 225). Some activity at the castle in the mid-

2.18 Sketch of the seal of Nicholas Comyn as bishop of Ferns in 1512 (right). A note states that 'this episcopal see bears, sapphire, two keys, saltier-ways [*sic*] suppressed by a mitre with labels in fess, topaz' (after Harris and Ware 1764, i, 435)

fifteenth century is indicated by the chance discovery there of a silver groat of Edward IV (1461–70) (Bradley and King 1990, 61), but little else of note has been found there from this period.

Bishop Neville died in 1503 and was replaced the following year by Oxford-educated Edmund Comerford (fig. 2.17), who passed away at Easter in 1509 (Leslie 1936, 5; Cotton 1848, vol. ii, 334). Limerickman Nicholas Comyn was elected bishop after Comerford's death, but was transferred to the sees of Waterford and Lismore in 1519 (Leslie 1936, 5). Like his predecessor Comerford, Comyn was a graduate of Oxford University, where he was also ordained in 1505 (Davis 2000, 158 and n51). In Walter Harris's 1764 edition of James Ware's Works is a sketch of the seal of Nicholas Comyn as bishop of Ferns in 1512 (Harris and Ware 1764, i, 435; fig. 2.18). There was certainly an international dimension to the education and formation of some of the clerics of Ferns, but it may be something of a stretch chronologically to think that the William Lacy who was abbot of Ferns in 1507 (Grattan Flood 1916, 32) was the same William Lacy, an Englishman of the diocese of Ferns, who was admitted as a chaplain and 'familiar of the master' (of the Hospitallers) in the Aegean in August 1456 (O'Malley 2016, 45). Nonetheless, the two men were almost certainly related and the fact that some of Ferns' ecclesiastics lived into their eighties suggests that Abbot William may indeed have spent time with the Hospitallers overseas in the 1450s.

THE NEW ENGLISH

The MacMurrough Kavanaghs, still titular kings of Leinster, continued to occupy most of north Wexford and resisted all crown attempts to regain control. They administered their territories on the basis of Gaelic laws and customs. Sweetman found little evidence for activity at Ferns Castle in the sixteenth century (Sweetman 1979, 241), but constables continued to be appointed and Cathaoir MacMurrough (MacInnycross), the MacMurrough, held that position in the 1530s. Richard Butler, 1st viscount Mountgarrett, was appointed constable in 1538 (Grattan Flood 1916, xi, 33). He was to be the last Anglo-Irish constable (1538–50); all subsequent officials were New English settlers (Goff 1987, 125), who seem to have come and gone with some frequency. Ferns was key to any government attempt to rein in the control and influence of the Irish in the region (especially the Kavanaghs, as the MacMurrough dynasty were increasingly called).

In 1536 a renewed offensive was launched by Lord Deputy Leonard Grey who seized Ferns Castle using guns and cannons (Colfer 2013, 68). Grey described the castle in 1536 as being 'one of the ancientest and strongest castles within this land', but three years later his successor Anthony St Leger wrote that it was in 'sore decay' (Grattan Flood 1898, 31, 229). In 1537 Bishop John Purcell II – who had been involved in the Lambert Simnel affair in Dublin in 1488 – was said to have assisted Cathaoir MacMurrough Kavanagh to burn the town of Fethard in the south of the county (Leslie 1936, 5).

Caher Mac Art proposed to the government that north Wexford be shired as County Ferns and that, as sheriff, he would administer English law and customs there, but this offer was not accepted (Goff 1987, 125). In 1543, however, a major step was achieved in the crown policy of surrender and regrant. The Kavanaghs agreed to recognize crown authority at the castle and manor of Ferns, and to cultivate their land in the English fashion. This move served to progress crown attempts to anglicize the people and the land and to stabilize relations with the Kavanaghs, at least temporarily. In March 1550, however, Caher Mac Art briefly seized Ferns Castle from Butler once more (Moore 1987, 8; O'Byrne 2009). The following year, Anthony Colclough was made constable of Ferns Castle (McCormack and Clavin 2009), but by 1553 Francis Agard was in possession of the castle and the lands attached to it (Morrin 1861, 303). Nicholas Heron became seneschal of the Kavanaghs and constable of the castle in 1558 and was granted the lands previously held by Agard (Grattan Flood 1916, 33; Goff 1987, 127–8). Heron's position was funded by collecting rents and dues in Gaelic areas as well as crown lands around Ferns. English Catholic mercenary Thomas Stukley purchased lands from Heron and was constable of Ferns Castle briefly in 1567–8 (Izon 1956, 80–1). Stukley was replaced as constable of Ferns Castle by Nicholas White (Clavin 2009) after Stukley had been imprisoned in Dublin Castle for aiding and

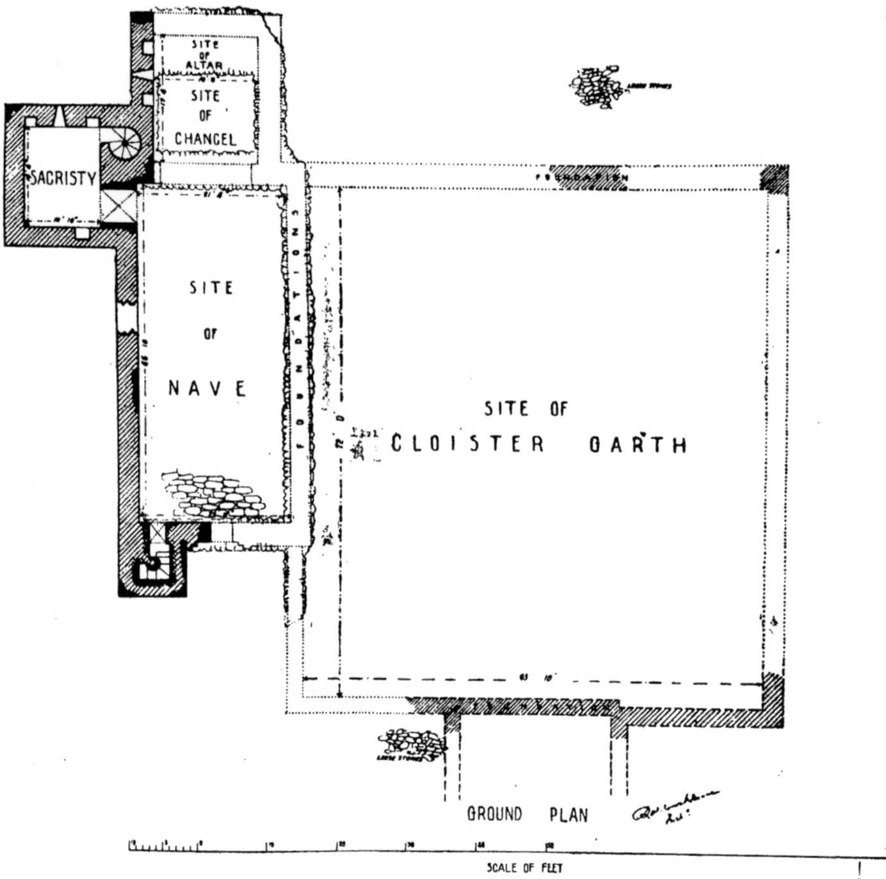

2.19 Ferns: ground plan of remains of St Mary's Abbey by Robert Cochrane, 1910. 'The dark hatched lines indicate where the facing and rebuilding of the masonry was executed in 1846' (after Cochrane 1910, 52, pl. 1)

abetting local Kavanagh rebels in Wexford (Clavin and Barry 2009). Among the payments made to White for the period 1568–72 was 8*s.* 10*d.* for the 'Physician Apothecary' (SP Ire., 1572, vol. 35, no. 43: PROI).

Abbot Purcell died in 1539 and was succeeded by William Doyle. Doyle was the last abbot of St Mary's, as it was suppressed in April of that year (Grattan Flood 1916, 32). A picture of the devastation of Ferns in the mid-sixteenth century can be gleaned from the Dissolution documents: 'church and hall worth nothing above repairs … lands waste and unprofitable by war of the Kaverners [Kavanaghs] … lands not well occupied by reason of war' (White 1943, 353–76); at the site of St Mary's itself 'there are no buildings in the precinct save the abbey church and a hall; these are necessary for the farmer, and are worth nothing above repairs' (White 1943, 371). A range of monastic properties were parcelled out to new landholders. A plan of the abbey church drawn by Robert Cochrane in 1910 includes sections of the 'cloister garth', which he was able to identify at that time (fig. 2.19).

Heron added the abbey and its lands to his Ferns property portfolio in 1561, but sold the whole lot in March 1569 to Thomas Masterson, a New English Catholic from Cheshire (Goff 1987, 128). Masterson maintained Heron's confrontational approach with the Kavanaghs, taking possession of the abbey lands in the face of strong resistance. The Kavanaghs allied with the Butlers in rebellion although the Butlers lost control of their vast estates for a time. Masterson was confirmed as seneschal and constable in the 1570s, but the castle was burned by Fiach McHugh O'Byrne in 1577 (Hore 1900–11, vol. vi, 56).

Various archdeacons, deans and bishops of Ferns are mentioned through the mid-sixteenth century (tables 2.1, 2.2). Alexander Devereux (bp 1539–66) was succeeded as bishop by his brother John (bp 1566–78), but after John retired the see remained vacant for some years (Leslie 1936, 6). There was mention in 1570 of a collegiate residence for the chapter house (Hore 1900–11, vol. vi, 239–40), but no detail survives. An attempt that year to move the cathedral to New Ross came to nothing. Five years later the cathedral was burned by Fiach McHugh O'Byrne (Hore 1900–11, vol. vi, 243).

'A HOTBED OF THIEVES AND ROGUES'?

The castle remained in hands loyal to the government, and Sir William Pelham, lord justice and chief governor of Ireland, stayed there overnight in January 1580 (Hore 1900–11, vol. vi, 60). In 1583 the queen granted to Thomas Masterson a lease for sixty years of the lands of Ferns as well as the site of the late 'Abbey or Monastry of Ferns, with all the structures and houses within that site, together with [various] parcels of lands' (Hore 1900–11, vol. vi, 81). A map prepared in 1579 shows the barony of Ferns with 'Ferns the shire town' depicted centrally and the rough boundaries sketched of 'Abbeyland' and two portions of 'Bishopsland of Ferns' (fig. 2.20). Thomas Masterson's name is written towards the top of the barony at Clohamon. The Mastersons' castle overlooked the River Slaney on their manor at Clohamon 10km to the north-west of Ferns. By 1588 Thomas Masterson was elderly and infirm, and was consequently relieved of the constableship and ward of Ferns Castle (Hore 1900–11, vol. vi, 94). He died in 1590 and was replaced as constable and seneschal by his son Sir Richard (Hore 1900–11, vol. vi, 81). By mid-decade, Fiach MacHugh O'Byrne and his allies had wreaked such havoc in north Wexford that Richard Masterson called for assistance from the lord deputy, Sir William Russell, who rode to Ferns Castle on 22 April 1595 and rested the night there (Hore 1900–11, vol. vi, 94). O'Byrne died in May 1597, but Masterson, still seneschal and constable of Ferns, was soon accused of being in collusion with some of O'Byrne's followers and

2.20 Map drawn in 1579 of 'Wicklow, Ireland: the newly made counties of Wicklow and Ferns' (comprising parts of the modern counties of Wexford, Wicklow, Carlow and Dublin), with annotations by Lord Burghley. Also named are Camolin, Mileshogue, Slieveboy and several other places (The National Archives, UK: MPF 1/69)

fostering the rebellious Kavanaghs. Ferns was described at that time as 'a hotbed of thieves and rogues who revelled at tables under the very walls of Ferns Castle' (Hore 1900–11, vol. vi, 99; Atkinson 1893, 498). Accusations against Masterson appear to have been unfounded, however, and he and his brothers were pardoned. It was confirmed, in fact, that he had 'effected good service against Fiach in April 1597; he brought in to the lord deputy one day twelve heads of that rebel's followers, besides seven prisoners taken at the same time, whom he committed to Wexford Castle (Hore 1900–11, vol. vi, 99; Pat. Rot. 39 Eliz.; Fiant no. 6160, 14 Nov. 1597).

Hugh Allen was appointed bishop in 1582 and remained in office until the end of the century (Harris and Ware 1764, i, 206; Leslie 1936, 6–7), by which time Ferns was described as 'an ancient ruined town' (Hogan 1878, 56). A thousand years after the foundation of the church of Ferns, the see of Ferns was finally united with the see of Leighlin in *c.*1600 (Leslie 1936, 7).

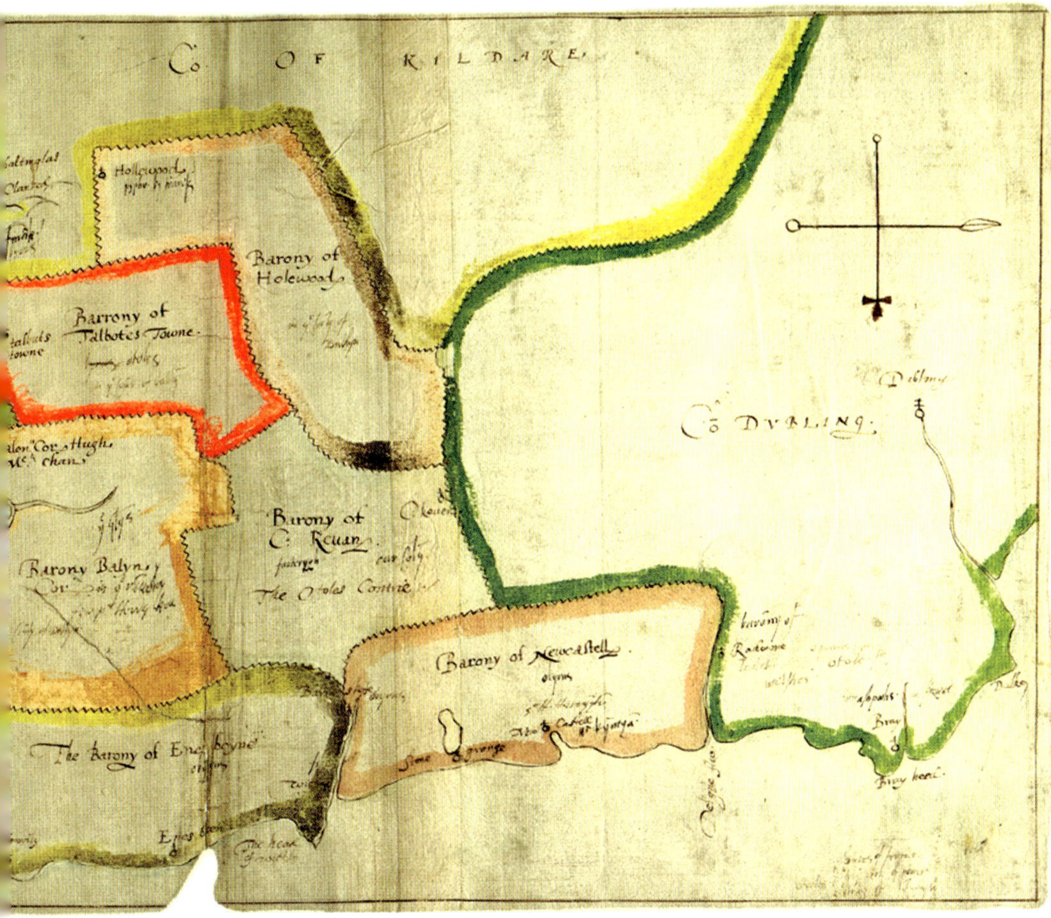

CONCLUSIONS

The rollercoaster ride experienced by Ferns over the course of more than a millennium was, in many respects, a microcosm of Ireland's medieval history and archaeology. As such, Ferns lends itself well to a case study such as this. At the end of the day, though, why did Ferns go from caput to caput? Was its ultimate decline due to its distance from the sea? It is possible that Glascarrig operated as the port for Ferns, but it may still have been the challenge of accessing Ferns from the sea that made Strongbow select Wexford as his caput in Ireland rather than the traditional Uí Chennselaig capital. On this point, Adrian Empey has remarked that Ferns 'had none of the advantages presented by Wexford, which combined access to the sea with the command of the Slaney estuary' (Empey 2017, 54n41). Ferns was not walled and it was not on a river. Ultimately, therefore, it was surpassed by New Ross and by Wexford town, which became the county capital.

BIBLIOGRAPHY

AClon.: Murphy, D. (ed.). 1896. *The annals of Clonmacnoise*. Dublin.

AFM: O'Donovan, J. (ed.). 1848–51. *Annals of the kingdom of Ireland by the Four Masters*. 7 vols. Dublin.

Anon. 1864. 'Proceedings, July Meeting'. *Journal of the Kilkenny and South-East of Ireland Archaeological Society*, new ser., 5, 109–38.

Anon. 1891. *Calendar of the ancient deeds and muniments preserved in the Pembroke Estate Office, Dublin*. Dublin.

Anon. 1893. *Calendar of the Patent Rolls preserved in the Public Record Office. Edward I, 1281–1292*. London.

Anon. 1894. *Calendar of the Patent Rolls preserved in the Public Record Office. Edward II, 1307–1313*. London.

Anon. 1897. *Calendar of the Patent Rolls preserved in the Public Record Office. Richard II, 1381–1385*. London.

Anon. 1903. *Calendar of the Patent Rolls preserved in the Public Record Office. Edward III, 1345–1348*. London.

Anon. 1906. *The thirty-eighth report of the deputy keeper of the public records and keeper of the state papers in Ireland*. Dublin.

Anon. 1908. *Calendar of the Patent Rolls preserved in the Public Record Office. Henry III, 1247–1258*. London.

Anon. 1909a. *Calendar of the Patent Rolls preserved in the Public Record Office. Edward III, 1354–1358*. London.

Anon. 1909b. *Calendar of the Patent Rolls preserved in the Public Record Office. Henry IV, 1408–1413*. London.

Anon. 1911. *Calendar of the Patent Rolls preserved in the Public Record Office. Edward III, 1358–1361*. London.

Anon. 1912. *Calendar of the Patent Rolls preserved in the Public Record Office. Edward III, 1361–1364*. London.

Anon. 1914. *Calendar of the Patent Rolls preserved in the Public Record Office. Edward III, 1370–1374*. London.

ATig.: Stokes, W. (ed.). 'The annals of Tigernach'. *Revue Celtique*, xvi (1985), 374–419; xvii (1896), 6–33, 119–263, 337–420; xviii (1897), 9–59, 150–97, 267–303, 374–91.

Atkinson, E.G. 1893. *Calendar of State Papers relating to Ireland of the reign of Elizabeth, 1596, July–1597, December*. London.

AU: *Annala Uladh, Annals of Ulster; otherwise Annala Senait, Annals of Sénat: a chronicle of Irish affairs, 431–1131, 1155–1541*, ed. W.M. Hennessy and B. MacCarthy. 4 vols. Dublin, 1887–1901.

Barry, T. 2007. 'The origins of Irish castles: a contribution to the debate'. In Manning, C. (ed.), *From ringforts to fortified houses: studies on castles and other monuments in honour of David Sweetman*, 33–9. Bray.

Beglane, F. 2015. *Anglo-Norman parks in medieval Ireland*. Dublin.

Beresford, D. 2009. 'Barrett, Patrick'. In *Dictionary of Irish Biography* at www.dib.ie/biography/barrett-patrick-a0409, accessed 14 May 2022.

Bhreathnach, E. 2019. 'The *Vita Apostolica* and the origin of the Augustinian canons and canonesses in medieval Ireland'. In Browne, M. and Ó Clabaigh, C. (eds), *Households of God: the regular canons and canonesses of St Augustine and of Prémontré in medieval Ireland*, 1–27. Dublin.

Bhreathnach, E. and Dowling, G. 2021. 'Forming an episcopal see and an Augustinian foundation in medieval Ireland: the case of Ferns, Co. Wexford'. *Proceedings of the Royal Irish Academy*, 121C, 191–226.

Bradley, J. and King, H. [1990]. 'Urban Archaeology Survey, part 11: County Wexford'. Unpublished report prepared for the OPW, Dublin.

Brand, P. 2009. 'Quantock (Cantok), Thomas'. In *Dictionary of Irish Biography* at www.dib.ie/biography/quantock-cantok-thomas-a7540, accessed 18 May 2022.

Brewer, J.S. and Brodie, R.H. (eds). 1920. *Letters and papers, foreign and domestic, of the reign of Henry VIII. Vol. 1: Part II: 1513–14*. London.

Busby, K. 2017. *French in medieval Ireland, Ireland in medieval French: the paradox of two worlds*. Turnhout.

Butler, R. (ed.). 1849. *The annals of Ireland by Thady Dowling*. Dublin.

Byrne, P. 2018. 'Tile found in Ferns may date back to Strongbow'. *Gorey Guardian*, 18 August.

Caley, J., Ellis, H. and Bandinel, B. (eds). 1817–30. William Dugdale: *Monasticon Anglicanum*. 6 vols. London.

Clavin, T. 2009. 'White, Sir Nicholas'. In *Dictionary of Irish Biography* at www.dib.ie/biography/white-sir-nicholas-a9006, accessed 20 May 2022.

Clavin, T. and Barry, J. 2009a. 'Stukeley (Stucley), Thomas'. In *Dictionary of Irish Biography* at www.dib.ie/biography/stukeley-stucley-thomas-a8365, accessed 20 May 2022.

Clavin, T. and Barry, J. 2009b. 'Garvey, John'. In *Dictionary of Irish Biography* at www.dib.ie/biography/garvey-john-a3430, accessed 20 May 2022.

Cloney, S. 1989. 'Some stone artifacts of south-west Wexford'. *Journal of the Wexford Historical Society*, 12 (1988–9), 92–7.

Coleman, E. 2016. '"Powerful adversaries": the Knights Templar, landholding and litigation in the lordship of Ireland'. In Browne, M. and Ó Clabaigh, C. (eds), *Soldiers of Christ: the Knights Hospitaller and the Knights Templar in medieval Ireland*, 184–94. Dublin.

Colfer, B. 1987. 'Anglo-Norman settlement in County Wexford'. In Whelan, K. and Nolan, W. (eds), *Wexford, history and society: interdisciplinary essays on the history of an Irish county*, 65–101. Dublin.

Colfer, B. 2002. *Arrogant trespass: Anglo-Norman Wexford, 1169–1400*. Wexford.

Colfer, B. 2004. *The Hook Peninsula, County Wexford*. Cork.

Colfer, B. 2013. *Wexford castles*. Cork.

Collins, D. 2018. 'The origins of the lordship of Leinster and the role of William Marshal: perceptions and reality'. PhD, MU.

Connolly, P. 1987. 'Irish material in the class of Ancient Petitions (SC8) in the Public Record Office, London'. *Analecta Hibernica*, 34, 1–106.

Connolly, P. 1998. *Irish exchequer payments, 1270–1446*. Dublin.

Connolly, P. 1995. 'Irish material in the class of chancery warrants, ser. I (C81) in the Public Record Office, London'. *Analecta Hibernica*, 36, 135, 137–61.

Corlett, C. 2011. 'A previously unrecorded cross-slab from Ferns, Co. Wexford'. *Journal of the Royal Society of Antiquaries of Ireland*, 141, 199–200.

Corlett, C. 2018. 'A knight on the tile'. *Archaeology Ireland*, 32:4, 23–4.

Cotton, H. 1848. *Fasti ecclesiae Hibernicae: the succession of the prelates and members of the cathedral bodies in Ireland*. Dublin.

Cox, R. 1689. *Hibernia Anglicana*. London.

Crawford, H. 1923. 'A descriptive list of Irish shrines and reliquaries. Part I'. *Journal of the Royal Society of Antiquaries of Ireland*, sixth ser., 13:1 (June).

Crooks, P. (ed.). *CIRCLE: a calendar of Irish chancery letters* (http://chancery.tcd.ie).

CS: *Chronicum Scotorum: a chronicle of Irish affairs ... to 1135 and supplement ... 1141–1150*, ed. W.M. Hennessy. London, 1866.

CSMA: Gilbert, J.T. (ed.). 1884. *Chartularies of St Mary's Abbey, Dublin, ... and annals of Ireland, 1162–1370*. 2 vols. London.

Curtis, E. 1936. 'Rental of the manor of Lisronagh, 1333 and notes on "betagh" tenure in medieval Ireland'. *Proceedings of the Royal Irish Academy*, 43C3 (Feb.), 41–76.

Davis, V. 2000. 'Irish clergy in late medieval England'. *Irish Historical Studies*, 32:126 (Nov.), 145–60.

Dawes, M., Devine, M., Jones, H. and Post, M. 1974. 'Inquisitions post-mortem, Richard II'. In *Calendar of Inquisitions post mortem, vol. 16: Richard II* (London). *Online* www.british-history.ac.uk/inquis-post-mortem/vol16, accessed 3 Apr. 2019.

De Paor, M.B. 2001. *Saint Moling Luachra: a pilgrimage from Sliabh Luachra to Rinn Ros Broic above the stream-pools of the Barrow*. Dublin.

Doherty, C. 1986. 'Saint Máedóc and Saint Molaisse'. *Bréifne*, 6, 363–74.

Doherty, C. 2002. 'The transmission of the cult of St Máedhóg'. In Ní Chatháin, P. and Richter, M. (eds), *Ireland and Europe in the early Middle Ages: texts and transmission/ Irland und Europa im früheren Mittelalter: Texte und Überlieferung*, 268–83. Dublin.

Dolley, M. 1987. 'Coinage to 1534: the sign of the times'. In Cosgrove, A. (ed.), *A new history of Ireland*, vol. ii: *medieval Ireland, 1169–1534*, 816–26. Oxford.

Doyle, I. 2016. 'Telling the dancer from the dance: the archaeology of early medieval Wexford'. In Doyle, I. and Browne, B. (eds), *Medieval Wexford: essays in memory of Billy Colfer*, 35–61. Dublin.

Dryburgh, P. and Smith, B. (eds). 2005. *Handbook and select calendar of sources for medieval Ireland in the National Archives of the United Kingdom*. Dublin and London.

Dunning, P.J. 1961. 'Irish representatives and Irish ecclesiastical affairs at the Fourth Lateran Council'. In Watt, J.A., Morrall, J.B. and Martin, F.X. (eds), *Medieval studies presented to Aubrey Gwynn SJ*, 90–113. Dublin.

Eames, E. and Fanning, T. 1988. *Irish medieval tiles: decorated medieval paving tiles in Ireland with an inventory of sites and designs and a visual index*. Dublin.

Empey, A. 2017. 'The evolution of the demesne in the lordship of Leinster: the fortunes of war or forward planning?'. In Bradley, J., Ó Drisceoil, C. and Potterton, M. (eds), *William Marshal and Ireland*, 41–77. Dublin.

FA: Radner, J.N. (ed. and trans.). 1978. *Fragmentary annals of Ireland*. Dublin.

Flanagan, M.T. 1996. 'Irish and Anglo-Norman warfare in twelfth-century Ireland'. In Bartlett, T. and Jeffery, K. (eds), *A military history of Ireland*, 52–75. Cambridge.

Flanagan, M.T. 1998, 'Strategies of lordship in pre-Norman and post-Norman Leinster'. In Harper-Bill, C. (ed.), *Anglo-Norman Studies, xx: proceedings of the Battle Conference in Dublin, 1997*, 107–26. Woodbridge.

Flanagan, M.T. 1999. 'John de Courcy, the first Ulster plantation and Irish church men'. In Smith, B. (ed.), *Britain and Ireland, 900–1300: insular responses to medieval European change*, 154–78. Cambridge.

Flanagan, M.T. 2005. *Irish royal charters: texts and contexts*. Oxford.

Flanagan, M.T. 2009. 'Aífe (Aoife, Eva)'. In *Dictionary of Irish Biography* at www.dib.ie/biography/aife-aoife-eva-a0069, accessed 16 May 2022.

Frame, R. 2022. *Plantagenet Ireland*. Dublin.

Gallagher, N. 2009. 'Rodyard (Rudyard), William de'. In *Dictionary of Irish Biography* at www.dib.ie/biography/rodyard-rudyard-william-de-a10130, accessed 20 May 2022.

Goff, H. 1987. 'English conquest of an Irish barony: the changing patterns of land ownership in the barony of Scarawalsh, 1540–1640'. In Whelan, K. and Nolan, W. (eds), *Wexford, history and society: interdisciplinary essays on the history of an Irish county*, 122–49. Dublin.

Graham, B.J. 1988. 'Medieval timber and earthwork fortifications in western Ireland'. *Medieval Archaeology*, 32, 110–29.

Grattan Flood, W.H. 1898. *History of Enniscorthy*. Enniscorthy.

Grattan Flood, W.H. 1916. *History of the diocese of Ferns*. Waterford.

Gwynn, A. and Hadcock, R. 1970. *Medieval religious houses: Ireland*. Dublin.

Hand, G.J. 1966. 'The status of the native Irish in the lordship of Ireland, 1272–1331'. *Irish Jurist*, new ser., 1, 93–115.

Hand, G.J. 1967. *English law in Ireland, 1290–1324*. Cambridge.

Hanmer, M. 1633. *Chronicle of Ireland*. Dublin.

Harris, W. and Ware, J. 1764. *The whole works of Sir James Ware concerning Ireland, revised and improved. Newly translated into English, revised and improved with many material additions and continued down to the beginning of the present century by Walter Harris*. 2 vols. Dublin.

Hayes Somers, M. 1997. 'A prosopography of Irish scholars'. *Medieval Prosopography*, 18, 139–87.

Hogan, E. 1878. *The description of Ireland … in anno 1598*. Dublin and London.

Hore, P. 1900–11. *History of the town and county of Wexford*. 6 vols. London.

Hore, P. 1910. 'Ferns, County Wexford'. *Journal of the Royal Society of Antiquaries of Ireland*, 40, 297–315.

Hughes, K. 1966. *The church in early Irish society*. London.

Hunt, J. 1974. *Irish medieval figure sculpture, 1200–1600: a study of Irish tombs with notes on costumes and armour*. 2 vols. Dublin.

Irish Times, 8 Sept. 1931.

Izon, J. 1956. *Sir Thomas Stucley,* c.*1525–1578: traitor extraordinary*. London.

Kavanagh, J. 2007. 'Ferns Upper, Ferns. Multi-period'. In Bennett, I. (ed.), *Excavations 2004: summary accounts of archaeological excavations in Ireland*, 466–7, no. 1806. Dublin.

Kavanagh, J. 2009. '2006:2104 – Ferns Upper, Wexford'. In Bennett, I. (ed.), *Excavations 2006: summary accounts of archaeological excavations in Ireland*: www.excavations.ie/report/2006/Wexford/0016857, accessed 9 May 2022.

Keating, G. 1908. *Foras Feasa ar Éirinn; or, The history of Ireland*. London.

Kelly, B. and Corlett, C. 2020. 'The fretful crosses of Ferns'. *Archaeology Ireland*, 34:2, 39–42.

Kelly, F. 2004. 'Sir John Rhŷs Memorial Lecture. Thinking in threes: the Triad in early Irish literature'. *Proceedings of the British Academy*, 125, 1–18.

Kenney, J.F. 1997. *The sources for the early history of Ireland: ecclesiastical*. Dublin.

Laing, L. 2006. *The archaeology of Celtic Britain and Ireland,* c.*AD400–1200*. Cambridge.

Leland, T. 1773. *The history of Ireland from the invasion of Henry II, with a preliminary discourse on the antient state of Ireland*. 3 vols. Dublin.

Leslie, J.B. 1936. *Ferns clergy and parishes: being an account of the clergy of the Church of Ireland in the diocese of Ferns, from the earliest period, with historical notices of the several parishes, churches etc.* Dublin.

Liebermann, F. and Pauli, R. (eds). 1885. *Giraldus Cambrensis: Libri de rebus a se gestis (Excerpta) (1177–1199).*

Luard, H.R. (ed.). 1872–84. *Matthew Paris: Chronica majora.* 7 vols. London.

Lucas, A. 1986. 'The social role of relics and reliquaries in ancient Ireland'. *Journal of the Royal Society of Antiquaries of Ireland*, 116, 5–37.

Lydon, J. 1987. 'A land of war'. In Cosgrove, A. (ed.), *A new history of Ireland*, vol. ii: *medieval Ireland, 1169–1534*, 240–74. Oxford.

Lynch, J. (ed. J.F. O'Doherty). 1944. *De Praesulibus Hiberniae: potissimis catholicae religionis in Hibernia serendae, propagandae et conservandae authoribus … Joanne Lincheao …* Dublin.

Mac Geoghegan, J. 1844. *The history of Ireland, ancient and modern.* Dublin.

Mac Niocaill, G. 1966. 'The origins of the betagh'. *Irish Jurist*, new ser., 1, 292–8.

Mac Niocaill, G. 1972. *Ireland before the Vikings.* Dublin.

Mac Shamhráin, A. 2009. 'Cathal'. In *Dictionary of Irish Biography* at www.dib.ie/ biography/ cathal-a1556, accessed 15 May 2022.

Mac Shamhráin, A. 2013. 'Ailbe Ua Máel Muaid, Uí Chennselaig and the *Vita Sanctorum Hiberniae*'. In Duffy, S. (ed.), *Princes, prelates and poets in medieval Ireland: essays in honour of Katharine Simms*, 309–38. Dublin.

MacDonnell, A.P. 1904. *The thirty-sixth report of the Deputy Keeper of the Public Records and keeper of the State Papers in Ireland.* Dublin.

MacErlean, J. 1914. 'Synod of Raith Breasail: boundaries of the dioceses of Ireland [AD1110 or 1118]'. *Archivium Hibernicum*, 3, 1–33.

Mahr, A. and Raftery, J. 1932–41. *Christian art in ancient Ireland.* 2 vols. Dublin.

McCormack, A.M. and Clavin, T. 2009. 'Colclough (Colcloght), Sir Anthony'. In *Dictionary of Irish Biography* at www.dib.ie/biography/colclough-colcloght-sir-anthony-a1820, accessed 20 May 2022.

McGettigan, D. and Mac Shamhráin, A. 2009. 'Áed Menn'. In *Dictionary of Irish Biography* at www.dib.ie/biography/aed-menn-a0046, accessed 15 May 2022.

McLoughlin, C. and Stafford, E. 2020. 'Medieval Ferns, Co. Wexford: from monastic centre to medieval town'. In Corlett, C. and Potterton, M. (eds), *The town in medieval Ireland in the light of recent archaeological excavations*, 85–100. Dublin.

McLoughlin, C. 2020, 'From early to late: uncovering medieval Ferns'. *Archaeology Ireland*, 34:2, 30–4.

McNeill, C. (ed.). 1950. *Calendar of Archbishop Alen's register, c.1172–1534.* Dublin.

Meyer, K. (ed.). 1906. *The Triads of Ireland.* London.

MIA: Ó hInnse, S. (ed. and trans.). 1947. *Miscellaneous Irish annals (AD1114–1437).* Dublin.

Mills, J. (ed.). 1905. *Calendar of justiciary rolls, 1295–1303.* Dublin.

Mills, J. (ed.). 1914. *Calendar of justiciary rolls, 1305–7.* Dublin.

Mills, J. 1892. 'Tenants and agriculture near Dublin in the fourteenth century'. *Journal of the Royal Society of Antiquaries of Ireland*, 21, 54–63.

Monk, M. 2018. 'Arable agriculture and secular settlement in early medieval Ireland'. *Ulster Journal of Archaeology*, 3rd ser., 74, 48–61.

Moore, D. 1987. *'English action, Irish reaction': the MacMurrough Kavanaghs, 1530–1630.* Maynooth.

Moore, M. (comp.). 1996. *Archaeological inventory of County Wexford.* Dublin.

Morrin, J. (ed.). 1861. *Calendar of patent and close rolls of chancery in Ireland, Henry VIII to 18th Elizabeth*. Dublin.

Moss, R. 2014. *Medieval,* c.*400*–c.*1600: art and architecture of Ireland*. New Haven, CT.

Mullally, E. (ed.). 2002. *The deeds of the Normans in Ireland: La Geste des Engleis en Yrlande. A new edition of the chronicle formerly known as The song of Dermot and the earl*. Dublin.

Murphy, M. and Potterton, M. 2010. *The Dublin region in the Middle Ages: settlement, land-use and economy*. Dublin.

Murray, G. 2005. 'A note on the provenance of the *Breac Maodhóg*'. *Journal of the Royal Society of Antiquaries of Ireland*, 135, 136–7.

O'Byrne, E. 2009. 'MacMurrough Kavanagh, Brian'. In *Dictionary of Irish Biography* at www.dib.ie/biography/macmurrough-kavanagh-brian-a5270, accessed 20 May 2022.

Ó Carragáin, T. 2010. *Churches in early medieval Ireland*. London.

Ó Corráin, D. 1972. *Ireland before the Normans*. Dublin.

O'Keeffe, T. 1997. 'Diarmait Mac Murchada and Romanesque Leinster: four twelfth-century churches in context'. *Journal of the Royal Society of Antiquaries of Ireland*, 127, 52–79.

O'Keeffe, T. 2015. *Medieval Irish buildings, 1100–1600*. Dublin.

O'Keeffe, T. 2021. *Ireland encastellated,* AD*950–1550: insular castle-building and its European context*. Dublin.

O'Keeffe, T. and Carey Bates, R. 2016. 'The abbey and cathedral of Ferns, 1111–1253'. In Doyle, I. and Browne, B. (eds), *Medieval Wexford: essays in memory of Billy Colfer*, 73–96. Dublin.

O'Keeffe, T. and Coughlan, M. 2003. 'The chronology and formal affinities of the Ferns donjon, Co. Wexford'. In Kenyon, J. and O'Conor, K. (eds), *The medieval castle in Ireland and Wales: essays in honour of Jeremy Knight*, 133–48. Dublin.

O'Malley, G. 2016. 'Authority and autonomy: relations between Clerkenwell, Kilmainham and the Hospitallers central convent after the Black Death'. In Browne, M. and Ó Clabaigh, C. (eds), *Soldiers of Christ: the Knights Hospitaller and the Knights Templar in medieval Ireland*, 23–46. Dublin.

O'Meara, J.J. (trans. and intr.). 1982. *Gerald of Wales: The history and topography of Ireland*. London.

Ó Riain, P. 2006. *Feastdays of the saints: a history of Irish martyrologies*. Brussels.

Ó Riain, P. 2011. *A dictionary of Irish saints*. Dublin.

Orpen, G.H. 1968. *Ireland under the Normans*. 4 vols. Repr. Oxford.

Orpen, G.H. (ed.). 1892. *The song of Dermot and the earl, an Old French poem*. Oxford.

O'Sullivan, A., McCormick, F., Kerr, T.R. and Harney, L. 2013. *Early medieval Ireland,* AD*400–1100: the evidence from archaeological excavations*. Dublin.

O'Toole, F. 2013. *A history of Ireland in 100 objects*. Dublin.

Otway-Ruthven, A. 1968. *A history of medieval Ireland*. London.

Plummer, C. (ed. and trans.). 1922. *Bethada Náem nÉrenn: Lives of Irish saints, edited from the original MSS with introduction, translations, notes, glossary and indexes*. 2 vols. Oxford.

Potterton, M. 2005. *Medieval Trim: history and archaeology*. Dublin.

Potterton, M. 2019. 'A second Pale? The growth and decline of Anglo-Norman Wexford, *c.*1200–1400'. In Shine, D., Potterton, M., Mandal, S. and McLoughlin, C. (eds), *Carrick, County Wexford: Ireland's first Anglo-Norman stronghold*, 18–77. Dublin.

Price, L. 1966. 'The origin of the word *betagius*'. *Ériu*, 20, 185–90.

Rae, E.C. 1987. 'Architecture and sculpture, 1169–1603'. In Cosgrove, A. (ed.), *A new history of Ireland*, vol. ii: *medieval Ireland, 1169–1534*, 737–77. Oxford.

Riley, H.T. (ed.). 1853. *The Annals of Roger de Hoveden, comprising the history of England and of other countries of Europe, from AD732 to AD1201*. London.

Scott, A. and Martin, F. (eds). 1978. *Expugnatio Hibernica by Giraldus Cambrensis*. Dublin.

Sharp, J. and Stamp, A. 1910. 'Inquisitions post-mortem, Edward II'. In *Calendar of Inquisitions post-mortem, vol. 6: Edward II* (London): www.british-history.ac.uk/inquis-post-mortem/vol6, accessed 21 Mar. 2019.

Sharpe, R. 1991. *Medieval Irish saints' Lives*. Oxford.

Sheehy, M.P. (ed.). 1962–5. *Pontificia Hibernica: medieval papal chancery documents concerning Ireland, 640–1261*. 2 vols. Dublin.

Simington, R.C. 1953. *The Civil Survey, AD1654–1656, vol. ix: county of Wexford*. Dublin.

Simms, K. 1998. 'Literacy and the Irish bards'. In Pryce, H. (ed.), *Literacy in medieval Celtic societies*, 238–58. Cambridge.

Stokes, W. (ed.). 1905. *Félire Óengusso Céli Dé: the martyrology of Oengus the Culdee*. London.

Sweetman, D. 1979. 'Archaeological excavations at Ferns Castle, County Wexford'. *Proceedings of the Royal Irish Academy*, 79C10, 217–45.

Sweetman, H. (ed.). 1875–86. *Calendar of documents relating to Ireland, 1171–1307*. 5 vols. London.

Theiner, A. 1864. *Vetera monumenta Hibernorum et Scotorum historiam illustrantia*. Rome.

Thomas, A. 1992. *The walled towns of Ireland*. 2 vols. Dublin.

Traquair, P. 1998. *Freedom's sword: Scotland's wars of independence*. London.

Turner, R.V. 1988. *Men raised from the dust: administrative service and upward mobility in Angevin England*. Philadelphia.

Twemlow, J.A. 1904. *Calendar of entries in the papal registers relating to Great Britain and Ireland: Papal Letters, vol. 6: AD1404–1415*. London.

Twemlow, J.A. 1921. *Calendar of entries in the papal registers relating to Great Britain and Ireland: Papal Letters, vol. 11: AD1455–1464*. London.

Twemlow, J.A. 1933. *Calendar of entries in the papal registers relating to Great Britain and Ireland: Papal Letters, vol. 12: AD1458–1471*. London.

Twemlow, J.A. 1960. *Calendar of entries in the papal registers relating to Great Britain and Ireland: Papal Letters, vol. 14: 1484–1492*. London.

Valante, M. 2015. 'Fleets, forts and the geography of Toirdelbach Ua Conchobair's bid for the high-kingship'. In McAlister, V. and Barry, T. (eds), *Space and settlement in medieval Ireland*, 48–63. Dublin.

Virtuani, P. 2016. 'Unforgiveable trespasses: the Irish Hospitallers and the defence of their rights in the mid-thirteenth century'. In Browne, M. and Ó Clabaigh, C. (eds), *Soldiers of Christ: the Knights Hospitaller and the Knights Templar in medieval Ireland*, 195–205. Dublin.

Whelan, B. 1979. 'Report on animal remains'. In Sweetman, D. 1979. 'Archaeological excavations at Ferns Castle, County Wexford'. *Proceedings of the Royal Irish Academy*, 79C10, 244–5.

Whelan, K. 2018. *Religion, landscape and settlement in Ireland, from Patrick to present*. Dublin.

White, N.B. 1943. *Extents of Irish monastic possessions, 1540–1541*. Dublin.

CHAPTER THREE

The changing monastic and political landscape of Ferns in context, twelfth to fifteenth century

ANNE-JULIE LAFAYE

INTRODUCTION

This chapter explores the impact of the Anglo-Norman colonization of Ireland on the monastic landscapes of the south-east of the country, with a particular focus on Ferns, from the twelfth to the fifteenth century. The late twelfth and thirteenth centuries were the most successful period for the newcomers, and the time during which most changes occurred, both politically and economically, and with regard to religious foundations. Even before the Anglo-Norman arrival, however, changes were taking place, with the twelfth century in particular a period of transition, especially in relation to Ireland's ecclesiastical and monastic organization (Ó Corráin 2004, 13–19; Bhreathnach 2019, 1–27). This chapter looks at the broader picture of monastic foundations before and after the arrival of the Anglo-Normans, from their physical imprint to their role in their founders' political and economic strategies. In each instance, attention is paid to the monastic landscape of Ferns, in particular its place in the kingship of Diarmait Mac Murchada, from the perspective of his religious patronage there, as well as with regard to what happened after the Anglo-Normans arrived: what changed, and what did not change, in the south-east of Ireland generally, and in Ferns in particular?

CHANGING MONASTIC LANDSCAPES IN THE PRE-ANGLO-NORMAN PERIOD

The twelfth century was a transitional period for ecclesiastical and monastic organization in Ireland. Religious reform came from the Continent and led to the establishment of a diocesan system, with Ferns becoming one of the five diocesan seats of Leinster in 1111, at the Synod of Ráith Bressail – a status confirmed in 1152 at the Synod of Kells. As elsewhere across Ireland, the early medieval monastic landscape of the south-east was characterized by a multitude of small ecclesiastical foundations. Those that grew into the main monastic centres in the diocese of Ferns were Ardcavan, Begerin and Ferns itself. Many more sites have been identified both in Ferns and in the adjacent dioceses of Leighlin, Kilkenny (later Ossory) and Glendalough (united with Dublin in 1204): the Archaeological Survey records 180 monastic sites in counties Wexford, Wicklow, Carlow, Laois, Kilkenny and Kildare, the most important among them being Aghaboe (Co. Laois), Kildare (Co. Kildare), Killeshin (Co. Laois), Leighlin (Co. Carlow) and St Mullins (Co. Carlow) (Gwynn and Hadcock 1970). These early sites were characterized by one or more circular enclosures centred on the church, as would have been the case in Ferns (see ch. 8).

While it is not clear from surviving records whether a monastic community existed in Ferns before the twelfth century, there is plenty of evidence for the existence of an early medieval church settlement, with the survival of three versions of the life of St Máedóc, also known as St Aidan, Ferns' patron saint (Ó Riain 2011, 431–6; chs 2, 8). The core of the early ecclesiastical site at Ferns is now marked by St Edan's Cathedral (Church of Ireland) and its graveyard, to the east of the town. In the graveyard, four sections of high crosses dating to the ninth/tenth century, including a decorated base and shaft, are the only surviving material evidence of the early ecclesiastical site; however, as examined in detail in Chapter 8, excavations and geophysical surveys across Ferns have identified sections of what are likely to have been the inner and outer enclosures of the early monastic site, as well as additional potential enclosing ditch(es), that may have formed an annex to the outer enclosure, or a third, broader enclosure (fig. 7.2). Archaeological investigations have also apparently confirmed that the innermost enclosure was abandoned either just before or because of the establishment of St Mary's Augustinian priory (fig. 3.4), which was placed on top of it (Bhreathnach and Dowling 2021; Shine et al. 2021; ch. 9).

A crucial aspect of the twelfth-century reform was the movement towards a standardized monastic way of life, notably the adoption of the Augustinian rule by many existing communities (Bhreathnach 2019). This was associated with a reorganization of the monastic landscape. The arrival of continental religious orders coincides with the transition from early monastic sites defined by circular enclosures to new physical and architectural forms. St Mary's Abbey was founded before 1162 by Diarmait Mac Murchada, king of Leinster, and his original charter to the Augustinian canons survives (Flanagan 2005). His widespread religious patronage ensured he had a significant role in changing the monastic landscape of Ireland in the twelfth century, both in Ferns and in the rest of his kingdom. Mac Murchada had extraordinary aspirations as a medieval ruler, and religious patronage was a key aspect of this (O'Keeffe 2003; chs 4, 6). As king of Leinster, he regularly used ecclesiastical patronage to further his military and political ambitions. He was involved in establishing communities of Augustinian canons at Ferns and at Dublin (All Saints' Priory, *c.*1166), and a convent of Arrouasian canonesses at St Mary de Hogges, *c.*1146, also in Dublin, as well as the nunneries of Aghade (Co. Carlow) and Kilculliheen (Co. Waterford), both in 1151 (Collins 2021, 86–97). He also endowed existing sites, commissioning, for example, a large sculpted portal for Killeshin Church (O'Keeffe 1997, 54).

3.1 Baltinglass, Co. Wicklow: remains of Cistercian abbey (image courtesy of Keith Smith)

Mac Murchada was the first Irish king to establish a Cistercian monastery, at Baltinglass in 1148 (Nicholls 1985; fig. 3.1). The Cistercians had arrived in Ireland just six years earlier in 1142, founding Mellifont Abbey in modern-day Co. Louth, of which Baltinglass was a daughter house. Mac Murchada established Baltinglass with a view to strengthening his grip on the provincial kingship of Leinster, providing the monastery with a strategic grant of eight parcels of land in the modern counties of Carlow, Kildare, Laois and Wicklow. These are listed in a charter confirming the Baltinglass possessions granted by John, lord of Ireland, in 1185, and referring specifically to the earlier grant made by Mac Murchada and his men (Nicholls 1985).

The Cistercians were the first order to bring to Ireland the claustral plan, in which three ranges of domestic buildings were organized around a cloister. They became exceptionally influential in terms of monastic planning and architecture across Europe. The so-called 'Fontenay Plan', named after the first abbey established by St Bernard of Clairvaux, and comprising a double-aisled cruciform church and domestic ranges organized according to their functions around the cloister, spread through the Cistercian network across Europe and was adopted at Irish sites such as Mellifont, Baltinglass and later foundations (Stalley 1987, 51–61; fig. 3.2), influencing the

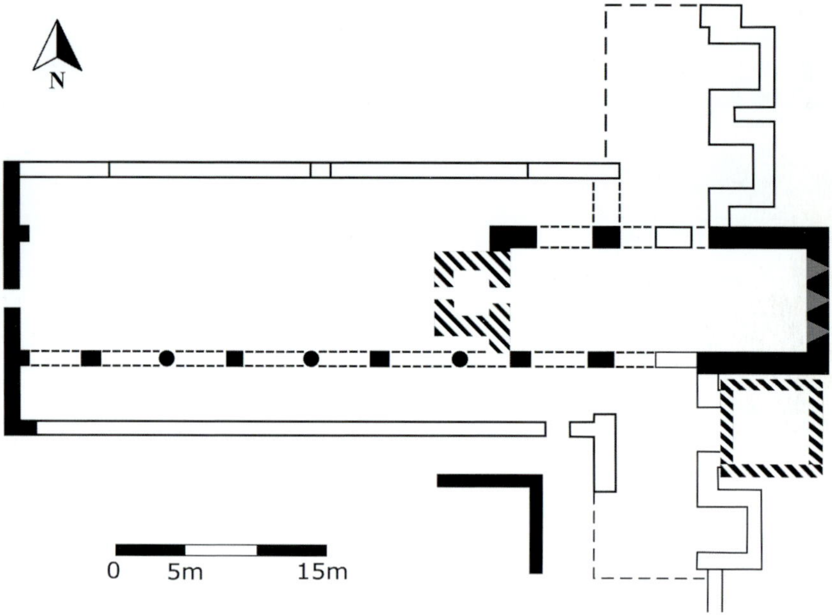

3.2 *(above)* Baltinglass, Co. Wicklow: ground plan of abbey church

3.3 Jerpoint, Co. Kilkenny: remains of Cistercian abbey (image courtesy of Keith Smith)

3.4 Ferns: remains of St Mary's Augustinian abbey (image courtesy of Keith Smith)

architecture of other orders, such as the Augustinian canons and later on the mendicants. Mac Murchada was not the only Irish king to found Cistercian abbeys – for example, Jerpoint was likely founded by the king of Ossory Domnall Mac Gilla Pátraic before 1165, or by his son in the later 1160s (Gwynn and Hadcock 1970, 122; fig. 3.3). Jerpoint was a daughter house of Baltinglass and mother house to Killenny, another pre-Anglo-Norman abbey founded by one of Mac Murchada's liegemen, Dermot O'Ryan, though it appears to have become officially affiliated to the Cistercian order in 1185 only, likely functioning as a Benedictine community beforehand (Gwynn and Hadcock 1970, 117; Butler and Bernard 1918). The grant was confirmed by Mac Murchada with a charter between 1162 and 1165; however, by 1227 the abbey was in dire financial difficulty and united to Graiguenamanagh (Duiske), also in Co. Kilkenny, of which it became a grange called 'Oldabbey' (see White 1943, 195, for its possessions at the Dissolution) – an example of the varying fortunes of such foundations, when inadequately endowed.

In Ferns, as already noted, the re-organization of the monastic landscape saw the foundation of St Mary's on top of the early monastic enclosure. The archaeological investigation of the site discussed in Chapter 9 may help shed light on whether its placement had symbolic significance. However, it was not the only change experienced by Ferns in the twelfth century, as it further grew as a centre of both ecclesiastical and secular importance. Indeed, as well as becoming the episcopal seat of a diocese that corresponded approximately to the core kingdom of the Uí Chennselaig dynasty, by the time of Mac Murchada's reign it had also become the *caput* or capital of the dynasty (see ch. 2). The status of Ferns was strengthened by Mac Murchada when he established his residence there, and its strategic importance was signalled by the fact that in 1166 Mac Murchada himself burned it 'for fear that the men of Connacht would burn his castle and his house' (*AFM*, 1161).

St Mary's Abbey (fig. 3.4) was a royal foundation and, considering the status of Ferns, it might have been expected to flourish and extend accordingly; however, the small Romanesque church commissioned by Mac Murchada did not outgrow its original walls, and until recently there had been no obvious signs that a claustral complex had been built, mirroring the large Cistercian abbeys established in the region. A stone enclosure (since disappeared) surveyed by Robert Cochrane in the early twentieth century, however, had suggested the existence of a cloister, which was seemingly confirmed in a geophysical survey conducted in 2015 by the 'Monastic Ireland: landscape, community and settlement' project (Bhreathnach and Dowling 2021). The recent excavations led by the IAFS uncovered evidence for walls lining up with Cochrane's enclosure, which have been revealed to represent the walls not of a claustral arcade, but of eastern and southern building ranges (as well as potentially a western range or western boundary wall); with these excavations not yet concluded, the evidence for the existence of a claustral arcade and ambulatory, while currently limited, may yet come to light (Cochrane 1910, 11–12, plan at 52; Shine et al. 2021, 39–41; 2022, 55–7; see ch. 9). Dates of AD1176–1269 for organics from the basal fill of the inner ditch of the early monastic enclosure during the IAFS excavations indicate that the ditch was backfilled around the time of the construction of St Mary's; however, artefacts recovered during the excavations suggest the ranges were constructed between the twelfth and fourteenth centuries, and further specialist analyses are required to determine whether the ranges and possible cloister were laid out when the church was built *c.*1160 or shortly thereafter. This is crucial as a date in the twelfth century would make St Mary's the earliest example of a claustral plan in an Augustinian context in Ireland (and not much later than the first Cistercian examples to occur in this country). If that is the case, Mac Murchada may well have been influenced by what the Cistercian monks of his Baltinglass foundation had built there. Tadhg O'Keeffe and Rhiannon Carey Bates have suggested that St Mary's was established to serve as a royal sepulchral chapel, the burial place of Mac Murchada, with the primary role of the canons to pray for his soul, and that it was modelled on Cormac's Chapel in Cashel, which had been commissioned by Cormac Mac Carthaig, king of Munster, and built in 1127–34 (O'Keeffe and Carey Bates 2016; see ch. 6 for O'Keeffe's updated analysis on the architecture of St Mary's Abbey following the excavation). There is evidence that with St Mary's and his caput of Ferns,

Mac Murchada was making a statement about the type of king he wanted to be, his aspirations to be high-king of Ireland and his territorial ambitions for his kingdom. The lands he granted to the canons of St Mary's were dispersed throughout his own demesne land and were therefore under his direct control. The dedication to St Mary, and not to St Aidan, the founder of the earlier monastery, suggests his wish to link his royal foundation to the Universal church, to make 'a statement of change' and, perhaps, to develop Ferns as a settlement in the manner of the great cathedral towns of Britain and the Continent (O'Keeffe and Carey Bates 2016).

All of this goes to demonstrate some of the ways in which changes were happening in Ireland even before the arrival of the Anglo-Normans. The landscapes of monasticism and of kingship were evolving, with Mac Murchada and Ferns at the forefront of changes. More dramatic changes loomed into focus when Mac Murchada's expansionist policies brought him into conflict with rival provincial kings, especially the O'Conors of Connacht. His enemies joined forces and he was stripped of his kingship and forced out of Leinster in 1166. He returned in 1167 and by 1170 Richard de Clare (Strongbow) and his men had helped him regain his kingdom. The arrival of Anglo-Norman mercenaries also put into motion a new process of conquest and colonization shortly before Mac Murchada died in Ferns in 1171. What happened to St Mary's and Ferns following the arrival of the Anglo-Normans? What happened to those already-changing monastic landscapes when the political geography of the region dramatically transformed too?

MONASTIC LANDSCAPES UNDER THE ANGLO-NORMANS: CHANGE AND CONTINUITY

Strongbow married Mac Murchada's daughter Aífe and, when her father died in 1171, he became lord of Leinster. When Strongbow too died five years later in 1176, William Marshal inherited the lordship of Leinster, having married Stongbow's daughter Isabel. Mac Murchada had led the way with Cistercian and Augustinian foundations, and the newcomers followed suit. William Marshal and his followers all included monastic patronage as a key element in their broader strategy for territorial control and economic development of the land they acquired.

The Anglo-Normans became patrons of existing foundations and were involved in their enlargement, such as at Jerpoint, the charter for which was confirmed by John as lord of Ireland (Flanagan 2005). Some of these existing communities were not keen to allow foreigners to take control of their affairs; the abbot of Baltinglass, for instance, Ailbe Ua Máel Muaid (Albin O'Mulloy), who became the last Irish bishop of Ferns in 1186, preached against English clergy at a synod in Dublin in 1185 (FitzGerald 1908, 384). Nonetheless, Anglo-Norman lords established their own, large monastic foundations that they endowed with extensive estates. Marshal founded the Cistercian

3.5 Tintern, Co. Wexford: remains of Cistercian abbey (image courtesy of Keith Smith)

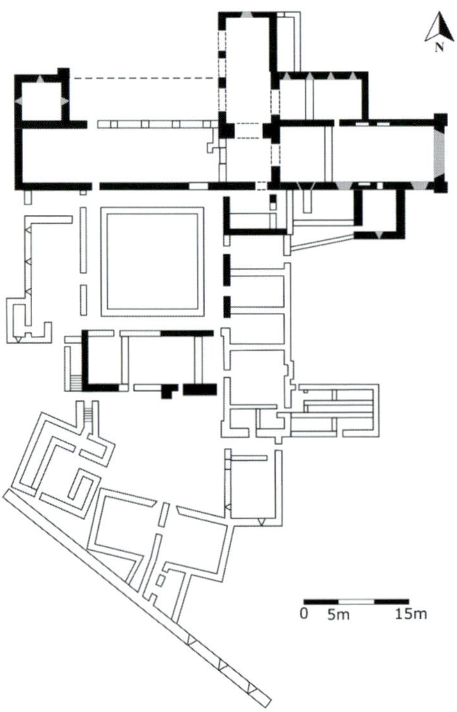

3.6 Kells, Co. Kilkenny: ground plan of Augustinian priory

abbey of Tintern de Voto in 1200, after vowing to do so if he landed safely following a rough sea crossing. The monks, who came from Tintern abbey in Wales, were granted thirty carucates (*c.*3,600 acres), with sitting tenants removed to make way for the newcomers (Bernard 1916; fig. 3.5). The coming of the Anglo-Normans also marked a new phase for Augustinian foundations, which were comparable to Cistercian houses in relation to planning, architecture and the size of their priories (Browne and Ó Clabaigh 2019). The largest Augustinian foundation was Kells Priory in Co. Kilkenny, founded by Geoffrey Fitz Robert, who came to Ireland with Marshal (Clyne 2007; fig. 3.6).

One of the main differences between the old and the new monastic foundations was that the latter were part of an overall plan that involved an economic reorganization of the land, with division into agricultural and administrative units – manors – and the foundation of settlements – boroughs – designed to attract settlers from England, Wales, France, Flanders and elsewhere (Lyttleton and O'Keeffe 2005). At Kells, for instance, Fitz Robert also established a borough, which became his manorial caput, and where he built a castle. On an Ordnance Survey map of the late nineteenth century we can still see the Anglo-Norman features of the medieval borough, which was planned, like others throughout Ireland, with a castle, streets and burgage plots, a market place, a mill, a parish church and a religious house – the Augustinian priory (Clyne 2017). Among the other boroughs founded around this time in Wexford are Clonmines (associated with Tintern), New Ross and, of course, Ferns (Colfer 2017).

Augustinians canons and Cistercian monks had been embedded in Ireland a full generation before the arrival of the Anglo-Normans. Conversely, it was even longer *after* the *adventus anglorum* that the mendicant orders established themselves there, from the 1220s onwards. The Franciscans, Dominicans, Carmelites and Augustinian friars went on to play a crucial part in the strategies of both Anglo-Norman and Irish lords. They were popular among all social classes and ethnicities and, ultimately, they became the most successful orders of the thirteenth century and of the later Middle Ages in Ireland generally (Ó Clabaigh 2012; Lafaye 2018). The mendicant orders established themselves in towns first because their main purpose was to preach to the faithful, and they embraced an ideal of poverty, depending on the generosity of the laity and alms-giving as their sole resource. As such, they controlled no large estates or properties. They were particularly well suited to the development of the urban network by the Anglo-Normans: there were, for instance, fewer cost implications for the patron of the town, with no significant land-grant needed beyond the site of the precinct.

They were seen by some as a stabilizing force between colonial and native worlds, often placed on the periphery of a borough, giving access to their church to burgesses from within the walls and rural populations living in the surrounding countryside (Lafaye 2018). At Castledermot in south Kildare, for example, the friary was just

a)

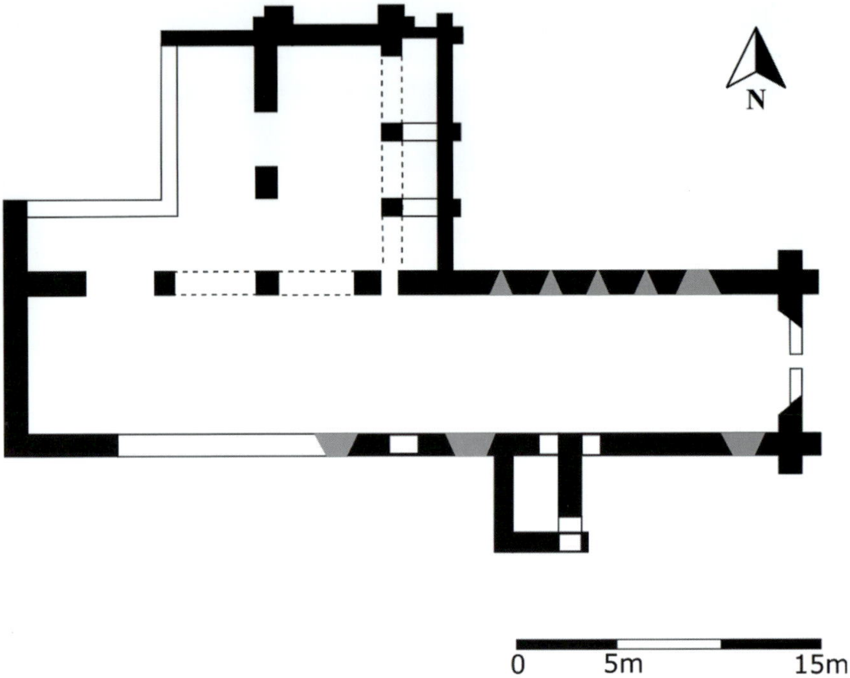

b)

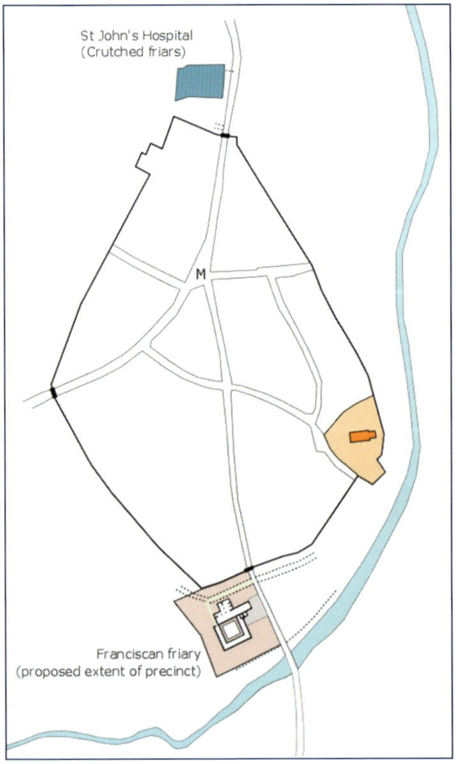

3.7 Castledermot, Co. Kildare: plans of **a)** Franciscan friary and **b)** town

3.8 Ferns: castle viewed from south (image courtesy of Keith Smith)

outside the southern gate of the walled borough, providing a conduit linking town and country (fig. 3.7). Mendicant friaries also followed the claustral plan, although on a smaller scale and in a more compact manner that the Cistercians and the Augustinian canons, because of the urban context in which they settled and their mendicant lifestyle (Lafaye 2021). As well as Castledermot, no fewer than fifteen mendicant friaries were established in the southern half of the Leinster lordship in the thirteenth and fourteenth centuries. These were in many important settlements of the region, under the patronage of both Anglo-Norman and Irish lords: the Dominicans came to Kilkenny (1225), Athy (Co. Kildare, 1253–7), Arklow (Co. Wicklow, 1264), Rosbercon (Co. Wesford, 1267) and Aghaboe (Co. Laois, 1382); the Franciscans settled in Kilkenny (*c.*1234), New Ross (*c.*1256), Wexford (1260) and Wicklow (pre-1272); the Augustinian friars in New Ross (late thirteenth century/pre-1320), Tullow (Co. Carlow, 1314) and Clonmines (Co. Wexford, *c.*1317); and the Carmelites in Leighlinbridge (*c.*1272), Knocktopher (fourteenth century) and Horetown (fourteenth century site unknown).

After the arrival of the Anglo-Normans, therefore, a reorganization of secular and monastic landscapes took place in south-eastern Ireland, particularly in the southern parts of the lordship of Leinster, in south Kilkenny and Wexford. As Mac Murchada's dynastic caput and a diocesan seat, Ferns represented a striking example of the changing monastic and political landscapes of the twelfth century and of the grand ambitions of a provincial king, even before the Anglo-Normans set foot in Ireland. After Mac Murchada's demise in 1171, Strongbow appears to have recognized the strategic importance of Ferns, especially as he worked to establish his authority and to attract followers to settle in Leinster (ch. 2). Control of Ferns was necessary to keep at bay the Meic Murchada, who continued to lay claim to Ferns, and remained a threat to the Anglo-Norman settlement of Leinster throughout the thirteenth century, re-emerging in their role as leaders of the Irish septs attacking the Leinster colony in the 1270s (Frame 1998, 241–5). Strongbow founded Ferns as a borough, and his heir William Marshal erected a masonry castle there (ch. 2; fig. 3.8) and kept it as part of his demesne land. That there were no great plans for Ferns to be developed as a very large borough is indicated by the limited number of burgages granted for settlers there: 160, the same as Carlow, but much fewer than the 506 in Marshal's newly established borough and port of New Ross (French and Hore 1910, 306). It is perhaps not surprising, then, that no mendicant community was established in Ferns.

At Ferns, the ecclesiastical foundation at St Mary's continued to exist after the coming of the Anglo-Normans. Though the upstanding remains of the Romanesque church suggest that it did not undergo any further development beyond the twelfth century, the latest excavation results have shown that at least two building ranges were built to the south of the church between the twelfth and the fourteenth century, and therefore possibly after the arrival of the Anglo-Normans. Considering the fact that the church was not extended, however, and that a western range or a stone cloister may not have existed, it is clear that it remained a foundation of limited size, or was possibly unfinished. This is particularly striking when compared to large Augustinian foundations such as Kells (fig. 3.6). For reasons that are not yet clear, it appears that neither the Meic Murchada nor others continued to endow St Mary's after Mac Murchada's death. The community was probably competing for patronage with the bishop and the canons of the newly established cathedral chapter – and the canons of St Mary's had to rely on the old twelfth-century land grants from Mac Murchada throughout the period and until its suppression in 1538. A few abbots are mentioned in fifteenth-century papal letters. All were Irish, which makes sense if the main purpose of St Mary's was as Mac Murchada's sepulchral chapel, but it may also explain the lack of any patronage from Ferns' Anglo-Norman lords (Twemlow 1912; 1933; 1966). An inventory of the abbey taken at the Dissolution suggests that claustral buildings did exist: the abbey was described as a 'church and belfry, dormitory, chapter-house, hall and other buildings' – and in possession of *c.*600 acres and 'other interests' (Gwynn and Hadcock 1970, 176). Three years later, there were 'no buildings in the precinct save the abbey church and a hall' (White 1943, 371–3).

The Meic Murchada continued to lay claim to Ferns as their caput until the sixteenth century but were not always in possession of it, and the history of the settlement from the thirteenth century onwards is marked by violence and destruction (ch. 2). In the years 1276/7, Gaelic leaders attacked the lands and property of the Anglo-Irish settlers, laying waste to forty-nine burgages in Ferns and 148 in Wexford town, while in 1317 St Mary's was plundered and burnt by Irish forces during the Bruce Wars. In 1324, according to an inquisition into the property of Aymer de

3.9 Aghaboe, Co. Laois: friary and church viewed from west (photograph courtesy of Laois County Council)

Valence, lord of Wexford, the castle, burgages and manor of Ferns were worth nothing, 'being waste by reason of the war of the Irish' and 'being wasted by the Irish felons' (French and Hore 1910, 306; ch. 2).

An interesting comparison to Ferns is Aghaboe in Co. Laois. Like Ferns, this was an early monastic site founded in the sixth century (by St Canice) and may have been an early seat of the diocese of Ossory, before it was moved to Kilkenny in 1111. Kilkenny was a daughter church of Aghaboe, which was St Canice's principal church. The importance of Aghaboe as an early monastic centre is reflected in the abbots of Aghaboe having kept the title of *comharba cainnigh* ('Canice's successors') until the early twelfth century (Gwynn and Hadcock 1970, 28; Mac Airt and Mac Niocaill 1983). Despite Kilkenny emerging as the diocesan seat, Aghaboe became a relatively important manor after the arrival of the Anglo-Normans. A motte castle was built near the early monastic site and what remained one of the principal churches of Ossory was served by a community of Augustinian canons. By the middle of the fourteenth century the manor was back under the control of the Meic Gilla Pátraic, former kings of Ossory, who captured the castle in 1349 and in 1382 established there a Dominican friary, which itself would have been some evidence of the friary's patrons' ambitions for Aghaboe (Flynn 1975; Ó Clabaigh 2012, 59; fig. 3.9). Indeed, as lords of Ossory the Meic Gilla Pátraic and their lordship thrived, with Aghaboe developing as a settlement and a relatively important economic centre (Edwards 2001, 77–97).

3.10 Ferns: medieval building east of cathedral (image courtesy of Keith Smith)

Aghaboe was located further north in a region never fully colonized and one that was back under Irish control very quickly, while Ferns was within a more densely settled area in Wexford, though at the same time outside the most economically thriving part of the colony.

Aghaboe did not survive as a settlement, however, while Ferns withstood the tests of time, in part, perhaps, due to its status as a diocesan capital. Change and continuity at Ferns are reflected in its fortunes as a bishop's seat. The last Irish bishop, Ua Máel Muaid, was appointed in 1186 *after* Anglo-Norman colonization had begun. As we saw, he had protested the arrival of English clergy, and later was involved in a series of disputes with Marshal concerning Ferns diocesan land being encroached upon by him and his followers (O'Byrne 2009; ch. 2). Nonetheless, he appears to have developed a rather good relationship with the Anglo-Norman colonizers, with King John even nominating him for the vacant metropolitan see of Cashel in 1206. Ua Máel Muaid was bishop spanning five decades until his death in 1223. After this time, only Anglo-Norman bishops were appointed. The cathedral at Ferns was rebuilt during the episcopacy of John St John, the successor to Ua Máel Muaid, and some Gothic architectural details survive that are consistent with a date in the second quarter of the thirteenth century (O'Keeffe and Carey Bates 2016). Also built during the time of Bishop St John, the large building to the east of the cathedral remains enigmatic (fig. 3.10). O'Keeffe and Carey Bates suggest it originally housed the effigy of St John (now inside the cathedral), but they also propose that Ua Máel Muaid was responsible for organizing the chapter of the cathedral, and Edel Bhreathnach in her own study of Ferns asks whether it could have been a – very grand and impressive – chapter house, commissioned by St John (Bhreathnach and Dowling, 2021).

CONCLUSION

While the political and economic impact of the Anglo-Normans is of course undeniable, with regard to the monastic landscape of Ferns and the south-east region as a whole it is clear that important changes had begun to take place well before Mac Murchada decided to seek help overseas. He played a crucial role in the implementation of these changes, through his widespread patronage of the 'new' monastic orders that established themselves in Ireland from the first half of the twelfth century onwards, namely the Augustinian Regular Canons and Canonesses and the Cistercians. Their arrival went hand-in-hand with a reorganization of the existing monastic landscape, through the grant of vast landed estates, and the construction of new churches and monasteries, often on the site of earlier ecclesiastical settlements – as was the case in Ferns. Mac Murchada, along with other contemporary Irish kings, used religious patronage as part of his territorial and political strategies, and monastic foundations such as St Mary's Abbey in Ferns were as much statements about his aspirations as a ruler as they were pious endeavours.

The Anglo-Normans, when they arrived, brought in political changes and a new economic organization, but continued in the Irish kings' footsteps when it came to religious patronage and territorial strategies, endowing existing foundations and establishing new ones. As far as Ferns is concerned, its development and ongoing relevance after the coming of the Anglo-Normans was mostly linked to its episcopal status, and the relative power of its bishops. The effect of the dramatic political changes that took place in the kingdom of Leinster from the late twelfth century onwards and the difficulties of the Meic Murchada in holding on to power in and around Ferns were not as positive for St Mary's Abbey, however, which does not seem to have thrived beyond its original status.

BIBLIOGRAPHY

AFM: O'Donovan, J. (ed.). 1848–51. *Annals of the kingdom of Ireland by the Four Masters*. 7 vols. Dublin.

Bernard, J.H. 1916. 'The foundation of Tintern Abbey, Co. Wexford'. *Proceedings of the Royal Irish Academy*, 33, 527–29.

Bhreathnach, E. 2019. 'The *Vita Apostolica* and the origin of the Augustinian canons and canonesses in medieval Ireland'. In Browne and Ó Clabaigh (eds), *Households of God*, 1–27. Dublin.

Bhreathnach, E. and Dowling, G. 2021. 'Forming an episcopal see and an Augustinian foundation in medieval Ireland: the case of Ferns, Co. Wexford'. *Proceedings of the Royal Irish Academy*, 121C, 191–226.

Browne, M. and Ó Clabaigh C. (eds). 2019. *Households of God: the regular canons and canonesses of St Augustine and of Prémontré in medieval Ireland*. Dublin.

Butler, C.M. and Bernard, J.H. 1918. 'The charters of the Cistercian abbey of Duiske in the county of Kilkenny'. *Proceedings of the Royal Irish Academy*, 35C, 1–188.

Carrigan, W. 1905. *History and antiquities of the diocese of Ossory, vol. 1*. Dublin.

Clyne, M. 2007. *Kells Priory, Co. Kilkenny: archaeological excavations by T. Fanning and M. Clyne*. Dublin.

Clyne, M. 2017. 'Kells and its priory'. In Bradley, J., Ó Drisceoil, C. and Potterton, M. (eds), *William Marshal and Ireland*, 78–105. Dublin.

Cochrane, R. 1910. 'Ferns, Co. Wexford'. In *78th Annual Report of the Commissioners of Public Works in Ireland*, 3–6, 16–17. Dublin.

Colfer, B. 2017. 'Monastery and manor: William Marshal's settlement strategy in Co. Wexford'. In Bradley, J., Ó Drisceoil, C. and Potterton, M. (eds), *William Marshal and Ireland*, 249–67. Dublin.

Collins, T. 2021. *Female monasticism in medieval Ireland: an archaeology*. Cork.

Edwards, D. 2001. 'Collaboration without Anglicization: the MacGiollapadraig lordship and Tudor reform'. In Duffy, P.J., Edwards, D. and FitzPatrick, E. (eds), *Gaelic Ireland, c.1250–c.1650: land, lordship and settlement*, 77–97. Dublin.

FitzGerald, Walter. 1908. 'Baltinglass Abbey, its possessions and their post-Reformation proprietors'. *Journal of the County Kildare Archaeological Society*, 5:6 (July), 378–414.

Flanagan, M-T. 2005. *Irish royal charters: texts and contexts*. Oxford.

Flynn, T. 1975. *The Dominicans of Aghaboe (c.1382–c.1782)*. Dublin.

Frame, R. 1998. *Ireland and Britain, 1170–1450*. London.

French, C. and Hore, F.H. 1910. 'Ferns, County Wexford'. *Journal of the Royal Society of Antiquaries of Ireland*, 40, 297–315.

Gwynn, A. and Hadcock N. 1970. *Medieval religious houses: Ireland*. London.

Lafaye, A.-J. 2018. 'Spiritual renewal and changing landscapes: the mendicant orders in Ireland, 13th–16th century'. In Lyttleton, J. and Stout, M. (eds), *Church and settlement in Ireland*, 119–41. Dublin.

Lafaye, A.-J. 2021. 'Dominican friaries in the medieval landscapes of Britain and Ireland: a comparative study'. In Giraud, E. and Linde, C. (eds), *A companion to the English Dominican province from its beginnings to the Reformation*, 69–111. Leiden.

Lyttleton, J. and O'Keeffe, T. (eds), 2005. *The manor in medieval and early modern Ireland.* Dublin.

Mac Airt, S. and Mac Niocaill, G. (eds). 1983. *The Annals of Ulster.* 1st ed. Dublin. *CELT: The Corpus of Electronic Texts*: https://celt.ucc.ie/published/T100001A, accessed 17 Feb. 2023.

Nicholls, K. 1985. 'The charter of John, Lord of Ireland, in favour of the Cistercian abbey of Baltinglass'. *Peritia*, 4, 187–206.

O'Byrne, E. 2009. 'O'Mulloy (Ua Máel Muaid), Ailbe (Aulbin)'. *Dictionary of Irish Bibliography*: www.dib.ie/biography/omulloy-ua-mael-muaid-ailbe-aulbin-a6901, accessed 17 February 2023.

Ó Clabaigh, C. 2012. *The friars in Ireland, 1224–1540.* Dublin.

Ó Corráin, D. 2004. 'The synod of Cashel, 1101: conservative or innovative?' In Edwards, D. (ed.), *Regions and rulers in Ireland, 1100–1650*, 13–19. Dublin.

O'Keeffe, T. 1997. 'Diarmait Mac Murchada and Romanesque Leinster: four twelfth-century churches in context'. *Journal of the Royal Society of Antiquaries*, 127, 52–79.

O'Keeffe, T. 2003. *Romanesque Ireland: architecture, sculpture and ideology in the twelfth century.* Dublin.

O'Keeffe, T. and Carey Bates, R. 2016. 'The abbey and cathedral of Ferns, 1111–1253'. In Doyle, I. and Browne, B. (eds), *Medieval Wexford: essays in memory of Billy Colfer*, 73–96. Dublin.

Ó Riain, P. 2011. *A dictionary of Irish saints.* Dublin.

Shine, D., Mandal, S., Lynch, L. and O'Meara, D. 2021. '"Discovering St Aidan's monastery": preliminary archaeological excavation report'. Unpublished report.

Shine, D. and Mandal, S. 2022. '"Discovering St Aidan's monastery": preliminary archaeological excavation report'. Unpublished report.

Stalley, R. 1987. *The Cistercian monasteries of Ireland: an account of the history, art and architecture of the White Monks in Ireland from 1142 to 1540.* London and New Haven, CT.

Twemlow, J.A. (ed.). 1912. *Calendar of papal registers relating to Great Britain and Ireland: vol. 9, 1431–47*, 430–6: www.british-history.ac.uk/cal-papal-registers/brit-ie/vol9/pp430-436, accessed 17 Feb. 2023.

Twemlow, J.A. (ed.). 1933. *Calendar of papal registers relating to Great Britain and Ireland: vol. 12, 1458–71*, 108–11: www.british-history.ac.uk/cal-papal-registers/brit-ie/vol12/pp108-111, accessed 17 Feb. 2023.

Twemlow, J.A. (ed.). 1966. *Calendar of papal registers relating to Great Britain and Ireland: vol. 14, 1484–92*, 220–3: www.british-history.ac.uk/cal-papal-registers/brit-ie/vol14/pp220-223, accessed 17 Feb. 2023.

White, N.B. 1943. *Extents of Irish monastic possessions, 1540–1541.* London.

CHAPTER FOUR

The cult of relics and expressions of wealth at eleventh- and twelfth-century Ferns

KATE COLBERT

The early ecclesiastical site of Ferns (*Ferna*) is located in the northern half of Co. Wexford; it lies in a small valley near the eastern foothills of the Blackstairs Mountains, *c.*10km south of the border with Co. Wicklow and *c.*13km east of Co. Carlow (fig. 4.1). The site itself is situated on a gentle slope *c.*100m south-west of a small stream, and 1km west of the River Bann. The church and graveyard are bounded by a national road (N11) to the north and a local road to the south, giving the site a wedged shape where they meet to the west (fig. 4.2). A thirteenth-century stone castle built by the Marshals, possibly on the site of an earlier ringwork castle, stands on a low hill *c.*400m to the west of the cathedral. St Peter's Church, built in the sixteenth century but with the fabric of several earlier churches, is *c.*200m to the north-east (Bhreathnach and Dowling 2021, 195). The core of the upstanding archaeological remains at Ferns are St Edan's Cathedral (Church of Ireland), which includes the chancel of the thirteenth-century cathedral and is thought to stand on the site of the early medieval church (Moore 2012), the remnants of a medieval chapter house 17m to the east, the ruins of the Augustinian St Mary's Abbey 68m south-east and a holy well *c.*110m north-east of the cathedral, as well as four (possibly five) high crosses, a smaller granite cross and two cross-slabs . A geophysical survey conducted as part of the 'Monastic Ireland' project in 2015 revealed two concentric curvilinear ditches, *c.*60m apart, representing the eastern end of the original early medieval ecclesiastical enclosure (Bhreathnach and Dowling 2021, 212–13). Extensive prehistoric activity around Ferns has also been identified through excavations in the surrounding townlands. An early Bronze Age flat cemetery was uncovered *c.*70m north-west of St Edan's, and an early Iron Age ring-ditch, as well as a late Bronze Age pit, were found in the townland of Ferns Lower, *c.*800m from the church (ibid., 195–6).

Ferns was one of the most important churches in early medieval Leinster, patronized by the powerful Uí Chennselaig from an early stage, if not from the outset, though it was not quite on a par with the two most powerful churches in the province, Kildare and Glendalough, which were of 'national' importance. Nevertheless, Ferns features prominently in documentary sources from the early medieval period. As will be discussed below, careful analysis of this material has revealed more nuanced information about the site, and about the trans-regional cult of its founding saint,

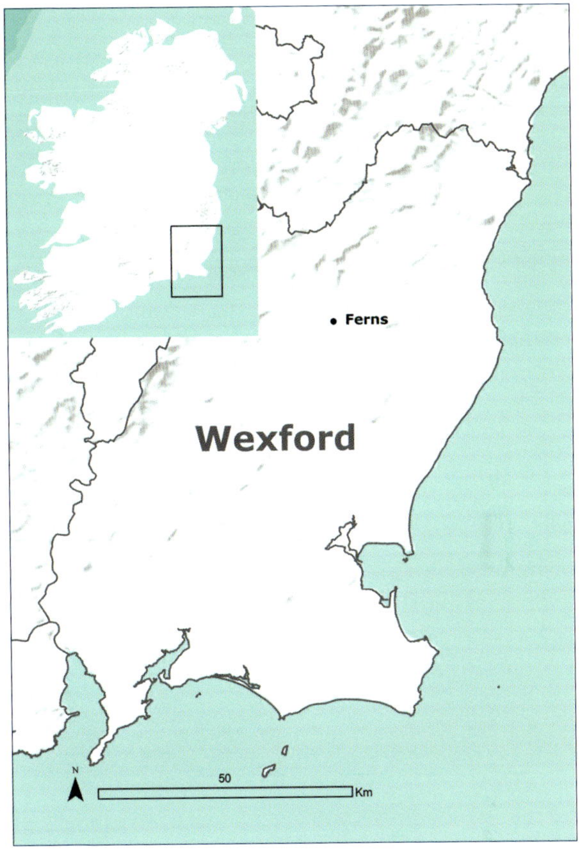

4.1 Ferns: location map (base map © ESRI)

4.2 (*below*) Ferns: site layout and relevant associated features (base map © OpenStreetMap)

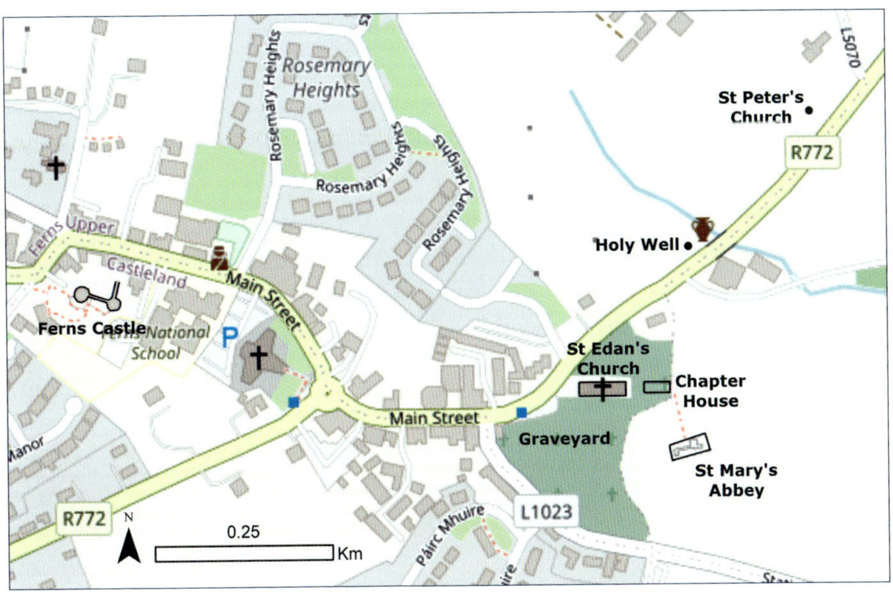

Máedóc. Excavations conducted in advance of public works and improvements to infrastructure over the last few decades have also provided a wealth of additional archaeological information on Ferns and the surrounding area. Furthermore, the large geophysical survey of the fields surrounding the ruins of St Mary's Abbey, a short distance to the south-east of the cathedral, has provided a tantalizing glimpse of a rich and complex array of archaeological features that lie just below the surface (Bhreathnach and Dowling 2021; ch. 9). One area of study that has yet to be analysed in detail, however, is the cult of relics at Ferns. It is hoped that this essay will shed more light on its presence at Ferns, how it influenced the site socio-politically and how it might manifest archaeologically, particularly through investment in stone sculpture.

HISTORICAL AND HAGIOGRAPHICAL BACKGROUND

Ferns was reputedly founded in the late sixth/early seventh century by Aedán mac Sétna, more commonly known by the hypocoristic name, Máedóc. He is recorded as being born on Inis Brechmaighe in Magh Slécht, Co. Cavan, and is also considered the patron saint of the churches of Drumlane, Co. Cavan, and Rossinver, Co. Leitrim (Breen 2009). The deaths of Ferns' abbots, bishops, *princepes* (superiors), *comharbaí* and *airchinnigh* (hereditary successors and administrators, respectively) are regularly recorded in the annals from *c.*620 onward, beginning with Máedóc himself (*AFM 1*, M624.3; *AU*, U625.3; *Chron. Scot.*, CS625; *ATig.*, T627.8). It was burned, raided or plundered at least seven times – including once by its own patron, Diarmait mac Murchada, in 1166 (*AFM 1*, M834.8, M838.11; *AU*, U835.5, U839.10, U930.1, U1042.1; *Chron. Scot.*, CS834, CS839, CS 929, CS1041; *AFM 2*, M917.9, M919.18, M928.9, M1041.14, M1166.14; *ATig.*, T1041.5, T1166.1; *AI*, AI930.1, AI1166.8). In the ninth–eleventh centuries, Ferns was headed by a hereditary family, the Uí Laidgnéin, a 'discard' branch of the Uí Chennselaig (Bhreathnach and Dowling 2021, 196). During this time, it also had close affiliations with Kildare, Tech Moling and Tamhlacht (possibly Tallaght, Co. Dublin). Lachtnán mac Mochtigern was bishop of Kildare as well as superior/abbot of Ferns (*AFM 1*, M873.3; *AU*, U875.1); Laighnen was *comharba* of Ferns and Tamhlacht (*AFM 2*, M937.5); Cairbre mac Laidgnéin and his descendant, Cairpre Conchobhar Ua Laidgnéin, were abbot and *airchinneach* of both Ferns and Tech Moling, respectively (*AFM 2*, M965.5, M1043.2; *AU*, U1043.4). Three battles or skirmishes also took place at Ferns, at least two of which were fought by members of the monastic community itself (*AFM 1*, M764.6; *AU*, U769.2, U783.6, U817.5). Notably, Cathal mac Dúnlainge, who led the community of Tech Munnu against Ferns in 817, is named king of Uí Chennselaig and prior (*secnap*) of Ferns in his obituary two years later (*AU*, U819.5).

Ferns was the seat of Uí Chennselaig ecclesiastical and political power from at least the eleventh century, though likely earlier, considering the Uí Chennselaig controlled

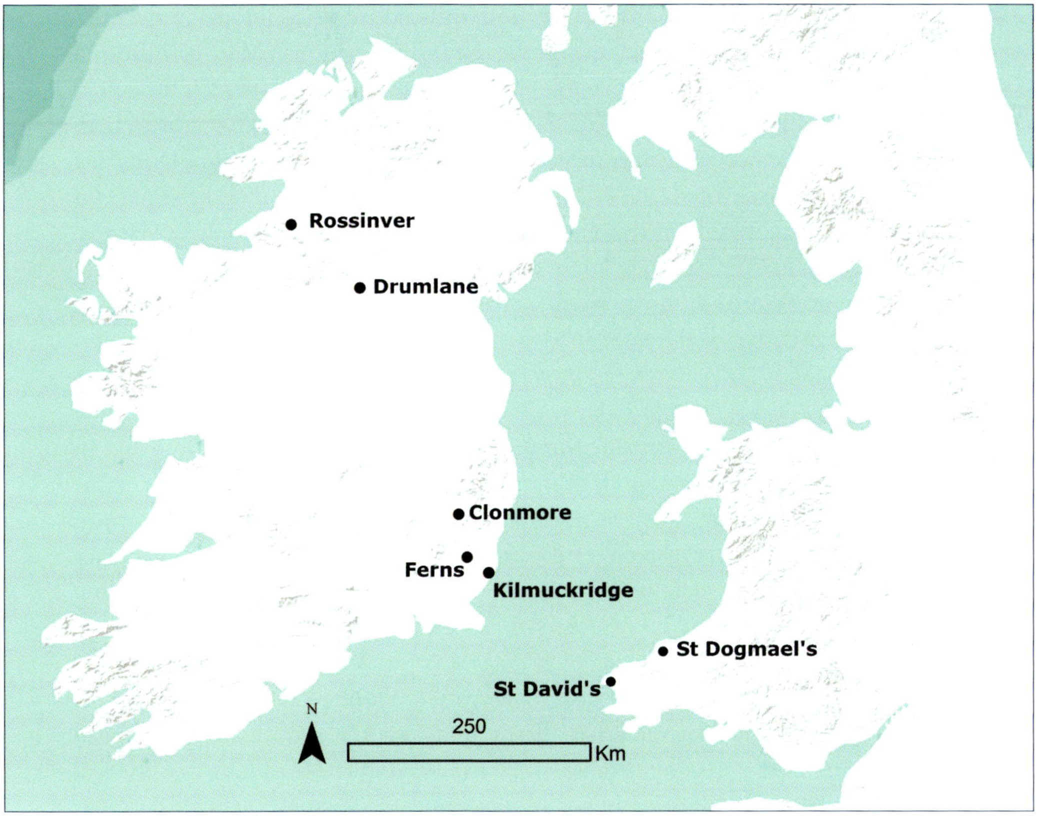

4.3 Ferns: map showing relevant sites mentioned in the text (base map © ESRI)

much of the territory that is now Co. Wexford from probably the eighth century (Byrne 1987a, 148).[1] The Uí Chennselaig dynasty is thought to have originated in the ancient local kingdom of the Uí Felmeda, near Rathvilly, Co. Carlow (MacCotter 2008, 131). They had achieved a measure of power by the late sixth century, and the kingdom of Uí Felmeda may have been the early caput of the Uí Chennselaig (ibid.). Several of its early kings were of Uí Felmeda lineage, most notably Brandub mac Eochu (d. 605, more below; Ó Riain 2011, 431; Gleeson 2014, 735–6). From the seventh century onward, however, this region came to be dominated by the Uí Dúnlainge, and the Uí Chennselaig were pushed eastward (Mac Shamhráin 1996,

1 Ardamine, *c.*18km to the north-east, may have also been a seat of Uí Chennselaig kingship, at least during the first few decades of the eighth century. Colcu mac Bresail, of the Síl Cormaic branch of the Uí Chennselaig (Byrne 1987a, 148; Culleton 1999, 52), is referred to as the king of *Ard Ladrann* in the Annals of Ulster (U722.2). His son, Áed, however, is titled king of Leinster (*AU* U738.4). He fell in the battle of *Áth Senaig* against Áed Allán and the Uí Néill in 738 (ibid.), and was the last Uí Chennselaig king of Leinster until the revival of their power in the eleventh century (Byrne 1987a, 148).

70–2; Gleeson 2014, 735–6). The power and influence of Ferns peaked in the mid-eleventh–twelfth centuries, starting with the rise of Diarmait mac Máel-na-mBó and his restoration of Uí Chennselaig kingship over Leinster in 1042. Likewise, the cult of Ferns' patron saint, Máedóc, flourished during the eleventh and twelfth centuries, both at Ferns and in the northern kingdom of Uí Bréifne, where his churches of Drumlane and Rossinver were situated (fig. 4.3). It was also during this time that the saint's cult at Ferns seemed to have been in competition with the cult of a different St Máedóc, that of Clonmore, Co. Carlow, 27km to the north – and this included their respective relic collections. Moreover, it was starting in the eleventh century that we see written evidence of confraternal ties cultivated between Ferns and the major ecclesiastical centre of St David's, in Pembrokeshire, Wales. The Welsh ecclesiastic (and later bishop of St David's) Sulien is thought to have taken a copy of the Life of St Máedóc of Ferns back with him to Wales sometime in the late eleventh century after studying in Ireland, possibly at the invitation of Diarmait mac Máel-na-mBó (Byrne 1987b, n. 21, 40; Mac Shamhráin 1996, 151). Sulien is credited with translating a lost Irish copy of the Life into Latin, now the earliest surviving copy, as well as the passages that place Máedóc in Wales as a student of St David (Doherty 2002, 270). The close relationship between Ferns and St David's is reinforced in a twelfth-century gloss of the *Martyrology of Oengus* that may suggest ongoing pilgrimage activity between St David's and Ferns during the early medieval period (Stokes 1905, 54–5; Doherty 2011, 265).

Like many other Irish churches, Ferns underwent a significant hierarchical reorganization in the opening decades of the twelfth century, becoming an episcopal see after the Synod of Ráith Bressail in 1111 and the establishment of diocesan boundaries. It has been suggested that Diarmait mac Murchada (d. 1171) had ambitions to make Ferns the ecclesiastical capital of Leinster, though such aspirations were unrealistic and, ultimately, did not come to fruition, as archepiscopal status was given to Dublin in 1152 (Doherty 2002, 273). The ecclesiastical layout at Ferns likewise underwent a reorganization in the twelfth century. St Mary's Abbey was built by Mac Murchada, possibly in the 1140s or early 1150s, though it was chartered as an Augustinian house between 1160 and 1162 (O'Keeffe 1997, 60; Bhreathnach and Dowling 2021, 201). Notably, the abbey was built on top of the earlier inner ecclesiastical enclosure, indicating that it had already been backfilled by this time (Bhreathnach and Dowling 2021, 202; ch. 8). Ferns was the primary burial place of the Uí Chennselaig elite, and St Mary's may have been constructed by Mac Murchada as a royal sepulchral chapel (ibid., 199, 203). Despite its episcopal status and royal patronage in the twelfth century, however, Ferns' position was in decline by the end of the thirteenth century as economic power had shifted away to other centres such as Waterford and New Ross (ibid., 225).

THE CULT OF RELICS AT FERNS

Though it most likely originated earlier, it was in the mid-eleventh century that the cult of Máedóc of Ferns came to prominence. Unsurprisingly, this correlated with the rise to power of the Uí Chennselaig, of whom Máedóc was the patron saint. The rise of the Uí Chennselaig in Leinster also roughly coincided with the consolidation of Uí Ruairc power in Bréifne, and Charles Doherty (2002, 269) has argued that it was their patronage of Máedóc's churches of Drumlane and Rossinver that introduced his northern cult into the eleventh-century Latin Life of Máedóc, though this text deals primarily with the affairs of Leinster and Ferns. While royal patronage would have been an important factor in its development, however, Edel Bhreathnach and Ger Dowling (2021, 197) have suggested that the trans-regional spread of Máedóc's cult is unlikely to be based on a link between the Uí Chennselaig and Uí Ruairc, as there is no obvious connection between the two. Rather, it was probably transmitted primarily through hagiography, relics associated with Máedóc and, perhaps, ecclesiastical links. It is worth noting that, around the same time we first see hagiographical evidence of the intertwining of Máedóc's northern and southern cults, we also see the appearance of northern ecclesiastical families in the annalistic entries relating to Ferns, first in 1050 and then again in 1059 (ibid., 196–7; *AFM* 2, M1050.2, M1059.6; *ATig.*, T1059.10). Indeed, the latter was an obituary for Conaing Ua Fairchellaig, *airchinneach* of Drumlane and 'successor of Máedóc in Connacht and Leinster' (*AFM* 2, M1059.6; *ATig.*, T1059.10). This honorific is not repeated in any other annalistic entries, however, and it is unclear if Conaing Ua Faircheallaigh actually held any power or position at Ferns.

There is also evidence for intense competition between the saint's cult at Ferns and that at Clonmore in the eleventh and twelfth centuries, contained within the hagiographical material of the period. Significant portions of the Lives of Máedóc of Ferns were taken up with appropriating much of the *acta* that were ascribed to Clonmore's founding saint in the eleventh-century additions to the *Bóroma* saga, as well as promoting a notably similar collection of saints' relics. The ecclesiastical site of Clonmore was supposedly founded in the seventh century by Áed mac Éogan, who was also known as Máedóc. This Máedóc was a saint of the Uí Dúnlainge, a major political rival of the Uí Chennselaig for much of the early medieval period. Indeed, it would not be surprising if enmity between the two churches existed prior to the eleventh century, given the location of Clonmore within Uí Felmeda territory (the previous seat of the Uí Chennselaig), and the potentially socio-politically charged circumstances of its foundation (Colbert 2021, 101). Certainly, there was tension between Ferns and Clonmore in the mid-eleventh century, as this was when political power in Leinster was shifting away from the Uí Dúnlainge, patrons of Clonmore, to the Uí Chennselaig, patrons of Ferns (ibid., 119; Mac Shamhráin 1996, 94–6).

Clonmore's ecclesiastical identity was inextricably bound to its relic cult, and it claimed to possess a corporeal relic from *every* saint in Ireland. While this was clearly an exaggeration, Clonmore was nonetheless reputed to house one of the most substantial collections of corporeal relics in early medieval Ireland. Moreover, the proliferation of ninth- to twelfth-century poems, martyrologies, hagiographies, genealogies and sagas involving Máedóc Ua Dúnlainge and his church, its saints and its clergy, or otherwise extolling the virtues of Clonmore must have served to increase its renown (Colbert 2020a, 269–70; 2021, 100–1, 112, 115–16, 118–20). Given this, it is no wonder that many of the episodes from the Lives of Máedóc of Ferns were 'written as a means of subsuming a rival cult' (Doherty 2002, 269).

According to the earliest surviving version of the Latin Life of Máedóc of Ferns, which was probably composed during the reign of Mac Máel-na-mBó (d. 1072; ibid., 269–70), the care of Clonmore and its community was given to Máedóc of Ferns, and he single-handedly drove off the forces of Áed mac Ainmerech, king of the Uí Néill (d. 598; Plummer 1910, 301, §24). In a later passage, however, Máedóc of Ferns instead aids Brandub mac Eochu, Uí Chennselaig king of Leinster, in this task (ibid. 309–10, §54). This is an alternative version of the events recounted in the *Bóroma* saga, in which Máedóc Ua Dúnlainge of Clonmore is a key player (O'Grady 1892, 370–1, 377; Stokes 1892, 56–7, 78–9). The redactor of this Life addresses this by simply placing Máedóc of Ferns at Clonmore, and removing Máedóc Ua Dúnlainge from the narrative entirely. Furthermore, near the end of the Life, Máedóc of Ferns is depicted as a companion of Brigit of Kildare, as well as Fínán Lobhar ('the leper'), another saint closely tied to, and supposedly buried, at Clonmore (Plummer 1910, 310, §56; 1922 i, 274–5; ii, 266, §253–5; Colbert 2021, 101). This passage may be significant in that it seems to be an attempt by Ferns to undermine Clonmore's affiliation – and emphasize its own ties – with Kildare, one of the most powerful and politically important churches in early medieval Leinster (and, indeed, Ireland), in addition to appropriating one of Clonmore's early saints, if not Máedóc Ua Dúnlainge's successor outright, Fínán Lobhar (Colbert 2020a, 266–7; Colgan 1645, 276). Undoubtedly, the redactor of this Life intended to show Máedóc of Ferns as belonging to the top echelon of Leinster saints, on par with Brigit.

The rivalry between these two churches obviously continued into the twelfth century, because the compiler of the twelfth-century glosses to the *Martyrology of Oengus* felt it necessary to specify that St Onchú and his collection of saints' relics 'went to Cluain Mór Máedóc – i.e., Máedóc Ua Dúnlainge of Leinster, and not Máedóc of Ferns' (Stokes 1905, 70–1; for more on Onchú, see Colbert 2021, 100–1). Furthermore, a longer, twelfth-century version of the Latin Life of Máedóc of Ferns, which likely reflects the political concerns of Mac Murchada, contains similar accounts of the aforementioned episodes involving Clonmore, Áed mac Ainmerech, Brandub mac Eochu, Brigit of Kildare and Fínán Lobhar, but this time Clonmore is declared to belong to Máedóc of Ferns outright (Doherty 2002, 271–2; Plummer 1910, 149, §24, 161, §55, 162 §57). This Life also contains additional episodes involving Máedóc of Ferns and Brandub mac Eochu, and changes the passage in which Máedóc acquires the lands of Ferns so that it is Brandub himself that grants Máedóc the land (translated from Latin):

> Then, again the king said to St Moedhog: 'Behold, I offer myself to you, that I may be buried in your churchyard, and that my family may be buried with you'. And the king gave great offerings to St Moedhog, as well as the field in which the man of God built a monastery, which is called Ferna. [It is Ferns] in which St Moedhog was buried, and king Brandubh and his race after him will always be buried there (Plummer 1910, 151, §26).

This passage has important implications for the existence of corporeal relics at Ferns, and as a place of royal burial, which will be discussed later. While the eleventh-century Life of Máedóc makes no specific mention of his burial place, it is reasonable to presume that burial at Ferns was implied, both in the light of the passage above and considering that the earlier Life is likewise focused primarily on the affairs of Leinster and Ferns.

While the evidence indicates that the rivalry between the saints' cults at Ferns and Clonmore was, at least in part, politically motivated, it is unclear to what extent their respective relic collections played a role in this competition. The textual sources for Clonmore are explicit in relation to the presence of relics and reliquaries, particularly in the twelfth century (Colbert 2021, 112–14). The documentary and archaeological evidence together indicate that there were probably three reliquary foci at Clonmore – a *scrín mór* (large shrine), most likely a portable and highly decorated house-shaped shrine containing the majority of the church's corporeal relic collection, a separate stone sepulchre containing the bodies of Clonmore's three main saints, namely Máedóc Ua Dúnlainge, Onchú and Fínán Lobhar, and a simple composite stone shrine that was presumably erected over the original grave of Clonmore's founding saint (ibid.). Relics did indeed feature frequently in the hagiographies of Máedóc of Ferns, but the archaeological evidence for a relic cult at Ferns is thin, as will be discussed below. The eleventh-century Latin Life of Máedóc of Ferns makes no mention of relics, with the potential exception of one passage (conflated in later hagiographies) in which a Roman was healed of his paralysis by means of a clove he found in the mouth of Máedóc's dead body (Plummer 1910, 310, §55). However, the twelfth-century Latin Life states that Máedóc's relics (*reliquias*) continued to perform miracles after the saint's death (ibid., 162, §59). A passage from a later Irish translation of this twelfth-century Life goes further, stating that 'by the earth (of his sepulchre), by his clothing and by his relics (*thaisibh*)', Máedóc continued to perform miracles on earth (Plummer 1922 i, 189; ii, 183, §40). Additionally, this Life changes an episode dealing with the theft of a sheep so that the thief in question must swear his innocence upon relics (*mionn*), rather than directly to Máedóc, as in previous versions (ibid., §36). The term *taise* refers specifically to corporeal relics, typically the dead body of a saint, while *mi(o)nn* indicates a relic that is used as an insignia of ecclesiastical rank and authority, usually an object associated with a saint (Wycherley 2015, 205–9). In the most important Irish version of the Life of Máedóc of Ferns, dating to the sixteenth or seventeenth century but containing twelfth-century material written by Gilla Mochuda Ó Caiside, relics feature prominently throughout the text, which also reflects the shift in focus to Máedóc's cult at his northern churches, as discussed above (Plummer 1922 i, xxxiii–iv; Doherty 2002, 274–5; Murray 2007, 265). Almost immediately in this Life, Máedóc is referred to as *Máedócc na mionn*, 'Máedóc of the relics' (Plummer 1922 i, 191; ii, 185, §7). Máedóc's relics are mentioned in multiple passages, usually either to warn against swearing false oaths upon them or, by their virtue, as a reminder of obeisance owed to Máedóc and his *paruchia*. Two lengthy passages in particular are devoted to describing the 'seven chief famous relics' (*mhionna*) of Máedóc of Ferns, which are the Brec (i.e., the *Breac Máedóc*, which still exists), the *Bachall Bhrandaibh* ('Staff of Brandub'), the white staff, the white bell or 'bell of the hours', the bell of the brooch, the *Mac Ratha* and Máedóc's 'beauteous wonder-working' reliquary (ibid., i, 244–7; ii, 237–9, §§195–8). The second passage names each of the churches to which these relics were bequeathed – the *Bachall Bhrandaibh* went to Ferns, while the two bells and reliquary (*ministir*) went to Drumlane. The Brec, white staff and *Mac Ratha* went to Rossinver, as well as Máedóc's own bodily remains (*thaisi*), in contradiction to the twelfth-century Latin Life (ibid., i, 266–71; ii, 258–63, §§231–43).

These passages demonstrate that a relic cult almost certainly existed at Ferns, at least by the twelfth century, if not earlier. It likely centred on the secondary relics of its founder, Máedóc – objects that had come in contact with and/or were used by the saint in life – though it is possible his corporeal relics were venerated there as well. By contrast, the relic collection at Clonmore was, as far as we know, entirely corporeal, and emphasized the veneration of Irish saints as a communal whole, which was atypical of most other relic cults across Ireland and the rest of Europe in the early medieval period (Colbert 2021 121–2; Crook 2011, 25–40). In this regard, perhaps Ferns was not competing with Clonmore directly in terms of the materiality of its relic collection, particularly as it is not entirely certain what corporeal relics, if any, were actually housed at Ferns. From the hagiographies, however, it is clear that the two churches were in competition regarding the pre-eminence of their respective saints – and it can be inferred for the associated revenue from pilgrimage as well (Ó Carragáin 2003, 146). As mentioned above, one of the relics connected with Máedóc of Ferns is the *Breac Máedóc* (fig. 4.4), a house-shaped reliquary dating to the second half of the

4.4 The *Breac Máedóc*; note the metal rings on either side through which a strap would have been looped for easy transport (© National Museum of Ireland)

eleventh century that was reputed to have once contained a sizeable collection of corporeal relics (Murray 2007, 265). Considered an insignia (*mionn*) of Máedóc in itself, it is tempting to see the *Breac Máedóc*, with its relics of Roman saints Stephen, Lawrence and Clement, as well as the ankle of St Martin of Tours, and 'some of the hair of the Virgin Mary, and many other relics of saints and holy virgins' (Plummer 1922 i, 266; ii, 258, §232) as Ferns' answer to the *scrín mór* at Clonmore. A collection of relics brought back from Rome would probably have been considered one of the only trumps to possessing the relics of every Irish saint (e.g., Wycherley 2015, 193).

The caveat to this is that there is no explicit evidence that the *Breac Máedóc* was ever housed at Ferns. That said, it is possible that it was kept at Ferns at some point, even if temporarily. House-shaped shrines, like the *Breac Máedóc*, were meant to be transportable, allowing for wider dispersion of a saint's cult (Crook 2011, 25; Ó Floinn 1989, 53–4; 1997, 147–8). Indeed, the *Breac Máedóc* has loops on either side of the reliquary so that a strap can be threaded through, allowing it to be carried easily (fig. 4.4). Relics often accompanied church leaders while on circuit or at assemblies, and Niamh Wycherley (2015, 38–9, 173) has argued that the exchange of a particular relic, or group of relics, between its possessors created 'intangible, but nevertheless concrete, ties of allegiance and adherence' that were in turn used to generate internal bonds. It would not be surprising if such a bond existed between Máedóc's three principal churches, at least in the eleventh and twelfth centuries, when we see both the appointment of northern clerics to Ferns in the mid-eleventh century, and the intermingling of his northern and southern churches in the hagiographies of the eleventh and twelfth centuries. Thus, it is reasonable to suggest that, perhaps at one time, Máedóc's relics were shared between his churches, and there would have been cause on occasion to move some or all of the relics between them. One possible scenario is that they were used during formal processions while on circuit. Such processions have been associated with church foundation rituals (albeit probably invented) that were usually connected with a patron saint and periodically re-enacted 'to reaffirm the sanctity of a site and its legal status as a sanctuary' (Ó Carragáin 2009, 218; Aitchison 1994, 265–81). The incorporation of Máedóc's insignia (*mhionna*) into such rituals would undoubtedly lend them an additional air of authority. Alternatively, the relics of a saint were sometimes moved between churches when one was replacing another as head of that saint's *paruchia*, such as when the relics of St Colmcille were moved from Iona in Scotland to Kells, Co. Meath, in 878 (Stalley 2020, 98). Moreover, perhaps it is not coincidental that the *Breac Máedóc* was crafted around the same time that the two political powers patronizing the centres of Máedóc's cult, the Uí Chennselaig in Leinster and the Uí Ruairc in Bréifne, were contemporaneously rising to prominence. Bhreathnach and Dowling (2021, 197) have suggested that the *Breac Máedóc* was made in Dublin, which was under the control of the Uí Chennselaig from 1052 to 1072 (*AU*, U1052.8, U1072.4; *AFM* 2, 1052.8, M1072.3), so it could be speculated that Ferns, through the patronage of the Uí Chennselaig, had a hand in commissioning the reliquary, though it ultimately ended up at Rossinver, and then Drumlane (Murray 2005, 136).

DISCUSSION

From the written evidence, it is highly likely that there was a cult of relics at early medieval Ferns. It is possible that some or all of Máedóc's relics were shared between his three primary churches at some point, but the *Bachall Bhrandaibh*, or 'Staff of Brandub', was presumably housed at Ferns by the twelfth century. It is named as one of Máedóc's seven *mhionna* and, as such, would have been an insignia of office and a symbol of ecclesiastical authority, representing both St Máedóc and Ferns (Wycherley 2015, 168). The *Bachall Bhrandaibh* would have also fulfilled a semi-legal role in swearing oaths, exacting tribute, settling legal disputes and creating binding contracts, in addition to being an object of popular devotion (ibid., 193, 209). While references to secondary relics outnumber those of corporeal relics from the eighth/ninth century onwards, however, it must also be emphasized that a saint's final resting place was considered the 'primary locus of his power' and thus, typically, was the most important site in that saint's cult (ibid., 37–8, 171). Consequently, possessing the bodily remains of its founding saint was taken as proof of a church's authority and legitimacy, and often used as a means of securing territorial rights. Indeed, this emphasis on the relics of the founder as a source of ecclesiastical and spiritual authority posed a challenge to Armagh's claims to primacy in that it did not have the remains of Patrick. To circumvent this, Armagh's lawyers and hagiographers justified Armagh's claims based on its possession of relics brought from Rome, in addition to possessing the insignia (*mhionna*) of Patrick (ibid., 168; Bieler 1979, 186, §§18–19).

In the case of Ferns, the twelfth-century Latin Life of Máedóc *did* claim that it possessed the saint's body, though this is contradicted by later Lives. Coupled with the intense rivalry between its saint's cult and that at Clonmore – which had a large collection of corporeal relics in addition to the body of its founding saint – Ferns surely must have possessed more relics than just the *Bachall Bhrandaibh* if it expected to surpass Clonmore in this regard. This supposition is supported by the comment made in the twelfth-century glosses to the Martyrology of Oengus, that Onchú's collection of relics went to Clonmore and not to Ferns. This comment suggests that Ferns was making a similar claim for a large collection of corporeal relics at the time, though whether this took the form of a founder's tomb or shrine, the *Breac Máedóc* with its Roman relics (if shared between Máedóc's *paruchia*), something else entirely or a combination thereof must be left to speculation. Furthermore, the association between relic veneration and pilgrimage is well established, particularly as a means to acquire revenue, as well as to secure jurisdiction and affiliations. Moreover, as Wycherley states (2015, 195), 'pilgrimage to the sites of corporeal relics was an important facet of popular devotion'. Given this, and the apparent desire to overshadow the saint's cult at Clonmore, it would have benefited Ferns to enshrine Máedóc's corporeal remains, as well as erect a founder's tomb or shrine over his original grave, as shrine-tombs at founders' graves have been linked to pilgrimage activity (Herity 1993, 194). Even if Ferns' claim to Máedóc's body in the twelfth century was unfounded, a cenotaph (an empty grave that commemorates an individual buried elsewhere) could have served as a focus for pilgrimage and devotion. Cenotaphs were a prominent feature of monastic cemeteries in early medieval Ireland, for which we have both documentary evidence, e.g., *The Life of Colmán of Lynn* (Meyer 1911), and excavation evidence from sites like Inishmurray, Co. Sligo and High Island, Co. Galway (O'Sullivan and Ó Carragáin 2008; Scally 2014). Considering this, it is somewhat confounding that there is little (surviving) archaeological evidence for such

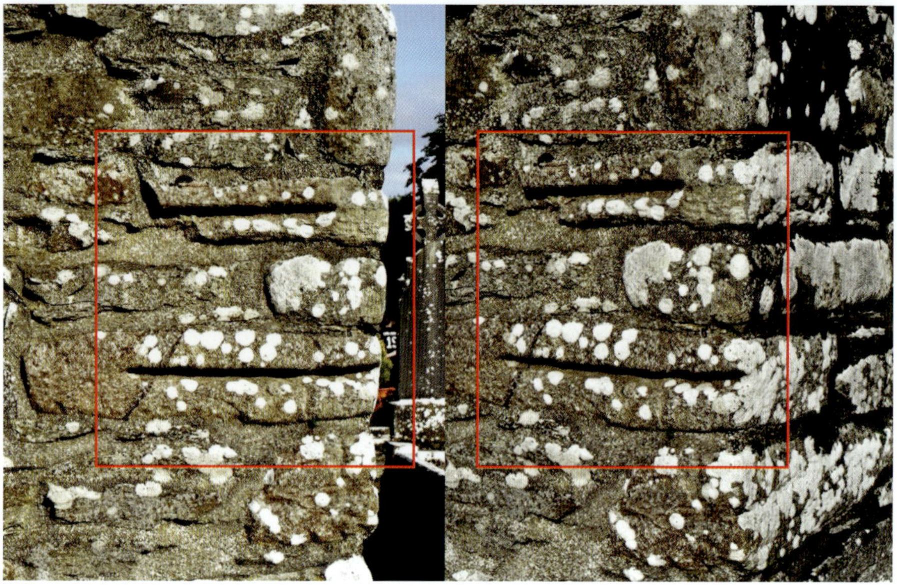

4.5 Monasterboice, Co. Louth: composite shrine posts incorporated into the wall of the South Church, with panel slots highlighted

investment at Ferns. The *Bachall Bhrandaibh* is lost, and though the *Breac Máedóc* survives, its connection to Ferns is tenuous at best. Churches with ties to relic cults often left behind archaeological traces in the form of stone sculpture such as shrines and cross-slabs, though this does not appear to be the case at Ferns. It may be worth examining what little sculpture Ferns did produce, however, and exploring potential links to its cult of relics. Despite claiming to be Máedóc's final resting place (at least in the twelfth century), there is presently no evidence at Ferns for a founder's tomb, shrine or cenotaph. However, this does not necessarily preclude the existence of one at some time. Slabs from earlier shrines sometimes get reused in later periods, like at Monasterboice, Co. Louth, where the posts of a composite stone shrine were built into the fabric of the eleventh/twelfth-century South Church (fig. 4.5). Additionally, three shrine posts in the graveyard of Clonmore had been incorporated into the rows of modern headstones, and were only recently identified (Colbert 2021, 100). Thus, a closer inspection of the graveyard and surviving buildings may yet reveal similar evidence at Ferns. Finally, there could have been shrines at Ferns made of material that did not survive, such as wood (more below).

During the early medieval period, ecclesiastical cemeteries and their associated relic cults typically developed in tandem, and an increase in burials *ad sanctos* ('among saints') from the ninth century onwards reflected the popular appeal of relic veneration in Ireland (Ó Carragáin 2010, 83; Wycherley 2015, 64–5). The desire for burial 'near the bones of the saints' frequently led to graves being crowded closely around saints' tombs or shrines (O'Brien 1992, 136). This practice is evident from excavations of early cemeteries at Illaunloughan, Co. Kerry and Teach Molaise at Inishmurray, Co. Sligo (White Marshall and Walsh 2005, 64–6; O'Sullivan and Ó Carragáin 2008), as well as from the sizeable collections of early medieval grave markers at two other major cult centres in Leinster: Glendalough (Co. Wicklow) and Ferns' rival, Clonmore.[2] Of course, the popularity of burial *ad sanctos* was not the only cause of prolific cross-slab production; royal patronage was also a significant driving factor, as evidenced at other ecclesiastical sites associated with elite burial such as Clonmacnoise, Co. Offaly, Iniscealtra, Co. Clare and, again, Glendalough (Ó Floinn 1995). Considering Ferns was known as the resting place of Uí Chennselaig kings, and the perceived permanence of stone as an artistic medium, the paucity of early medieval grave markers at Ferns seems counterintuitive. Despite this, only one grave marker of early medieval date has been found (fig. 4.6).

4.6 Ferns: early medieval slab showing an atypical variation of the *flabellum/labarum* motif (image courtesy of Christiaan Corlett)

The slab, discovered relatively recently by Christiaan Corlett (2011), probably dates to the twelfth century and features what may be interpreted as a skeuomorphic representation of a *flabellum* (liturgical fan) or, perhaps, a *labarum* – a banner or standard usually displaying a cross- or hexafoil-decorated disc mounted on a metal pole – but with the unusual inclusion of a small Latin cross incised in outline at its apex. As far as is known, this particular motif only appears on two other Irish stones, both associated with Kilmuckridge (*Cill Mucrois*), 16km to the south-east – a Welsh foundation that had come under the jurisdiction of Ferns after the Synod of Ráith Bressail in 1111. Significantly, it is also found on a late eleventh-/early twelfth-century cross-slab at St David's in Pembrokeshire, Wales (Colbert 2020b, 75–6; Edwards 2007a, 441). Rarity aside, this addition likely served merely as an extension or reinforcement of the metaphors for the Resurrection already represented by *flabella* and *labara*, examples of which follow a similar distribution pattern to that of marigolds and the related cross-of-arcs, which are found frequently along the west

2 Glendalough and Clonmore house the largest and second-largest collections of cross-slabs in Leinster respectively.

4.7 Ferns: three plain high crosses positioned, from left to right, to the west, north and north-west of St Edan's Cathedral (© Photographic Archive, National Monuments Service, Government of Ireland)

coast of Ireland, as well as in parts of Britain with Irish cultural influences (Newman and Walsh 2007, 178, 182; Edwards 2007b, 187, 190, 197). It is important to note, however, that marigolds and crosses-of-arcs are rare in the south-east of Ireland, yet very common in south-west Wales. Furthermore, there is also a high concentration of stones carved with *flabella/labara* in Pembrokeshire – along with the cross-slab from St David's described above, this motif is especially characteristic of sculpture from St Dogmael's (*c.*53km north-east of St David's) and associated churches. Thus, it seems likely that the design on the slab at Ferns, along with those at Kilmuckridge, was influenced by sculpture found along the south-west coast of Wales – not only because of strong hagiographic and socio-political ties, but also by virtue of proximity, as the coasts of Wexford and Pembrokeshire are only 80km apart (Colbert 2020b). Furthermore, while artistic exchange with south-west Wales is expressed on only one slab at Ferns, it is, arguably, also evident in the carved stones at its daughter house, Clone, which has three stones carved with either a Maltese cross or cross-of-arcs (ch. 5). Nevertheless, the slab at Ferns provides the only physical evidence at present of the close ties between Ferns and churches in south-west Wales during the early medieval period, particularly St David's, which features so prominently in the hagiographies.

Turning now to crosses, Ferns is like other large Irish ecclesiastical sites in that it produced multiple high crosses, at least four but possibly five. Three granite crosses are plain, each with imperforate rings and raised edge-moulding that form the shape of a

4.8 Ferns: fragments of the two decorated high crosses: the 'Mac Murchada' cross (above) and a newly discovered fragment from a possible fifth high cross (below); images courtesy of Christiaan Corlett

cross with widely curved arm-pits (fig. 4.7). A fourth cross shaft and a stone fragment that may have belonged to a fifth cross are decorated with panels of fret patterns and interlace (Kelly and Corlett 2020, 40; fig. 4.8). These latter two belong to the mainstream of high-cross design in Ireland, and probably date to the ninth or tenth

4.9 Ferns: small granite cross, part of a composite monument, with tenons at its base and top

century. The plain crosses cannot be closely dated, though they are stylistically typical of many high crosses in the south-east. The decorated crosses likely had imperforate rings as well, considering they are also made of granite (e.g., Kelly 1986, 64); however, the stark contrast in design suggests that they are from a separate carving episode to that of the plain crosses. It is tentatively postulated here that the plain high crosses at Ferns were produced in the eleventh or twelfth century, and perhaps coincided with the peak of Ferns' relic cult. As Roger Stalley stated (2020, 98), 'there was clearly a relationship between cross making and ecclesiastical politics', and the socio-political landscape of eleventh- and twelfth-century Ferns was especially dynamic. Moreover, there is evidence that carved crosses were linked to ecclesiastical status and that, in the early twelfth century, fierce competition between churches to secure episcopal sees prompted the expansion and reorganization of many sites, as well as renewed high-cross construction (ibid.). Significantly, the erection of high crosses was also sometimes preceded by the arrival of relics, as it was in the late ninth century at Kells, Co. Meath, and at Tuam, Co. Galway in the mid-twelfth century (ibid.), and it is not difficult to see something similar occurring at Ferns. The same argument could also be made for its decorated ninth-/tenth-century crosses – that they may have been associated with the arrival of relics – but, regardless, the restructuring of Ferns in the early twelfth century may account for the production of the plain high crosses, if not the enhancement of Ferns through relics as well.

A relatively small granite cross, sometimes categorized as a high cross (though this is debatable as the criteria for what constitutes a high cross are not always clearly defined), stands at the east end of the possible chapter house at Ferns. It is 1.1m high, 44cm wide and 33cm thick; its visible east face has an unpierced ring that has been recessed so as to define the shape of the cross head (fig. 4.9). There is a tenon at its base and a smaller, rounded tenon at the top, presumably for a capstone. The bottom tenon was probably inserted into a base, but the tenon at the top is notable, as capstones are rare on solid-ringed crosses (Kelly 1986, 59). Like the other crosses at Ferns, its imperforate ring is typical of free-standing crosses in the region, and it is similar enough in style and execution to the three plain high crosses that they could be roughly contemporary, though the capstone could also indicate an earlier date, perhaps more in line with the decorated high crosses. A few metres to the north and likewise

4.10 Ferns: thick cross-slab, also part of a composite monument, with a possible tenon (highlighted) and mortise at its base and top respectively

bolted to the east wall of the chapter house is a cross-slab with, coincidentally, the same maximum dimensions as the cross above. It was first recorded standing in the churchyard at Ferns (Ffrench 1895, 404–5), but was moved to the chapter house in recent decades by the National Monuments Service. The cross-slab is a thick, well-dressed and slightly tapering granite stone, carved in relief on what is now its east face with a ringed Latin cross with widely curved arm-pits, all defined by edge-moulding. The cross is framed by a wide, flat border along the edges of the stone face, into which the cross arms and stem extend. There is a rectangular hollow, *c.*30cm long, 20cm wide and 6cm deep, on the top of the stone. This could be a mortise, but as it is relatively shallow, it is also possible that it served a different function. A small 'lip' of stone below the moulding at the base of the slab might be the remnants of a tenon (fig. 4.10). If so, then the cross-slab may have likewise been inserted into a base. The edge-moulding and widely curved arm-pits of the cross mirror that seen on the three plain high crosses; the morphology of the slab itself – thick, well-shaped and slightly tapering – may indicate a late twelfth-century date (Colbert 2020a, 67, 113).

Neither the cross nor the slab are in situ, so it is unclear what functions they served. However, there is little doubt that both were intended to act as focal points in the ecclesiastical landscape, particularly as they are composite monuments, with one possibly featuring a capstone reminiscent of some sculptured high crosses. Either one or both monuments could have been erected on a boundary or an entrance to one of the ecclesiastical enclosures. Alternatively, they may have marked important locations, or commemorated events within the monastery, which 'were often intended to preserve particular memories about the exemplary life of the founding saint' (Ó Carragáin 2020; Colbert 2020a, 163–6), so it may be worth noting that in the hagiographies, Máedóc was known for erecting crosses as well as performing lengthy cross vigils (Plummer 1910, 143, §9, 145, §13, 299, §13; Plummer 1922 ii, 178, §8, 203, §66, 274, §266). These two monuments may have also served as foci for devotional practices such as prayers, penitence and confession. Moreover, these practices were not limited to ecclesiastics; the laity participated in such devotional rituals as well, which are a common theme of pilgrimage (Ó Carragáin 2009, 216; Colbert 2020a, 165). In this regard, the cross and slab may have been actively engaged with during pilgrimage rounds or, potentially, formal ecclesiastical processions, possibly in imitation of Máedóc's cross vigils, though this suggestion is speculative. While there is little evidence to indicate that these carved stones are tied directly to the cult of relics at Ferns, they may have facilitated devotions and veneration to St Máedóc.

SUMMARY AND CONCLUSIONS

Based on the evidence put forth above, we can presume there was a cult of relics at Ferns during the early medieval period, one that was competing with that at Clonmore in the eleventh and twelfth centuries, if not earlier. Relic veneration at Ferns presumably centred on the secondary/contact relics of its founder, as the only relic known to be connected specifically to Ferns is the *Bachall Bhrandaibh*, an insignia that would have symbolized the saintly authority of Máedóc and that of his church. Veneration of corporeal relics could have featured as well, perhaps through the presence of a reliquary (possibly one shared between Ferns and Máedóc's northern churches of Drumlane and Rossinver) and/or a tomb-shrine dedicated to Máedóc. However, the caveat to this latter suggestion is that unlike many other Irish churches associated with relic cults, Ferns did not produce any stone shrines, founder's tombs or accompanying burials *ad sanctos*, or at least none that has survived. It also differs from other major ecclesiastical centres known for elite burial, such as Clonmacnoise, Iniscealtra and Glendalough, in that only one early medieval grave marker has been found at the site. Indeed, at present, there is little archaeological data on the burial and commemoration practices of early medieval Ferns,[3] though it was clearly a prestigious place of burial. Moreover, the range of archaeological features that have already been excavated in the area immediately around Ferns highlights its importance as a focus for settlement and burial from the Bronze Age to present day (Bhreathnach and Dowling 2021, 196; for more detail, see ch. 8). The small granite cross and cross-slab in the chapter house likely served as devotional foci within the ecclesiastical landscape, possibly marking locations or events associated with St Máedóc, though there is little evidence to connect them directly with the cult of relics. It has been established that there was sometimes a relationship between the erection of high crosses and the acquisition of relics, however, so it is possible that one of the two periods of high-cross construction at Ferns was related to its relic cult. On balance, without further evidence, this suggestion remains speculative.

The presence of sculpture within an ecclesiastical landscape was often considered a measure of the relative wealth and power – and therefore, jurisdiction – of a community's respective church and patron and, perhaps, of the cult of their saint (Williams et al. 2015). For example, in the aforementioned case of Tuam, when the site was expanded and embellished with relics and sculptured high crosses in the mid-twelfth century, the clergy and their patron, Turlough O'Conor, the king of Connacht, 'were following ancient precedent, giving the monastery a physical presence on a par with places like Armagh, Kells or Clonmacnoise' (Stalley 2020, 98). Yet what little sculpture in which Ferns invested is relatively modest and unambitious, albeit competently executed. A poor survival rate does not satisfactorily account for the dearth of stone sculpture at an important site like Ferns, especially considering the wealth, power and influence it wielded in Leinster throughout much of the early medieval period. While it seems probable that at least some new pieces of early medieval sculpture will be revealed in the future, either through conservation works, archaeological investigation or chance discovery, prior experience indicates that if Ferns had invested in stone sculpture on a significant scale, many more examples would have already come to light. Thus, it may be concluded that Ferns was investing most of its wealth in other media.

Though surviving evidence for alternative avenues of investment are likewise thin, the obvious example is the *Bachall Bhrandaibh*, which was no doubt richly ornamented. Another example is a finely wrought bronze book clasp, decorated with enamel and millefiori glass, that was found in the field east of the cathedral, near St Mary's Abbey, in 1931 (Lacey 2017, 34; fig. 4.11). The clasp is thought to date from the eighth or ninth century, and may have been produced at Ferns (ibid.). Archaeological evidence for early medieval millefiori and decorative glass production has been uncovered at high-status sites such as Garranes, Co. Cork, Lagore, Co. Meath, Dunmisk, Co. Tyrone, Armagh, Iona and, possibly, Clonmacnoise (Laing

3 This is the current state of knowledge at the time of writing; however, ongoing excavations at Ferns may shed new light on the matter.

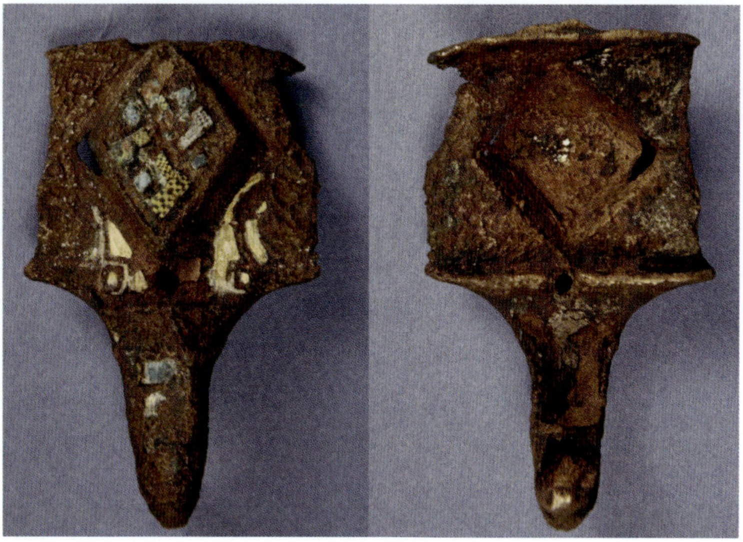

4.11 Ferns: front and back of bronze, enamel and glass book clasp, thought to date to the eighth/ninth century, recovered from the field east of St Edan's Cathedral, near the ruins of St Mary's Abbey (© National Museum of Ireland)

2006, 125). Recent excavations at Ferns revealed large-scale metalworking activity, primarily centred on the late twelfth/early thirteenth century, though the size and extent of the smithy indicated phasing as well as longevity, which implies that metalworking was taking place at Ferns earlier as well (McLoughlin 2020, 34). Moreover, while much of the metallurgical waste uncovered was of an industrial nature, the discovery of several early medieval stick pins (which were typically made of bronze) indicates that high-end metalwork may have also been produced at Ferns in the early medieval period (ibid.; Laing 2006, 165). Yet, regardless of what items were actually made on-site, it seems that Ferns was indeed investing in luxury goods (and possibly manuscript production as well) – just not, to any great extent, monumental carved stone.

Ferns obviously had the ambition and wealth to promote the cult of its saint and associated relics. However, the lack of investment in stone sculpture at Ferns is at odds with well-established, albeit broad patterns evident at many important ecclesiastical sites across Ireland and Britain in which sculpture production, as a public expression of power and wealth, is often related to socio-political changes (e.g., Gondek 2006). As we have seen above, this included the arrival (*adventus*) of relics, and the accompanying pomp and ceremony led some churches to monumentalize the occasion in stone (Wycherley 2015, 85; Stalley 2020, 98). Yet Ferns flourished for centuries without ever choosing to invest in artistically ambitious sculpture, demonstrating that such correlations between investment in sculpture and socio-political shifts cannot always be assumed. Furthermore, significant collections of sculpture are notably absent at all of the major church sites in south-east Ireland (Colbert 2020a, 322). Lismore produced seven carved stones, though no high crosses, while Emly, Cork and Cloyne – the region's other great ecclesiastical centres, and the seats of bishops – have virtually none. This was obviously a deliberate choice, as access to resources would not have been an issue. Certainly, stone was not the only material from which sculpture was carved during the early medieval period and, undoubtedly, we are seeing only a partial picture due to the use of other, perishable materials like wood. This suggests that sculptural lacunae do not necessarily indicate a fundamental difference in the organization of religious and/or devotional space at sites like Ferns. Rather, this contrast may have more to do with archaeological visibility. That these churches, including Ferns, maintained their pre-eminence in rich overkingdoms, with no shortage of resources, for several centuries without any major investment in carved stones indicates that the production of carved stones and, in particular, ambitious sculpture, was clearly not considered essential in terms of expressing the prestige, status or authority of a site. Thus, we cannot always expect the distribution of carved stones to be a direct and straightforward reflection of the distribution of ecclesiastical, or indeed royal, power and resources. This is something to bear in mind as we continue to seek a better understanding of the character of early medieval relic cults, as well as the distribution of carved stones in Ireland.

BIBLIOGRAPHY

AFM1: Ryan, E. (ed.) and O'Donovan, J. (trans.), *Annals of the Four Masters 1*: celt.ucc.ie//published/T100005A/index.html, accessed 9 Apr. 2022.

AFM2: Priour, M. and Beechinor, S. (eds) and O'Donovan, J. (trans.), *Annals of the Four Masters 2*: celt.ucc.ie//published/T100005B/index.html, accessed 9 Apr. 2022.

AI: Färber, B. (ed.) and Mac Airt, S. (trans.), *Annals of Inisfallen*: celt.ucc.ie/published/T100004/index.html, accessed 9 Apr. 2022.

Aitchison, N.B. 1994. *Armagh and the royal centres in early medieval Ireland: monuments, cosmology and the past*. Woodbridge.

ATig.: Purcell, E. and Ó Corráin, D. (eds) and Mac Niocaill. G. (trans.), *Annals of Tigernach*: celt.ucc.ie//published/T100002A/index.html, accessed 9 Apr. 2022.

AU: Bambury, P. and Beechinor, S. (eds) and Mac Airt, S., Mac Niocaill, G., Hennessy, W.M. and Mac Carthy, B. (trans.), *Annals of Ulster, AD431–1201*: celt.ucc.ie//published/T100001A, accessed 9 Apr. 2022.

Bhreathnach, E. and Dowling, G. 2021. 'Forming an episcopal see and an Augustinian foundation in medieval Ireland: the case of Ferns, Co. Wexford'. *Proceedings of the Royal Irish Academy*, 121C, 191–226.

Bieler, L. (ed. and trans.). 1979. *The Patrician texts in the Book of Armagh*. Dublin.

Breen, A. 2009. 'Máedóc (Áed, Áedán, Mogue)'. In *Dictionary of Irish Biography* at www.dib.ie/biography/maedoc-aed-aedan-mogue-a5307, accessed 9 Apr. 2022.

Byrne, F.J. 1987a. *Irish kings and high-kings*. London.

Byrne, F.J. 1987b. 'The trembling sod: Ireland in 1169'. In Cosgrove, A. (ed.), *A new history of Ireland, vol. ii: medieval Ireland, 1169–1534*, 1–42. Oxford.

Chronicon Scotorum. Färber, B. and Murphy, R. (eds) and Hennessy, W.M. and Mac Niocaill, G. (trans.): celt.ucc.ie//published/T100016/index.html, accessed 9 Apr. 2022.

Colbert, K. 2020a. 'Early medieval sculpture in south-east Ireland: identities, landscapes and memory'. PhD, UCC.

Colbert, K. 2020b. 'Artistic and cultural transmission across the Irish Sea: the "marigold" stones of Wexford and their Welsh connections'. In Thickpenny, C., Forsyth, K., Geddes, J. and Mathis, K. (eds), *Peopling insular art: practice, performance, perception*, 71–83. Oxford.

Colbert, K. 2021. 'Exploring "the Angels' Graveyard": relics, sculpture and ecclesiastical power at Clonmore'. *Medieval Archaeology*, 65:1, 98–125.

Colgan, J. 1645. *Acta sanctorum Hiberniae*. Repr. 1948. Dublin.

Corlett, C. 2011. 'A previously unrecorded cross-slab from Ferns, Co. Wexford'. *Journal of the Royal Society of Antiquaries of Ireland*, 141, 199–200.

Crook, J. 2011. *English medieval shrines*. Woodbridge.

Culleton, E. 1999. *Celtic and early Christian Wexford*. Dublin.

Doherty, C. 2002. 'The transmission of the cult of St Máedhóg'. In Ní Chatháin, P. and Richter, M. (eds), *Ireland and Europe in the early Middle Ages: texts and transmission*, 268–83. Dublin.

Doherty, C. 2011. 'Was Sulien at Glendalough?' In Doherty, C., Doran, L. and Kelly, M. (eds), *Glendalough: City of God*, 261–77. Dublin.

Edwards, N. 2007a. *A corpus of early medieval inscribed stones and stone sculpture in Wales, vol. II: south-west Wales*. Cardiff.

Edwards, N. 2007b. 'Early medieval sculpture in south-west Wales: the Irish Sea connection'. In Moss, R. (ed.), *Making and meaning in Insular art*, 184–97. Dublin.

Ffrench, J.F.M. 1895. 'Excursions in County Wexford'. *Journal of the Royal Society of Antiquaries of Ireland*, 5:4, 403–11.

Gleeson, P. 2014. 'Landscapes of kingship in early medieval Ireland, AD400–1150'. PhD, UCC.

Gondek, M. 2006. 'Investing in sculpture: power in early historic Scotland'. *Medieval Archaeology*, 50, 105–42.

Herity, M. 1993. 'The forms of the tomb-shrine of the founder saint in Ireland'. In Spearman, R.M. and Higgitt, J. (eds), *The age of migrating ideas: early medieval art in northern Britain and Ireland*, 188–95. Gloucester.

Kelly, B. and Corlett, C. 2020. 'The fretful crosses of Ferns'. *Archaeology Ireland*, 34:2, 39–42.

Kelly, D. 1986. 'Irish high crosses: some evidence from the plainer examples'. *Journal of the Royal Society of Antiquaries of Ireland*, 116, 51–67.

Lacey, B. 2017. 'Archaeological excavations and the history of Ferns, Co. Wexford'. MA, UCC.

Laing, L. 2006. *The archaeology of Celtic Britain and Ireland, c.AD400–1200*. Cambridge.

MacCotter, P. 2008. *Medieval Ireland: territorial, political and economic divisions*. Dublin.

Mac Shamhráin, A. 1996. *Church and polity in pre-Norman Ireland: the case of Glendalough*. Maynooth.

McLoughlin, C. 2020. 'From early to late: uncovering medieval Ferns'. *Archaeology Ireland*, 34:2, 30–4.

Meyer, K. (ed.). 1911. *Life of Colmán of Lynn*. Dublin.

Moore, M. 2012. WX015-003003. SMR database, National Monuments Service: webgis.archaeology.ie/historicenvironment, accessed 9 Apr. 2022.

Murray, G. 2005. 'A note on the provenance of the Breac Maodhóg'. *Journal of the Royal Society of Antiquaries of Ireland*, 135, 136–8.

Murray, G. 2007. 'The Cross of Cong and church metalwork from Romanesque Ireland'. PhD, UCC.

Newman, C. and Walsh, N. 2007. 'Iconographical analysis of the Marigold Stone, Carndonagh, Inishowen, Co. Donegal'. In Moss, R. (ed.), *Making and meaning in Insular art*, 167–83. Dublin.

O'Brien, E. 1992. 'Pagan and Christian burial in Ireland during the first millennium AD: continuity and change'. In Edwards, N. and Lane, A. (eds), *The early church in Wales and the West*, 130–7. Cardiff.

Ó Carragáin, T. 2003. 'A landscape converted: archaeology and early church organization on Iveragh and Dingle, Ireland'. In Carver, M. (ed.), *The cross goes north: processes of conversion in northern Europe, AD300–1300*, 127–52. Woodbridge.

Ó Carragáin, T. 2009. 'The saint and the sacred centre: the early medieval pilgrimage landscape of Inishmurray'. In Edwards, N. (ed.), *The archaeology of the early medieval Celtic churches*, 207–26. Leeds.

Ó Carragáin, T. 2010. *Churches in early medieval Ireland: architecture, ritual and memory*. New Haven.

Ó Carragáin, T. 2020. 'Landscapes, myth-making and memory: ecclesiastical landholding in early medieval Ireland'. In Wooding, J.M. and Olson, L. (eds), *Prophecy, fate and memory in the early and medieval Celtic world*, 34–51. Sydney.

Ó Floinn, R. 1989. 'A fragmentary house-shaped shrine from Clonard, Co. Meath'. *Journal of Irish Archaeology*, 5, 49–55.

Ó Floinn, R. 1995. 'Clonmacnoise: art and patronage in the early medieval period'. In Bourke, C. (ed.), *From the isles of the north: early medieval art in Ireland and Britain*, 251–60. Belfast.

Ó Floinn, R. 1997. 'Insignia Columbae I'. In Bourke, C. (ed.), *Studies in the cult of Saint Columba*, 136–61. Dublin.

O'Grady, S.H. (ed.). 1892. *Silva gadalica (I–XXXI): a collection of tales in Irish with extracts illustrating persons and places*, 1. London.

O'Keeffe, T. 1997. 'Diarmait Mac Murchada and Romanesque Leinster: four twelfth-century churches in context'. *Journal of the Royal Society of Antiquaries of Ireland*, 127, 52–79.

Ó Riain, P. 2011. *A dictionary of Irish saints*. Dublin.

O'Sullivan, J. and Ó Carragáin, T. 2008. *Inishmurray: monks and pilgrims in an Atlantic landscape*. Cork.

Plummer, C. (ed.). 1910. *Vitae Sanctorum Hiberniae*, 2. Oxford.

Plummer, C. (ed. and trans.) 1922. *Bethada náem nÉrenn, Lives of Irish saints*. 2 vols. Oxford.

Scally, G. 2014. *High Island (Ardoileán), Co. Galway: excavation of an early medieval monastery*. Dublin.

Stalley, R. 2020. *Early Irish sculpture and the art of the high crosses*. London.

Stokes, W. (ed.). 1892. 'The Boroma'. *Revue Celtique*, 13, 32–125.

Stokes, W. (ed.). 1905. *Félire Óengusso Céli Dé: the Martyrology of Oengus the Culdee, critically edited from ten manuscripts, with a preface, translation, notes and indices*. London.

White Marshall, J. and Walsh, C. 2005. *Illaunloughan Island: an early monastery in County Kerry*. Bray.

Williams, H., Kirton, J. and Gondek, M. 2015. 'Introduction: stones in substance, space and time'. In Williams, H., Kirton, J. and Gondek, M. (eds), *Early medieval stone monuments: materiality, biography, landscape*, 1–34. Woodbridge.

Wycherley, N. 2015. *The cult of relics in early medieval Ireland*. Turnhout.

CHAPTER FIVE

Clone Church, Co. Wexford: an archaeological survey

CHRISTIAAN CORLETT

The church of Clone[1] is situated in the parish of Clone within the barony of Scarawalsh, part of the ancient territory of Uí Chennselaig[2] and just 2.25km south of Ferns. According to W.H. Grattan Flood, the church was dedicated to St Aidan (Grattan Flood 1916, 39), which seems plausible considering its proximity to Ferns, but virtually nothing of the early history of this site is known. The church at Clone is situated on an east-facing slope, overlooking a small, well-defined valley to the north-east and east (fig. 5.1). This valley is host to a small stream that is a tributary of the River Bann (itself a tributary of the River Slaney), which forms the western boundary of the present townland of Clone. Approximately 260m to the east is an enclosure site (WX015-025), possibly a ringfort. The standing remains at Clone primarily consist of a Romanesque church, a sundial, three cross-slabs as well as numerous architectural fragments. The church is situated within a modern rectangular enclosure that is relatively modest in size and contains several nineteenth-century headstones. One uninscribed headstone near the church is decorated with early prehistoric art.

ROMANESQUE CHURCH

Much of the church building (WX015-023001-) is no longer standing, and the reason for this is indicated by George Kinahan, who stated that part of the church had been pulled down a few years previous to provide material for the construction of the present wall around the church and graveyard (Anon. 1889, 9). This is supported by the fact that several carved stones can be seen clearly in the graveyard wall and the gate piers. John O'Donovan, however, writing in 1840, indicates that the church at that time was already in poor condition:

> all clad in a thick vesture of ivy, but the east gable is totally destroyed, even its foundations not being traceable. The south was in good preservation and is near 20 feet in height but contains no features; the north wall is much injured (Herity 2014, 147).

1 RMP WX015-023; National Monument 665. **2** Formerly Uí Dega, which would subsequently provide the name for the late medieval deanery of Oday.

5.1 Clone Church: aerial view (© National Monuments Service of Ireland)

A significant amount of poorly documented repair and reconstruction of the church was carried out in 1956, funded by Wexford County Council and then Bord Fáilte Éireann.[3] The church came into State Guardianship in March 1996. A portion of the south wall collapsed in 2016, and at the time of writing (2022) the Office of Public Works are carrying out significant conservation works at the church. A study of the building by the author prior to this work identified the level of previous repairs from 1956 and to provide a much clearer picture of the original church as constructed in the twelfth century. Additional information has come to light during the present conservation project.

The church consists of a unicameral rectangular building 14.7m long and 5.7m wide, with no surviving evidence for any differentiation between the nave and chancel. The rubble-built walls are substantial and range between 1.2m and 1.3m wide. The interior of the church falls in level from west to east, which is somewhat unusual but clearly deliberate and would have presented anyone entering the church via the west door with an elevated view of the altar at the east end of the church.

3 The site was inspected on 6 June 1956 by Patrick J. Hartnett, then an archaeological officer with Bord Fáilte Éireann. His brief report to Percy Le Clerc, Inspector of National Monuments at the Office of Public Works, indicates that Wexford County Council were very concerned about the condition of the church, due in part to a thick growth of ivy, as well as alder and whitethorn on the walls. Le Clerc provided specifications for the repairs to the church. He also loaned two OPW stone masons to undertake the work and they appear to have started in mid-August 1956. Le Clerc does not appear to have taken an active role in supervising the works. Instead, they were overseen by Revd Joseph Ranson of Enniscorthy. The only record of the progress of the works is contained in two letters from Ranson to Le Clerc, dated 3 September and 25 October 1956 (OPW works file).

5.2 Clone Church: view from the south-west, November 2010

The north wall averages 2m in height, and largely represents a 1956 rebuild along the line of the original wall, the lower portions of which had survived and were retained. The east-end wall stands 1.1m high. As noted above, O'Donovan recorded that the east gable was already missing in 1840. Indeed, the present east end of the church was almost entirely rebuilt as part of the 1956 repairs undertaken by Wexford County Council. Externally there is a foundation plinth visible, which is evidently original, and presumably guided the rebuilding of the east end at this location. We have no documentary or illustrative record of the former east window, but architectural fragments recently found at the site give a good impression of its form and will be discussed below.

The height of the south walls varies and is lowest at the east end (1.1m high), and generally rises to the point (*c.*5m high) at which it meets the west gable. The east end appears to have been rebuilt in 1956, while much of this western section of the wall is original, the uppermost courses as well as much of the south-west angle were reconstructed as part of the works carried out that year.[4] There is a noticeable build-line in the masonry some 1.5m above the external ground level (fig. 5.3). Above this line are some slightly larger stones than those used in the lower courses. One explanation is that the south wall incorporates the lower sections of walling of an

4 In 2016 a portion of the upper section of the west end of the south wall collapsed. This appears to correspond with an area of the 1956 repairs.

5.3 Clone Church: view of the south wall showing the build-line in the masonry

earlier stone church on the site. It seems more likely in this case, however, that the build-line represents a short break in the original construction of this wall.

The west gable wall (presently some 7m high) is the most substantial part of the building that survives (fig. 5.4). It is built on a plinth that is evident internally and externally. There are some large stones at the base of the exterior of the west gable that may represent evidence for an earlier stone church that was partly used as building material for the present building, but this is not conclusive. Internally, there is a rebate some 5m above ground level, which may reflect the original height of the north and south walls of the building. The south wall was reconstructed in 1956 to this height at the south-east angle, perhaps guided by the presence of the internal rebate on the west gable. Externally, much of the face of the west gable was repaired in 1956, though a significant amount of the central portion above the west doorway is likely to be original masonry. Both the south-west and north-west angles and upper portions were built-up as part of the 1956 works to stabilize the wall. Notably, there are no quoin

5.4 Clone Church: view of the west gable of the church, November 2010

stones surviving in situ at any of the four angles of the church, yet throughout the graveyard there are numerous squared green-tuff blocks (Stephen Mandal, pers. comm.) that most likely served as quoins.

In the west gable is a trabeate doorway (fig. 5.5). It measures 2.2m high and inclines slightly, measuring 92cm wide at the base and 84cm at the top. The door frame is 63cm deep. A substantial flagstone (a greenish granite) forms a saddle stone and extends under both sides of the door frame, indicating that this is an original feature.

Externally the doorway has the surviving jambs of two orders (fig. 5.5), carved from single-piece stones that are very weathered, though the diagonal tooling remains visible in places. The inner order has an angle roll forming a slender engaged column with an incised herringbone pattern, whereas the outer order is squared and undecorated. Notably, the herringbone pattern is absent on the upper two jambs on either side of the frame, which have a plain angle roll instead. The squared outer order is heavier and blockier than an architrave that might typically extend above the doorway as a hood moulding or label, but the effect is very similar. A flat stone capped the northern side

(a)

(b)

5.5 Clone Church: exterior of west doorway **(a)** and detail of the double architrave **(b)**. Note that the stone capping the outer order on the northern (left) side has been reset flush with the face of the gable, and no longer projects to meet with the top of the architrave

5.6 Clone Church: west doorway in September 1956 **(a)** showing the cracked lintel (© National Monuments Service of Ireland). Note the flat stone capping the northern outer order of the doorway, which is also evident in George du Noyer's drawing from 1862 **(b)** (© Royal Society of Antiquaries of Ireland)

of the door, and is evident in a photograph from 1956, as well as a drawing by George Victor du Noyer in 1862 (fig. 5.6), but any counterpart on the southern side of the door had already been removed. This northern capping stone is still present but was set back flush with the main face of the wall in 1956 and no longer projects above the architrave. In fact, this stone was probably not in its original position anyhow, as it has the appearance of an impost that would normally be placed under the spring of an arch, directly on top of the capital of a column below, but we have no surviving evidence to confirm the former presence of capitals.

A large flagstone forms a flat lintel and has been rendered in cement externally. This lintel was inserted in 1956 to replace a former lintel (fig. 5.6) that was cracked sometime before 1883 (Kinahan 1883–4, 37). At a glance, the trabeate form of the doorframe appears to be original, and several earlier drawings and photographs of the doorway seem to confirm this. However, a closer inspection of the photographs prior to its restoration (figs 5.6, 5.7) indicate that this trabeated form is a later reconfiguration. First, there is no evidence that the architrave of the door jambs formed a flat hood or label across the door frame. Instead, the masonry above the

5.7 Clone Church: west doorway sometime prior to 1956 (© National Monuments Service of Ireland). Note the in-filled masonry above the previous lintel and the presence here of the bead-edged trapezoidal stone indicated with a red arrow

5.8 (*below*) Clone Church: carved stones presently arranged over the west door of the church (labelled A–H and shown in figs 5.9–5.13)

5.9 Clone Church: stone head A (*left*) and stone head B (*right*)

former lintel was clearly in-fill. Furthermore, a Romanesque stone decorated with beading can be detected in this photograph as forming part of this in-filled masonry (fig. 5.7). When the cracked lintel was removed in 1956, this in-filled masonry was repaired and the stone with the beading was removed and placed on a supporting corbel above the doorway (see below). In conclusion, then, it seems more likely that originally there was an open arch above the doorframe that was later in-filled above an inserted lintel. What is less clear is when this reconfiguration of the doorframe took place.

A series of carved stones, mostly comprising human heads, have been arranged in a horizontal line across the top of the doorway (fig. 5.8). As we shall see, this arrangement is not original and forms part of the 1956 reconstruction works, though the reason for rearranging the stones in this way is not clear. Starting at the north end, these consist of:

- a trapezoidal stone (impost?) with beading (fig. 5.16).
- head A appears to represent an unfinished human head, perhaps a trial piece (fig. 5.9).
- head B represents an animal head (fig. 5.9).

5.10 Clone Church: stone head C

5.11 Clone Church: stone head D

- head C sports a distinctive drooping moustache and is clearly a male figure (fig. 5.10).
- head D has a long slender face and wears a mitre; it must represent a bishop or archbishop (fig. 5.11).
- head E represents a human face (fig. 5.12).
- heads F and G represent two weathered faces.
- stone H features an animal with arched back in bold relief, in side-profile (fig. 5.13).

Prior to 1956, the carved heads were arranged in a staggered arc above the exterior of the doorway. This is clearly shown in a pencil drawing of the doorway by Du Noyer from 16 June 1862 (fig. 5.14), a photograph by Jane W. Shackleton from 1895 (fig. 5.14) and a photograph taken sometime prior to 1956 (fig. 5.7).

These images confirm that the heads C, D and E formed the upper three stones of the arrangement, with head D at the top of the arch, and heads C and E respectively flanking the left and right at a slightly lower level. Du Noyer interpreted stone head E as a female face and suggested that it represented the portrait of a queen or wife of a chieftain who he thought was depicted by head C on the other side of the bishop (Du Noyer 1864–6, 432). In his sketch of the doorway, he certainly depicts this head as having a more feminine appearance, which is not as evident today. However, he also shows the figure as wearing pointed headgear of some kind, which he appears to have interpreted as a crown. This crown-like feature is evident also on close inspection of Jane Shackleton's photograph from 1895, but is no longer discernible today, implying that the top of the head has been damaged. It appears that the animal head B was originally at the base of the arch on the south side of the door. It is depicted by Du Noyer with bulging eyes, a grinning mouth full of teeth and a human-like nose and he suggested that this was a court jester (1864–6, 432–3). If this is indeed the same carving, he was clearly mistaken in identifying this as a human head. In his sketch, the stone (H) with the animal in profile is depicted above animal head B and it was still in this position in 1956 (fig. 5.6).

5.12 Clone Church: stone head E

5.13 Clone Church: animal carving H

5.14 Clone Church: west doorway as photographed in September 1895 by Jane W. Shackleton **(a)** (RSAI Album 22/20/2) and drawn by George du Noyer in June 1862 **(b)** (© Royal Society of Antiquaries of Ireland; a painting of this sketch is preserved in the Royal Irish Academy: Du Noyer Sketches VII/48)

It is also clear that there was originally a carved stone at the base of the arch at the northern or left side, and Du Noyer (1864–6, 432) recorded that this had been moved to St Aidan's or St Mogue's well (WX015-003002-) at Ferns. This must be the stone head (WX015-003020-) that was built into the cap-house over the well around 1847. The bottom portion of this head is missing (fig. 5.15) and the remainder is very weathered, so that much of the detail is missing; however, it is clearly a human figure and appears to be wearing some form of headgear. Notably, the heads described above as A, F and G above were found within the adjoining graveyard in 1956.

Finally, there is the decorated stone slab that was placed above the doorway in 1956 (fig. 5.16). This stone can be detected in an earlier photograph (fig. 5.7), where it forms part of the in-filled masonry above the former lintel above the doorframe. It measures 33cm long and 7cm thick. It is trapezoidal and tapers to 25cm wide at one end, whereas the wider end is broken at one corner, but it can be estimated that it originally measured about 40cm wide. The upper edge of the stone is decorated with beading or pellets; there are eight beads along the narrow end. Its decoration is similar to the capitals of the Romanesque doorway at Kilbunny Church, Colin, Co. Waterford. Similar beading is also found on the outer order of the west doorway at Aghowle, Co. Wicklow (Corlett 2021). Given its trapezoidal shape, however, it seems unlikely that the stone at Clone formed a capital or abacus of a doorframe. Instead, the diagonal sides may reflect the splays of the internal embrasures of a two-light window, whereby it formed an impost of a central, double-splayed plinth dividing the embrasures. Such a double-splayed plinth can be seen dividing the embrasures of the two east windows at Aghowle (though this does not feature an impost). Alternatively, this stone may have been related to a fitting within the church, such as a shelf for a statue.

5.15 Ferns: stone head at St Aidan's Well

5.16 Clone Church: stone decorated with beading along the edge

(a) **5.17** Clone Church: internal embrasure of west doorway with the reconstructed rear arch **(a)** and Du Noyer's drawing of the embrasure showing the fragmentary remains of the arch in 1862 **(b)** (© Royal Society of Antiquaries of Ireland; a painting of this sketch is preserved in the Royal Irish Academy: Du Noyer Sketches VII/49) (b)

The internal embrasure for the door is 1.43m wide and has a rounded head. The top of the embrasure arch extends 50cm above the soffit of the doorframe. This arch was already in a poor state of preservation when Du Noyer sketched it in 1862 (fig. 5.17), and it was reconstructed in 1956 using cement blocks.[5] At the base of the inner embrasure, on the north side, there is a squared green-tuff block, similar to the stone used in the doorframe. This may have been placed here during the 1956 repairs, but it seems likely that the jambs and voussoirs of the entire inner embrasure were originally constructed with angular blocks of this stone. There is no evidence for the

5 This cement-block arch has a rounded profile, but the fragmentary stone arch recorded by Du Noyer implies that it had a segmental form, which suggests it was not the original and was perhaps contemporary with the insertion of the former lintel over the doorframe and the in-filling of the open arch above.

arrangement of the door, such as a hanging eye or spud, and no draw-bar holes for a locking mechanism survive, and such features are likely to have been removed during the course of the various modifications to the doorway.

WINDOW FRAGMENTS

There is no documentary or illustrative record of the former appearance of the east end of the church, which had collapsed sometime before 1840, and what survives today was almost entirely rebuilt in 1956. Therefore, we have no source material that might confirm the form of the east window, or the presence of windows at the east end of the north and/or south walls. However, there are several fragments that derive from window frames or their internal embrasures. The most obvious of these is the head of a window frame that may have formed part of the missing east window (fig. 5.18). This window opening would have measured 19cm wide. Notably, the internal splay of the soffit meets the edge of the outer reveal at a point, so the window opening did not have a formal frame. The exterior features an arched hood or label with a simple chamfer. This extends horizontally either side and may be indicative of a former string coursing on the exterior of the church, such as on the east façade of the Romanesque abbey church at Jerpoint, Co. Kilkenny.

One newly discovered stone is part of the jamb of a window frame (fig. 5.19). It preserves evidence for a flat frame (5cm deep) of the window itself and an outer reveal (8cm wide and 5cm deep), which has a chamfer on the outer angle: this indicates that the window had an external recessed surround, which is a feature of several of the windows at St Mary's Church in Ferns. This jamb is not a match for the lintel just described.[6] There is a second lintel at Clone, unshaped except for the rounded head of a window ope, 23cm wide, and the splay of the internal embrasure, indicating that it was originally positioned immediately inside the head of a window frame. It is evidently not a comrade of the window head just described.

It has been suggested by several commentators that the internal embrasure of a Romanesque window at St Peter's Church at Ferns came from either St Mary's Abbey at Ferns or the church at Clone (Leask 1955, 163; Moore 1996, 125, 156; O'Keeffe 1997, 76). The window embrasure at St Peter's has herringbone decoration that certainly compares with the design found on the west doorway at Clone. However, the window at St Peter's is carved from granite, which is not a feature at Clone and rules out the likelihood that it came from here. Furthermore, several carved stones have recently come to light among the rubble at Clone itself that belong to a former internal window embrasure of the church. They are the same green tuff, with the same

6 Notably, in Revd Ranson's letter to Percy le Clerc dated 25 October 1956 (see n. 3 above) he included a sketch of a round-headed window lintel (presently missing), which had an external reveal with a chamfer very similar to the one on this jamb.

5.18 (*above left*) Clone Church: round-headed window-frame lintel **5.19** Clone Church: jamb of a window found among the rubble. Despite being a single stone, it is very informative and tells us a lot about the form of the original window; it preserves part of the internal splay of the window and the depth of the frame. It also tells us that the window had an external reveal or casement, which was embellished with a chamfer

5.20 (*above left*) Clone Church: jamb with an engaged column and a matching voussoir, which likely formed part of the internal embrasure of the east window **5.21** Clone Church: jamb (bottom) of the internal embrasure of a window featuring an angle roll flanked on the splay (left) by a fillet. The upper stone here is a voussoir with a slightly broader angle roll that is flanked on the splay by a slender roll instead of a fillet. The different angle of the splay implies that this formed the rear arch of a different window embrasure

distinctive diagonal tooling as was used to carve the doorway at Clone. Several examples are matching jamb stones and voussoirs from an internal window embrasure. These have a heavy angle roll, flanked on both the face and the splay by a slender roll (fig. 5.20) that would have formed engaged columns on the inner angles of the embrasure, which likely continued across the rear arch. Despite being undecorated, these elaborate mouldings suggest that they belonged to the former east window of the

(a) **5.22** Clone: stone with angle roll (*above*) **(a)** and a chamfered stone with an incised bird, built into a gate pier to the south-west of the church **(b)** (b)

church. Other fragments simply feature an angle roll that is flanked by a fillet on the splay (fig. 5.21). These clearly belong to two different window embrasures, implying that the church had at least three windows. While the conservation works are on-going it has not been possible to catalogue these carved stones fully, but this will be possible in due course and will hopefully provide some clue as to the likely dimensions of the windows.[7]

Some 350m to the south-west of Clone church is a field gate on the roadside, flanked by two stone-built pillars. One of the pillars has at least three stones that undoubtedly originated at Clone Church. One of these is a simple angular block, while a second has an angle roll of a simple engaged column (fig. 5.22a). This does not appear to have belonged to either a doorway or a window, and points to the presence of some other decorative feature within the church. The third stone (WX015-070----) is of interest for having an incised image of a bird, perhaps a peacock, though the abstract form makes it difficult to confirm the likely species that is depicted (fig. 5.22b). It appears to be placed between two widely spaced, horizontal lines that may represent a frame, and it is conceivable that the bird formed part of a larger composition. The angle of the stone to the right of the bird has a narrow chamfer (3cm wide), indicating that it was associated with an architectural feature. It is possible, of course, that this is not a Romanesque carving, but some later graffiti.

SUNDIAL

One of the most unusual features from Clone is the stone sundial (WX015-023004-), now on display at the OPW visitor centre beside Ferns Castle. It consists of a stone

7 Further carvings were incorporated (and partly concealed) within the graveyard wall in 1956.

5.23 Clone Church: head of sundial

pillar that measures 1.63m tall and 11cm thick. The shaft is 35cm wide and constricts at the base (29cm wide) to accommodate a socket. The semi-circular head measures 51cm across. An incised arc (radius 26cm) indicates the line of the semi-circle where the head meets the shaft (fig. 5.23). Twelve lightly incised lines radiate from the centre of the semi-circle, and though these form eleven segments, the intent was clearly to create a twelve-part division. There are two holes through the thickness of the stone. The upper hole is perpendicular, whereas the lower one is set at a 70-degree angle. The holes served as sockets for the gnomon that cast the shadow on the dial. It is not clear if these represent the sockets for a single or, more likely, successive gnomons. When Du Noyer visited the site in 1862 he described the ancient sundial as being situated on 'the bank of the stream 200ft [61m] ESE of the old church of Clone'.[8]

STONE SOCKET

In 1862 Du Noyer sketched (fig. 5.24) a stone he described as a granite block that represented 'either a very rude font or holy water stoup or the base of a small stone

8 Du Noyer's note attached to a painting of the sundial held in the RSAI.

cross' and he noted that it was situated 'on the brow of the glen E of the old church 150 feet [*c*.46m] distant from the church', which roughly corresponds to the same area in which he found the sundial. He described the stone as measuring 2 feet six inches

(a)

5.24 Clone Church: photograph from September 1956 of the sundial and the missing stone socket **(a)** (© National Monuments Service of Ireland). This is presumably the same stone sketched by Du Noyer in 1862 **(b)** (RSAI Du Noyer Album 3; a painting based on this sketch is preserved in the Royal Irish Academy: Du Noyer Sketches VII/51). Kinahan's conjectural drawing, published in 1883, proposes that this base originally hosted the sun dial **(c)** (© Royal Society of Antiquaries of Ireland)

(b)

(c)

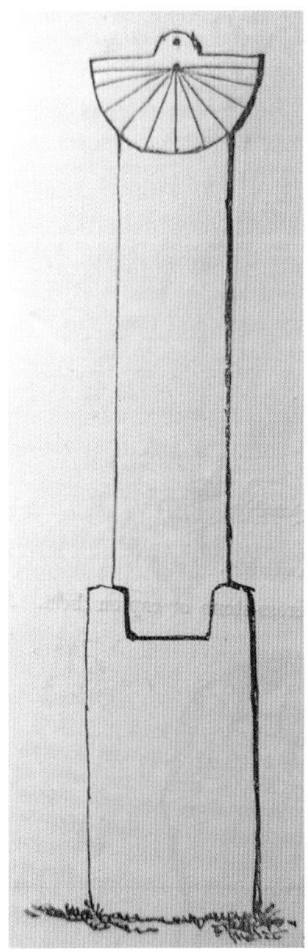

5.25 Clone Church: cross-slabs A (*left*) and B (*right*)

(a) **(b)**

5.26 Clone Church: cross-slab C **(a)**, and a photograph from 1939 **(b)** showing the stone in its original position in the field (© National Monuments Service of Ireland)

(75cm) tall and 12 inches (30cm) wide. The hollow he described as '9 inches [22.9cm] long, 4½ [11.5cm] wide and 4½ [11.5cm] deep'. Du Noyer (1864–6, 443) refers to this as 'The ancient font at Clone'. Kinahan (1883–4, 9) shows it as the base of the sundial in a conjectural drawing (fig. 5.24), though he describes the stones as 'dismantled'. The stone also appears alongside the sundial in a photograph from 1956 (fig. 5.24). Unfortunately, the whereabouts of this stone are not known today. Du Noyer's suggestion that it represents a font seems unlikely, and a more plausible explanation is that it served as a stone socket. However, the bottom of the shaft of the sundial is wider (29cm) than the recorded width of the socket (22.9cm), rejecting Kinahan's suggested link between the two. This can only be confirmed with the relocation of the socket, but for the time being it is tempting to suggest that the socket reflects the former presence of a stone cross at Clone.

CROSS-SLABS

There are three cross-slabs from the site (fig. 5.25). Cross-slab A (WX015-023003-) is presently situated beside the doorway. It measures 41cm high, 8cm thick, 18cm wide at the base and 21.5cm wide at the top. The top of the stone is occupied by a Maltese cross in false relief, with a central cup. Cross-slab B (WX015-023006-) is an unshaped granite stone that measures 73cm long, 48cm wide, 17cm thick (fig. 5.25). The stone is rounded at the top and tapers towards the base. At the top of the stone is a Maltese cross is false relief. The cross is within a circle 33cm by 34cm across. There is a central boss with a shallow cup at its centre. The original location of these cross-slabs is not recorded. Cross-slab C (WX015-023012-) is an irregular stone that measures 1.02m long, 35cm wide and 26cm thick (fig. 5.26). An incised Maltese cross is contained within a circle 29cm across. This cross-slab was formerly situated on a small mound (*c.*3m across and 30cm high) some 80m south-east of the church (WX015-024- - - -) and appears to have been in this position when it was drawn by Du Noyer (1864–6, 443; Royal Irish Academy: Du Noyer Sketches VII/50). The cross was then facing west.

STONE MORTAR

Presently situated near the door of the church is a stone mortar (WX015-023005-). The unshaped, rounded block measures 88cm by 53cm across and 23cm thick (fig. 5.27). The steep-sided basin is bowl-shaped and measures 30cm by 28cm across and is broken through the base of the stone. The original find location of this stone is not recorded.

5.27 Clone Church: stone mortar

5.28 Clone Church: stone used as a grave marker close to the west doorway. The decoration is consistent with art more typically found in Neolithic passage tombs, though no megalithic tombs are known in the area

PASSAGE-TOMB ART

Some 5m west of the church is an example of prehistoric art (WX015-023014-) that has been reused as a headstone, probably around the turn of the nineteenth century. This was first discovered by Barry Lacey and Michael Moore as recently as August 2018. It comprises a stone 54cm and 18cm thick, standing 54cm tall, with a slightly pointed top. It is decorated on the east face with four incised, nested arcs, which resemble passage-tomb art (fig. 5.28). No other examples of passage-tomb art have been documented in Wexford, and the closest comparison is a stone formerly from Tornant Upper, Co. Wicklow, and now in the National Museum of Ireland (NMI 1929:1404). However, another example of early prehistoric art, in the form of cup marks, is situated at Artramon, near Castlebridge (WX037-005003-) and, together with the example at Clone, appear to form part of a pattern, previously noted in south Wicklow, of early prehistoric art being reused in historic graveyards as burial markers in the eighteenth and nineteenth centuries (Corlett 2014).

DISCUSSION

Clone Church represents a unicameral building constructed in the middle of the twelfth century and it features distinctive Romanesque carvings. Before we discuss the church building itself, it is worth exploring several other features, namely the three cross-slabs and a sundial, which are likely to represent the earlier history of the site, prior to the twelfth century. The prehistoric art can be excluded from this discussion as it would be better placed elsewhere in a study of prehistoric archaeology in the region (chs 1, 12).

Sundials are generally quite rare at pre-Anglo-Norman churches in Ireland, although examples are known from some high-profile sites, such as Kells, Co. Meath, Monasterboice, Co. Louth, Nendrum, Co. Down and Clogher, Co. Tyrone. These typically take the form of free-standing stone pillars, as at Clone. All of these examples are semi-circular, although the D-shaped head of the Clone sundial is unusual. In this respect, the Clone sundial probably compares best with the ornate sundial at Kilmalkedar, Co. Kerry. The twelve-fold division of the Clone dial is also unusual, but compares with a sundial from Bangor, Co. Down (Hamlin 1987, 31–2). The Clone sundial is remarkably similar to a sundial at St Beuno's Church at Clynnog Fawr in Gwynedd, Wales. The date of sundials from Ireland is unclear. An example from Clogher, Co. Tyrone, may well be of pre-tenth-century date (ibid., 39), whereas the majority of others could conceivably date to the eleventh or twelfth century. If so, this suggests that they are in some way related to the widespread liturgical reforms of the Irish church during the twelfth century.

The three cross-slabs from Clone are broadly like one another. They are all relatively small and feature similar incised Maltese crosses. Such crosses are very unusual in south Leinster and are practically unknown elsewhere in Wexford. Notably, no similar cross-slabs have been found at nearby Ferns. This raises the important question of their significance. First, they belong to a form that has been dated elsewhere to as early as the seventh century (for example, see Herity et al. 1997), although a similar date in south-east Leinster cannot be presumed. If so, then there may be reasons to consider that the ecclesiastical site at Clone had some direct association with St Máedóc himself and the time he spent in Uí Chennselaig and at Ferns. All three cross-slabs appear to have been intended as upright rather than recumbent stones. While it is possible that they represent burial markers, this should not be taken for granted, and like cross-slabs at other early Christian sites, it is possible that they served some other function related to the use of sacred space around the church. It is worth noting, therefore, that until quite recently Cross-slab C was situated some 80m south-east of the church. In the 1860s the sundial was beside the stream some '200ft ESE' of the church, and the missing stone base (perhaps related to the sundial or a missing cross) was originally located on the brow of the glen 46m from the church. This strongly suggests that a large space around the church was organized in a way that we might expect to find at sites that were central to a *turas* or rounds of stations associated with pilgrimage. In east Leinster, the finest example of this is at Glendalough, where the upper lake features an organized landscape of stations associated with St Kevin and the origins of the site (Corlett 2017, 34–47). It is tempting to suggest that Clone was similarly associated with the origins of St Máedóc in Ferns.

The church at Clone consists of a single-phase building constructed in the mid-twelfth century. There is suggestive but not conclusive evidence for an earlier stone church incorporated into this building, and there are no obvious later modifications, though the infilling of the arch and the insertions of a flat lintel over the doorframe may have been carried out at some point during the later medieval period.[9] The unicameral and undifferentiated plan of the church compares with another Romanesque church at Aghowle, Co. Wicklow, which may have been constructed in the 1150s (Corlett 2021, 160–2). The church at Aghowle features a trabeate west doorway, which has previously been compared to the doorway at Clone, however it has been demonstrated here that this was not the original form of the doorframe, which instead is likely to have had a more conventional arched opening above. There are other differences between these two sites. First, at Aghowle, the architectural details such as the door and window frames, as well as the jambs and voussoirs of the eastern window embrasures and the quoins on each of the four angles are carved from locally sourced granite. At Clone, the stone of choice was green tuff, which was used to carve

9 Though not discussed here, historical evidence indicates that the church continued in use until the early seventeenth century, so the lack of obvious later medieval alterations to the building is curious.

the surviving window fragments, the west doorframe and the stone heads formerly placed over the doorway. It seems likely that the internal embrasure of the doorway (both the jambs and the voussoirs) was also carved from green tuff, and the large quantity of green-tuff blocks scattered around the site implies that this was used for the quoins also, though none has been found in situ. There are parallels for the widespread use of green tuff throughout Wexford for important architectural details such as doorways, windows, chancel arches and quoins, including at Kilmakilloge near Gorey, Templeshannon in Enniscorthy and Ballybrennan near Bree, and closer to home at St Mary's Augustinian priory at Ferns. Tadhg O'Keeffe noted that it is not inconceivable that the church at Clone became a cell of St Mary's, which was founded around 1162 by Diarmait Mac Murchada, then king of Leinster (O'Keeffe 1997, 54). While a connection with Mac Murchada seems likely, there is no historical evidence to suggest that Clone was connected with the Augustinian priory of St Mary's in Ferns (Bhreathnach and Dowling 2021). Instead, a more likely explanation is that Clone was built as a parish church in the mid-twelfth century, as part of an attempt by Ferns to maintain its rights as the head of a diocese, which it had successfully claimed at the Synod of Ráith Bressail in 1111 and again in 1152 at the Synod of Kells, when Ferns became part of the archdiocese of Dublin. Indeed, it is highly likely that Mac Murchada had a very direct role in sponsoring the construction of stone churches that reflected the evolving parish system, centred on Ferns. Furthermore, it is possible that in so doing Mac Murchada and the diocese of Ferns were confronting any rival attempts by the nearby Hiberno-Norse town of Wexford to make a bid for the seat of the diocese, which Dublin had successfully done in 1152 at the expense of the diocese of Glendalough.

There may be another explanation for the building of the Romanesque church at Clone. In order to account for the presence of the carved figures, we must examine their potential significance beyond a purely aesthetic one. First, such carved heads are not found at any other surviving Romanesque church in the county, and perhaps more telling is the fact that none is known from Ferns either. This means that they served a specific purpose and may have been intended to commemorate people and/or an event, and it is tempting to suggest that such an event was associated with Clone itself. While stones with animal carvings are commonly found in Romanesque churches elsewhere, their presence at Clone may provide a clue as to the overall meaning of the carvings. In the Lives of Máedóc there is a story that attempts to explain the origins of how he came to establish the church at Ferns. For example, in the vernacular *Betha Máedóc* (1), an abbreviated version of the late twelfth-century Latin *Life*, we are told:

> Once the king of Uí Cennselaig was on a plundering expedition, and Moeog met him, and the king gave him alms, and proceeded to his house. And disease and grievous sickness overtook him, so that it seemed to him as if his spirit

> departed from him. And hell was revealed to him, with horrible animals attacking him, and one animal with its breath dragged the king and drew him to its very mouth, when he saw the poor man putting the alms, which the king had given him, into the beast's mouth. But it did not cease to drag the king, till the poor man brought down his bachall on the mouth of the beast. The king awoke, and told all that he had seen. 'Send for Moeog', said they, 'and thou shalt learn everything from him'. 'It is fitter that I should fare to the servant of God', said the king; and he went to where Moeog was. 'This is the man to whom I gave the alms', said the king, 'and who freed me from the maw of the beast'. And the king gave him Ferns in perpetuity (Plummer 1922 ii, 179–80).

Perhaps the animal over the door was intended to represent the beast of the king's dream, and the heads above the door were intended to represent the individuals in the story, such as the Uí Chennselaig king and St Máedóc, and Clone may even have been considered to be the actual location of this event. This is pure speculation, of course, and there may be other stories associated with St Máedóc (perhaps not even documented in the Lives) that are represented by these carvings, or they may relate to the contemporary twelfth-century events and people of Ferns, such as Mac Murchada and Ioseph Ua hÁeda, bishop of Ferns from *c.*1155 to 1185.

The symbolism of the heads above the doorway may never be fully resolved, and equally difficult to answer is the question as to the original form of the doorway. Clearly, the presentation of the doorway and the carved heads resulting from the interventions undertaken in 1956 is very misleading. It has been argued above that the flat lintel above the doorframe (the broken lintel replaced in 1956) was not original, and that formerly there was an open arch above the doorway. What is less clear is the original arrangement of the carvings above this open arch, other than those that survived in the mid-nineteenth century. The doorway was already severely disfigured by the time it was first drawn by Du Noyer in 1862, and one of the heads had just been removed to Ferns to form part of the cap house constructed over St Aidan's Well. It is quite likely that other carved heads had been removed in previous years. Nonetheless, we have no evidence to confirm that the heads formed a continuous arch over the doorway, such as the outer order of the doorways at St Tola's Church at Dysert O'Dea[10] and St Caimin's Church on Iniscealtra, Lough Derg, both in Co. Clare (fig. 5.29). This is certainly possible, but it is worth noting that this arrangement is rare in Irish Romanesque doorways, and there is nothing comparable known from

10 The Romanesque doorway at Dysert O'Dea is not in its original position and was reconstructed in its present one at some point in the late medieval period, or perhaps in the seventeenth century. It is also clear that the outer order of heads has been incorrectly reassembled, perhaps combining carvings from both a doorway and a chancel arch. Another Romanesque doorway featuring an arch of carved heads can be found at Inchagoill on Lough Corrib, Co. Galway, but this was reconstructed in the mid-nineteenth century and its authenticity is not clear.

5.29 Romanesque doorways at Dysert O'Dea **(a)** and on Iniscealtra **(b)**, Lough Derg, Co. Clare. Though much more elaborate, the continuous arc of carved heads forming the outer order of the arch may give an impression of the original form of the heads above the doorway at Clone Church **(b)**

Ferns or elsewhere in Wexford. Rather than the ornate inner orders of the doorway at Dysert O'Dea, the heads over the doorway of Clone Church may have been simply arranged over a single-order arch with a plain angle roll, as a continuation of the upper jambs of both sides of the frame, which have plain angle rolls that contrast with the herring-bone pattern of the main body of the door jambs below.

CONCLUSION

The archaeological remains at Clone strongly suggest that the church here has early origins, and perhaps it was founded by St Máedóc during his time at Ferns. There are indications that the site developed into an important pilgrimage site, presumably because of a long-standing association with St Máedóc, and this was reinforced in the middle of the twelfth century with the construction of a Romanesque church, which probably served as a parish church in the newly established and evolving diocese of Ferns.

BIBLIOGRAPHY

Anon. 1889. 'Proceedings'. *Journal of the Royal Society of Antiquaries of Ireland*, 19, 3–23.

Bhreathnach, E. and Dowling, G. 2021. 'Forming an episcopal see and an Augustinian foundation in medieval Ireland: the case of Ferns, Co. Wexford'. *Proceedings of the Royal Irish Academy*, 121C, 191–226.

Corlett, C. 2014. *Inscribing the landscape: the rock art of south Leinster*. Dublin.

Corlett, C. 2017. *Glendalough*. Wicklow.

Corlett, C. 2021. 'An archaeological survey of Aghowle Church, Co. Wicklow'. *Journal of Irish Archaeology*, 30, 141–66.

Du Noyer, G.V. 1864–6. 'Early Irish and pre-Norman antiquities'. *Proceedings of the Royal Irish Academy*, 9, 423–44.

Grattan Flood, W.H. 1916. *History of the diocese of Ferns*. Waterford.

Hamlin, A. 1987. 'Some northern sundials and time-keeping in the early Irish church'. In Rynne, E. (ed.), *Figures from the past: studies on figurative art in Christian Ireland*, 29–42. Dublin.

Herity, H., Kelly, D. and Mattenberger, U. 1997. 'List of early Christian cross-slabs in seven north-western counties'. *Journal of the Royal Society of Antiquaries of Ireland*, 127, 80–124.

Herity, M. 2014. *Ordnance Survey letters. Wexford: letters relating to the antiquities of the county of Wexford containing information collected during the progress of the Ordnance Survey 1840*. Dublin.

Kinahan, G.H. 1883–4. 'Clone, near Ferns, Co. Wexford'. *Journal of the Royal Society of Antiquaries of Ireland*, 16, 37–8.

Leask, H.G. 1955. *Irish churches and monastic buildings, 1: the first phases and the Romanesque*. Dundalk.

Moore, M.J. 1996. *Archaeological inventory of County Wexford*. Dublin.

O'Keeffe, T. 1997. 'Diarmait Mac Murchada and Romanesque in Leinster: four twelfth-century churches in context'. *Journal of the Royal Society of Antiquaries of Ireland*, 127, 52–79.

Plummer, C. 1922. *Lives of Irish saints*. 2 vols. Oxford.

CHAPTER SIX

The architecture of sacral kingship in twelfth-century Ferns: the church of St Mary's Abbey

TADHG O'KEEFFE

An Augustinian community resided in Ferns from the early 1160s in an abbey dedicated to St Mary. According to a charter of 1160/2, the abbey was patronized by Diarmait Mac Murchada (Flanagan 2005, 284–9). It is not known whether the abbey was founded de novo as Augustinian, its regular canons introduced to Ferns from elsewhere in Ireland, or was an existing monastery in which the rule of St Augustine was adopted under the influence or direction of Mac Murchada. The consensus is that the latter is more likely than the former (Bhreathnach and Dowling 2021, 11–12; see also O'Keeffe 1997, 56–63). If so, it raises another question: was the abbey's church, of which there are substantial remains, built around 1160, or was it already extant and then became Augustinian?

I argue in this essay that the church was built by Mac Murchada in the later 1130s, and that it was a royal chapel in the tradition of Cormac's Chapel in Cashel, Co. Tipperary, its architecture articulating the concept of sacral kingship. The church's design suggests that, from the outset, it accommodated within its walls space for a small community of clerics. Given the later embrace of the Augustinian monastic observance at St Mary's, there would be a prima facie case for regarding such a community as monastic, but clergy serving a royal chapel could have been secular.

CATHEDRAL AND ABBEY

By the time that the Augustinian way of life was first observed there, Ferns had been a diocesan centre for half a century, its ecclesiastical jurisdiction reaching to the boundary of the kingdom of Uí Chennselaig. The first, early twelfth-century, cathedral would probably have been an eleventh-century or earlier church, rather than a brand new building. One can make such an assertion with confidence because it is apparent that the creation of dioceses in 1111 did not precipitate a building-boom but led, rather, to a redesignation-boom, with extant churches elevated to cathedral status. The Anglo-Normans did not build a new cathedral at Ferns until a couple of decades into the thirteenth century. This should not surprise us. They were actually quite slow to replace the old cathedrals which they inherited after 1169 with new cathedrals. The process was delayed perhaps by the need to create (or finalize a pre-invasion process of creating) a fully functioning parochial network, and develop a prebendary system (O'Keeffe 2015, 144).

Whatever the nature of the cathedral of Ferns at the start of the 1160s, the newly established Augustinian abbey was within earshot of it. Mac Murchada's charter of 1160/2 bestowed rights and privileges on the canons, and it granted some authority to their neighbour, the bishop, in the installation of their abbot. But the abbey and cathedral were separate institutions, operating independently of each other. The pre-invasion Augustinian community was not, in other words, the cathedral chapter; native Irish cathedrals did not have chapters (Nicholls 1973, 102–11). And when a cathedral chapter was created after the invasion, probably during the episcopate of Bishop Ailbe Ua Máel Muaid (d. 1223), the native-born bishop whom the Anglo-Normans appointed, it was a secular chapter, not a monastic chapter, despite the physical proximity of the cathedral and the abbey (O'Keeffe and Bates 2016, 73–96).

Historical evidence of a regular community remaining at Ferns through the Middle Ages is provided by an occasional reference to an abbot (ch. 2), and by the record of the abbey's dissolution in the mid-sixteenth century (summarized in Gwynn and Hadcock 1970, 175–6). Archaeologists are always reluctant to gainsay documentary evidence, but the archaeology of the site would indicate that something is not quite right here.

The physical evidence indicates that the abbey's glory days, so to speak, did not last very long, and perhaps lasted a few decades at most. The abbey church dates from the twelfth century. It saw no alteration of any significance after the invasion, other than some late medieval rebuilding at the top of its western tower, even though the cathedral was rebuilt in the 1220s and 1230s on a large scale with high-quality moulded stonework. Not only was its relatively small liturgical space retained from the twelfth century, but there is no evidence that changes were made to its very modest fenestration to improve lighting (O'Keeffe 2003, 57–63; see also O'Keeffe and Bates 2016, 80–1). With its chancel too cramped to have accommodated comfortably a choir for a standard twelve-strong Augustinian community, and no evidence of any special entrance for a community of canons other than through the west door, it is difficult to believe that this church was deemed sufficiently fit for monastic purpose over a period of three centuries and more for it to be spared enlargement or replacement. Yet, it seems that it was.

Given that the church is twelfth-century and was not of an architectural type that one finds in claustral contexts, the existence of a cloister court with its associated buildings, the fragmentary remains of which were recorded by Robert Cochrane over a century ago (fig. 6.1; Cochrane 1910, 3–6, 16–17), is a puzzle (ch. 9). Excavation might provide clarity, but the available evidence indicates that the church was built first – both the plan of the site and the metrological analysis of the complex presented

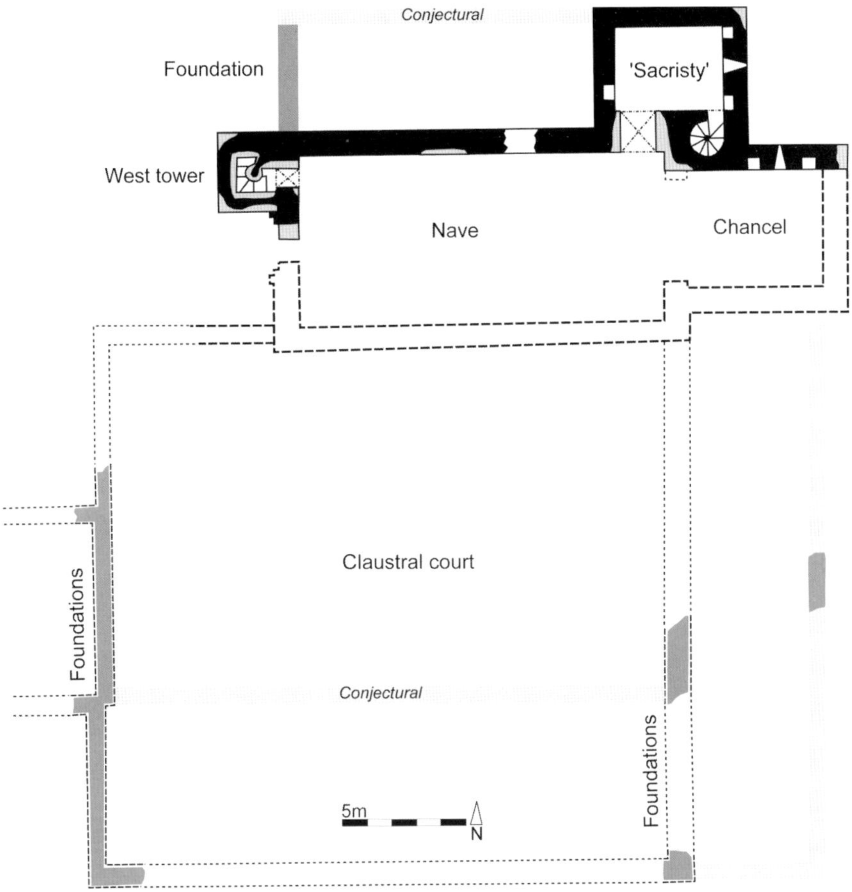

6.1 Ferns: plan of St Mary's Abbey (after Cochrane 1910), with the addition of the foundation north of the western tower

in Chapter 9 certainly indicate that – and that the claustral range was laid out in advance of a planned-for rebuilding of the church, but that the entire project was abandoned, leaving the claustral ranges only part finished. Excavation might produce evidence that the ranges were indeed occupied by monastics during the centuries in which the abbey seems from the documentary record to have remained active, but, in that event, I would anticipate the discovery of evidence that the cloister and its buildings were of low quality. The central court might have been walled and the buildings roofed to make them habitable, but I would be surprised, given that the church was left untouched, if there was evidence of an arcade of dressed stone, a well-appointed chapter house, a first-floor dormitory with latrines, or a first-floor refectory.

The date at which the cloister was laid out is a terminus ante quem for the date of the church. A date of *c.*1160 for the cloister would make sense, for that is when the rule was introduced to Ferns. A pre-1160 date for the church would be consistent with the chronological hints in the church's architecture. It is possible that the Anglo-Norman arrival at the end of the 1160s derailed what was an ambitious project earlier in the 1160s to build claustral ranges and then modify or enlarge the existing church.

AN ANALYTICAL DESCRIPTION OF THE CHURCH

The modern visitor to St Mary's sees a nave-and-chancel church. It is missing its entire south side. Usefully, though unfortunately, this allows the visitor to see most of the building in cross-section (fig. 6.2). Two other structures stand attached to this building. First, at its west end is a tower, its lower part square and its upper part round. It projects from the north side of the nave's former west wall, and it is entered from inside the nave. Second, attached to the north side of the junction of the nave and chancel, and entered from the nave, is a small, two-storeyed, square-plan building. This was identified by Cochrane as a 'sacristy' (1910, 16). There was a third structure, but all that survives above ground is a short, grass-covered, foundation: it is – or, rather, was – a building attached to the north side of the nave and running parallel to it.

The nave

The nave measured 14m by 6.4m internally. Its roof structure must have been made of timber, for its walls were insufficiently thick to carry a vault across its span. The wall-head was at least 8.5m off ground-level, so the apex of the roof was at least 13m above ground-level. This was an exceptionally tall nave by twelfth-century Irish standards. The surviving north wall seems to have been built in a series of stages: the lower 1.5m or so – the original ground-level is uncertain – has narrow stones and has a clear 'line' at the top, and above that the wall rises for an additional 7m or so, but with a narrow (20–30cm) horizontal course of narrow stones about halfway up that height. One can see some roughly vertical bands or zones of masonry in the wall, but the horizontal courses provide compelling evidence that the wall was built from the bottom up along its full length, and not in vertical sections.

Entry to the nave was from the west, through a two-ordered doorway. Two features of the nave's surviving north wall require explanation. First, a break in the wall looks to be the site of a second doorway; it is not easily explained otherwise. External doorways in the north walls of naves tend to be further west. This break was not, I will argue below, the site of an external doorway, but that of an internal doorway which connected the nave to a roofed space to its north. Second, the north wall of the nave has no fenestration. The north walls of small churches in Ireland were rarely fenestrated like their corresponding south walls, and were sometimes windowless. But

6.2 Ferns: St Mary's Church, from the south

such walls were generally lower and shorter than the north wall at Ferns. The explanation I offer below is that the north wall of the nave was actually a partition wall rather than an outside wall. I will refer to it hereafter, for clarity, as 'the partition wall'.

The west tower

The tower which projects from the north side of the west wall of the nave was tight against the outer order of the west doorway. Post-medieval fabric repair makes it difficult to determine the dates of the tower and the doorway relative to each other, but there is no reason to doubt their contemporaneity. The lower half of the tower is square. At the point at which it clears the much-broken top of the partition wall, it changes shape, from square to round (fig. 6.3). Today, the interior of the tower has a clockwise spiral stairs with stone steps. This is an insertion. In the nineteenth century, the interior walls of the tower were lined with brick. A circular brick newel was built. The stair-flags were inserted into the brick lining and into the newel. Lest there be any suspicion that the stairs might be original, as Cochrane (1910, 5) maintained, and that the brick newel was inserted solely to add stability, one can see the underside of the steps as one ascends to the top of the tower, whereas in the other, undoubtedly twelfth-century, stairs in the church (discussed below), the roof has a corkscrew vault. An original stairs inside the west tower would almost certainly have had a vaulted roof also. The tower, then, was originally ascended by ladders in the manner of a classic Irish Round Tower.

6.3 Ferns: west tower, viewed from the north-west

Three openings in the tower face eastwards into the church (fig. 6.4). The first is the doorway into the tower at ground level. This was the original site of entry to the tower from inside the church, but it is not clear how much fabric is original. There is evidence of repair, which is consistent with Cochrane's labelling of his plan of the church. I think that the arch, made of rubble voussoirs, might be original. The jambs are certainly more recent.

Directly above the doorway is the second opening. This too was a doorway, even though there is no structural trace of a floor onto which it may have led. It is an original, twelfth-century, opening. Slightly larger than the one below, its jambs have been altered, but its arch, which is identical to the arch below, seems to be original. The interior south corner of this doorway has in-situ dressed stones, their twelfth-century date confirmed by their diagonal tooling (fig. 6.5). Did this doorway open onto a gallery for which there is no remaining evidence? Or did it provide a vantage point for looking into the body of the church, and a setting in which whoever stood in that doorway could be seen by those inside the church?

6.4 Ferns: west tower, viewed from the interior of the nave

6.5 Ferns: original stonework in the first-floor doorway of the west tower

6.6 Ferns: original stonework in the second-floor doorway of the west tower

Higher up again is the third opening, also facing into the church. It is positioned where the tower changes shape externally, so its bottom part is in the square tower and its top part is in the round tower. Internally, though, the tower is still square at this level. Examination of the fabric of the tower, especially when viewed from the nave, might lead one to think that the round part of the tower is later than the square part below, and that this particular opening was made when the tower was extended upwards as a cylinder. But I am not sure that the round part of the tower is later (except at the very top). In any case, close study of this opening suggests that the square-to-round transition is part of the original build. Original stonework survives on its interior north side and is like that of the 'floating' doorway below, with narrow joints and diagonal dressing. It also has a roll-moulding flanked by a double-quirk (fig. 6.6), an articulating device which first appears in the mid-1130s in Kilmalkedar, Co. Kerry, and is commonly found from the 1140s. Even though it appears too narrow to have been a doorway, its position would suggest that it was. The moulded stonework would suggest that it was a doorway of higher status than one below it. The question of how it 'worked' is a difficult one to answer.

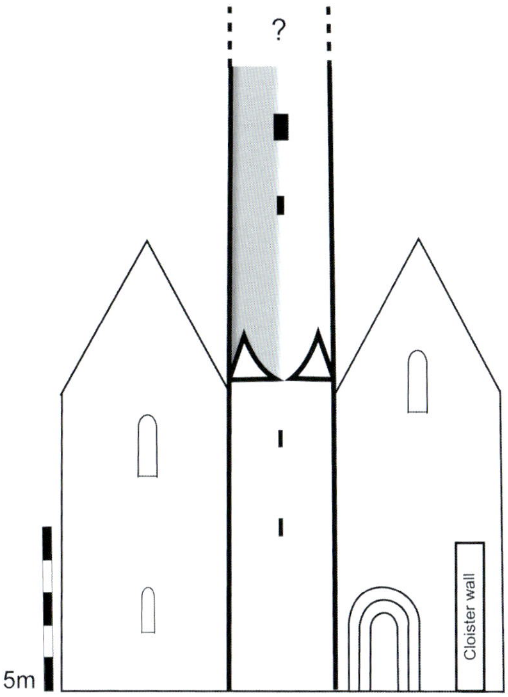

6.7 Ferns: west elevation of St Mary's, conjectural

6.8 Ferns: west elevation of St Mary's today

The north side of the partition wall

On the north side of the west tower, buried in the grass, are remains of a wall which ran northwards for about 4m, continuing the line of the nave's west wall. This was not a boundary wall, but was the wall of a building. It terminates at a point which lines up with the north wall of Cochrane's 'sacristy' (see fig. 6.1). Thus, it defines a rectangular area on the north side of the nave. This allows the north wall of the nave to be interpreted as a partition wall rather than as an outside wall, as noted above. And it also explains the west tower. If we reconstruct the space bisected by the partition wall, the west tower's position makes sense: it was in the centre of the west façade of the church (fig. 6.7). The oddly lop-sided appearance of the west end of the church today (fig. 6.8) is therefore a consequence of the loss of the northern half of the church.

The vaulted chancel

The chancel measured 4.47m by 5.3m internally. The east and south walls are represented by foundations only. The surviving north side is very intriguing (fig. 6.9). It has three parts: the lower wall, which is featureless, the upper wall, which is fenestrated, and the vault. Each of these requires a commentary.

6.9 Ferns: interior north wall of the chancel of St Mary's

First, in the lower part of the wall, one can see the site of the predella, the step in front of the altar, and a blocked opening. The step was still there, though quite broken, when Cochrane surveyed the church. There was very little space between it and the chancel arch. So, if there was a choir, as the church's post-1160/62 monastic function would imply, it must have extended to the west of the chancel arch. This would not have been an odd arrangement in itself, for monastic choirs were not always confined to the eastern limbs of their host churches. A designated choir in St Mary's would have necessitated a screen running across the width of the nave, somewhere near to its east end. If there was one, the entry to Cochrane's 'sacristy' would have been on the east side of that screen.

Second, above the blank wall is a central window, flanked by small niches. The rear of the window, which faces into the chancel, has neatly dressed stones with no mouldings, and no capitals or imposts separating the uprights from the arch. In contrast, the little niches have roll-mouldings on their uprights and have inward-facing

6.10 Ferns: detail of the vaulting in the chancel of St Mary's

moulded imposts. Cochrane noted that these small niches were restored, and one can certainly see evidence of alterations. At issue is whether they were restored, in which case they are still in their original positions, or were inserted later. One notes that the arrangement of the niches and the central window is not quite symmetrical, with the niche on the left (the west), which is very slightly the smaller of the two, being closer to the central window than is the niche on the right. The window itself appears to be in its original position, but these niches could have been inserted later. Given that they have moulded stonework, unlike the window they flank, it is possible that they originally flanked the original east window. However, why would they have been moved? The functions of the niches are not obvious. They are a little too high off ground-level to have been storage for sacred vessels. One suggestion which I would offer, but with little conviction, is that there was a portable Easter sepulchre below the window and tightly set against the north wall of the chancel (for such sepulchres, see O'Keeffe 2015, 117–20), and that the niches were associated with it.

Third, the upper part of the wall preserves the evidence that the chancel was barrel-vaulted. That vault, long collapsed, was made in four short segments, defined by three

6.11 Cashel, Co. Tipperary: detail of the nave vault, Cormac's Chapel

6.12 The barrel-vaulted roof, with transverse arches, of St Sernin, Toulouse

6.13 Ferns: the base of the vault on the south wall of the sacristy, the white line marking the uneven surface from which the vault springs

square-sectioned transverse arches. One can see clearly how the vault was made. The chamfered springer stones of the arches were as long as the other stones in those arches, and therefore they project (unseen) back into the wall, but they also sit on a narrow (10cm-wide) ledge. These arches defined short vault-cells. The stones in those cells were wedged in place between the arches (fig. 6.10), indicating that the arches and the cells were made at the same time. It might seem self-evident that this is how they would have been built, but actually it is not: transverse arches could in principle be erected first, and in many cases they probably were. The nave of Cormac's Chapel in Cashel is the most likely model for the use of transverse arches in the Ferns chancel vault. It is difficult to think of an alternative. But there are some significant differences: the Cashel arches have responds and capitals, and are more substantial, and they are in the nave rather than in the chancel. The link between Ferns and Cashel is conceptual as much as it is formal. The Cashel vault is a miniature version of a more substantial vault, for it has more transverse arches than it needs: it has six short vault bays defined by seven transverse arches along a length of less than 9m (fig. 6.11), but in France, where this type of vaulting was common, the same number of transverse arches will normally service a barrel-vault more than four times that length (fig. 6.12). In other words, the Cashel vault is a scaled-down version of a larger vault. That is in keeping with that chapel's overall character: Cormac's Chapel is monumental in conception but small-scale in execution. The Ferns vault repeats the overkill of transverse arches, but without the scaled-down monumentality of the Cashel chapel.

The Ferns vault has two unusual features, both suggesting that it is not a primary feature. First, the narrow ledge on which the transverse arches were placed was not surfaced evenly. One gets the impression that the arches were placed on top of a broken wall. To move briefly into Cochrane's 'sacristy', for it is relevant here, one sees the same thing: its collapsed vault, which does not have transverse arches, appears also to have rested on broken walling on both its north and its south sides, and the latter is the same wall on which the chancel vault sits (fig. 6.13). Second, transverse arches in European churches were always aligned very exactly with openings below them, but at Ferns the arches are aligned only approximately with the window and the niches. Were the vault part of the original imagining of the church, these would surely have been aligned. Mortar analysis might allow us someday to determine the chronological relationship between the walls of the east end of the church and the vaulting, but visual inspection suggests an interval between them. Comparisons between the plans of St Mary's and Cormac's Chapel, discussed below, suggest it was a short interval.

Above the chancel vault was another room, accessed via Cochrane's 'sacristy' by stairs (see below). That upper room was narrower than the chancel: its outer walls were not flush with the chancel's outer walls. The builders took a risk in building the upper room in this manner, and their miscalculation probably explains why the vault over the chancel no longer survives. The side walls of the upper room were built above the

6.14 View of the roof of the chancel, showing (on the right-hand side) the outer wall of its upper room resting on the haunch of the vault

haunches of the chancel vault (fig. 6.14), but haunches were not designed to take such weights. I have seen no other example of a vault supporting a wall in this manner. Either it was never done, or there was a collapse any time it was done. The roof-type chosen for that upper room is not known, but it was probably of stone, like that of Cormac's Chapel. The additional weight loaded onto the side walls by a stone roof would have increased the likelihood of collapse.

The chancel arch no longer survives. A wide roll-moulding on an ex-situ stone stored in the base of the western tower might have come from it. Part of the arch's abutment projects on the north side, and the foundation of one of its responds survives on the south side. These two pieces of evidence are together important: it is the surviving respond-foundation on the south which allows us to describe the projecting wall on the north as an abutment, and that in turn allows us to visualize a chancel arch about 4.5m high at its apex. Establishing that height is important, even if it is an approximate measurement. It is apparent that the east wall of the nave had quite an expanse of masonry above the arch (and possibly even a rood, because an in-situ support for a wooden beam survives). Also, it means that the barrel-vaulted roof

6.15 The interior east wall of the 'sacristy'

of the chancel would not have been visible from most of the nave: anybody who walked through the arch into the chancel would probably have been surprised by how high its roof was relative to the height of the chancel arch.

Robert Cochrane's 'sacristy'

A two-storeyed structure, almost square in plan with a formerly barrel-vaulted lower chamber, projects from the north side of the junction of the nave and chancel. Access to its interior is from the nave, while spiral stairs (with a corkscrew barrel vault) gave access to its upper chamber as well as to a room above the chancel. The way the vault sits on an uneven wall has already been mentioned. The outer wall of the room above the vault was set back slightly, just like the room over the chancel, so here too the haunches of the vault might have been expected to carry the weight of walls, and here too it might explain the collapse of the vault. The east wall of the lower chamber has a window flanked by blind arches (fig. 6.15), and the arrangement is almost identical to what one finds on the north wall of the chancel. The opposite wall (the west wall) has a wall cupboard with a shelf, presumably for sacred vessels.

There is a straightforward interpretation of this structure: the lower storey was indeed a sacristy, and the stairs led to two upper rooms, one over the sacristy and one over the chancel, with the priest and his assistants descending from them into the body of the church. Parallels with Cormac's Chapel suggest a different interpretation.

ST MARY'S ABBEY CHURCH REINTERPRETED

Comparisons between St Mary's at Ferns and the Augustinian abbey church of St Saviour's at Glendalough, Co. Wicklow, built between 1153 and 1162, have already been discussed in print (O'Keeffe 2003, 57–63; fig. 6.16). The Glendalough church also has a 'room' on the north side of its nave, almost of the same size as that at Ferns (as indicated by shading in the simplified outline plans in fig. 6.16). If the gap in the north wall of the Ferns nave is indeed the site of a doorway, it parallels that at Glendalough. Also, each church had stairs leading from their north sides towards spaces above their barrel-vaulted east ends. There are also some important differences between the two churches. St Saviour's was more heavily ornamented. It had no tower. The room on the north side of St Saviour's was a single space without partition, whereas there were two spaces on the north side at Ferns, one a 'room' and the other Cochrane's 'sacristy', with no connecting doorway between them. Finally, two reconstructed doorway gaps in Glendalough's south wall suggest processional doorways for its Augustinian canons, whereas Ferns has no such doorways, but there is no accommodation for a community of canons on the south side of the church, whereas Ferns had a claustral area.

These differences notwithstanding, the apparent similarities between the two churches, combined with their Mac Murchada associations (O'Keeffe 1997), might suggest that both churches are explained and understood, and that idiosyncrasies of each of them, especially St Mary's, the more idiosyncratic of the two, are no more than wilful deviations from the norm. As the older of the two, Ferns is the one to which we should turn to understand both. Making sense of Glendalough based on an interpretation of Ferns is a project for another day.

To understand St Mary's, we need to look to the two surviving royal chapels in Munster, St Flannan's 'Oratory' in Killaloe, Co. Clare, and, especially, Cormac's Chapel. Detailed analyses and interpretations of the buildings at Killaloe and Cashel are presented elsewhere, along with supporting references (O'Keeffe 2024, passim), so a summary will suffice here.

At Killaloe, around 1100, Muirchertach Ua Briain erected St Flannan's 'Oratory', so-called. It was a small, two-storeyed, stone-roofed, chapel of nave-and-chancel plan. Only the nave survives, but its form was repeated in the chancel. The lower storey of

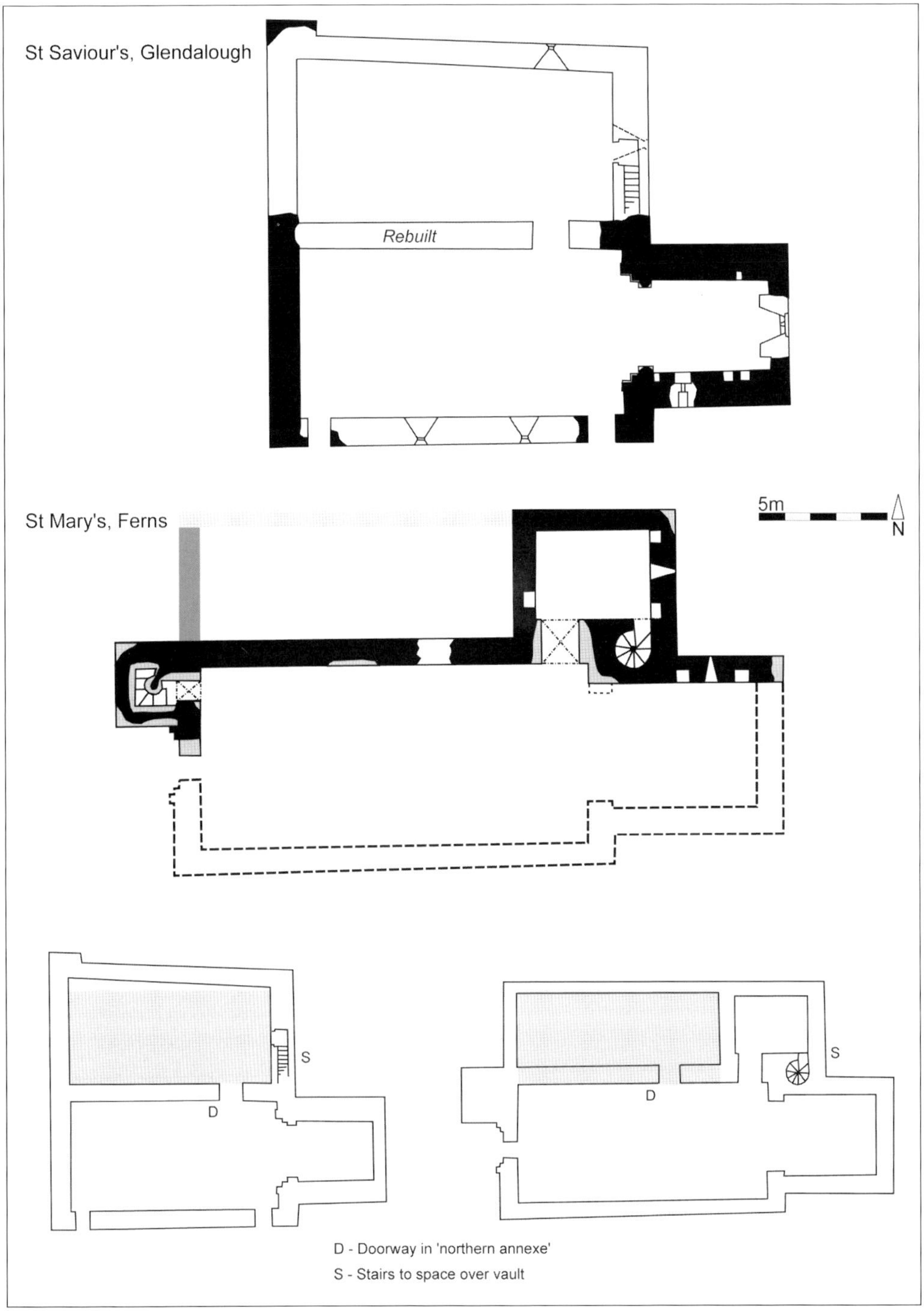

6.16 Plans of St Mary's, Ferns, and St Saviour's, Glendalough, highlighting some points of comparison

6.17 St Flannan's Oratory, Killaloe, from the west

the nave has round barrel vaulting. The upper storey, which was accessible by ladder, has a pointed barrel vault. The chapel was erected inside the ecclesiastical site which was Killaloe, overlooked by the secular royal site of Kincora, only a few hundred metres away. The chapel's architecture was in the reliquary-chapel tradition, and its dedication to the local saint would be consistent with that. Its description as a 'royal chapel' is intended to speak of more than just its patronage: it appears to have been a

6.18 Cashel, Co. Tipperary: Cormac's Chapel from the south-east **6.19** Cashel, Co. Tipperary: cross-section through Cormac's Chapel, looking east, showing the chancel-opening and altar niches at the east end of the upper nave. The vault of the upper chapel begins at floor level, which is unusual, but is a consequence of how the chapel adopted the stone-roofed, double-vaulted, format. In many *Doppelkapellen* the upper chapel is a little less elaborate than the lower chapel, as in this case

private chapel, rather than a conventional congregational church. Its west doorway was the work of a mason from Norman England, possibly one sent to Muirchertach's employ by William II. Beside the chapel at the time of its construction was the church which would be redesignated the cathedral after 1111, and later substantially rebuilt. After 1111, then, Killaloe had, side-by-side, a small vaulted and stone-roofed chapel, built under royal patronage, and a cathedral (fig. 6.17).

In 1127, when Cormac Mac Carthaig was restored to the kingship in Cashel, he also built a vaulted and stone-roofed chapel (fig. 6.18), and it too stood beside a cathedral. Cormac's Chapel, as it has been known since it was consecrated in 1134, copied the form of the Killaloe chapel in having superimposed vaulted spaces under a stone-roof. It was, it would seem, an antagonistic copying: the intention was not to flatter by imitation the royal chapel of the rival Uí Briain dynasty but, rather, to appropriate its architectural principle and create something more substantial.

Cormac's Chapel had features not found in Killaloe, including transverse arches in its nave barrel vault, and a rib vault in its chancel. It also possessed a pair of towers flanking the east side of its nave, one (the north) having an altar at ground-floor level and the other (the south) a spiral stairs with a corkscrew barrel vault to give access to the upper level. That upper level was actually a chapel in itself. Cormac's Chapel was, in other words, a double-chapel, a type of building described in the literature as a *Doppelkapelle*. There had been no upper chapel in Killaloe. Cormac took the Killaloe model, made the upper space accessible, and gave it a liturgical purpose.

Three features of Cormac's Chapel's architecture indicate that there was an upper chapel. First, access was by a high-grade, newel-turned, spiral stairs, entered from the nave via a doorway with a tympanum. Second, ashlar was used in the upper level and there is evidence of painting. Third, and most interesting from the perspective of Ferns, the wall which separated the large upper room (over the nave) from the smaller upper room (over the chancel) has an opening archway, albeit door-like in scale, which is flanked by niches (fig. 6.19). This is liturgical architecture: there are Norman-English parallels for east windows or chancel arches being flanked by comparable niches, with those niches being associated with altars. The dividing wall between the two parts of Cormac's Chapel's upper part was, therefore, a screen wall between a nave and a chancel.

The best parallel for the Cashel wall is the east wall of the Ferns 'sacristy' (fig. 6.15). It is apparent from this that the room on the north side of the chancel of St Mary's was not a sacristy at all, but a chapel. Thus, St Mary's was a form of double-chapel, its two liturgical spaces side-by-side rather than superimposed. There are hints that it was an actual variation on Cormac's Chapel. In both Cashel and Ferns, the 'second' chapel was vaulted, had paired altar niches, and was accessed from the nave. The transverse arches in Ferns, and the likelihood of external stone-roofing, reinforce the connection.

The room on the north side of the nave's partition wall is not explained by reference to Cashel. This might have been the space for clergy serving the chapel, in which case we might have the model for St Saviour's at Glendalough. I am inclined to think, though, that it was liturgical rather than residential, and to wonder whether the wall at its east end, separating it from Cochrane's supposed, but now debunked, sacristy, is a later insertion, its niche for sacred vessels recycled from elsewhere in the building.

The link with Cormac's Chapel helps us to date the double-chapel of St Mary's. The Cashel chapel was consecrated shortly after Mac Murchada became king. A date early in his reign would make sense for Ferns: power is best asserted at the moment of ascent. Was Mac Murchada represented among the nobles of Ireland who attended the consecration of Cormac's Chapel? Was he there himself? Whatever the case, Cormac's Chapel was available as a source from 1134, and that would point to a late 1130s date for Ferns.

Why might Mac Murchada have imitated Cormac's Chapel? To answer that question, we need to look closely at what Cormac Mac Carthaig's chapel said of him. As well as standing beside a cathedral, Cormac's *Doppelkapelle*, with its superimposed chapels connected by stairs (as distinct from an aperture in the floor dividing them), conformed to the model of an episcopal double-chapel. Cormac, it should be noted, was remembered in his obituary in 1138 as 'bishop of the kings of Ireland'. But his *Doppelkapelle*'s location at the heart of a royal citadel also suggests that its family tree includes the mid-ninth-century Sacra Capella of the Great Palace of Constantinople, derived ultimately from the Holy Sepulchre, and the earlier thirteenth-century Gothic Ste-Chapelle in Paris. Thus, Cormac's Chapel was a monument of sacral kingship. Cormac's characterization as Solomon in *Visio Tnugdali*, and his chapel's use in inauguration ceremonies modelled on those of German emperors, underscore this. Mac Murchada's royal chapel must have been built with similar, sacral kingship, intent. All that we are missing from St Mary's to complete the formal parallel between it and Cormac's Chapel is a tomb. Cormac had an external *arcosolium*, a tomb niche, readied for his burial. A place of burial was probably readied for Mac Murchada. Might it have been on the north side of the altar, underneath the window and the two blind niches (fig. 6.9)?

The western tower, its meaning and significance

The western tower is puzzling. Insofar as it has been discussed in the literature, it is regarded as a bell-tower (Moss 2015, 188). The way it is circular above the roof of the church would point to a kinship with the Glendalough churches of St Kevin and Trinity, both of late eleventh- or early twelfth-century date, but the Ferns scheme is not fully explained by reference to Glendalough.

Towers, always round, invariably stood free of their associated churches in tenth- to twelfth-century Ireland, either to the north-west or to the north-east. The Ferns tower is unusual in several ways. First, it was attached to its associated church. Second, there is evidence that it was not at the side of the façade, imitating the placement of the freestanding towers, but was in the middle (see fig. 6.7). Third, it has a square-plan lower part. Taking these together, one visualizes a tower not unlike the tower-porches of eleventh- and twelfth-century Europe, albeit slenderer and with a circular upper part. But it was not an entrance tower. Its doorways look into the church, one at ground-level, and two higher up. The dialogue between its elevated doorways and the church interior is like that between a Round Tower and its church: one could look into the church at Ferns from an elevation, just as one could look to a church doorway from the elevated vantage point of a Round Tower doorway. The absence of evidence for a gallery at the west end of the Ferns nave is significant here, for it removes the only viable alternative to my favoured explanation for Round Tower doorways, and for the Ferns doorways, which is that these were display doorways, elevated so that those who stood within them could look towards the liturgical focus, but also be seen from below. The explanations I have offered elsewhere for Round Towers thus fit Ferns: it is in the Round Tower family and has similar functions and symbolism (O'Keeffe 2004). It is appropriate to discuss briefly the Irish Round Tower, and to restate my argument that the description of them as bell-towers misses their point completely.

Records of the loss of relics when Round Towers were damaged or destroyed suggest that they contained altars, and were therefore consecrated (for example, see Yasin 2012, 249). So too does the evidence of mass fatalities in towers: gatherings of people inside churches and towers when ecclesiastical centres were attacked suggest that sanctuary was being sought, and the deaths indicate (as is known to have been the case in the Middle Ages) that sanctuary was not always observed by assailants (for violations of sanctuary, see Shoemaker 2011; for Ireland, see Hughes 1966, 191, 197, 264). Also, evidence of the consecrated status of the Round Tower are the records of royal killings at Kells in the late eleventh century and at Devenish in the late twelfth. Finally, one should note that the doorways of Round Towers are sometimes more elaborate than the doorways of their associated churches, suggesting the towers had liturgical functions requiring the elaboration of their points of entry. Also, one should note that the windows of Round Towers often ascend clockwise in imitation of procession, even though the internal floors were connected by ladder.

The presence of altars, coupled with the evidence of royal patronage (directly at Cashel and Clonmacnoise, and indirectly at Kells and Devenish), points to the imperial, Carolingian and Ottonian, architectural tradition of northern Europe as the natural context in which to seek the formal and conceptual origins of the Irish Round Tower. The two towers shown on the Plan of St Gall of *c.*820 are especially interesting because they stand relative to the plan's church as Irish Round Towers do relative their churches, and the plan further records an altar at the summit of each (Horn and Born 1979, 129–31). These were, then, elevated circular chapels. The specific dedications of those altars to SS Michael and Gabriel underscore how, from at least the time of St Martin of Tours, western church towers of all types, freestanding or attached, symbolized the protection of the faithful but were also the loci of Resurrection liturgies, in which capacity they recalled the Anastasis rotunda of the Holy Sepulchre in Jerusalem (for a description of St Martin of Tours, see Van Dam 1993, 312; for the Holy Sepulchre symbolism, see Heitz 1986, 90–100).

The best formal parallels for the Irish Round Towers are in the German lands of the tenth century, where cylindrical towers were built in pairs and were attached to *Westwerken* (Lobbedey 2002, 65–75). These towers did not have altars themselves, but they were associated with the altars inside the *Westwerken*. The fact that the Irish towers contained bells does not mitigate against this: in medieval England, for example, bell-towers sometimes had chapels, often with St Michael dedications (Norton 1998, 7–9; Stocker and Everson 2006; Shapland 2019). In fact, one reason why the suggestion of an Italian origin – Ravennate or Roman – for the Irish Round Tower must be rejected is the absence of altars from the southern European towers.

What we see at Ferns, then, is evidently a late variation on the Irish Round Tower, but one that is oddly more faithful, in principle at least, to the register of northern European (often royal or imperial) buildings in which the Irish Round Towers must be contextualized. What are the implications of this? I wonder whether, by joining a Round Tower to the west end of his church, Mac Murchada is telling us, across the centuries, that the church of St Mary's was royal too.

Cormac's Chapel did not have a Round Tower, but its north tower deliberately referenced Muirchertach's Round Tower at Cashel with the same adversarial intent that inspired his chapel's imitation of St Flannan's oratory. The Cormac's Chapel tower was entered through an elaborate opening facing the chancel, it contained an altar, and it was capped with a stone roof. Might his knowledge of Cashel and the way in which Cormac Mac Carthaig played with the concept of a traditional Round Tower have inspired Diarmait Mac Murchada to integrate a tower into the design of his own royal chapel in Ferns?

CONCLUSION

This chapter is a work-in-progress rumination on a remarkable site, some secrets of which will doubtless be revealed by excavation. For now, the near-certainty is that the church pre-dates the claustral enclosure (ch. 9). That enclosure might date from *c.*1160 when the rule of St Augustine was introduced to Ferns. If that is the case, the date of the church needs to be pushed back in time. I suggest that the date is moved to the late 1130s, and that St Mary's abbey church is understood as a close cousin of Cormac's Chapel. This reinterpretation of the Ferns church moves it from the margins to the centre of the narrative of Irish architectural history. It suggests that it was built, following Cormac's Chapel, as a monument of sacral kingship.

BIBLIOGRAPHY

Bhreathnach, E. 2012. 'Benedictine influence in Ireland in the late eleventh and early twelfth centuries: a reflection'. *Journal of Medieval Monastic Studies*, 1, 63–91.

Bhreathnach, E. and Dowling, G. 2021. 'Forming an episcopal see and an Augustinian foundation in medieval Ireland: the case of Ferns, Co. Wexford'. *Proceedings of the Royal Irish Academy*, 121C, 191–226.

Cochrane, R. 1910. 'Ferns, Co. Wexford'. In *78th Annual Report of the Commissioners of Public Works in Ireland*, 3–6, 16–17. Dublin.

Flanagan, M.T. 2005. *Irish royal charters: texts and contexts.* Oxford.

Gwynn, A. and Hadcock, N. 1970. *Medieval religious houses: Ireland.* London.

Heitz, C. 1986. 'The iconography of architectural form'. In Butler, L.A.S. and Morris, R.K. (eds), *The Anglo-Saxon church: papers on history, architecture and archaeology in honour of Dr H.M. Taylor*, 90–100. London.

Horn, W. and Born, E. 1979. *The plan of St Gall*, 1. Berkeley, Los Angeles and London.

Hughes, K. 1966. *The church in early Irish society*. Ithaca.

Lobbedey, U. 2002. 'Les Westwerke de l'époque ottonienne en Allemagne du Nord'. In Christian Sapin (ed.), *Avant-nefs et espaces d'accueil dans l'église entre le IVe et le XIIe siècle*, 67–75. Paris.

Moss, R. 2015. 'Augustinian canons (canons regular, Austin canons)'. In Moss, R. (ed.), *Art and architecture of Ireland, i: Medieval,* c.*400*–c.*1600*, 187–95. Dublin.

Nicholls, K.W. 1973. 'Mediæval Irish cathedral chapters'. *Archivium Hibernicum*, 31, 102–11.

Norton, C. 1998. 'The Anglo-Saxon cathedral at York and the topography of the Anglian city'. *Journal of the British Archaeological Association*, 151, 1–42.

Ó Carragáin, T. 2010. *Churches in early medieval Ireland.* New Haven and London.

O'Keeffe, T. 1994. 'Lismore and Cashel: reflections on the beginnings of Romanesque architecture in Munster'. *Journal of the Royal Society of Antiquaries of Ireland*, 124, 118–51.

O'Keeffe, T. 1997. 'Diarmait Mac Murchada and Romanesque Leinster: four twelfth-century churches in context'. *Journal of the Royal Society of Antiquaries of Ireland*, 127, 52–79.

O'Keeffe, T. 2003. *Romanesque Ireland: architecture and ideology in the twelfth century.* Dublin.

O'Keeffe, T. 2004. *Ireland's round towers: buildings, rituals and landscapes of the early Irish church.* Stroud.

O'Keeffe, T. 2012. 'Augustinian regular canons in twelfth- and thirteenth-century Ireland: history, architecture and identity'. In Burton, J. and Stober, K. (eds), *The Regular Canons in the medieval British Isles*, 460–74. Turnhout.

O'Keeffe, T. 2015. *Medieval Irish buildings, 1100–1600.* Dublin.

O'Keeffe, T. 2024. *Medieval Irish architecture and the concept of Romanesque: building traditions in eleventh- and twelfth-century Europe*. London.

O'Keeffe, T. and Carey Bates, R. 2016. 'The abbey and cathedral of Ferns, 1111–1253'. In Doyle, I. and Browne, B. (eds), *Medieval Wexford: essays in memory of Billy Colfer*, 73–96. Dublin.

Ryan, M., Mooney, K., Prendergast, F. and Masterson, B. 2004. 'Church Island: a description'. In Mac Shamhráin, A. (ed.), *The island of St Patrick: church and ruling dynasties in Fingal and Meath, 400–1148*, 106–24. Dublin.

Shapland, M.G. 2019. *Anglo-Saxon towers of lordship*. Oxford.

Shoemaker, K. 2011. *Sanctuary and crime in the Middle Ages, 400–1500*. New York.

Stocker D.A. and Everson, P. 2006. *Summoning St Michael: early Romanesque towers in Lincolnshire*. Oxford.

Van Dam, R. 1993. *Saints and their miracles in late Antique Gaul.* Princeton NJ.

Yasin, A.M. 2012. 'Sight lines of sanctity at late Antique martyria'. In Wescoat, B.D. and Ousterhout, R.G. (eds), *Architecture of the sacred: space, ritual and experience from Classical Greece to Byzantium*, 248–80. Cambridge.

CHAPTER SEVEN

St Mary's Abbey, Ferns: an archaeological survey

CHRISTIAAN CORLETT

INTRODUCTION

St Mary's Abbey (fig. 7.1) was founded between 1160 and 1162, with the support of Diarmait Mac Murchada, then king of Leinster. The abbey was founded for the Augustinian Canons Regular, who were a relatively new introduction to Ireland at this time. The foundation charter (Flanagan 2005, 284–9) makes it clear that it was established as a royal chapel, and perhaps intended as the mortuary chapel of Mac Murchada himself, who died at Ferns in 1171. Despite local tradition asserting that he was buried in the nearby graveyard, beside the remains of an elaborate high cross dating from the late ninth or early tenth century, it is most likely that he was buried here in St Mary's. The royal charter names a variety of lands elsewhere in Wexford that were designed to support the abbey (Bhreathnach and Dowling 2021, 14–16), but these were not as extensive as the lands Mac Murchada granted to the Cistercians when he founded Baltinglass Abbey (Nicholls 1985). However, St Mary's was never intended to serve the same function as the great Cistercian monasteries and, being closely associated with the seat of the diocese and the cathedral nearby, it did not seek total independence or separation, and therefore did not require the same resources to be self-sufficient. Quite possibly Mac Murchada envisaged that St Mary's would not require an extensive endowment because it would be directly and generously patronized by himself and his heirs as a royal foundation. Of course, this was not to be. The abbey seems to have struggled financially throughout the later medieval period, but it did at least survive, with much of its estates intact, until it was finally closed in 1538. An extent made at Ferns in January 1541 found that 'There are no buildings in the precinct save the abbey church and a hall' and the jury concluded that 'these are necessary for the farmer, and are worth nothing above repairs' (White 1943, 371). Given that the jury all had Gaelic names and were clearly local, it might be wise to take this brief account with a pinch of salt.[1] It would certainly be a mistake to assume that this reflects a dilapidated monastery that, by the beginning of the sixteenth century, had been reduced to a shell of its former self. It would also be an error to dismiss the former abbey church as of minor significance based on the partial ruins that survive.

1 The Kavanaghs appear to have frustrated the crown's attempts to secure possession of the abbey until 1552 (Bradshaw 1974, 73).

7.1 Ferns: St Mary's Abbey, viewed from the west-south-west

At first glance, the remains of the abbey are quaint but modest. It stands isolated in a field and gives a false impression of a small and discrete site. A belfry projects from the western end of the church and dominates the scene, distracting attention from what little remains of the nave and chancel. The lower level of this tower is square in plan, but where it clears the roof level of the nave it changes to circular, so that the upper portion resembles a round tower. The roof above the western nave of the church was most likely a timber one. However, over the chancel at the eastern end there was an elevated barrel-vaulted ceiling, above which was at least one storey. To the north of the chancel is a small building with the remains of another elevated vaulted ceiling that supported at least one storey above. Previous writers have generally referred to this structure as a sacristy. It is suggested here, however, that this is a chapel, and the implication of this will be discussed. Today there are no obvious traces of the cloister in the field to the south of the church, but the remains are known to survive in the ground. The church received only a brief mention by Harold Leask (1955, 163–4) in his study of Irish Romanesque churches, while Françoise Henry commented that this was 'a very strange ruin' (1970, 176), though her brief description does not betray what perplexed her about the church. More recently the church was described by Tadhg O'Keeffe (1997) and again in a joint paper by O'Keeffe and Carey Bates (2016).

As we shall see, by the end of the eighteenth century, when we have the earliest visual records, the abbey church had suffered large-scale collapse and/or demolition and much of the stone had already been carried off site. The church has reduced further since that time, though the surviving ruins give a somewhat misleading impression of a solid structure. We are left with a fragmentary and incomplete ruin, and there are no humps and bumps in the surrounding field to even suggest that the abbey may have extended much beyond the footprint of the church. However, the complete lack of any rubble of the missing portions of the church should be a warning about how much the site has been sanitized in recent centuries. This is significant in terms of trying to gain a better understanding of the church, because, as is evident from all previous discussions, it is difficult to look beyond the skeletal and emaciated remains we see today and reimagine the full-bodied church that may have stood here at the end of the twelfth century and throughout the late medieval period. If we can overcome our biased first impression of the ruins that greet us only then can we begin to recognize that this was once a large and complex structure.

ANTIQUARIAN COMMENTARY

Gabriel Beranger visited Ferns in 1780 and left us with a brief but intriguing description of the abbey:

> the remains of an ancient building which has a square tower (D) which appears to have been 3 stories high. It has on the top of the wall at one end (E) a round tower, but that as well as D is stuffed full of turf to the verry doors and inaccessible within (Harbison 2004, 141).

Beranger's drawing does not survive, but we are fortunate that it was copied some years later by Austin Cooper (fig. 7.2). This confirms the logical conclusion that Beranger's round tower 'E' is the one still standing at the west end of the nave and clarifies that his three-storey square tower 'D' is the structure on the north side of the chancel. It is clear that substantial parts of the church were already missing by 1780 and though the east end of the chancel and a portion of its south wall still stood at that time, they too disappeared soon after. These small details are important and confirm that the east end of the chancel had a straight end. This is corroborated by another drawing by Cooper (fig. 7.3), this time an original one by the artist himself, showing the church from the

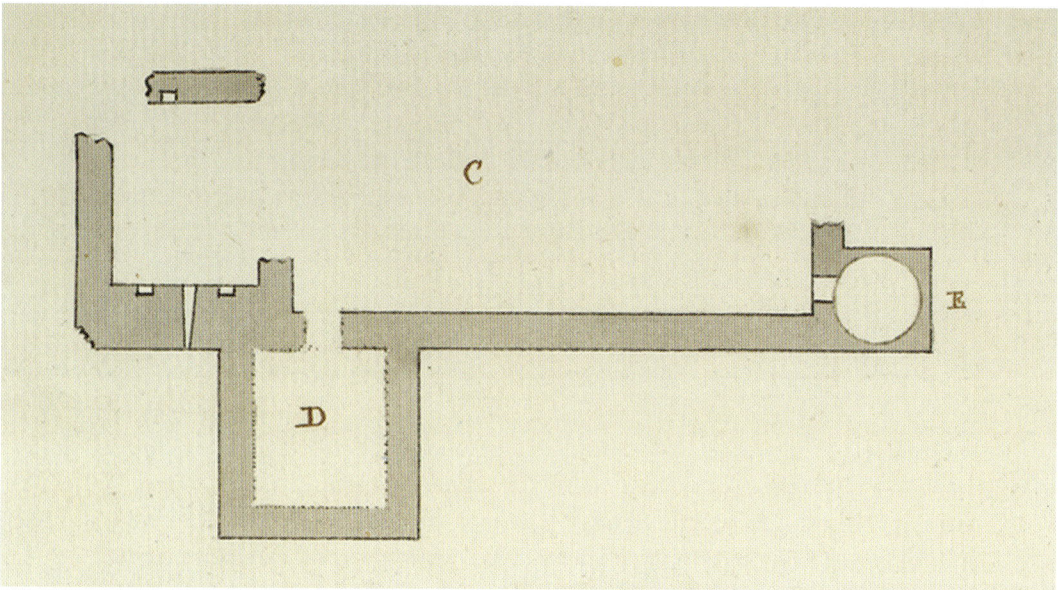

7.2 Ferns: Austin Cooper's 1799 copy of Gabriel Beranger's plan from 1780 (NLI Coo 2122 TX (4)25). The plan of the church is not significantly different to the remains that survive today, except that the east end of the chancel and part of the south wall (both shown here on the *left*) were still standing at that time

south-east, and depicting a tall east end of the chancel, with an opening where the east window should be,[2] and a tall but slender portion of the south wall. Beranger's contention that the square north tower (his tower D) stood three storeys high is interesting, but perhaps misleading. Cooper's own drawing (dated 26 August 1787, but based on a drawing during a visit in June 1786) depicts the church from the south-east, but does not conclusively show the northern compartment rising above its present height. Perhaps a more elevated portion had collapsed during the intervening six years. Another view recorded a few years later (fig. 7.4), this time from the north-west, was published by Jonathan Fisher (1795). In this view we can see the internal elevation of the east end of the northern compartment and the little first-floor window above the remains of the barrel-vaulted ceiling spanning the ground floor. This is precisely how the internal elevation survives today, and rather than representing three floors as suggested by Beranger, we know that the ground floor had an elevated ceiling, with a first floor over the vault. Perhaps Beranger saw evidence for two floors above the vault, but it seems more likely that he presumed there were two floors under the high vaulted ceiling. That said, it is still conceivable that originally there was another level, perhaps even two, above the first floor of the northern compartment.

2 It is curious, however, that Beranger's plan does not illustrate this window.

7.3 Ferns: Cooper's painting of St Mary's Abbey church (*left*), viewed from the south-east, with the cathedral in the background (NLI Coo 2122 TX (2)8). The tall south wall of the chancel, recorded by Beranger six years earlier, is still standing. Note the low wall extending to the left (i.e., south) of the chancel, which probably reflects part of the former claustral range, which no longer survives

7.4 Ferns: view of St Mary's Abbey church from the north-west by Jonathan Fisher, published in 1795

7.6 Ferns: tower at the west end of the nave, viewed from the south-west, perhaps dating from 1840 (RIA Du Noyer Sketches IV (27)). Du Noyer's details of the windows are both on the south side of the square portion of the tower. The middle window here is the lower south window, while that on the right is at the top of the square portion of the tower

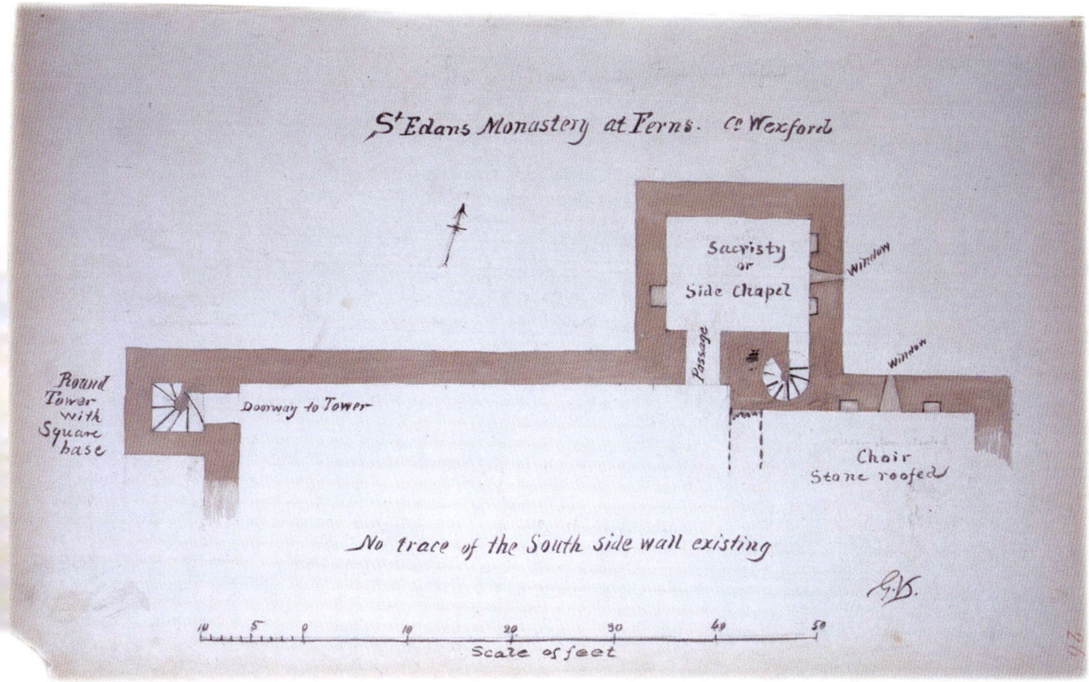

7.5 Ferns: plan of St Mary's Abbey church by Du Noyer, perhaps dating from 1840 (RIA Du Noyer Sketches IV (26))

Sometime later, George Victor du Noyer recorded a plan and several views of the church. The drawings are undated, but we know from the dates of drawings of the nearby castle and granite crosses that Du Noyer was in Ferns in 1840, 1848 and 1862, and there may also have been other unrecorded visits. By now, the east end and south wall of the chancel, recorded by Beranger and Cooper, had long disappeared and in effect the remains of the church were reduced to what survives today. Du Noyer's plan and south-western view of the tower (figs 7.5, 7.6) may have been recorded around 1840, as it seems to pre-date repairs undertaken in 1846 (discussed below), whereas an overall view of the church from the south-east (fig. 7.7) may have been drawn in 1862 as it appears to show the 1846 interventions.

The person responsible for the repairs in 1846 was the then owner Mrs Butler-Bryan (Hore 1911, 173). In fact, these interventions are very much visible today, but we are also fortunate that they are confirmed ('for the guidance of future investigators') in the *Seventy-eighth annual report of the Commissioners of Public Works in Ireland* (Anon.[3] 1910, 13). In particular, the jambs of the niches flanking the north window in the chancel and the arch of the doorway into the north chapel were restored. At the

3 The author was most likely Robert Cochrane.

7.7 Ferns: view of St Mary's Abbey from the south-east (Royal Society of Antiquaries of Ireland; the pencil sketch on which this water colour is based is held by the Royal Irish Academy). This view may date from 1862 as it appears to show repairs undertaken in 1846

west end of the nave, the jagged wall was built up square. Indeed, every surviving corner of the chancel and the north chapel appears to have been previously robbed of its quoins and was squared off with inferior masonry. The tower was also repaired at this time. For example, the jambs and arches of the doorways at both the ground- and first-floor levels were repaired. A clearly modern granite doorway above was inserted, the interior of the tower was lined virtually throughout with brick, and a new level with four tall windows was added to the top to provide a viewing area. The quoins of the south-western and north-western angles had been removed previously and the scars were repaired at this time, which is still detectable in the masonry.

The church was taken into state care in 1880, but it was not until 1909 that conservation works were undertaken by the Office of Public Works. In the end, the repairs were minimal. Butler-Bryan's interventions were retained, and it appears that

7.8 Ferns: St Mary's Abbey church, viewed from the south

for the most part the OPW simply consolidated the standing remains. They did also use this as an opportunity to carry out 'excavations' to calculate the likely extent of the southern side of the church:

> Starting with these remains [i.e., the surviving northern half of the church] as a basis, a ground plan of what was surmised to be the original church was projected on paper, and excavations were made for the remaining walls in the position indicated. The result was the discovery of the foundations/of the original west and south walls of the church and the chancel (ibid., 11–12).

As a result, the OPW confidently rebuilt a few courses of masonry above the foundations of the south side of the church to give some impression of the layout of the church.[4] The term 'excavations' in this instance meant literally digging, and not archaeological investigation. Therefore, without a detailed record of what they found and obviously lacking any of the scientific rigour that would apply today, we need to

4 It is interesting to note that on his earlier plan of the church (fig. 7.5) Du Noyer wrote on the drawing that there was 'no trace of the south side wall existing'. This illustrates just how much of the structure had been

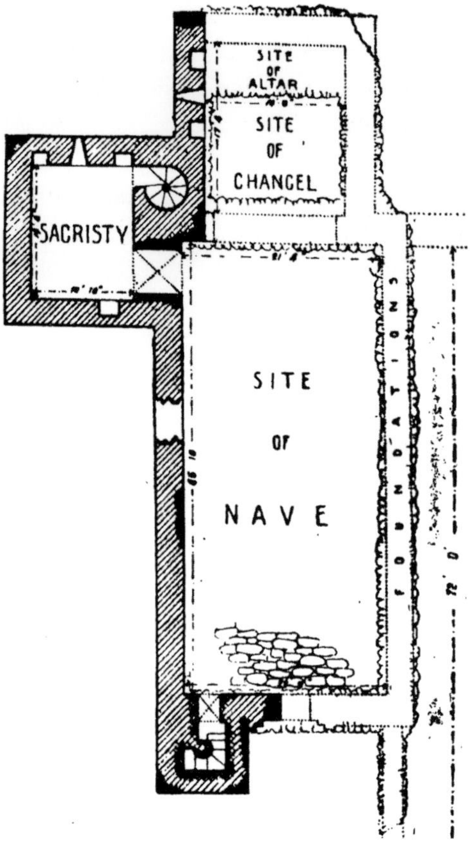

7.9 Ferns: plan of St Mary's Abbey by Robert Cochrane, reproduced in the *Seventy-eighth annual report of the Commissioners of Public Works in Ireland* (1909–10), where the north chapel is mistakenly identified as a sacristy

be somewhat circumspect about the actual meaning of what they found. We should not take the findings at face value, and we cannot be certain of what other evidence may have been found and dismissed without further comment.

TOWER

Starting at the west end of the church, the eye-catching tower stands some 17m tall, but the uppermost 4.5m (including the slender windows here) are modern, dating from 1846. Therefore, we can say that the tower originally stood at least 12.5m tall.[5] The tower is not contained within the footprint of the nave. Instead, it projects 2.38m from what survives of the external face of the west end of the nave. At around 7m above the ground the tower changes from square to a cylindrical or drum shape.

completely removed and how the southern side of the building we see today is entirely a product of the 1909 'excavations' to locate the foundations of the wall here. 5 The line between the original and the modern masonry (clearly seen within the tower rather than from the exterior) is very irregular, so it appears that the modern portion was not built on the original top of the tower, implying that a portion of the tower, perhaps the

O'Keeffe (1997, 59) remarked that the tower appears to be 'added to the original west wall of the church and is later than the portal' and in a later joint paper (O'Keeffe and Carey Bates 2016, 76) restates that this is a later addition, but there appears to be nothing to confirm this and there can be little reason to doubt that the tower was part of the original design.

At ground-floor level is a round-headed doorway. The frame of this doorway has been rebuilt, presumably because they had been significantly robbed of its original stone, but the arch may be original. Today, the interior of the tower is lined with brick, and this facilitated the insertion of a spiral staircase virtually the full height of the tower, as far as the small viewing platform, just below the large openings at the top. This work dates from 1846. In a paper read before the Royal Irish Academy in July 1864, Du Noyer provided a useful observation that must pre-date the insertion of the present staircase, presumably at the time he planned the church (fig. 7.5), which, as suggested above, may have been done in 1840. First, he mentioned only the ground- and first-floor doorways, and not the uppermost doorway we see today. Secondly, he noted that the spiral stairs then terminated at the point at which the tower changed from square to circular. At this point Du Noyer stated that the upper circular portion of the tower 'is then divided into two apartments, the upper one lighted by four narrow, flat-headed windows' (Anon. 1864–8, 132). The four narrow windows Du Noyer mentions are not the four large windows that we now see at the top of the tower. As noted, this portion of the tower was added in 1846. Instead, Du Noyer was referring to four slender windows below this level. The spiral staircase that we see today appears to be entirely modern and, although it may incorporate steps from this earlier stairs, this is not clear today. Indeed, it is also not entirely clear if the staircase that Du Noyer saw was original. For example, 2.8m above the bottom of the tower is a ledge[6] that can be traced around the four sides of the square interior, and there seems little doubt that this was designed to accommodate a wooden floor, i.e., the first floor. It seems likely, therefore, that the original means of ascending the tower was by ladder. This first-floor level roughly corresponds to the first-floor doorway of the tower and windows at both the south and west sides.[7] The external frame of this first-floor doorway is also missing, but part of the internal green-tuff frame (Stephen Mandal, pers. comm.), particularly on the south side, is intact (fig. 7.10). The purpose of a doorway at this level is not immediately obvious. There is no evidence for corbels or joist holes in the north wall of the nave that would suggest that there was gallery at this end of the church, which would be accessed from the tower at this level. In fact, the purpose of this door becomes apparent as we climb to the next level of the tower.

The brick lining within the tower has concealed any evidence for a timber level immediately above the first-floor doorway, but it seems likely that there was one just

roof level, had already collapsed. **6** The internal faces of the tower step back above the ledge, which allowed the insertion of the brick lining within the tower above this level. **7** The south window has green-tuff jambs and is unchanged since it was recorded by Du Noyer *c.*1840 (fig. 7.6).

7.10 Ferns: east side of the western tower, facing into the nave of the church, and (*right*) the internal embrasure of the first-floor doorway. Note the finely cut green tuff forming the south side of the frame. There seems little doubt that the external frame was similarly constructed, but this stone has been robbed in antiquity

below a window on the south side (fig. 7.12) near the top of the square portion of the tower.[8] It is also clear that there was an elaborate east-facing window at this level. This can be seen on the exterior where we today see a tall, narrow opening with a modern granite surround,[9] referred to by some writers as a doorway to the former roof of the nave (fig. 7.10). That this is a window is evident from within the tower, where we can see the remains of an original tall[10] window embrasure with a narrow splay (fig. 7.11). The angle of the green-tuff jambs on the north splay of the embrasure[11] has a slender roll flanked on both sides by a narrow fillet. This form of elaboration seems completely unnecessary on the internal embrasure of a window hidden high up within the tower where it could not be seen. The jamb does appear to be original and *in situ*, however, and the modern brick lining within the tower is built up against the face of the jamb.

8 This window also has green-tuff jambs. Du Noyer's drawing, *c.*1840, seems to depict an ashlar-built window that is somewhat different to the one we see today (fig. 7.6). **9** The external face of the tower is also substantially repaired at this point and the granite surround was likely introduced in 1846. **10** The northern jamb of the window splay is 1.6m tall, though a small stone at the top of the jamb may not be original. **11** The southern splay is entirely modern.

7.11 (*above*) Ferns: internal embrasure of the upper doorway of the tower. Note the narrow splay of the embrasure on the left (north) which features an angle roll flanked by fillets
7.12 Ferns: two windows with green-tuff jambs on the south side of the square portion of the tower. The lower window lights the level of the 'first-floor' doorway, while the upper one at the top of the square portion of the tower is positioned where Du Noyer recorded that the internal stone stairs originally terminated

If we accept that this is an original window, it is notable that it would have faced over the former roof of the church, rather than the interior. The fact that this window has an embellished internal embrasure is highly relevant, and the most likely explanation is that this space[12] served as an anchor hold for an anchorite, with an east-facing window (and perhaps a small altar underneath) for prayer. Above this window there is the evidence for a string course that projected from all four sides of the interior to support a timber floor above, which may represent the sleeping accommodation within the lower portion of the drum section. There was likely another floor level

12 The internal dimensions at this level are 1.45m east–west and 1.35m north–south, which is quite representative of the floor levels throughout the tower.

above this, corresponding to the four slender windows facing the cardinal points. There is no obvious evidence for the original roof level, which may be concealed by the masonry of viewing platform that was added to the top in 1846.

This brings us back to the first-floor doorway below. If the second floor functioned as an anchor hold, the doorway below may have been positioned to allow the anchorite to participate in ceremonies within the church. It may also have provided a place in which communication would be permitted, at a remove, between someone in the church and the anchorite within the tower. It is unfortunate that the doorframe facing into the church is missing, as it is likely that it would have been given special treatment.[13] It might also have accommodated a screen that reduced the visibility of the anchorite from within the church.

NAVE

The detailed analysis of the tower above has provided us with new insights before we have even begun to examine the church itself. So let us now turn our attention to the nave adjoining the tower. The nave is 14.5m east–west, and assuming that the reconstructed foundations on the southern side were correctly identified by the OPW in 1909, this would indicate that it was 6.35m north–south. The only substantive part of the nave still standing is the north wall. The west end of the north wall of the nave survives as a tall, blank section of masonry, some 6m high[14] and 90cm thick (figs 7.13, 7.14). It is notable that there is no evidence for a north doorway or any windows. Towards the east end is an irregular breach that is 1.3m wide at the base but is much wider higher up. It is tempting to suggest the former presence of a window here may be the reason for this breach, but it is notable that Beranger's plan from 1780 shows an uninterrupted wall (fig. 7.2). The main feature of the north wall can be seen on its internal face. At 1.3m above the ground, there a distinct horizontal band of irregularly shaped grey conglomerate stones. Given that the interior of the church was probably rendered with plaster, this was hardly a decorative feature. O'Keeffe has suggested that the lower portion of the wall, beneath this band of conglomerate blocks, 'may be contemporary with the portal of the west wall, while much of the upper fabric may be contemporary with the Round Tower' (1997, 59). There is no corresponding build-line on the external face of the north wall, and rather than representing two entirely different building phases, it is more likely that the horizontal line of conglomerate blocks reflects a brief pause in construction.[15] At the east end of the north wall is a doorway (fig. 7.13), which will be discussed below. High above this doorway (4.7m above ground level) is a slender but broad stone projecting from the inner face of the

13 Below the sill of the door, facing into the nave, is a scar that might imply a sort of balcony feature or projecting ledge facing into the church. **14** This compares with the height of the side walls of the unicameral church at Aghowle in south-west Co. Wicklow (Corlett 2021, 48). **15** At Killadreenan near Newcastle, Co. Wicklow, the

7.13 Ferns: internal elevation of the north wall of the nave

7.14 Ferns: external elevation of the north wall of the nave

north wall, at exactly the point it meets the crossing wall that divided the nave from the chancel. It is possible that this supported a wooden beam that spanned the west end of the nave, and the logical conclusion for such a wooden beam in this position is that it carried a rood cross positioned directly above the now missing chancel arch, which will also be discussed below.

Aside from the reconstructed foundations of the south wall, nothing of this side of the nave survives, and we have no way of knowing the location of the doorway to the former cloister on the south side of the church, though evidence for this may still be forthcoming in any future archaeological excavations here. Unfortunately, we can never hope to establish whether the south wall had any windows, but we can speculate that the answer to this question is that it did, primarily on the basis that they would have been necessary to compensate for the absence of windows on the north side of the nave. We might also surmise, on the basis that the cloister was located on the south side of the nave, any windows here would likely have been elevated, to account for the cloister walk immediately outside the south wall of the church.[16] The logical conclusion is that the interior of the nave was tall, narrow and dark, and any natural light would have been provided by elevated windows on the south side and perhaps a window at the west end.

Indeed, the presence of the cloister on the south side rules out the likelihood that the church had a south doorway, as is sometimes found at Romanesque churches, such as Cormac's Chapel on the Rock of Cashel. This would imply that the now missing west doorway was the main portal of the church. In a Romanesque context, the main portal was very important, and we can expect that this was given special attention in terms of its architectural form and sculptural embellishment. Unfortunately, we have little tangible evidence to demonstrate this at St Mary's. Only a short section of the west end of the nave survives to the south of the tower (fig. 7.15). At a glance, the sudden termination of the wall appears to mark the north side of the west doorway, but this face was entirely rebuilt in 1846. Above this, the elevated overhang preserves the hint of a window splay, but this entire section of masonry was also substantially repaired in 1846. Therefore, the integrity of this doorway and the window above is highly questionable.[17] Externally, on what is today presented as the north side of the doorway, there are two green-tuff bases of a doorframe (fig. 7.15). Though projecting, they are embedded into the bottom of the wall. The outer base is very damaged and

exterior of the south wall of the nave has a similar feature, whereas the exterior of the north wall has a herringbone pattern (Corlett 2015, 22–3). More than likely this represented a brief pause in the construction of the walls, and certainly does not represent different phasing. **16** If we are to truly keep an open mind about the church, it is worth considering the possibility that there was an aisle on the south side of the nave, and that the cloister was situated immediately beyond this. **17** Indeed, Du Noyer's view (fig. 7.6) shows the tower prior to the 1846 repairs, and it is notable that the present window splay is not depicted, and the lower portion seems to extend further south than it does today. If this is accurate, it implies that the bases of the portal are not in situ and the doorway must have been to the south of their current position.

7.15 Ferns: surviving west end of the nave (*left*) with the squared end and elevated splay of a window, and (*right*) the two green-tuff bases of the west portal. The base on the left is disfigured and lacks any distinct shape, while that on the right is clearly bulbous

has no recognisable form, while the inner one is unmistakeably bulbous. O'Keeffe (1997, 57) suggests that these bases are *in situ*, but this seems unlikely, and the issue might only be clarified by archaeological investigation.

Before leaving the nave, it is worth drawing attention to one final feature here. At the west end of the north wall, on the exterior, are the foundations of a wall barely protruding above the grass. The wall extends for 3.7m due north of the west end of the tower. This may reflect the line of a wall that enclosed the precinct around the abbey. If so, all other remains of such a precinct wall are now gone. Another possibility is that it preserves the west end of an aisle that was attached to the exterior of the north wall of the nave. Such aisles provided an external sheltered area for pilgrims and can still be observed elsewhere in Europe. However, the complete lack of corbels or joist holes that would have secured a lean-to roof over such an aisle suggests this explanation is unlikely.

NORTH CHAPEL

At the east end of the north wall, at the point where the nave meets the chancel, is a doorway that provides access to the northern compartment, which, as we shall see, undoubtedly represents a chapel. As noted above, the inner and outer frames of this doorway were rebuilt in 1846. No doubt the frames had been previously robbed of their original stones, presumably green tuff. The core masonry of the arch and the sides of the doorway are original, however, and so we can be confident of the measurements of the doorway.[18] On the west side is a drawbar hole to lock the door from within.

The north chapel measures 3.27m north–south and 4.25m east–west. Immediately on entering the chapel from the nave, on the left (west) side of the doorway, is a niche.[19] The jambs and round-headed arch are formed with cut green tuff (fig. 7.16). Opposing slots roughly midway on either side clearly indicate that the niche was divided with a horizontal shelf, most likely a wooden one. The frame has a sunken surround to accommodate a door, which appears to have been hung from the southern (left) side. The evidence for a door suggests that this niche represents an aumbry for storing the liturgical vessels.

At the east side of the chapel there is a small window, flanked on either side by a round-headed niche (fig. 7.17), perhaps designed to display statues. The arrangement is like that found within the chancel (discussed below), however, rather than being placed at the same level, the niches here are positioned well below the elevated window. The green-tuff window frame (72cm high and 18cm wide) is formed by a single jamb on the south side and three on the north side, and it is spanned by a single

7.16 Ferns: round-headed niche on the west side of the north chapel, beside the doorway from the nave

18 2.6m high and 1.06m wide. **19** This niche measures 63.5cm wide, 49cm deep and originally about 87cm high, but the base has been robbed out.

7.17 Ferns: interior of the north chapel, accessed via a round-headed doorway from the nave (right). At the east is a window, flanked on either side by a small round headed niche. In the corner is a narrow doorway to a spiral stairs to the upper levels. Note the string course above the doorways and rounded vault forming an elevated ceiling of the chapel and a floor for the level above

lintel. The frame has an external surround (fig. 7.19), while the internal embrasure is quite narrow (just 52cm wide) and the internal sill plunges steeply.

The northern niche was heavily reconstructed in 1846. The jamb on the north side of the niche is formed by a single piece set vertically, which appears to be original. The three green-tuff voussoirs, including the springer, on the north side are original, but the key stone of the arch, the southern voussoirs, the southern jambs and the slate sill all appear to be inserted. The niche flanking the south side of the window is also partly repaired. The original jambs on the south side are missing, but the green-tuff voussoirs and northern jambs are intact.

On the south wall of the chapel is an elevated string course.[20] Above this is a shallow rebate,[21] which facilitates the springing of the vaulted ceiling (fig. 7.17). Only a small

20 This string course is 2.9m above the internal ground level. It averages 8cm thick and projects 10cm. On the opposing north wall, only a short section of the corresponding string course survives at the east end. The rest of the north wall survives to an average height of 2.4m and is substantially rebuilt. **21** The rebate is 78cm above the top of the string coursing.

7.18 Ferns: lower steps of the spiral stairs leading to the rooms above the vaulted ceilings of the north chapel and the chancel and (*right*) a similar spiral stairs within the tower flanking the south side of Cormac's Chapel on the Rock of Cashel

7.19 Ferns: narrow window lighting the east side of the spiral stairs (*left*) and (*right*) the exterior of the east window of the north chapel

7.20 Ferns: (*left*) east end of the first floor above the barrel vault of the north chapel and (*right*) exterior of the east window of the first floor of the north chapel

7.21 Ferns: external elevation of the east end of the north chapel. Note the elevated set-back below the upper window, which corresponds roughly with the top of the internal barrel vault. The top has been reconstructed to give the impression of a gable, but this is likely to be misleading

portion of the eastern end of the vaulted ceiling survives, and the soffit of this vault is 5.22m above the internal ground level. At the east end of the south wall is a narrow, round-headed doorway (fig. 7.17). The original frame has been robbed out and repaired, except for two original green-tuff voussoirs (including the springer) on the eastern side. Inside the doorway is a spiral stair with a rounded newel on the five lowest steps, which are in situ (fig. 7.18). Unfortunately, the steps above this have been robbed out. Lighting the east side of the stairs as it rises is a slender window with a triangular head (fig. 7.19). The jambs and head of the frame[22] have a narrow external chamfer that meets the internal splay to form a pointed edge. The stairs provide access to the level above the barrel vault and probably also to the level above the barrel vault over the chancel (discussed below). Only the east end of the first floor survives above the barrel vault and has sloping sides that are suggestive of a gable (figs 7.20, 7.21). However, this is misleading, and the sloping sides have been entirely reconstructed. Therefore, we cannot be certain whether it was the only level above the barrel vault. It features an east-facing round-headed window.[23] On the exterior of the east wall of the chapel is a sloped set-back, roughly the same height as the top of the internal barrel vault.

CHANCEL

As with the nave of the church, only the north side of the chancel remains. The eastern end of this wall was neatly squared off in 1846, thereby removing all trace of the scar of the east gable end of the church. The top of the foundations of the south wall of the chancel (including the south-eastern corner) was discovered in 1909, and partly reconstructed to show the line of the walls. If correct, these indicate that the chancel measured internally 5.4m east–west and 4.72m north–south.[24] At the western end of the chancel, an elevated portion of overhanging masonry projecting from the north wall is all that remains of the wall that divided it from the nave. Below this, the scar of this former dividing wall was patched up in 1846, thereby giving the false impression that there was no chancel arch. The overhanging masonry is 1.05cm thick and capable of accommodating an arch of up to three orders, but this is entirely speculative (fig. 7.22). Indeed, all evidence for the former chancel arch here is missing, except three loose fragments;[25] a base, a column and a capital, all of which belong to one order of the arch (fig. 7.22). The engaged column comprises a heavy angle roll that is unadorned. The base is simply a continuation of the column with only a series of incised horizontal bands forming a crude torus to punctuate the column from the

22 78cm high and 5.5cm wide. **23** The head of the internal embrasure is flat and evidently reconstructed. **24** Notably, the foundations of most of the east-end wall were not reconstructed in 1909, implying that little evidence survived or was found at that time. **25** Presently stored at the base of the west tower.

7.22 Ferns: this capital, column and base are the only surviving parts of the chancel arch. On the right can be seen the patched-up masonry where the chancel arch was removed, and the scar repaired

base, the body of which has incised zigzags creating a band of chevrons. Unlike the base, a plain, slender collar punctuates the junction of the column and the capital, which has a simple leaf pattern. Above this, the abacus has a band of incised saltire crosses.

The north side of the chancel is lit by a centrally placed window (fig. 7.24). This is quite small,[26] and is flanked by two niches, reminiscent of the similar arrangement within the north chapel, described above. The window frame is formed by a single jamb on the east side and three jambs on the west. Externally, the frame (except the sill) has a recessed surround. Internally, the narrow, splayed embrasure (1.52m high) inclines slightly and is formed by three large jambs on either side, simply embellished with a flat chamfer on the angle, though this does not follow through on the voussoirs of the rear arch (fig. 7.25). The window is quite elevated, and the sill of the embrasure is 2.02m above current internal ground level (fig. 7.23). The window is flanked on either side by a round-headed niche. Both niches were significantly reconstructed in 1846, and many of the stones are not original, or at least have been reused incorrectly

26 The window opening is 69cm high and inclines slightly (16.5cm wide at base and 15cm wide at top).

7.23 Ferns: north side of the chancel, including the first-floor room above the former barrel-vaulted ceiling

in the repairs. For example, the western niche (to the left of the window) has on its eastern side a single jamb-stone that features a roll on two angles: that on the eastern angle is concealed by the jamb of the adjoining window embrasure (figs 7.24, 7.33). This jamb must have been reused here in the 1846 repairs and no doubt originated elsewhere in the church. The eastern niche has also been repaired. The jamb on the west side has a weathered angle roll but is probably not original to the niche.[27] On the east side of the niche are three jambs. The lower jamb has an inverted cushion stop, immediately above which is a torus punctuating the bottom of the angle roll of the engaged column (fig. 7.25), which is notably more substantial than the mouldings on any of the other jambs here. The angle roll forming the top of the jamb is capped with a slender abacus that projects into the niche.

Directly above the window is a horizontal rebate (3.68m above the internal ground level) from which springs the surviving portion of the vaulted ceiling over the chancel.

27 The masonry between this jamb and the eastern jamb of the window is clearly modern.

7.24 *(above)* Ferns: window and flanking niches on the north side of the chancel

7.25 (*left*) Ferns: chamfer on the inner angles of the jambs of the window embrasure (note the chamfer does not continue over the rear arch) and (*right*) the eastern side of the niche flanking the east side of the window

7.26 Ferns: spring of the vaulted ceiling and two supporting ribs on the north side of the chancel. The corbel on the left (i.e., west) has different tooling and seems to be a modern replica. It is quite possible that there originally was a rib here, and there may also have been a fourth rib on the right (i.e., east) of the two surviving ones flanking the north window

7.27 Cashel, Co. Tipperary: flat ribs under the vaulted ceiling over the nave of Cormac's Chapel

This was evidently a rounded vault (similar to that spanning the north chapel) that was supported by at least two flat-sectioned transverse arches set deep into the vault (fig. 7.26).[28] These arches (especially the eastern one) are formed by horizontal blocks with alternating vertical pairs.[29] The bases of the springers are chamfered and feature small sockets (now in-filled with stones) which O'Keeffe (1997, 60) suggested accommodated metal tie-rods. Alternatively, they may have secured the temporary framework for supporting the arches while the vault was being constructed. It has been suggested by O'Keeffe and Carey Bates (2016, 77–8) that the vault may represent a later insertion to replace a timber ceiling that previously spanned the chancel. There is, however, no evidence that the vaulted ceiling over the adjoining north chapel is secondary, and there seems no reason to suggest that the vaulted ceiling of the chancel was not part of the original design. The best comparison for the flat arches at St Mary's can be found at Cormac's Chapel on the Rock of Cashel, where they are a feature of the vaulted ceiling over the nave (fig. 7.27). Indeed, the intact ceiling at Cashel gives us a very good impression of the former ceiling at Ferns.

Externally, the north wall features an elevated set-back, at the same level as that on the exterior of the east end of the north chapel and reflecting the top of the vault over the chancel. The lower portion of a narrow window is placed mid-way along the north wall of the upper level above the chancel (fig. 7.23). Unfortunately, this upper level is heavily truncated and there is no surviving evidence to confirm if there was another vaulted ceiling above this, perhaps with a stone roof, or if the upper storey simply had a timber-built roof.

Returning to the ground floor, the north window of the chancel is quite elevated, and this reflects a significant drop in ground level at the eastern end of the church, compared to the west end. Underneath the north window of the chancel, much of the internal face of the wall has been quite crudely repaired, most likely infilling gaps where stone was removed and robbed-out. This gives the impression of a flat, vertical face, but one large stone block (the face of which is broken) and several smaller stones near the ground project slightly into the chancel. The significance of this is not entirely clear, but on his plan of the church from about 1909 (fig. 7.9), Robert Cochrane depicts a dashed line across the chancel at this point to show the 'site of altar'. He does not elaborate in his written description, but the implication from this annotation of the plan is that he concluded the east end of the chancel had a raised floor to accommodate the altar. In fact, it is worth considering the possibility that there was a crypt beneath the chancel, and the 1846 repairs may have concealed the scar of the robbed-out vault that formerly spanned such a crypt.

28 A third rib is suggested by a single springer on the western side. However, this stone has punch dressing that is noticeably different to the diagonal tooling on the other carved stones here and throughout the rest of the building, implying that it is a later replacement, perhaps quite modern. However, based on the spacing of the other two ribs we can surmise that there was a third rib roughly in this position, and perhaps a fourth closer to the east end of the chancel. **29** The ribs are 26.5cm wide and project 10cm.

DISCUSSION

Even though nearly two-thirds of the abbey church is missing today, we can say a lot about its original form, even where features are missing. For example, the lack of original quoins is an issue throughout the church. These seem to have been robbed in antiquity, and the angles surviving today were all repaired in 1846. Though it is difficult to confirm, it is likely that they were originally green tuff, and evidence for their use as such can be found at Templeshannon in Enniscorthy and Ballybrennan near Bree (fig. 7.28). Such green tuff was also widely used in the Romanesque church at nearby Clone (ch. 5). Here at St Mary's, it was used almost exclusively for the windows and niches,[30] the arches supporting the vault over the chancel, and the few surviving fragments of the west doorway and the chancel arch. Clearly, a lot of architectural features, in particular doorframes, have been removed at some point since the dissolution of the abbey and in particular the green tuff appears to have been prized and presumably reused for building projects elsewhere. One example of this modern repurposing of green tuff is the cap house over St Aidan's Well, constructed in 1847, only a year after the repairs were undertaken throughout St Mary's. This square structure has a stone roof, which is built on a cornice that is supported on all four sides and angles by a series of twenty green-tuff corbels (fig. 7.29). These corbels all take the form of inverted cones. They are plain but preserve the diagonal tooling typical of Romanesque stone cutting. It is likely that these corbels originally supported a roof-level cornice of a nearby Romanesque church, perhaps St Mary's.

Until further fragments of the west doorway are discovered, it is not possible to speculate further, but given that this appears to have been the only entrance to the church, it seems safe to assume that it was given special treatment with relatively elaborate carvings. Only two basal stones survive, indicating a portal with at least two orders, but there may have been more. The bulbous base is a feature also found on the west doorway at Killeshin, Co. Laois, and at the base of a crossing arch at Baltinglass Abbey, Co. Wicklow (fig. 7.30), both closely linked with none other than Diarmait Mac Murchada. However, they are also a feature of the chancel arches of the Nun's Church at Clonmacnoise (Ní Ghrádaigh 2003) and St Carthage's Church at Rahan, Co. Offaly (FitzPatrick and O'Brien 1998), and the form need not be uniquely associated with Mac Murchada's patronage of church building.

The tower flanking the west doorway is particularly interesting. O'Keeffe and Carey Bates suggest that the first-floor doorway of the tower may have had 'a ritual use beyond bell-ringing' (2016, 81). This is an extension of O'Keeffe's argument elsewhere (2004) that the doorways of Irish round towers may have served ceremonial functions, hence they invariably face towards the contemporary church. The tower has

30 Yellow sandstone is also a feature of the niches, but everywhere this is found it seems to be the result of the 1846 repairs and it cannot be demonstrated conclusively that it is original to this church.

7.28 Green-tuff quoins surviving at (*left*) Templeshannon in Enniscorthy and (*right*) Ballybrennan near Bree

7.29 Ferns: green-tuff corbels reused to support the roof of St Aidan's Well, constructed in 1847. The provenance of these corbels is unclear, but it is tempting to suggest that they formed part of an elevated corbel table at the wall tops of either St Mary's Church, or perhaps the nearby cathedral

7.30 (*left*) Bulbous base of a crossing arch at Baltinglass Abbey, Co. Wicklow, and (*right*) the west portal at Killeshin, Co. Laois

7.31 Maastricht, Netherlands: rounded towers on the north-west and south-west angles of the early eleventh-century westwork of the Basiliek van Onze-Lieve-Vrouw (Basilica of Our Lady)

understandably attracted much attention. O'Keeffe suggests 'it sufficiently resembles Ireland's free-standing Round Towers of the tenth, eleventh and twelfth centuries to be regarded as an example of that type of monument' (1997, 57). Brian Lalor asked, 'if it is not an early medieval Round Tower, then what is it?' (1999, 229). Both ignored George Lennox Barrow who argued that 'The round portion may have been influenced by round towers, but it is not one itself' (1979, 196). Of course, the round upper section of the tower makes a tempting comparison with more conventional Irish round towers, but this is somewhat misguided. Indeed, the difference is best illustrated by the fact that the internal plan of the tower is square, even within the upper drum section, whereas the internal plan of round towers is, without exception, circular. It is argued above that the tower originally had timber floors throughout, and the level at the top of the square portion, with its elaborate east-facing window, served as an anchor hold. If so, this would certainly explain the potential 'ritual use' of the first-floor doorway as a place where an anchorite could participate, albeit at a remove, in the religious ceremonies taking place in the church. To the congregation attending services in the church, the very presence of an anchorite close behind them, who was enclosed in full-time prayer for their salvation, would have been a very powerful presence indeed. The mystery of this presence within the room, but not quite in the room at the same time, may have been heightened by a screen that inhibited a direct view of the recluse. This elevated doorway may also have provided a sufficiently distanced space for an anchorite to communicate when required and, as has been pointed out by Colmán Ó Clabaigh, a recluse may have to 'conduct necessary business with servants and benefactors, and to offer counsel and conversation to visitors' (2010, 174).

Whatever about the function of the space within the tower, its positioning directly beside the (now missing) west portal, the main doorway into the church, would undoubtedly have made a powerful statement to anyone approaching the abbey in the later twelfth century. In fact, this positioning of tower and portal evokes images of the westwork of continental church architecture. The early eleventh-century westwork of the Basiliek van Onze-Lieve-Vrouw (Basilica of Our Lady) in Maastricht in the Netherlands features engaged rounded towers at both the north-west and south-west angles (fig. 7.31). The overall effect is somewhat different to Ferns, but it demonstrates the use of circular or rounded towers elsewhere that might have influenced the intention of the Wexford tower. Throughout much of central Europe, the westwork had been an important architectural feature of churches since the ninth-century rule of Emperor Charlemagne and continued to evolve during the tenth century (for example, St Pantaleon's in Cologne) and throughout the eleventh century (for example, St Boniface's in Freckenhorst, Westphalia). This form of architecture is not evident in Ireland prior to the twelfth century, but the introduction of both Romanesque architecture and new religious orders, including the Augustinians, is a clear sign of continental influence arriving in Ireland on a scale not previously seen.

Cormac's Chapel on the Rock of Cashel is undoubtedly a product of this new influence, but other than several early Cistercian abbey churches, there are few examples that overtly display such external inspiration. At St Mary's in Ferns, however, there are subtle clues that the church here did not conform to more the conservative interpretation of Romanesque found at Monaincha, Co. Tipperary, or Kilmalkedar, Co. Kerry, but was attempting to emulate more closely fashions outside Ireland.[31] It also introduces the question, could the symmetry here at Ferns have been similarly completed with a second tower on the south side of the doorway? Only archaeological excavation might confirm this, but there is a strong case for suggesting that a tower on the south side of the doorway was part of the original plan, even if it was never implemented. Indeed, the evidence presented here that the north tower served as an anchor hold strengthens the suggestion that there was a second tower, as the canons here would likely have required a bell tower that was independent of the anchorite's cell. Even before we have set foot within the church, we already have a different impression of this church.

Though not obvious today, we can say with some certainty that the nave of the church was quite dark. The tall north wall does not appear to have had any windows, but the south wall may have had windows lighting this side of the nave. Given that there seems to have been a cloister on the south side, these southern windows must have been quite elevated and probably provided very limited light into the nave. It might also be expected that there was an elevated window above the former west portal.

An unusual feature of the church is the drop in floor level (50cm) from west to east, which is very noticeable standing at the west end of the church where the portal would have been. This is a feature, though less dramatic, at Clone church nearby, as well as the Cistercian abbey at Holycross, Co. Tipperary, but contrasts with the Cistercian abbey at Dunbrody in the south of the county, where the floor rises from the west towards the high altar at the east. As noted above, however, the present levels are somewhat deceiving. The height of the north window of the chancel above the ground suggests that the present ground level is significantly lower than the original floor level of the church. It is possible that the chancel (or at least the eastern part) originally had a suspended timber floor, which might have compensated somewhat for the different levels throughout the church. Another possibility is that the chancel was designed to accommodate a low crypt, such as an example under the chancel at Tuamgraney, Co.

31 In April 1161, Gilla na Náem Laignech, a former bishop of the neighbouring diocese at Glendalough in Wicklow (having resigned the see in 1157), died as the head of the Irish community or Schottenkloster of Wurzburg (Flanagan 2010, 97). However, Ó Riain (2011) suggests that this was a scribal error for Gilla na Náem, bishop of Cloyne. Regardless, this is just one example of documented direct ecclesiastical contact with central Europe prior to the arrival of the Anglo-Normans (and indeed the French Cistercians), and it should be no surprise that architectural influences from there should be present in Ireland, alongside nearer influences from Britain and western France.

7.32 Ferns: lightly incised chevron pattern on the base from the former chancel arch suggests that they were intended as guide-lines for a painted pattern

7.33 (*above*) Ferns: reconstructed niche flanking the west side of the north window of the chancel. Note the righthand side of the niche has a jamb stone with a pair of angle rolls and the righthand roll is partly concealed by the adjoining jamb of the window embrasure. This stone clearly originated elsewhere within the church, and one possibility is that it formed part of blind arcade, such as the arcades flanking the west doorway at Roscrea, Co. Tipperary (*right*)

Clare. This would explain the rough masonry, patched up in 1846, below the north window of the chancel, and it is suggested above that this represents the repaired scar of a robbed-out stone vault over a crypt. Ultimately, the former presence of a crypt can only be confirmed or ruled-out by archaeological excavation. It is generally agreed that St Mary's was a royal chapel, and if it was also intended, as has been suggested, as the mortuary chapel of Diarmait Mac Murchada, a mortuary crypt under the altar to accommodate a high-status tomb would be anticipated.

It is difficult to reimagine the chancel arch that divided the nave and chancel. With only a few stones of one of the piers surviving (and no voussoirs), we do not have sufficient information to propose a reconstruction based on how many orders or what scale the arch may have been. However, one feature does stand out in the surviving stones: they are quite plain with only light-touch decoration (fig. 7.32). This suggests that the arch did not have complex relief carvings, such as at St Saviour's Church at Glendalough, Co. Wicklow (Corlett 2017) or the Nun's Church at Clonmacnoise, Co. Offaly (Ní Ghrádaigh 2003). This might be interpreted as a deliberate display of restraint in terms of ornamental embellishment of the chancel. However, Augustinian churches elsewhere in Ireland during the period in question are not known for sculptural restraint, as is evident at both the aforementioned churches at Glendalough and Clonmacnoise. Instead, it is worth considering that this sculptural restraint was intentional because it was designed to complement an entirely different form of artistic expression, and the rather plain fragments of the chancel arch might reflect a preference for painted ornament.

The suggestion that the chancel arch was designed to be primarily decorated with paint is supported when we try to reimagine the chancel itself. Cooper's drawing from 1786 records the now-missing gable with a single, relatively small window lighting the altar. It may have been slightly bigger than the surviving north window, but it is tempting to suggest that the latter was originally mirrored by a similar window in the missing south wall.[32] The niches flanking the north window were certainly intended for the display of religious statues. The east window may also have had flanking niches, or perhaps a more elaborate blind arcade, such as we find at Cormac's Chapel, and the jamb stone with a pair of angle rolls reused in the niche flanking the west side of the north window may originally have formed part of such a blind arcade (fig. 7.33). Alternatively, such blind arcades are also an external feature of some Romanesque churches, such as the west façade at Roscrea, Co. Tipperary (fig. 7.33).

If we accept that the chancel had a relatively small, single-light east window in addition to the surviving small north window (and perhaps a similar south window), these would have provided very little light into the chancel and their small scale must have contrasted the tall, vaulted ceiling, supported on noticeably plain ribs. Furthermore, the lack of decorative carvings throughout is also very telling because it was so clearly deliberate. These features combined are highly suggestive of a chancel that was designed as a large canvas to accommodate frescoes with elaborate figurative scenes, while the plain embrasures of the windows, and simple mouldings of flanking niches, ribs of the ceiling, and perhaps the chancel arch, were painted with decorative colour schemes and patterns. Evidence for this can be found at Cormac's Chapel, but

32 Beranger's plan (fig. 7.2) records a short section of the south wall still standing in 1780. He depicts a single niche here but does not record a window. This might imply there was no window lighting the south side of the chancel, but this would be highly unusual and it is notable that his plan does not show the east window subsequently recorded by Cooper.

7.34 Cashel, Co. Tipperary: view of the east end of Cormac's Chapel, with the elevated towers flanking the tall chancel

perhaps the best example to illustrate what St Mary's may have resembled is St Mary's Church at Kempley near Gloucester (Thurlby 2022).

This brings us to the upper floor of the chancel. Only the north side survives today. Here we find a window, and we might confidently suggest that there was an opposing window on the south side, and perhaps an east-facing window. It is worth noting that the upper room is quite truncated, and though it is not possible to determine how much of the structure is missing, this east end of the church was originally taller than the nave, perhaps even forming a low tower. This is quite unusual in an Irish church context, and a more common arrangement would be a chancel that is somewhat smaller than its adjoining nave, such as at Monaincha, Co. Tipperary, or, in the case of contemporary Cistercian churches, the nave and chancel were typically of equal height.

The north chapel is of particular interest. It is accessed by a doorway from the nave, beside the chancel arch. Though previously referred to as a sacristy (Anon. 1910, 12), this is certainly incorrect. The ground floor has an east window with flanking statue niches and elevated vaulted ceiling, and there can be little doubt that it served as a chapel and not a sacristy. Such a space might have served as an anchor hold or chapel for an anchorite, as suggested for the north chapel of Cormac's Chapel (Ó Carragáin 2010, 290–1), but we have already seen evidence that implies an anchor hold in the west tower at St Mary's. Indeed, the presence of the staircase here providing access to the upper rooms of the chapel and (apparently) the chancel rules out any likelihood that this was a sufficiently segregated anchor hold. By the same token, the presence of this stairs also confirms that this would not have been a secure sacristy. As noted above, only the east wall survives of the room above the high elevated ceiling and the reconstructed impression of a gable here is entirely fabricated. This raises the fundamental question, could there have been a tall tower above the north chapel, rising high above the roof of the chancel. While this is somewhat speculative, the elevated set-back on the east face of the north chapel is indicative of a tall elevation that required horizontal division, a feature of the towers at Cormac's Chapel and the tall west façade at St Crónán's, Roscrea, though in both cases string courses are used to divide the elevations.

We have no upstanding remains of the south side of the chancel (other than the base of the wall reconstructed in 1909), but a south chapel, or at the very least a sacristy, would be anticipated here. In this way, a southern chapel or sacristy would have completed the symmetry of the north chapel and provided the church with a cruciform plan. Within more conventional Romanesque architecture in Ireland, a cruciform church is quite rare, though examples are known, such as Cormac's Chapel and St Carthage's Church at Rahan (FitzPatrick and O'Brien 1998, 57–60). However, with the Continental monastic influence that was becoming well-established in Ireland by the 1160s, a cruciform plan would be expected, and it is worth recalling that the large cruciform church at Mellifont Abbey, Co. Louth, was already consecrated a few years earlier, while the construction of the cruciform church at Baltinglass Abbey, Co. Wicklow, was nearing completion (Stalley 1987). Instead of a simple nave, chancel and curious northern compartment, the suggestion that St Mary's had a cruciform plan gives us another entirely new perspective of the overall building. Indeed, we can potentially take our new outlook one step further. If we can accept the possibility that a tower above the north chapel flanked the north side of the chancel, it would be symmetrically logical to expect that a similar tower flanked the southern side of the chancel. Such flanking towers were common throughout Europe during the twelfth century, and this is precisely the arrangement that we can see closer to home at Cormac's Chapel (fig. 7.34).

CONCLUSION

The relative simplicity of the surviving ruins of St Mary's Abbey church appears to have restrained commentators from completing a comprehensive analysis of the building. This has resulted in a failure to look beyond the standing remains and to attempt to understand the overall structure, including what no longer survives. If we begin to imagine a cruciform church, with a low tower over the chancel (and perhaps with a crypt below), north and south chapels extending off the chancel, with perhaps tall towers overhead, we now begin to reimagine a much more impressive church more in keeping with Cormac's Chapel at Cashel. Add to this the possibility that the west portal had a southern flanking tower mirroring the surviving north tower, and we now have a complex Romanesque church without parallel in Ireland, but with numerous precedents in continental Europe. The paucity of high-quality carvings has perhaps also led to dismissive views of the church, when in fact it seems clear that sculpture was deliberately sacrificed in order to prioritize a painted interior, particularly within the chancel.

BIBLIOGRAPHY

Anon. 1864–8. 'Proceedings and papers'. *Journal of the Royal Society of Antiquaries of Ireland*, 8, 109–39.

Barrow, G.L. 1979. *The round towers of Ireland: a study and gazetteer*. Dublin.

Bhreathnach, E. and Dowling, G. 2021. 'Forming an episcopal see and an Augustinian foundation in medieval Ireland: the case of Ferns, Co. Wexford'. *Proceedings of the Royal Irish Academy*, 121C, 191–226.

Bradshaw, B. 1974. *The dissolution of the religious orders in Ireland under Henry VIII*. Cambridge.

Corlett, C. 2015. 'Something fishy about the church at Killadreenan'. *Archaeology Ireland*, 29:2, 21–3.

Corlett, C. 2017. *Glendalough*. Wicklow.

Corlett, C. 2021. 'An archaeological survey of Aghowle church, Co. Wicklow'. *Journal of Irish Archaeology*, 30, 141–66.

Fisher, J. 1795. *Scenery of Ireland*. Dublin.

FitzPatrick, E. and O'Brien, C. 1998. *The medieval churches of county Offaly*. Dublin.

Flanagan, M.T. 2010. *The transformation of the Irish church in the twelfth century*. Woodbridge.

Harbison, P. 2004. 'Barralet and Beranger's antiquarian sketching tour through Wicklow and Wexford in the autumn of 1780'. *Proceedings of the Royal Irish Academy*, 104C, 131–90.

Henry, F. 1970. *Irish art in the Romanesque period (1020–1170AD)*. London.

Hore, P.H. 1911. *History of the town and county of Wexford, vol. 6: history of the towns and castles of Ferns and Enniscorthy with notes on some of the parishes*. London.

Lalor, B. 1999. *The Irish round tower: origins and architecture explored*. Cork.

Leask, H.G. 1955. *Irish churches and monastic buildings, vol. 1: the first phases and the Romanesque*. Dundalk.

Ní Ghrádaigh, J. 2003. 'But what exactly did she give?: Derbforgaill and the Nuns' Church at Clonmacnoise'. In King, H.A. (ed.), *Clonmacnoise studies*, 2, 175–207. Dublin.

Nicholls, K.W. 1985. 'The charter of John, lord of Ireland, to the Cistercian abbey of Baltinglass'. *Peritia*, 4, 187–206.

Ó Carragáin, T. 2010. *Churches in early medieval Ireland*. London.

Ó Clabaigh, C. 2010. 'Anchorites in late medieval Ireland'. In McAvoy, L.H. (ed.), *Anchoritic traditions of medieval Europe*, 153–77. Woodbridge.

O'Keeffe, T. and Carey Bates, R. 2016. 'The abbey and cathedral of Ferns, 1111–1253'. In Doyle, I. and Browne, B. (eds), *Medieval Wexford: essays in memory of Billy Colfer*, 73–96. Dublin.

O'Keeffe, T. 1997. 'Diarmait Mac Murchada and Romanesque Leinster'. *Journal of the Royal Society of Antiquaries of Ireland*, 127, 52–79.

O'Keeffe, T. 2004. *Ireland's round towers: buildings, rituals and landscapes of the early Irish church*. Stroud.

Ó Riain, D. 2011. 'A Glendalough bishop in Germany? The Four Masters and the three Gilla na Náems'. In Doherty, C., Doran, L. and Kelly, M. (eds), *Glendalough: City of God*, 177–82. Dublin.

Stalley, R. 1987. *The Cistercian monasteries of Ireland: an account of the history, art and architecture of the White Monks in Ireland from 1142 to 1540*. London and New Haven, CT.

Thurlby, M. 2022. 'Photo essay: painted masonry and ornament in English Romanesque architecture'. *Peregrinations: Journal of Medieval Art and Architecture*, 8:3, 88–128.

CHAPTER EIGHT

Chasing St Aidan's monastery at Ferns

BARRY LACEY, MICHAEL 'BODHI' ROGERS, DENIS SHINE, GER DOWLING, ANNE-JULIE LAFAYE, DAVID McILREAVY & STEPHEN MANDAL

INTRODUCTION

Ferns was an important place in the medieval period as the capital of the kingdom of Uí Chennselaig (chs 2, 3). Much of the town's renown derives from its association with Diarmait Mac Murchada, king of Leinster (d. AD1171), who established Ferns as his royal caput, and later infamously invited an Anglo-Norman mercenary force to Ireland. The importance of later medieval Ferns is reflected in its built heritage, which includes the remains of a thirteenth-century cathedral, the twelfth-century Augustinian foundation of St Mary's Abbey and the impressive thirteenth-century Marshal castle near the western limits of the town. The castle may have been largely built by William Marshal, 2nd earl of Pembroke (1190–1231), but it had several earlier incarnations during the later twelfth to the early thirteenth centuries (Corlett 2012). Perhaps unsurprisingly, it is the later medieval period that emerges most clearly from the results of modern archaeological investigations in the Ferns area, which includes about sixteen excavations in the vicinity of the castle alone (fig. 8.1; appendix 8.1).

In the last few years, excavations have also contributed greatly to our understanding of early medieval Ferns, illuminating, for instance, the potential circuit and dating of the boundary (termon/terminus) of Aidan's monastery. This work includes development-led excavations in Castleland (McLoughlin 2020; McLoughlin and Stafford 2020) and in advance of the Ferns Village Rehabilitation scheme by both TVAS Ireland Ltd and Irish Archaeological Consultancy Ltd (IAC) (Taylor and Hurley 2021; ch. 11), as well as recent investigations undertaken as part of an international research project by the Irish Archaeology Field School (IAFS) in the immediate vicinity of St Mary's Abbey (Shine et al. 2021; Shine and Mandal 2022; see also ch. 9). The latter work built on the results of a previous geophysical survey conducted in 2015 by the 'Monastic Ireland: landscape, community and settlement' project, which revealed a wealth of features in the field surrounding St Mary's Abbey, including segments of two very large enclosures that appear to mark the eastern boundary of the early monastery (Bhreathnach and Dowling 2021).

Prior to the 2015 geophysical survey, the nature and scale of the early monastic enclosure was largely unknown. This investigation, however, coupled with the results

8.1 Ferns: map featuring all archaeological excavations undertaken to date. A square indicates an excavation of the possible early medieval enclosures; numbers relate to Appendix 8.1 below

of previous excavations, prompted new ideas, with Ian Doyle (2016, 54), for instance, suggesting that the early enclosure was defined by an inner ditch measuring about 200m in diameter and an outer ditch some 300–350m across (fig. 8.2). More recently, following the discovery of a 115m-long segment of an early medieval ditch in Castleland (McLoughlin 2020; McLoughlin and Stafford 2020), Catherine McLoughlin speculated that this feature represents the western limit of the monastic enclosure, implying a much larger monastic site with a diameter in excess of 500m.

These discoveries relating to early medieval Ferns have coincided with a renewed interest in the study of the monastic landscapes of early medieval Ireland in general. Such studies have examined the formation and organization of monastic and ecclesiastical settlements, how they compared to monastic sites across Europe, and the transition that took place in the twelfth century (before and after the arrival of the Anglo-Normans) especially in the context of the broader ecclesiastical reforms taking place in Ireland. As at Ferns, research and community-led archaeological investigations at a number of other sites have expanded the archaeological evidence available to researchers, and complemented new knowledge generated from commercial

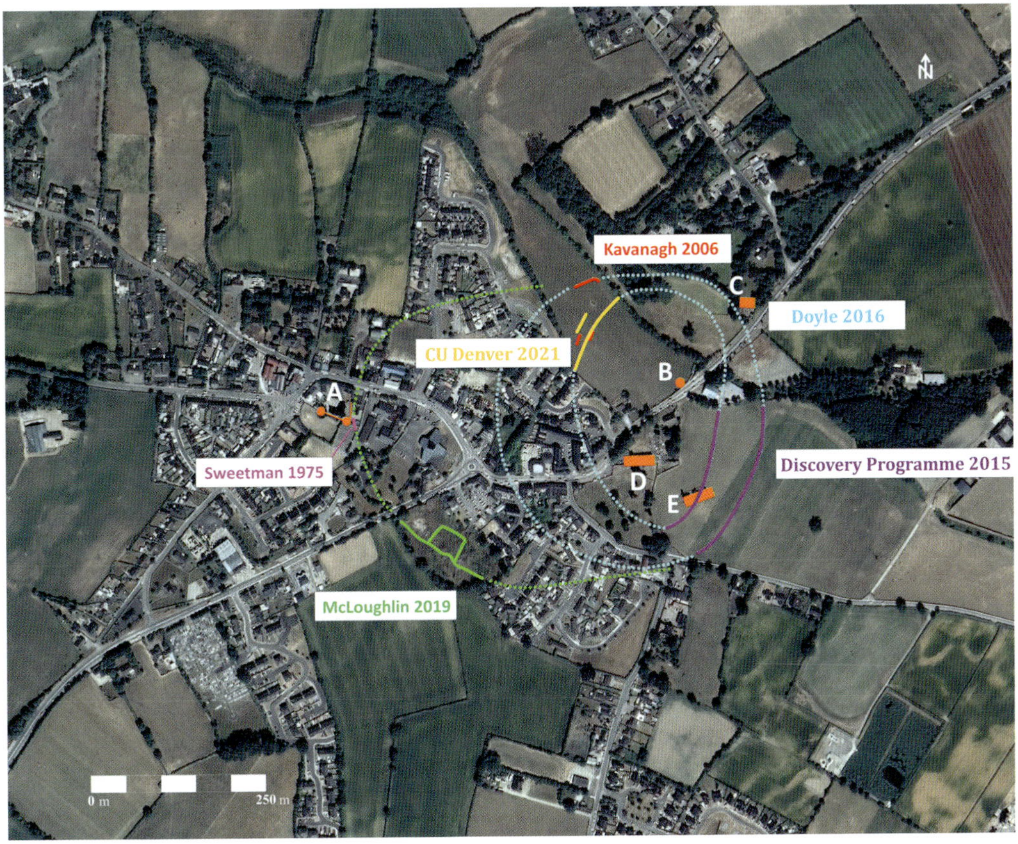

8.2 Ferns: map showing previously proposed circuits of the monastic enclosure, by Doyle (2016) and McLoughlin (2020), together with select major archaeological landmarks within the town (A: Ferns Castle; B: Mogue's Well; C: St Edan's Cathedral; D: St Peter's Church; E: St Mary's Abbey). Solid lines represent ditch sections confirmed through geophysics or excavations, while dotted lines map conjectured enclosure. Line colours correlate with text labels

archaeology in the last thirty years. In the past two decades in particular, questions and interpretations that first came to the fore in the 1980s – such as the concept of 'monastic towns' (e.g., Doherty 1980, 1985; Graham 1987, 1988), and the existence and exceptionalism of a 'Celtic monasticism' – have been explored and disputed by historians and archaeologists, who have developed new perspectives on the evolution, character, organization and fate of these early ecclesiastical settlements; this body of research has also highlighted the influence of, and connection with, sites across Europe and the role of noble or royal dynasties in the shaping of the 'monastic' landscape of early medieval Ireland (Etchingham 2011; O'Sullivan 2013; Bhreathnach 2014). The idea that all early ecclesiastical sites can even qualify as 'monasteries' – let alone monastic towns – has been challenged (Etchingham 2011). However, in the scope of this chapter and for ease of the discussion, the term 'monastic' will be used in relation

8.3 Ferns: map showing the completed (solid line) and planned (dotted line) geophysical areas in 2021 (together with the outline of the survey from 2015). The dashed line indicates areas to which access was not possible/permitted in 2021

to the early medieval site in Ferns. In the last decade, projects such as 'Monastic Ireland' (The Discovery Programme and Trinity College Dublin) and 'Making Christian Landscapes' (University College Cork) have brought together archaeologists and historians to explore early medieval ecclesiastical and monastic landscapes, leading to a number of surveys and publications (e.g., Bhreathnach and Dowling 2021; Bhreathnach 2019; Ó Carragáin and Turner 2016; Ó Carragáin 2017, 2021, 2022).

Among the sites excavated and surveyed in recent years, some offer particularly good comparative material for Ferns, which will be discussed further in the final section of this chapter: these sites include Clonfad in Co. Westmeath (Stevens 2012), Seir Kieran in Co. Offaly (Dowling 2022), Kilmacduagh in Co. Galway (Dowling 2015b) and, closer to Ferns, Taghmon in Co. Wexford – the latter of which was discussed with Ferns by Ian Doyle at the occasion of the volume published in memory of Billy Colfer (Doyle 2016). This evidence adds to that of the well-known larger sites, which represent further important comparable sites to Ferns, such as Armagh,

Clonmacnoise (Bhreathnach 2014, 183–200; King 2009; Murphy 2003) and Glendalough (Doherty et al. 2011). In turn, the investigations on the circuit and date of Ferns' early monastic enclosure presented in this chapter will add to the increasing corpus of evidence informing our understanding of early monasticism in Ireland, and indeed wider Europe.

To further establish the potential circuit of the monastic enclosure, a new campaign of geophysical investigations was initiated by the authors in the environs of Ferns in November 2021. The surveys, involving high-resolution magnetic gradiometry, were undertaken across six areas (with nine areas originally intended), totalling approximately ten hectares (fig. 8.3). This chapter presents the results of this latest phase of work, which, together with a detailed summary of previous and ongoing excavations in the town, provides new insights on the archaeology of Ferns and the potential route of the monastic enclosure; these new investigations will then be placed in the context of the landscape of early monasticism in Ireland through comparison with other sites that have undergone similar surveys and/or been excavated in recent years.

EARLY MEDIEVAL FERNS: UPSTANDING ARCHAEOLOGICAL EVIDENCE

It is beyond the scope of this chapter to provide a detailed summary of early medieval Ferns, and only minimal information is provided here to help contextualize the archaeological results (chs 2, 3; Bhreathnach and Dowling 2021).

The monastery at Ferns was reputedly founded sometime around the turn of the seventh century by St Aidan, also known as St Máedóc or St Mogue (d. 620–5), who was active in the sixth and seventh centuries (Culleton 1999). Several hagiographies have been written on St Aidan, who is believed to have been born in Inisbrefny, Co. Cavan, in the mid-sixth century. The date of his death on 31 January is generally agreed (Doherty 1986), but variously given as occurring in 620 or 625. His place of burial is also disputed as either Ferns or his birthplace at Inisbrefny (Culleton 1999). Having spent several years studying at St David's in Wales, Aidan returned to Ireland in *c.*580 to the 'Wexford region' before being granted land in the territory of the Uí Chennselaig by Beacc, a cousin of Brandubh mac Eochu (d. 605), king of Leinster. In around 598 he is recorded as establishing a monastery at Ferns and was consecrated as bishop the same year.

Many such foundations were established in Ireland in the same period, and over five thousand early churches are recorded (O'Sullivan et al. 2013, 140). Relatively few have been surveyed or excavated, however, and how many could be classified as 'early monasteries' is impossible to know. Some of those sites certainly developed into ecclesiastical centres associated with a founder-saint and marked physically by one or more circular enclosures. In Co. Wexford alone, thirty-two ecclesiastical enclosures have been recorded by the Archaeological Survey of Ireland. These are monumental in scale in the most prominent monasteries, such as at Clonmacnoise and Glendalough, where several early medieval buildings also survive. In Ferns, while several elements of the original monastery have been identified in the 2015 geophysical survey (Dowling 2015; Bhreathnach and Dowling 2021) and in archaeological excavations (e.g., McLoughlin and Stafford 2020; Taylor and Hurley 2021; Shine et al. 2021; ch. 9), the only surface remnants of Ferns' early medieval site are several high crosses (O'Keeffe 1997), cross-slab(s) and cross fragments or bases. None of these monuments is in its original location and they are now mainly found in the grounds of St Edan's Cathedral. A high cross and cross-slab are recorded in the graveyard to the south of St Edan's Cathedral, the latter of which is recalled locally as being related to the burial place of Diarmait Mac Murchada but dates to the ninth or tenth centuries (Harbison 1992 i, 89). A high cross base is also extant within St Mary's Abbey church. Some of the crosses were moved in the early twentieth century from roadside walls (Hore 1906, vol. vi, pp 172–3). However, their existence, together with early historical references, such as Viking raids on the monastery in AD835 and 839, indicate Ferns to have been a monastery of some importance (Culleton 1999; ch. 3).

Table 8.1 Summary of excavation data through sections of probable early medieval enclosures

Excavation	Ditch width	Ditch depth	Date	Shape	Ditch
Sweetman	2.5m	1.2m	Contained thirteenth- to fourteenth-century pottery	U-shaped	Outer(most)
Ryan	2.6m	1.7m	cal. AD384–535	V-shaped	Outer?
Kavanagh	5.2m* 5m	N/A 2m	N/A N/A	N/A V-shaped	Outer Outer(most)
McLoughlin	3m	1.5m	cal. AD659–851 cal. AD727–940	U-shaped	Outer(most)
Taylor	1.14m	0.92m	N/A	U-shaped (recut)	Inner
IAFS	2.4m (recut) 2.5m	1.2m 0.9m	cal. AD1176–269 cal. AD655–773	U-shaped (recut) U-shaped	Inner Outer
IAC	1.5m+	0.98m	cal. AD663–820	V-shaped	Unknown

(*this ditch was caught obliquely in testing, possibly exaggerating its width)

PREVIOUS ARCHAEOLOGICAL INVESTIGATIONS IN FERNS ON THE MONASTIC BOUNDARY

The catalogue of previous excavations at Ferns (up to the time of writing) presented in Appendix 8.1 was garnered from information published in summary form in the Excavations volumes (Bennett 1987–2012) and online at excavations.ie, together with published papers, unpublished technical reports and several bibliographies (for a previous summary, see Lacey 2017). All recorded excavations at Ferns were assessed to provide a complete picture of the local sub-surface heritage, before placing particular emphasis on investigations associated with the monastic boundary (table 8.1). In total forty-four excavations have been undertaken at various locations around the town, twenty-three of which have been deemed of 'no archaeological significance' (even in these cases of 'no archaeological significance', of course, the absence of archaeological evidence in a given location might in itself be a significant piece of evidence). Of the excavations undertaken to date, seven have assessed ditches that may be part of the monastic enclosure(s).

From 1972 to 1975 David Sweetman undertook archaeological excavations at Ferns Castle (Sweetman 1979). This was to facilitate a programme of conservation works, including on the castle keep, the ground floor and second floor of the south-east tower and the cellar of the south-west tower. Excavations also focused on the drawbridge area of the castle and the castle fosse, which was completely excavated at its southern end and partly excavated at its eastern extent. Additional investigations took place to the east of the castle to assess the potential for surviving outer defences; in this area a small, U-shaped rock-cut ditch (2.5m wide by 1.2m deep) orientated roughly north-north-east to south-south-west was recorded. The ditch contained a basal fill (40cm deep) described as a sticky brown filling with loosely packed shaley stones overlying it (Sweetman 1979, 224). Late thirteenth-/early fourteenth-century pottery sherds were found on top of this shale fill, providing a *terminus post quem* for the underlying fills. Based on more recent excavations in Castleland in 2019, McLoughlin suggested this ditch is a north-westerly extension of the outer monastic enclosure (McLoughlin and Stafford 2020, 96), despite the recovery of later medieval pottery from Sweetman's ditch fills.

The Castleland excavations (18E0526; described in detail in McLoughlin 2020; McLoughlin and Stafford 2020) followed a programme of eighteen test trenches that revealed a range of features including a large curving ditch (McLoughlin and Stafford 2020). Excavations in 2019 clarified that this ditch extended across the site in a north-west to south-east direction for 115m, averaging 3m in width and 1.5m in depth. Samples from the basal fills were dated to cal. AD659–851 and 727–940 (McLoughlin and Stafford 2020, 91). A sub-rectangular enclosure, measuring about 50m by 40m at maximum extent, adjoined the internal side of the putative 'monastic ditch'. The ditch defining this enclosure was 3m wide and had a maximum depth of 2.25m; an entrance was apparent at the enclosure's southern end. Basal fills from the sub-rectangular enclosure ditch were dated to cal. AD685–873, indicating that both it and the main 'enclosure ditch' are broadly contemporary. The remains of what may be a rectangular building, defined by a series of pit- and posthole-type features, were located within the enclosure. While no artefacts were recovered to provide a chronology, the structure had been truncated by later thirteenth-century activity.

Several pits, used to collect water, were also cut into the enclosure. These so-called 'well pits', which generally measured up to 2m in diameter and 1.8m in depth, often contained later medieval pottery. The presence of the well pits suggests that the enclosure ditch was backfilled by the later medieval period but must have remained visible or recognisable within the landscape as an entity capable of holding water. Towards the southern limit of the site, two late medieval structures and evidence of industrial activity was also uncovered. The latter activity included the remains of a smithy, consisting of an extensive area (40m by 8m) of hearths, pits and furnaces, with some 240kg of metallurgical waste recovered (McLoughlin and Stafford 2020, 93). In addition, a wide range of medieval ceramics, early medieval stick pins, nails and other ferrous objects, fragments of medieval glass and a plough coulter were among the recovered artefacts (McLoughlin and Stafford 2020, 93–4).

In 1998, during archaeological monitoring of works for the Ferns Sewerage Scheme, a V-shaped ditch was uncovered at the junction of Clone Road and Station Road. It was described as measuring approximately 2.6m wide at road level and was 1.7m deep below the surface hardcore. The ditch contained a tertiary fill of charcoal-rich brown soil, overlying a horizontal band of charcoal containing slag and what was described as a 'furnace bottom' (Ryan 2000, 8). A sample of alder charcoal from the ditch returned a date of cal. AD384–535 (UCD-0007; provided in the report as 1-sigma). This ditch has been interpreted as possibly forming part of the outer monastic enclosure (Doyle 2016, 54). A pit of unknown date was also uncovered about 5m to the west.

In 2006 archaeological testing conducted by John Kavanagh in the field immediately to the north of Mogue's Well revealed a multi-period site. A total of sixty-seven test trenches were opened, several of which contained various linear, circular and sub-circular features; a single, possibly prehistoric, cremation pit was also identified. Of note, two concentric ditches 5–6m wide and 15m apart were uncovered in the centre-west portion of the site and these were interpreted as belonging to a bivallate ringfort (Kavanagh 2009). These ditches have since been re-interpreted by Doyle (2016, 53–5) as part of the inner monastic enclosure, though the results of the 2021 geophysical survey combined with those of the 2015 survey suggest they may relate to the inner and outer enclosure ditches identified in 2015 (see below). Near the centre of the site, a substantial V-profiled ditch (5m by 2m deep) was also uncovered, extending east to west. The ditch contained a single, sterile soil fill and was traced across at least two trenches and found to terminate near the river. While no interpretation was given regarding the function of the ditch, Doyle (2016) suggested it formed part of the outer monastic enclosure, though it could be part of a much wider outer enclosure, relating to the medieval ditch in Castleland (McLoughlin 2020).

In 2019, in advance of proposed pavement rehabilitation, drainage and watermains installation, archaeological testing was undertaken throughout Ferns. A total of sixteen test trenches were excavated, including fifteen along the local road network and a single trench close to a stream at the north-eastern corner of the field containing St Mary's Abbey (Taylor and Hurley 2021). To facilitate a surface-water drainage outfall pipe, the latter trench was extended to an area some 3m in width and 121m in length for excavation in 2020. Based on Ger Dowling's (2015) geophysical survey, the pipe trench was anticipated to encounter enclosing elements of the monastic complex, as well as other linear anomalies. The excavations 'revealed evidence of possible prehistoric features, early medieval and medieval occupation in the form of ditches, gullies, pits, postholes and occupation layers/deposits' (Taylor and Hurley 2020, 1; see also ch. 11). One of the ditches appears to mark the line of the inner monastic enclosure as recorded during the geophysical survey (Bhreathnach and Dowling 2021). This ditch had a U-shaped profile and measured 1.14m wide and 92cm deep. It was devoid of artefacts but had been recut twice, with the second recut containing medieval pottery. Seven metres to the west, a slightly larger ditch, measuring 1.6–2m wide and 1.05m deep, was recorded, again with a V-shaped profile. This ditch also contained sterile fills and appears to correspond with an anomaly on the 2015 geophysics. The excavation also revealed the impressive remains of a horizontal timber mill, which was ultimately preserved in situ. Artefacts from the excavations included a range of medieval pottery, metal, slag, stone, animal bone, leather and worked wood, which are being assessed at the time of writing. Radiocarbon and dendrochronological dates for the excavation, as well as analyses of charred and waterlogged plant remains, pollen and insect remains are also ongoing (see ch. 11).

The archaeological testing on the road incorporated archaeological testing on Main Street and Station Road (including at the site of the ditch uncovered by Frank Ryan, as outlined above). Writing up the monitoring of the construction works for the Ferns Village Rehabilitation Scheme is ongoing at the time of writing (see below). However, the initial testing conducted by Kate Taylor on Station Road also uncovered a possible extension of the inner enclosure, when a ditch was recorded that appeared to align with an extrapolated extension of the inner enclosure from the 2015 geophysical survey. This ditch was beneath a later medieval occupation layer, providing a *terminus post quem* for the ditch. Evidence of this ditch was also thought to be found in a neighbouring trench. It was suggested that the ditch can be extrapolated to follow the sharp curve in Station Road and that this indicates that the line of the original enclosure may be preserved within the existing road layout. Dating and analysis of the ditch on Station Road are pending conclusion.

In 2021 the inaugural excavation season took place of a three-year research project led by the IAFS. These excavations are detailed elsewhere in this volume (ch. 9), so a summary only is given here, focusing on the enclosing ditches. In 2021 two cuttings (1 and 2) were opened to investigate geophysical trends identified by Dowling (2015), namely a rectangular feature immediately south of Mary's Abbey church (that was interpreted by Cochrane (1910) and O'Keeffe (1997) as a potential cloister (ch. 9)), and a possible double-aisled structure identified in the 2015 geophysics to the south-east of Mary's Abbey. These structures were positioned over the inner and outer ditch of the monastic enclosure respectively. The excavation confirmed an L-shaped feature in Cutting 1, as revealed by geophysical survey and depicted on historical mapping, to be the intact remains of two walls at right angles, one of which contained later medieval pottery within its lime-mortar bonding. These walls mark part of a claustral court adjoining St Mary's Abbey, further evidence of which was also found in excavations in 2022 in Cutting 3 (ch. 9). The partial remains of a walled double-aisled structure were confirmed in Cutting 2, with pottery and a coin within these features suggesting a *c.*twelfth to fourteenth century date.

In Cutting 1, the walls were constructed over a large medieval cesspit and the inner ditch of the monastic enclosure. The ditch, cut into natural clays, ran from a terminus along a north-west to south-east orientation within the cutting. The eastern side of the cut was heavily truncated, with the surviving portion of the ditch U-shaped in form and measuring a minimum of 2.4m in width by 1.2m in depth. The ditch contained three fills, with the uppermost one containing a selection of predominantly medieval finds, including nine sherds of twelfth- to fourteenth-century pottery among a range of other finds (ch. 9). A hazel sample from a basal fill returned a date of cal. AD1176–1269, apparently confirming that the ditch remained open until the twelfth century and may have been intentionally backfilled to accommodate the construction a claustral court at St Mary's around the time the abbey was built in the 1160s. The outer monastic ditch was only recorded at the north-east limits of Cutting 2 and, like the inner monastic ditch, it was heavily truncated. The ditch was broadly U-shaped in profile and measured *c.*1.5m wide by 90cm deep. The ditch contained two fills, both devoid of artefacts. A single radiocarbon date, from birch charcoal in the basal fill returned a date of cal. AD655–773, consistent with the ditch being part of the early medieval outer enclosure of Aidan's monastery. This outer monastic ditch was also identified in plan, but not excavated, in 2022 when a further two cuttings were opened. These 2022 excavations, while not directly related to the monastic enclosure, are discussed in Chapter 9.

Finally, at the time of writing, reporting on the archaeological monitoring of the construction works for the Ferns Village Rehabilitation Scheme is in progress by the IAC under the direction of David McIlreavy (consent C000709; licence E004633). As some of these monitoring works occurred adjacent to previously excavated segments of an early medieval ditch, such as that identified on Station Road, they merit inclusion here (McIlreavy and Lacey 2022). Unfortunately, the depth of works along most of Station Road does not appear to have been sufficient to further explore the potential ditch features identified by Taylor during previous testing (see above). Nonetheless, the monitoring works have confirmed that the medieval occupation layer recorded by Taylor extends north-west towards the graveyard. Elsewhere along the scheme, monitoring of works on Main Street, *c*.75m west of the cathedral, identified further elements of a ditch noted by TVAS during the preceding test-trench programme. Despite heavy truncation by modern services, the section of this feature excavated during the IAC programme of works survived as a curving linear feature, extending approximately north to south-west. The ditch was V-shaped, with a slight bowl-shaped base. The maximum recordable width and depth of the feature were 1.5m and 98cm respectively. Four fills were documented, including a basal fill containing occasional charcoal, a pig tooth and several pieces of slate. Charcoal from this deposit returned an early medieval date of cal. AD663–820. On the outer face of the ditch, a layer of 'slumped' material may derive from an original external bank. While it is tempting to suggest that this ditch could form part of the proposed inner enclosure circuit, extrapolation of its circuit (albeit based on a narrow exposed area) suggests that it may not be related to the inner enclosure, and could represent a separate linear feature dividing the monastic space, or an entirely different enclosing element. While the function of the ditch is still being considered, the date returned from the basal fill material does at least place the ditch firmly within the early development phase of this monastic landscape, and it is broadly congruent with dates on this enclosure for the IAFS excavation (table 8.2).

Table 8.2 Summary of published radiocarbon dates from excavations through sections of the probable early medieval enclosure, and the previously unrecorded enclosure (after McLoughlin and Stafford 2020; McIlreavy and Lacey 2022; Ryan 2000; Shine et al. 2021). For IAFS dates, calibration after OxCal. 4.1 (Bronk Ramsay 2009) using the IntCal09 dataset (Reimer et al. 2009) (note Ryan's date provided at 1-sigma level; all others shown at 2-sigma)

Excavation	Lab. code	Charcoal ID	Sample no.	14C age (BP)	Calibrated age (95.4% probability) (cal. BC/AD)	Possible ditch
Ryan	UCD-0007	*Alnus Glutinosa*/ Alder	–	1620±50	AD384–535	Outer
McLoughlin	UBA-42013	*Maloideae* (apple type)	–	–	AD727–940	Outer(most)
McLoughlin	UBA-42014	*Corylus*/Hazel	–	–	AD665–773	Outer(most)
IAFS	UBA-47031	*Betula*/Birch	2058	1317±25	AD655–773	Outer
IAFS	UBA-47033	*Corylus*/Hazel	1029	825±25	AD1176–1269	Inner
IAC	FTMC-KP43-3	*Maloideae* (apple type)	–	1279±28	AD683–820	Unknown

SURVEYS

The recent geophysical surveys at Ferns are as instructive as the excavations with regard to the scale and nature of some of the archaeological features within the town, including those that relate to the monastic boundary. Two broad phases of survey have been undertaken for research purposes, beginning in 2015, followed by an expanded survey in 2021 (which would be useful to continue in future seasons, subject to the permission of additional landowners).

In May 2015 an extensive programme of magnetic gradiometry and more limited electrical resistance survey was undertaken as part of the Monastic Ireland project in the area surrounding St Mary's Abbey (consent 15R4002: Dowling 2015; Bhreathnach and Dowling 2021). The survey area, comprising approximately four hectares in the townlands of Ferns Demesne and St Edan's Demesne, was found to contain a density of archaeological features that likely reflect multi-period activity spanning several centuries. Notably, the surveys identified two large concentric ditches (inner *c.*2m wide and outer *c.*3–4m wide) that were suggested to mark the eastern extent of the monastic enclosure. The outer ditch appears to underlie a possible 'double-aisled' structure, itself located at the approximate centre of what may be a sub-circular enclosure measuring some 65m in overall diameter. The geophysical signature of this 'building' indicated a structure *c.*12m by 10m with *c.*1m-wide masonry walls. Both the structure and the earlier outer monastic ditch were assessed by excavation in 2021 and 2022 (Shine et al. 2021; see above and ch. 9). Several other anomalies of archaeological potential occur around the double-aisled structure, notably the encircling enclosure, as well as numerous other linear, curvilinear and 'pit-like' features.

Directly adjacent to the south wall of St Mary's Abbey, the surveys identified a rectangular anomaly/structure that was originally mapped by Cochrane (1910) and proposed by O'Keeffe (1997, 60) to be the location of an associated cloister. The 'walls' outlining this possible structure were ill-defined, suggesting differential preservation and bands of rubble/building collapse in places. Excavations in 2021 indicated this anomaly may preserve the walls of claustral ranges (see above and ch. 9). The south-eastern portion of these 'range structures' was built over the possible inner monastic boundary.

A wide array of further anomalies were also apparent in the data retrieved, showing evidence of successive phases of agriculture, land-division and possible industrial activities, some of which could pre-date the monastic settlement itself or post-date the Dissolution in the sixteenth century (Dowling 2015). These features speak to the complex history of the site, which extends from prehistory to the modern era. They include several amorphous strongly positive responses, probably indicative of hearths, furnaces, kilns or other similar industrial-type features; pit and 'ditch-like' features possibly associated with field systems and enclosures/paddocks; and faint linear responses consistent with plough furrows (Dowling 2015). Of note was an anomaly

8.4 Ferns: map showing combined 2015 and 2021 geophysical survey results

interpreted as a roundhouse or ring-ditch, *c.*10m in diameter, and two parallel lines, *c.*7m apart and 90m long, interpreted as a trackway or droveway.

In November 2021 an expanded programme of magnetic gradiometry was undertaken in the immediate environs of Ferns, across six areas in the town totalling 10 hectares (21R0297; see also Dowling 2021; figs 8.4, 8.5). These surveys were undertaken by Ger Dowling on behalf of the University of Colorado, Denver, in collaboration with the IAFS and local archaeologist Barry Lacey. The 2021 programme built on the results of the previous geophysical survey at Ferns in 2015 and identified an impressive array of sub-surface features, many of which are of clear archaeological significance and seemingly relate to occupation and agriculture spanning several centuries or even millennia. Of particular interest to this chapter is the identification of possible segments of the northern circuit of the early monastic boundary.

Although the surveys conducted in 2021 are fully reported (Dowling 2021), it is important to note that access to two key fields (as well as significant areas of other

8.5 Ferns: map highlighting the lines of the possible early medieval enclosures, together with the 2015 and 2021 geophysical survey results and ongoing archaeological excavations

survey areas) was not possible at the time (fig. 8.3). Taken together, the results of the 2015 and 2021 surveys provide a significant new 'sub-surface map' of possible archaeological activity around both St Mary's Abbey and the town at large (figs 8.4, 8.5). The most noteworthy of the newly revealed features (for this chapter) are two closely set, curving ditches in Area 9; these may represent part of the northern circuit of the enclosure (see below). A wide array of other anomalies identified in Areas 5 and 6 also point to early medieval and later occupation and agriculture. Unfortunately, modern disturbance, interference or development impacted greatly on the survey results in Areas 1–4 (preventing any survey taking place in the case of Area 1). However, a subtle linear feature in Area 3 may represent a continuation of the early medieval ditch found in Castleland (McLoughlin and Stafford 2020). Alternative methods of geophysical prospection (for example, earth resistance) in these areas might provide better results.

CONTEXTUALIZING AND REINTERPRETING THE ENCLOSURE

The recent excavations and geophysical surveys at Ferns have added crucial new data, especially in the form of radiocarbon dates, allowing fresh conclusions to be drawn on the antiquity and circuit of the early monastic enclosure. As stated previously, two main circuits have been suggested for the monastic boundary to date, firstly by Doyle (2016), who proposed an inner enclosure *c.*200m in diameter and an outer enclosure *c.*300–350m in diameter (fig. 8.2), and latterly by McLoughlin (McLoughlin 2020; McLoughlin and Stafford 2020), who postulated a much larger monastic site, with an outer diameter of over 500m. Both putative circuits have merit, each supported by archaeological evidence. However, on the basis of the 2021 survey results and other evidence, an alternative layout may now be proposed. It is increasingly probable the early medieval enclosure at Ferns is more complex than originally anticipated, with the possibility that it had either additional outer enclosing circuits, and/or an annex to the outer enclosure, which, based on the new surveys, is more likely to be similar in shape to the smaller circuit originally proposed by Doyle (2016).

Of critical significance here is the identification in Area 9 of two curving ditches that, as mentioned above, could represent part of the northern circuit of the enclosure. Positioned about 15m apart, the 'new' ditches appear to correspond to the two concentric ditches initially found by Kavanagh (2006), who interpreted them as forming part of a bivallate ringfort, and later re-interpreted by Doyle (2016, 53–5) as forming part of the inner monastic enclosure. However, rather than representing just the internal circuit, the ditches in Area 9 may be a continuation of both the inner and the outer enclosure ditches mapped by Dowling (2015) around St Mary's Abbey. While the latter ditches at St Mary's Abbey lie about 60m apart at their eastern extent, the closer spacing of the Area 9 ditches (at 15m) may be due, in part, to the local topography, with its makers perhaps seeking to avoid the more steeply sloped terrain a short distance to the north-west.

This re-interpretation of the bivallate ditches encountered by Kavanagh (2006) as forming both the inner and outer monastic enclosures makes sense considering that these circuits are clearly formed only by single ditches in the St Mary's Abbey field (as also inferred by the 2021/2 excavations and the 2015 geophysical surveys) indicating that both ditches in survey Area 9 are unlikely to represent a single bivallate inner monastic enclosure, but instead are more likely to represent single-ditched outer and inner enclosures. This monastic enclosure is distinct from the circuit proposed by McLoughlin (2020) where the outer enclosure would be some 200m distant from the inner ditch.

A further segment of the monastic boundary was identified on Station Road during excavations by Ryan and by Taylor; indeed, Taylor proposed that a clear curve in Station Road itself preserves the line of the monastic boundary. Joining the different

8.6 Ferns: map showing the reinterpreted route of the monastic enclosures (inner, outer and outermost) based on all archaeological excavations and geophysical surveys. Image includes crop-mark as revealed on 2018 Google Earth pro imaging and shows the potential for the enclosure to be D-shaped (with the north-east limit formed by Barney's stream) or oval

strands of evidence together, including the geophysical surveys, the excavations by Taylor and the IAFS in St Mary's field, and the alignment of Station Road there is now increasing evidence that the monastic boundary was defined by two roughly concentric ditches, with diameters of *c.*315m and 175–220m respectively, the outer one being possibly preserved in the curving line of Station Road (fig. 8.6). This is in keeping with the evidence from other towns, such as Armagh, Duleek, Kells (Co. Meath), Kildare, Kilkenny and Lusk, where the modern street pattern can be seen to reflect the layout of the enclosures of the early monasteries that once dominated these places.

Evidence of a second 'outermost' ditch was also identified through archaeological testing by Kavanagh (2006) and interpreted by McLoughlin (2020) as joining her 115m-long segment of ditch, as well as the linear feature encountered in excavation by Sweetman (1979). Another possibility is that these elements join as a third enclosing circuit to Ferns. However, even further evidence for additional enclosing elements at Ferns is a crop-mark identified on Google Earth Pro aerial imagery, which could also align with the Castleland ditch, via Sweetman's ditch and the geophysical data from Area 3. Unfortunately, this crop-mark does not form a natural alignment with Kavanagh's outer ditch, although that possibility cannot be discounted. This wider ditch could form part of an entire third, or potentially even third and fourth enclosures, or it may have formed an annex or annexes to a smaller bivallate enclosure. Unfortunately, the failure of the geophysics to generate good data in the west side of the village makes it difficult to speculate further, although a subtle indication of an outermost ditch was observed in Area 3. Future surveys, with different techniques, at the western side of the village (especially where that crop-mark was identified) might provide further evidence about whether there was a third (or fourth), larger enclosing ditch around early medieval Ferns.

The excavations have more clearly dated the ditches as originating (as one might expect) in the seventh to ninth centuries; an outlier to this is the early date established by Ryan on Station Road, which is on the precipice of the arrival of Christianity to Ireland. The dates for the ditch in Castleland (cal. AD659–851 and 727–940) are slightly later than those from the 2021 excavations in Ferns Demesne by the IAFS (cal. AD655–773), as well as from the ditch excavated by IAC (cal. AD683–820). While the standard deviations do overlap to some extent, this difference could support the theory that the Castleland ditch is a later annex to the main outer enclosure(s), or a third enclosing element. Dating evidence from the IAFS excavations also indicates that at least portions of the innermost monastic ditch may not have finally been backfilled until the later medieval period, with the inner ditch in St Mary's field apparently not backfilled until around the time the abbey was founded in the 1160s.

Thirteenth- to fourteenth-century pottery was also found in Sweetman's possible outermost ditch. A similar pattern has been observed at the outermost ditch in Castleland, where the excavation of well pits into the ditch indicates the later medieval population was aware of the ditch's existence and its ability to catch water, although the ditch was at least partly backfilled centuries before this. Collectively, this evidence clearly indicates that at least some of the early medieval monastic boundaries survived and were known within the Ferns landscape for several centuries.

On the balance of probability, and based on evidence presenting itself in 2022, the inner circuit as shown on Figure 8.6 seems the most likely route for a bivallate monastic enclosure, joining as it does the most points of available evidence. This is not to discount the significant stretch of medieval ditch in Castleland to the west of the town, which might yet be shown to represent a third enclosing element external to the bivallate enclosure, or the crop-mark from 2018, which could join with the Castleland ditch or form an entirely separate enclosing element or monument. Similarly, the relationship between the monastic enclosing ditches and the curvilinear feature found by IAC close to the cathedral may yet be clarified, but unfortunately remains uncertain at the time of writing due the limited nature of the investigations carried out here (McIlreavy and Lacey 2022).

There are numerous examples of early ecclesiastical sites with three (or more) enclosures, with the innermost circuit usually directly surrounding the church, as is the case in Clonfad and Nendrum. Several archaeological excavations and surveys have revealed configurations comparable to Ferns, such as at Kilmacduagh, where a geophysical survey as part of the same Monastic Ireland project revealed, similar to Ferns, an inner and an outer enclosure (Dowling 2015b). At Clonfad, part of an inner and an outer enclosure were excavated, and the remaining parts of the circuit were confirmed by geophysics (Stevens 2012). At Seir Kieran, a geophysical investigation discovered two new ditched enclosures surrounding the modern church and graveyard, in addition to the upstanding double-banked enclosure (22R0008: Dowling 2022). In Wexford itself, of the thirty-two ecclesiastical enclosures in the Archaeological Survey, five are defined by two enclosures, identified from aerial photographs and Google Earth imagery. In Ferns, the impossibility of conducting the planned survey beyond the stream (known locally as Barney's Stream) means we can only speculate as to whether the enclosures continued beyond the stream, or if they stopped, forming D-shaped enclosures as observed at other early medieval ecclesiastical sites. In Clonfad, while not D-shaped, excavators found that the inner enclosure partly overlapped with the stream running to the south of the site; a similar scenario was suggested for Taghmon in Co. Wexford, where a stretch of ditch excavated in 2004 aligns with the possible enclosure of the ecclesiastical site that aerial photography had revealed, which itself converges with the curving section of a former stream (Hardy 2007; see also Colfer 2002, 152–3; Doyle 2016, 45). Similarly, extensive geophysical surveys and targeted research excavations in Clone, only 2.25km from Ferns, have concluded that the early medieval enclosure there is likely to be D-shaped (Shine et al. 2020; Shine and Lacey 2020, 2021; ch. 12). Finally, many of the monastic sites in Co. Offaly, including Seir Kieran, Drumcullen and Birr, are also thought to be D-shaped, with one side defined by a stream or river (see, for example, O'Brien 2006; O'Sullivan 1997; O'Sullivan et al. 2018).

The various archaeological investigations carried out in Ferns have also given some tentative clues to the further organization of the monastic space within the enclosures, and the activities taking place there, though further work is needed to explore the many potential archaeological features identified by the surveys. As noted, a sub-rectangular enclosure was uncovered during the Castleland excavation, which is broadly contemporary with the outermost ditch discovered there. A rectangular building was also located within the enclosure (McLoughlin 2020b, 12). The ditch feature identified during IAC's monitoring may yet be confirmed as an earlier sub-division of the monastic space; the function of this ditch would be interesting to clarify since it appears to have fallen out of use relatively early in the recorded history of the monastery.

That important early ecclesiastical settlements were divided into separated sections with specific functions and inhabited by groups of people with different roles and statuses has been established by historical sources and supported by archaeological investigations, such as at Dunmisk in Co. Tyrone (Ivens 1986). These are best known from sources relating to Armagh, where the circular enclosures were further divided into *trian*, which can be traced in the street patterns of the modern town (Bradley 1998, 44; McCullough and Crawford 2007, 1–2; Bhreathnach 2019, 39); the archaeological excavations in Clonfad have also provided some evidence of such subdivision, with excavations revealing an extensive metalworking site in the eastern side, mainly dedicated to the production of handbells, in the area between the inner and outer enclosure, corresponding to Armagh's 'Zone 2', where students, clerics and craft workers lived and worked (Stevens 2012, 121). In Ferns no solid evidence has yet been found pointing to industrial activity on a scale comparable to Clonfad, though the 2004 excavation to the west of the cathedral suggested that the area was used for metalworking on a limited scale during the medieval period (04E0663: appendix 8.1). A medieval smithy, although not early medieval, was also excavated in Castleland adjacent to the early medieval ditch (McLoughlin 2020b, 13; McLoughlin and Stafford 2020, 89).

CONCLUSIONS

Whatever is the correct interpretation of Ferns' bivallate or trivallate enclosure, and how the various ditches formed inner, outer, outermost or annex enclosures, what is certain is that the site is more complex than previously presented. The evidence presented in this chapter demonstrates that Ferns likely continued to grow as a monastic (or ecclesiastical) site from at least the sixth to the tenth century and beyond. The enclosure, even following the more conservative interpretation of the two 'smallest' circuits as the main boundaries of the monastery, would have measured 315m in minimum diameter, from north-west to south-east. For comparison, the outer enclosure at Clonfad was over 200m; at Kilmacduagh, based on the geophysical survey, possibly over 200m; Armagh 250m north–south; Clonmacnoise *c.*570m north–south (for a discussion of the enclosures, see Murphy 2003); Kells over 360m east–west by 280m north–south; Seir Kieran 320m north–south; Clone *c.*200m north–south. Of the thirty-two ecclesiastical enclosures identified in Co. Wexford for which we have relevant data, four have a diameter of under 50m, ten are between 50m and 100m, ten between 100m and 200m, two of a maximum of 250m, and two, like Ferns, of over 300m. Ferns would therefore fit on the high end of the scale, even with the smaller proposed outer enclosure.

Ferns' connection with the ruling dynasty ensured its initial success, and its reorganization in the twelfth century, as part of the church reforms and changes to the monastic landscape brought on by the arrival of continental religious orders such as the Cistercians and Augustinians secured its survival into the later Middle Ages. It is interesting to note, as a counterpoint, that all references to a settlement in Taghmon stop in the eleventh century, and the site appears not to have prospered any further; as Ferns emerged as the chief centre of the Uí Chennselaig dynasty from the middle of the eighth century, Taghmon ceased to align with the dynastic interests, while Ferns continued to flourish (Doyle 2016; Bhreathnach and Dowling 2021). The dating of the larger enclosure/annex, for instance, with a latest possible date in the middle of the tenth century, may reflect Ferns' continued development even before the twelfth-century transformations. This may have marked an enlargement of the outer enclosure, or the construction of a larger enclosure and the backfilling of the earlier one. Similar patterns have been observed at Clonmacnoise, where the enclosing ditch was backfilled in the eighth or ninth century and a larger enclosure was constructed (Murphy 2003, 19). Ascertaining the complexity and chronology of Ferns' early medieval enclosures requires additional research, both geophysical survey and excavation. What is clear on current evidence is that Ferns at different times had a number of enclosures, at least one of which continued to function throughout the early Middle Ages and seems to have gone out of use only when St Mary's claustral court was built on top of it (ch. 9).

BIBLIOGRAPHY

Bhreathnach, E. 2014. *Ireland in the medieval world, AD400–1000: landscape, kingship and religion*. Dublin.

Bhreathnach, E. 2019. 'The nature of pre-"reform" Irish monasticism'. In Bhreathnach, E., Krasnodębska-D'Aughton, G. and Smith, K. (eds), *Monastic Europe, AD1100–1700: communities, landscape and settlement*, 23–43. Turnhout.

Bhreathnach, E. and Dowling, G. 2021. 'Forming an episcopal see and an Augustinian foundation in medieval Ireland: the case of Ferns, Co. Wexford'. *Proceedings of the Royal Irish Academy*, 121C, 191–226.

Cochrane, R. 1910. 'Ferns, Co. Wexford'. In *78th Annual Report of the Commissioners of Public Works in Ireland*, 3–6, 16–17. Dublin.

Corlett, C. 2012. 'Ferns, Co. Wexford'. *Archaeology Ireland*, Heritage Guide 59. Dublin.

Culleton, E. 1999. *Celtic and early Christian Wexford*. Dublin.

Doherty, C. 1986. 'Saint Máedóc and Saint Molaisse'. *Bréifne*, 6, 363–74.

Doherty, C., Doran, L. and Kelly M. (eds). 2011. *Glendalough: City of God*. Dublin.

Doherty, C. 1980. 'Exchange and trade in early medieval Ireland'. *Journal of the Royal Society of Antiquaries of Ireland*, 110, 67–89.

Doherty, C. 1985. 'The monastic town in early medieval Ireland'. In Clarke, H.B. and Simms, A. (eds), *The comparative history of urban origins in non-Roman Europe*, 45–75. Oxford.

Dowling, G. 2015. 'Geophysical investigations at Ferns, Co. Wexford'. Unpublished technical report for the Discovery Programme.

Dowling, G. 2015b. 'Geophysical investigations at Kilmacduagh, Co. Galway'. Unpublished technical report for the Discovery Programme.

Dowling, G. 2021. 'Geophysical survey report, Ferns, Co. Wexford'. Unpublished technical report prepared for the IAFS and UCD, 21R0297.

Dowling, G. 2022. 'Geophysical survey report, Seir Kieran, Co. Offaly'. Unpublished technical report for Offaly County Council, 22R0008.

Doyle, I. 2016. 'Telling the dancer from the dance: the archaeology of early medieval Wexford'. In Doyle, I. and Browne, B. (eds), *Medieval Wexford: essays in memory of Billy Colfer*, 35–61. Dublin.

Etchingham, C. 2011. 'The organization and function of an early Irish church settlement: what was Glendalough?' In Doherty, Doran and Kelly (eds), *Glendalough*, 22–53. Dublin.

Graham, B.J. 1988. 'The definition and classification of medieval Irish towns'. *Irish Geography*, 21:1, 20–32.

Graham, B.J. 1987. 'Urbanization in medieval Ireland, *ca.*AD900 to *ca.*AD1300'. *Journal of Urban History*, 13:2 (Feb.), 169–96.

Harbison, P. 1992. *The high crosses of Ireland: an iconographical and photographic survey*. 3 vols. Bonn.

Hardy, C. 2007. '2004:1825: The Village Inn, 5–6 Joseph Street, Taghmon, Wexford'. In Bennett, I. (ed.), *Excavations 2004: summary accounts of archaeological excavations in Ireland*, no. 1825. Dublin.

Hore, P.H. 1900–11. *History of the town and county of Wexford*. 6 vols. London.

Ivens, R.J. 1986. '1986:72: Dunmisk Fort, Tyrone'. www.excavations.ie.

Kavanagh, J. 2006. 'Archaeological test excavation report at Ferns Upper, Ferns, County Wexford'. Unpublished excavation report, 06E0780.

King, H. 2009. 'The economy and industry of early medieval Clonmacnoise: a preliminary view'. In Edwards, N. (ed.), *The archaeology of the early medieval Celtic churches: proceedings of a conference on the archaeology of the early medieval Celtic churches*, 333–50. London.

Lacey, B. 2017. 'Archaeological excavations and the history of Ferns, Co. Wexford'. MA, UCC.

McIlreavy, D. and Lacey, B. 2022. 'Preliminary report on archaeological monitoring at Castleland, Ferns Upper and Ferns Demesne, Ferns, Co. Wexford (consent no. C000709)'. Unpublished report prepared by IAC Archaeology on behalf of Wexford County Council.

McLoughlin, C. 2020. 'From early to late: uncovering medieval Ferns'. *Archaeology Ireland*, 34:2, 30–4.

McLoughlin, C. 2020b. 'Preliminary archaeological excavation report, Castleland, Ferns, Co. Wexford'. Unpublished report, 18E0526.

McLoughlin, C. and Stafford, E. 2020. 'Medieval Ferns: from monastic centre to medieval town'. In Corlett, C. and Potterton, M. (eds), *The town in medieval Ireland in the light of recent archaeological excavations*, 85–100. Dublin.

Murphy, D. 2003. 'Excavation of an early monastic enclosure at Clonmacnoise'. In King, H.A. (ed.), *Clonmacnoise studies*, 2, 1–34. Dublin.

Ó Carragáin, T. 2017. 'Church sites and other settlements in early medieval Ireland: densities, distributions, interactions'. In Edwards, N., Ní Mhaonaigh, M. and Flechner, R. (eds), *Transforming landscapes of belief in the early medieval Insular world and beyond*, 457–92. Turnhout.

Ó Carragáin, T. 2021. *Churches in the Irish landscape, AD400–1100*. Cork.

Ó Carragáin, T. and Turner, S. 2016. *Making Christian landscapes in Atlantic Europe*. Cork.

O'Brien, C. 2006. *Stories from a sacred landscape: Croghan Hill to Clonmacnoise*. Cork.

O'Donnell, R. and Ó Carragáin, T. 2022. 'How did early church sites differ from one another? A comparative approach within the kingdom of Fir Maige, Ireland'. *Church Archaeology*, 21, 5–31.

O'Keeffe, T. 1997. 'Diarmait Mac Murchada and Romanesque Leinster: four twelfth-century churches in context'. *Journal of the Royal Society of Antiquaries of Ireland*, 127, 52–79.

O'Sullivan, A., McCormick, F., Kerr, T. and Harney, L. 2013. *Early medieval Ireland, AD400–1000*. Dublin.

O'Sullivan, M. 1997. *The illustrated guide to Seir Kieran, County Offaly*. Offaly.

O'Sullivan, M., Rodgers, M., Shine, D. and Mandal, S. 2018. 'Seir Kieran: place, pilgrimage and tradition in the monastic midlands'. *Offaly Heritage*, 10, 21–42.

Ryan, F. 2000. 'Archaeological findings from monitoring of Phase 1 of Ferns Sewage Scheme, Co. Wexford'. Unpublished excavation report, 98E0132.

Shine, D. and Lacey, B. 2020. 'Clone community archaeological excavation report'. Unpublished technical report prepared for the National Monuments Service and Wexford County Council.

Shine, D. and Lacey, B. 2021. 'Clone Church archaeological excavation report'. Unpublished technical report prepared for the National Monuments Service and Wexford County Council.

Shine, D. and Mandal, S. 2022. 'Discovering St Aidan's monastery: preliminary archaeological excavation report (December 2022)'. Unpublished technical report produced for the National Monuments Service.

Shine, D., Lacey, B., Corlett, C., Elliott, I. and Mandal, S. 2020. 'Clone, Ferns: a meadow of St Aidan?' *Archaeology Ireland*, 34:4. 24–9.

Shine, D., Lynch, L., Mandal, S. and O'Meara, D. 2021. 'Discovering St Aidan's monastery: preliminary archaeological excavation report (December 2021)'. Unpublished technical report produced for the National Monuments Service.

Stevens, P. 2012. 'Clonfad: an industrious monastery'. In Channing, J. and Stevens, P., *Settlement and community in the Fir Tulach Kingdom*, 107–34. Dublin.

Sweetman, P.D. 1979. 'Archaeological excavation at Ferns Castle. Co. Wexford'. *Proceedings of the Royal Irish Academy*, 79, 217–45.

Taylor, K. and Hurley, H. 2021. 'R772 Ferns Village Pavement Scheme Phase 2, Ferns, Co. Wexford'. (Formerly N11 Ferns Rehabilitation Scheme, Phase 2) Stage (iii) post-excavation assessment report for Wexford County Council. Unpublished excavation report.

APPENDIX 8.1

Summary of archaeological excavations undertaken in Ferns up to 2021

Please note **bold** entries identify excavations possibly associated with the early medieval monastery.

Note: * indicates reports titled as an archaeological assessment, reflecting archaeological monitoring, testing or excavation

	Licence/ consent	Townland	ITM	Director/ author	Title	Description	Report	Publication
1	**E000107**	**Castleland**	**701687 649891**	**David Sweetman**	**Ferns Castle**	**Excavations focused on facilitating a programme of conservation works at the castle keep, the ground floor and second floor of the south-east tower, the cellar of the south-west tower and the drawbridge area. The castle's fosse was completely excavated at its southern extent and partly excavated at its eastern extent. Additionally, to the east of the castle a small rock-cut ditch was uncovered. Finds were primarily of a later medieval date.**	**Sweetman 1979**	**Sweetman 1979**
2	93E0158	Ferns Upper	701820 649908	Rosanne Meenan	N/A	Non-archaeological significance.	Available at Excavations.ie	N/A
3	95E0067	Castleland	701804 649784	Margaret Gowen	N/A	Slot trench containing large amounts of *c.*thirteenth-century pottery and a single spud stone. A backfilled quarry pit with masonry chippings, containing no datable material, was also recorded.	Gowen 1995*	N/A
4	96E0192	Ferns Upper	701578 649918	Sarah McCutcheon	N/A	Non-archaeological significance.	McCutcheon 1996	N/A
5	98E0132	Multiple – Ferns Village	702175 649930	Mary Henry	Pre – Construction Testing on the Ferns Sewerage Scheme	In the south-east corner of a field adjacent to Mogue's Well a series of linear cuts, possible post holes and burnt spreads were uncovered. A small amount of Bronze Age pottery was recovered from the fills within the cuts.	Henry 1998	N/A
6	**98E0132**	**Multiple – Ferns Village**	**702158 649673**	**Frank Ryan**	**Monitoring of Phase 1 of Ferns Sewerage Scheme**	**Several features were uncovered including: a shallow trench within a medieval layer; pit of unknown date; Iron Age ditch; limestone culvert; a single Bronze age pit; Iron Age Barrow (refer also to licence number 99E0450); possible ringfort.**	**Ryan 2000**	**Ryan and Buckley 2012**
7	98E0273	Castleland	701704 649908	Florence Hurley	N/A	Portion of castle's northern fosse uncovered.	Hurley 1998*	N/A
8	99E0450	Ferns Lower	702472 649477	Frank Ryan	N/A	Iron Age ring barrow containing the cremated remains of several individuals both adult and children.	Ryan 2000b	Ryan and Buckley 2012
9	99E0527	Castleland	701611 649759	Claire Walsh	N/A	Grouping of shallow pits with no established chronology.	Walsh 1999*	N/A

	Licence/ consent	Townland	ITM	Director/ author	Title	Description	Report	Publication
10	99E0527 (ext.)	Castleland	701611 649759	Angela Wallace	N/A	Portion of an irregular ditch, pits and possible post and stake holes. No established chronology or function.	Wallace 2000	N/A
11	99E0538	Ferns Upper	701976 649947	Avril Purcell	Archaeological testing for housing development MacMurrough Court	Non-archaeological significance.	Purcell 1999*	N/A
12	01E1182	Castleland	701734 649856	Michael Tierney and Stuart Elder	N/A	Non-archaeological significance.	Tierney and Elder 2001	N/A
13	01E1208	Ferns Upper	702069 649980	Maurice Hurley	N/A	Charcoal spread with no established chronology.	Hurley 2001	N/A
14	03E0254	Ferns Upper	702038 649862	Cathy Sheehan	Testing for redevelopment of Aldercourt Estate Area	Cluster of linear features, pits and postholes with no established chronology, together with a single medieval pit.	Sheehan 2006*	N/A
15	03E1813	Castleland	701682 649911	Catherine McLoughlin	N/A	Ferns Castle's northern fosse uncovered.	McLoughlin 2004,* 2005 and 2006	N/A
16	04E0628	Castleland	702020 649745	Brian Halpin	N/A	Non-archaeological significance.	Halpin 2004	N/A
17	04E0663	Ferns Upper	702053 649877	John Kavanagh	N/A	Possible Bronze Age cremation pits, medieval ditches, furrows and metal-working area and a post-medieval structure.	Kavanagh 2007	N/A
18	05E0662	Castleland	701933 649722	John Kavanagh and Kevin Murphy	N/A	Post-medieval farmyard.	Kavanagh and Murphy 2005*	N/A
19	05E1010	Ferns Upper	701565 649968	Catherine McLoughlin	N/A	Non-archaeological significance.	McLoughlin 2005b*	N/A
20	05E1118	Castleland	701933 649722	Brian Halpin and Mark Andrews	N/A	Post-medieval courtyard.	Halpin and Andrews 2005	N/A
21	05E1195	Castleland	701615 649516	Emmet Stafford	N/A	Non-archaeological significance.	Stafford 2005	N/A
22	06E0360	Ferns Upper	701873 649873	Catherine McLoughlin	N/A	Non-archaeological significance.	McLoughlin 2006b	N/A

	Licence/ consent	Townland	ITM	Director/ author	Title	Description	Report	Publication
23	06E0492	Ferns Lower	702169 649304	Red Tobin	N/A	Non-archaeological significance.	Tobin 2006*	N/A
24	**06E0780**	**Ferns Upper**	**702069 649980**	**John Kavanagh**	**N/A**	**A single possible prehistoric cremation pit; two concentric ditches possibly associated with a bivallate ringfort; medieval agricultural field systems; portion of a large east to west orientated ditch of unknown date.**	**Kavanagh 2009**	**N/A**
25	06E0968	Ferns Upper	701604 650049	Emmet Stafford	N/A	Non-archaeological significance.	Stafford 2007*	N/A
26	06E0987	Castleland	701623 649849	John Kavanagh	N/A	Non-archaeological significance.	Kavanagh 2006	N/A
27	06E1011	Castleland	701721 649910	Catherine McLoughlin	N/A	Non-archaeological significance.	McLoughlin 2007	N/A
28	08E0835	Ferns Upper	701942 649822	Ellen O Carroll	N/A	Non-archaeological significance.	O Carroll 2008	N/A
29	09E0509	Ferns Upper	701511 649931	Emmet Stafford	N/A	Non-archaeological significance.	Stafford 2009	N/A
30	11E0044	Multiple – Ferns Village	702152 649620	Mary Henry	N/A	Non-archaeological significance.	Henry 2011	N/A
31	E004633	Multiple – Ferns Village	701595 649663	Catherine McLoughlin	N11 Ferns Pavement Rehabilitation Scheme	Non-archaeological significance.	McLoughlin 2016	N/A
32	18E0319	Castleland	701774 649907	Catherine McLoughlin	N/A	Non-archaeological significance.	Available at Excavations.ie (2018a Report)	N/A
33	18E0335	Ferns Upper and Newtown	701071 650218	Catherine McLoughlin	N/A	Non-archaeological significance.	Available at Excavations.ie (2018b Report)	N/A
34	E004953	Ferns Demesne	702191 649764	Catherine McLoughlin	N/A	Minor quantity of disarticulated human bone in the base of a pit close to St Mary's Abbey during monitoring for the insertion of an interpretive panel.	Available at Excavations.ie (2018c Report)	N/A

	Licence/ consent	Townland	ITM	Director/ author	Title	Description	Report	Publication
35	18E0749	Multiple – Ferns Village	702175 649895	Catherine McLoughlin	N/A	Non-archaeological significance.	Available at Excavations.ie (2018d Report)	N/A
36	19E0191	Castleland	701647 649909	John Kavanagh	N/A	Non-archaeological significance.	Available at Excavations.ie	N/A
37	19E0254	Castleland and Ferns Upper	701818 649895	Thaddeus Breen and Edel Barry	N/A	Non-archaeological significance.	Available at Excavations.ie	N/A
38	19E0321	Ferns Upper	701792 649971	Catherine McLoughlin	N/A	Post-medieval ditch and furrows.	Available at Excavations.ie (2019 Report)	N/A
39	**C000709 E004633 R000395**	**Multiple – Ferns Village**	**702092 649696**	**Kate Taylor**	**R772 Ferns Village Pavement Scheme Phase 2**	**Potential prehistoric features; early medieval ditches; medieval pits; ditches and dump layers; medieval watermill; post-medieval features.**	**Taylor and Hurley 2021**	**This volume**
40	21E0116	Ferns Upper	701856 649877	Yvonne Whitty	N/A	Non-archaeological significance.	Available at Excavations.ie	N/A
41	20E0738	Castleland	701748 649789	Faith Bailey	N/A	Non-archaeological significance.	Bailey and Lacey 2021	N/A
42	**18E0526**	**Castleland**	**701847 649699**	**Catherine McLoughlin**	**N/A**	**Early medieval ditch with adjoining sub-rectangular enclosure; later medieval settlement and industrial activity.**	**McLoughlin 2018 (testing report)**	**McLoughlin 2020; McLoughlin and Stafford 2021 This volume**
43	**C000967 E005108 R000521**	**Ferns Demesne**	**702236 649747**	**Linda Lynch and Denis Shine**	**Discovering St Aidan's Monastery**	**Twelfth-century priory; early medieval enclosure; medieval structure.**	**Shine et al. 2021**	**This volume**
44	**C000709, E004633**	**Multiple – Ferns Village**	**702027 649787**	**David McIlreavy**	**R772 Ferns Village Pavement Scheme Phase 2**	**Early post-medieval structure associated with St Mogue's Well, section of post-medieval road surface, ditches and pits, including features previously encountered during TVAS testing. A curvilinear enclosure encountered near the cathedral may relate to the early medieval monastery, but is not confirmed as forming part of any monastic enclosure.**	**Pending**	**McIlreavy and Lacey 2022**

CHAPTER NINE

The archaeology of the Augustinian abbey of St Mary, Ferns: the cloister

DENIS SHINE, TADHG O'KEEFFE, STEPHEN MANDAL, LINDA LYNCH & DANIEL O'MEARA

INTRODUCTION

The importance of Ferns to the student of medieval Ireland is disproportionate to its relatively modest size. The historian knows it as a major ecclesiastical site of the early Middle Ages associated with St Aidan, as the capital of Diarmait Mac Murchada's twelfth-century kingdom and as a major regional centre of Anglo-Norman power under the Marshal and de Valence families. The medieval archaeologist knows it for its important collection of monuments, among them the early medieval high crosses, the early thirteenth-century Anglo-Norman cathedral and the curious Gothic structure to its east, the stone castle of the thirteenth century, and the Augustinian abbey of St Mary. In the last few years the below-ground archaeology at Ferns has been increasingly accessed and assessed, with geophysical prospecting and excavations throughout the town yielding important information that is already proving transformative. This body of research includes an excavation (and associated surveys) at the site of St Mary's abbey itself.

Founded in the third quarter of the twelfth century, and home to a community of canons regular, the abbey has almost entirely disappeared above ground, with only its ruined church – itself half-destroyed – still standing. In the early twentieth century, Robert Cochrane undertook a comprehensive survey of Ferns and its monuments, including a record of some foundations of a walled courtyard to the south of the church (Cochrane 1910, 3–6, 16–17). Evidently the remains of a cloister, the walls of that enclosure are no longer visible above ground. However, in July 2021 the Irish Archaeology Field School (IAFS) commenced a research and teaching excavation in the environs of St Mary's as part of a three-year project (fig. 9.1). In the first season of excavation, two cuttings were opened on land adjacent to the abbey church for the purpose of investigating the early medieval monastic enclosure and two possible medieval structures identified in geophysical surveys at the site by Ger Dowling in 2015 (Bhreathnach and Dowling 2021; see also Shine et al. 2021). Cutting 1 was made to assess a rectangular anomaly identified by geophysics immediately south of the abbey church, and which was apparently associated with the supposed cloister.

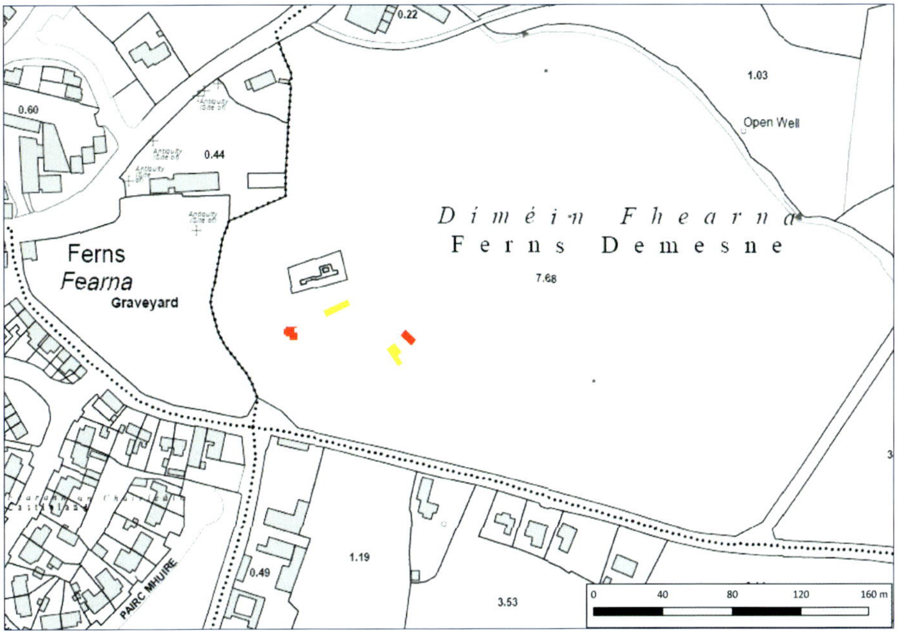

9.1 Ferns: location of 2021 cuttings (in red) and 2022 cuttings (in yellow) on the 1:2500 OS map (© Ordnance Survey Ireland/Government of Ireland copyright permit no. MP 000723)

Cutting 3 was also excavated across this feature in June 2022. Unfortunately, at the time of writing, post-excavation analysis of Cutting 3 is on-going and so findings can only be referenced here in the briefest terms to supplement the excavation findings from Cutting 1. Collectively, the excavations are contributing to this preliminary assessment of the abbey's now-lost claustral ranges.

The excavations are part of a larger research project which, while spearheaded by the St Mary's excavation, began at Clone (2.25km from Ferns) when excavation of another of St Aidan's early monasteries was undertaken in 2019 and 2021 (ch. 12) (Shine et al. 2020, 24–9; Shine and Lacey 2020; Shine and Lacey 2021). These excavations have been undertaken in tandem with a number of non-invasive surveys by the IAFS and their partners, including 3D lidar scanning on Ferns Castle, St Mary's and St Edan's Cathedral by the University of Colorado, Denver (UoCD) (ch. 14), detailed geophysical surveys throughout Ferns by Dowling in November 2021 (ch. 8) and successive seasons of geophysical survey around Clone Church by Irish Geophysical and Archaeological Services (ch. 12; Elliott 2021; Elliott 2022). Several of these research projects, such as the excavation at Clone and at St Mary's abbey, have been supported or partly funded by the Rediscovering Ancient Connections: the Saints Project (hereafter Ancient Connections). Ancient Connections is an 'inter-reg' cross-border arts and heritage project linking north Pembrokeshire and north Wexford. This cross-border project is intended to revive the ancient links between communities in

Pembrokeshire and Wexford and hopes to motivate both communities to rediscover their shared heritage and trade knowledge, experience and skills.

DISCOVERING ST MARY'S ABBEY

Long a significant place within the lands of the Uí Chennselaig, Ferns experienced significant growth as a caput during the reign of Mac Murchada. In addition to building a castle (or 'stone house'), he introduced the rule of St Augustine to Ferns around 1160 and made an endowment to the newly constituted Augustinian community (Bhreathnach and Dowling 2021; ch. 3). By then, Ferns was already an episcopal centre, having been chosen by the synodians at Ráith Bressail in 1111 to have the mother church of the diocese, which embraced the Wexford region. It retained its diocesan status after the invasion, as was normal for the dioceses chosen by pre-invasion synodians. A native Irishman, Ailbe Ua Máel Muaid (d. 1223), held the see while the Anglo-Normans were in control, and his successor, John St John (d. 1253), built the present cathedral[1] (O'Keeffe and Bates 2016, 73–96; see also McFall 1957). In contrast, little is known of the early history of St Mary's Augustinian abbey, immediately south of the cathedral. In 1317 it was plundered and burnt by Irish forces during the Bruce Wars. During the fifteenth century, the position of abbot was disputed, at a time when the Kavanaghs had re-established Gaelic control over Ferns and its castle (Gwynn and Hadcock 1970, 175–6; ch. 2). An inventory of the abbey taken at the Dissolution suggests that claustral buildings did exist: the abbey was described as a 'church and belfry, dormitory, chapter-house, hall and other buildings' – and in possession of *c.*600 acres and 'other interests' (Gwynn and Hadcock 1970, 176). Three years later, there were 'no buildings in the precinct save the abbey church and a hall' (White 1943, 371–3).

Today the only abbey building remaining above ground is the church, of which just the north portion survives. Between later fabric alterations and insertions, and the removal of jagged edges in the context of conservation, the ruins are less easy to read than one would like for a building of such historical importance. The architecture of the church is discussed in detail elsewhere in this book (chs 6, 7) and a brief description will suffice here.

The church was a nave-and-chancel building, the former measuring 14m by 6.4m internally, and the latter, originally barrel-vaulted, 4.47m by 5.3m internally (fig. 9.2). A square turret projects from the west end of the nave, its shape changing to cylindrical at the wall-head. A small two-storeyed square building (described as a sacristy by Cochrane (1910)) projects northwards from the junction of the nave and chancel, but

1 The cathedral went on to have an illustrious history, including being burnt by Fiach MacHugh O'Byrne in 1575, and then restored by him in 1577. The building was extensively reconstructed in 1817 to its current form, but retains much of its medieval fabric and features (see McFall 1957).

was entered at ground-level from the east end of the nave. To the west of this 'sacristy' and parallel to the nave was, apparently, an additional walled-in space, possibly a domestic space akin to that found in St Saviour's at Glendalough, a monastery that is also Augustinian and founded around the time that the rule of St Augustine was introduced to Ferns. The one-time presence of a cloister to the south of the church was noted above. Yet, although St Mary's clergy was reformed, the design of the church was incompatible with a conventional reformed-monastery cloister, for there was no access – apparently – into the church from the south side.

It is not known how much of the interior of the church or of the ground immediately outside it was cleared away in 'excavations' carried out over a century ago (Cochrane 1910). The probability is that valuable evidence of the church's history, including any trace of a pre-twelfth-century church, was lost at that time. In contrast, the archaeological potential of the ground outside the present church enclosure is very considerable. Within this field, which contains the abbey ruins, a number of organizations have conducted research in recent years. In 2020, Kate Taylor of Thames Valley Archaeological Service Ireland (TVAS) excavated a trench 121m in length (varying from 2.8 to 4.8m in width), to facilitate the installation of an outflow pipe for Transport Infrastructure Ireland. The excavation 'revealed evidence of possible prehistoric features, early medieval and medieval occupation in the form of ditches, gullies, pits, postholes and occupation layers/deposits' (Taylor and Hurley 2021). The excavation also recorded a ditch in the location of the inner monastic enclosure as recorded in Dowling's 2015 geophysical survey, as well as the impressive remains of a medieval horizontal mill and associated stone structure, which was ultimately preserved in situ (ch. 11). In October 2021 DigVentures was commissioned and funded by Ancient Connections to undertake a targeted programme of ground-penetrating radar (GPR) survey around St Mary's (as well as geophysical surveys at other sites in Wexford). This was conducted in two main areas, one directly over the 'rectangular feature' – the area identified below as the cloister – to the south of St Mary's, and the other in the area around the TVAS excavations, close to where the horizontal watermill was discovered. This survey revealed several interesting anomalies, including a possible square building close to the site of the TVAS excavations, which was conjectured as being associated with the watermill discovered by TVAS, or potentially an early ecclesiastical church building (ch. 10; see also Wilkins and Teale 2022, 6). Of more interest specifically to this chapter, this GPR survey also revealed possible building remains directly south of St Mary's, which could be related to the possible cloister. The strongest anomaly, potentially marking 'building remains', was located in the area in which an eastern range would once have stood, while rubble activity was also recorded in the area that would contain a northern building range, should such structures survive at the site.

Finally, in 2021 Dowling, on behalf of the IAFS and UoCD, and in collaboration with local archaeologist Barry Lacey, undertook an extensive programme of magnetic

9.2 Ferns: drone shot of St Mary's Abbey church, also showing Cutting 1 mid-excavation

gradiometry in the immediate environs of Ferns (Dowling 2021). This new survey was undertaken across six areas in the town, totalling ten hectares, and it included the eastern limits of the St Mary's field, not previously surveyed in 2015. Collectively the 2021 surveys provide a significant 'sub-surface map' of possible archaeological activity around St Mary's Abbey and in the general area to the south-east of the town (ch. 8). Within St Mary's field, the surveyed anomalies suggest medieval, post-medieval and prehistoric occupation and agriculture around the site and in surrounding fields; this activity appears to be part of an extensive multi-period archaeological landscape that extends continuously from known prehistoric and early medieval archaeological excavations conducted to the north and south of the site (ch. 1; see also Kavanagh 2004; 2006; 2006b; Ryan 1998; Ryan and Buckley 2012, 273–90).

THE IAFS EXCAVATIONS

The IAFS excavation initially took place over six weeks from July to August in 2021 (Shine et al. 2021), with a second four-week season also undertaken from June to July 2022 (Shine and Mandal 2022); at the time of writing, post-excavation analysis is on-

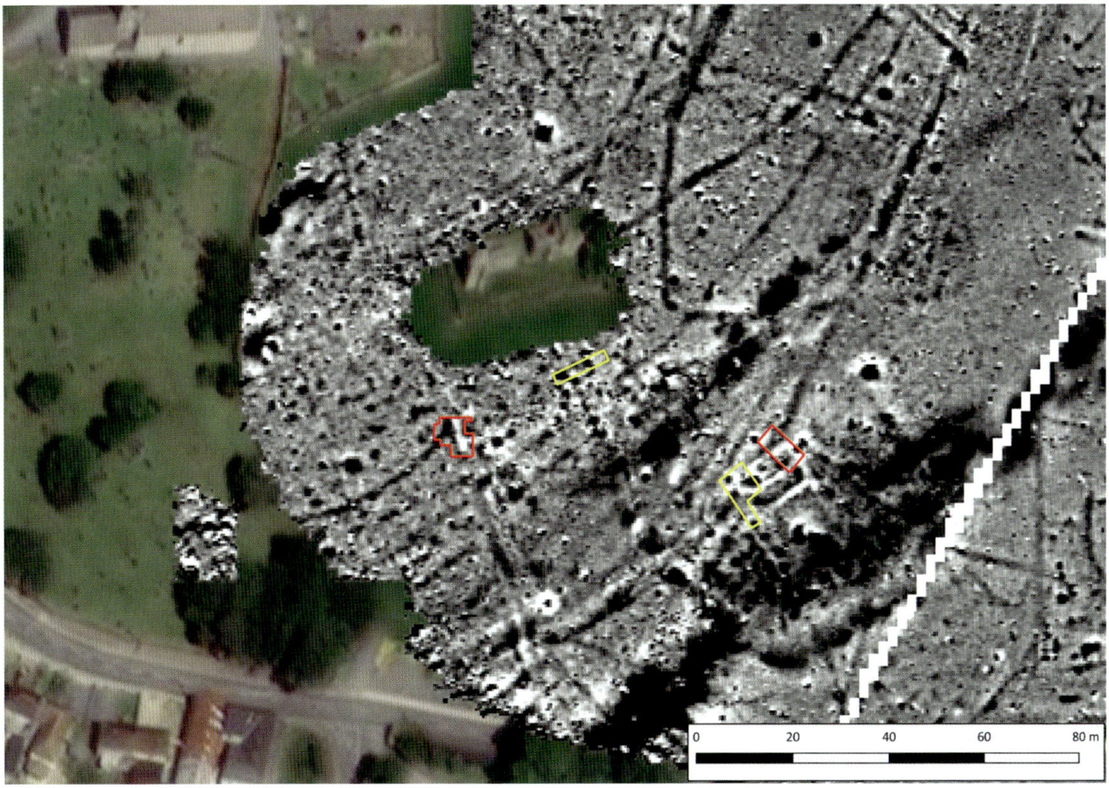

9.3 Ferns: location of 2021 cuttings (in red) and 2022 cuttings (in yellow) on the 2015 geophysical survey: background image courtesy of Ger Dowling

going and so only preliminary findings are available for inclusion here. The aim of the 2021 excavation was to investigate geophysical trends, first identified by Dowling (2015), relating to possible medieval structures and the early monastic enclosure (fig. 9.3). To assess these anomalies, Cuttings 1 and 2 were opened in 2021, followed by Cuttings 3 and 4 in 2022. Cutting 3 was also excavated to assess GPR trends identified by DigVentures and, more importantly, to test the eastern side of the site of the cloister to determine whether portions of an eastern range were intact. A third and final four-week season is planned for the summer of 2023.

Cutting 1: general description

Cutting 1 and later Cutting 3 were excavated to investigate a rectangular feature immediately south of St Mary's Abbey church (fig. 9.3). The first excavations in Cutting 1 confirmed two masonry walls at approximate right angles in this location. These walls were partly built over both the inner monastic enclosure and a large cesspit, the two other features considered of greatest archaeological significance within the cutting.

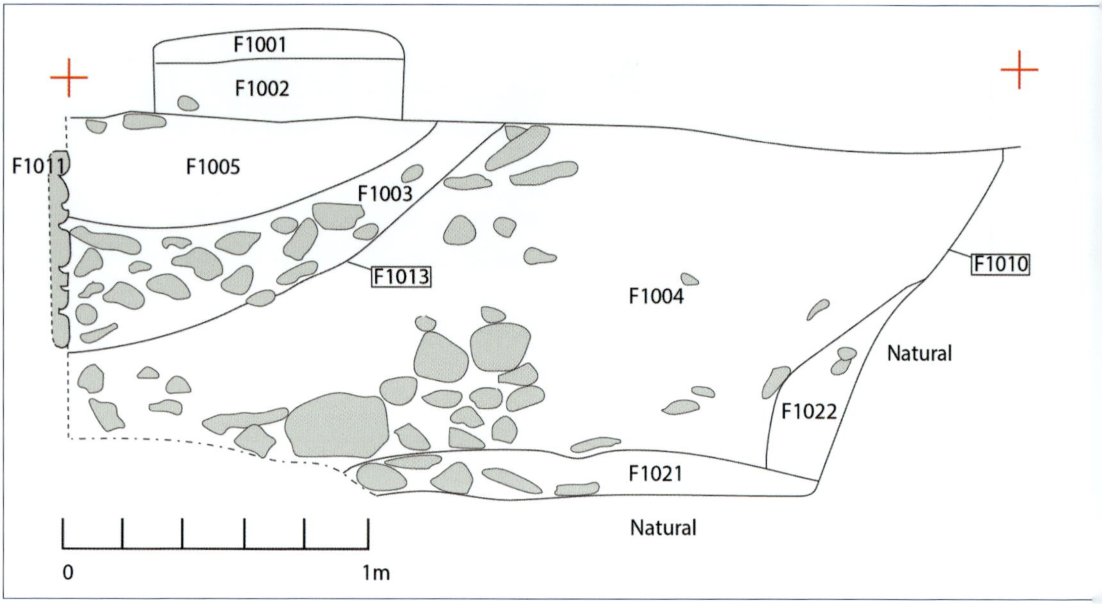

9.4 Ferns: section drawing of the inner monastic enclosure ditch and associated fills, which is also truncated by probable wall foundation cut

The ditch was found to be heavily truncated (with no eastern edge) but still measured >2.4m wide and 1.2m deep in maximum extent, although it narrowed markedly within the cutting as it approached a possible terminus, which may mark an entranceway to the monastery (fig. 9.5). The 2015 geophysical survey, which identified the ditch as a curvilinear anomaly, also recognized a defined gap in the ditch at this location (Dowling 2015). The positioning of the claustral walls (and St Mary's Abbey generally) adjacent to, and over, a possible entrance to the early medieval monastery poses intriguing questions as to whether the placement of the abbey had a symbolic significance in the re-ordering of the landscape. A radiocarbon date from a hazel sample from the basal fill of the ditch of cal. AD1176–1269 (table 9.1) suggests that the enclosure was backfilled around the time St Mary's Abbey was founded in the 1160s, which suggests that the builders were aware of its existence. A range of predominantly later medieval finds were also recovered from the tertiary ditch fill, including nine sherds of twelfth- to fourteenth-century pottery, a possible spacer/pottery waster, a medieval iron nail and a (presumably intrusive) piece of clay pipe; animal bone, iron slag and a tooth from a human infant were also recovered from this tertiary fill, with both underlying ditch fills being entirely sterile. The range of finds indicates that the tertiary fill was placed in the ditch to put it out of use some time in the twelfth to fourteenth century.

The cesspit in Cutting 1 was one of several other pits and linear features in the cutting. While only partly excavated, it merits description based on the finds it

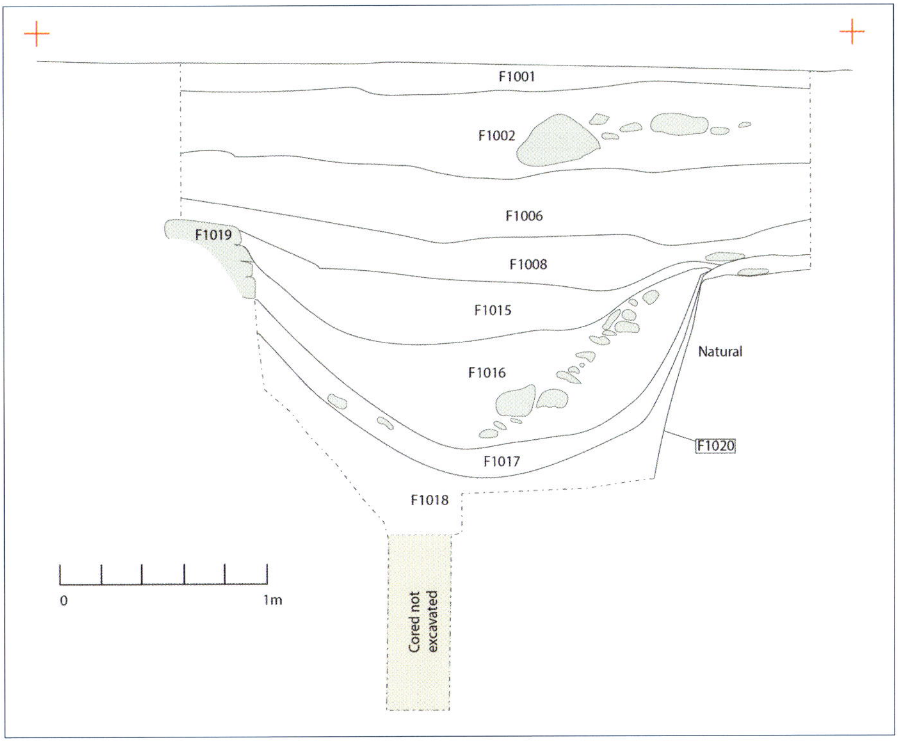

9.5 Ferns: section drawing of cess pit with associated fills and overlying deposits; also showing (*below*) the reconstructed ceramic lamp (or rushlight/candle holder) that was recovered from the pit

9.6 Ferns: drone shot of Cutting 1, showing western and southern claustral walls, as well as the inner monastic enclosure ditch to the walls immediate west: note the different construction between the western and southern wall

included, with the lower fills in particular containing coprolites, plant remains and a wooden paddle, indicating good organic preservation. The pit was not bottomed, due to safety constraints, but coring revealed it to be at least 80cm deeper than the limit encountered during excavation (fig. 9.5). The secondary fills of the cesspit also contained some of the more noteworthy ceramic artefacts from the 2021 excavation, including a 'Face-Man' jug and ceramic lamp or rush light/candle holder; these were found in addition to a substantial quantity of pottery, medieval iron nails, and some iron slag. The face-man jug consisted of twenty-two sherds, probably from the same vessel, of which eight could be reassembled to form a twelfth- to fourteenth-century Wexford-Type Coarseware jug rim with a partial face figure. The ceramic lamp or rush/candle holder consists of seven pieces of Leinster Cooking Ware pottery (fig. 9.5), which were reassembled, and is of particular interest due to its rarity, with only about two dozen such artefacts known from Ireland (Clare McCutcheon, pers. comm.; see also ch. 13). Another two small sherds of Leinster Cooking ware from the 2021 excavations, including one from Cutting 2, may also originate from lamps or rush holders.

Table 9.1 Radiocarbon dates for St Mary's Abbey excavations. Calibration was after OxCal. 4.1 using the IntCal09 dataset (Bronk Ramsey 2009, 337–60; Reimer et al. 2009, 1111–50). *The Carbon-13 stable isotope value (δ13C) was measured on prepared graphite using the AMS spectrometer; the radiocarbon date has therefore been corrected for isotopic fractionation. However, the AMS-measured δ13C value can differ from the δ13C of the original material and it is therefore not shown

Lab. code	Charcoal ID	Sample no.	δC13 (‰)	14C Age (BP)	Calibrated age (95.4% prob.) (cal. BC/AD)	Description
UBA-47030	*Corylus*/hazel	2050	*	1284±27	AD662–796	Doubled-aisled structure
UBA-47031	*Betula*/birch	2058	*	1317±25	AD655–773	Outer enclosure
UBA-47033	*Corylus*/hazel	1029		825±25	AD1176–1269	Inner enclosure

Cuttings 2 and 4: the double-aisled structure

Cutting 2 was excavated to assess a possible double-aisled structure (WX015-003033-), again initially identified in the 2015 geophysical survey, which suggested that this structure was constructed over a large enclosing feature, interpreted as the outer enclosure of St Aidan's monastery (fig. 9.7). While neither of these features are the focus of this chapter, their archaeological significance merits brief inclusion. The E-Shaped anomaly was confirmed during excavation in 2021 as a structure, preserved below ground in the form of very partial wall remains, including two short segments of poorly arranged masonry, and 'rubble'-filled wall cuts/trenches that have been extensively 'robbed out' of any surviving masonry. A single radiocarbon date of cal. AD662–796 (on *Corylus*/hazel charcoal) was obtained from the backfill of one of the wall cuts (table 9.1). This date is inconsistent with finds from other wall cuts, such as frequent sherds of medieval pottery including Leinster Cooking Ware, Wexford-Type Coarseware, Wexford-Type Ware and Minety-Type Ware; the pottery clearly indicates a twelfth- to fourteenth-century date, which is supported by the recovery of a thirteenth-century silver Long-Cross-Type King Edward II coin from one wall cut. It is probable that the apparent radiocarbon-date discrepancy occurred as that wall cut was placed through the outer monastic enclosure, leading to the introduction of early medieval charcoal.

Previously, Bhreathnach and Dowling (2021; see also Dowling 2015) speculated on the form and function of the 'double-aisled structure', suggesting it served as the residence of Diarmait Mac Murchada, as a diminutive form of eleventh- to twelfth-century stone castle, as a hall listed among the abbots' possessions in the Dissolution assessment of St Mary's Abbey or as a post-medieval pile-house or as a seventeenth-

9.7 Ferns: (*top*) drone shot of Cutting 2 during recording, note the outer monastic enclosure ditch in the top left and the wall foundation cuts in the centre and far right, which also contain fragments of poorly constructed wall; (*bottom*) drone shot of Cutting 4 mid-excavation, note the keyhole-shaped kiln towards the top-centre

century plantation castle. The excavation appears to have confirmed a medieval origin, but the function of this intriguing building was not clarified during the 2021 excavations. With the aim of ascertaining the building's function, Cutting 4 was excavated in 2022, targeting the western gable of the 'double-aisled structure', as well as its adjoining northern central and southern 'walls'. Unfortunately, the evidence for each of these walls was ephemeral, with the masonry even more poorly preserved than the severely quarried out remains documented in Cutting 2 in 2021. Enough intact masonry and rubble-filled trenches were identified, however, to plan the basic layout of the structure, while the recovered artefacts confirmed a twelfth- to fourteenth-century date. The western limits of the structure also contained a circular feature, initially identified in geophysical prospection and interpreted as a possible stairwell or stair turret (Bhreathnach and Dowling 2021). This feature was considered essential to interpreting the function of the building. While analysis is continuing at the time of writing, this circular anomaly has been confirmed as a stone-lined keyhole kiln, with a circular chamber measuring 1.6m in diameter. Crucially, the kiln is bonded into the central spine of the double-aisled structure and, based on an initial assessment of recovered artefacts, appears also to be twelfth- to fourteenth-century in date. While the kiln fills gave no obvious indication of its function and post-excavation analyses are on-going, the feature has been tentatively interpreted as associated with pottery or tile manufacture, based on the recovery of several pottery wasters.

The other feature of great archaeological interest in Cutting 2 is the outer monastic ditch, which, depending on accepted conjectures of the enclosure (Doyle 2016, 35–61), might also have extended further west (Ryan 1998; Ryan and Buckley 2012) and north-west in the town (McLoughlin 2020, 33–4; see also McLoughlin and Stafford 2020, 85–100) (ch. 8). The ditch was heavily truncated by a second linear feature, but still measured approximately 2.5m wide by 90cm deep with a U-shaped cut. A single radiocarbon date (from *Betula*/birch charcoal) from the basal fill of the ditch returned a date of cal. AD655–773 (table 9.1); this date is clearly consistent with this ditch being part of the early medieval outer enclosure of Aidan's monastery and is broadly congruent with dates from other excavated sections of the possible outer monastic enclosure (ch. 8). Cutting 4 was also placed over the outer circuit of the early medieval enclosure, where this feature was confirmed in plan, but not excavated.

Cuttings 1 and 3: the cloister

Two abutting walls were recorded on the site in the early twentieth century, which clearly marked the south-west corner of a courtyard, identifiable as a cloister courtyard (Cochrane 1910; O'Keeffe 1997). This courtyard was further identified during the 2015 geophysical survey, and later during a 2021 GPR survey.

During the excavation of Cutting 1, which examined these abutting walls, the north–south wall was recorded for a distance of 6.4m within the cutting, its stones

9.8 Ferns: plan of Cutting 1 at the conclusion of excavations

surviving to a variable height of four to five courses (laid on an average of one to two foundation courses). Averaging 90cm in width and constructed of roughly dressed local stone on its outer faces, the wall contained a rubble wall-core with evidence of both lime mortar and clay bonding (fig. 9.8). Crucially, one sherd of Wexford-Type Coarseware was recovered from the wall bonding during mortar sampling of the wall face. Wexford-Type Coarseware is a variation of Dublin-Type Coarseware, which typically dates from the late twelfth to thirteenth century. The chronology indicated by this find is consistent with both possible dates for the cloister – *c.*1160, when the Augustinian rule was introduced to Ferns, or after the invasion – without pointing clearly to one over the other (ch. 6). The wall was clearly reinforced, with additional foundation courses laid, where it overlay soft underlying geology, such as the cesspit.

The second, east–west, wall appeared to overlie natural clay, and survived typically to one course only. Architecturally, this wall was constructed very differently from the north–south wall, as it consisted of large roughly cut angular local stones of varying sizes (*c.*40cm by 33cm by 26cm in average maximum dimensions). At its western extent, close to where the two walls join, two elongated stones dressed on their exterior sides and lying perpendicular to each other appear to outline what may have been an ope. A small feature of four large stones with some smaller flat 'infilling' stones was positioned toward the western exposed extent of the wall. This feature was in linear formation 10cm from the wall and running parallel to it. The function of this feature was not ascertained as only four stones were exposed. The stones could form part of a bench or, considering their location at the west side of the south wall, they could be associated to a laver; alternatively, the placement of the stones could be coincidental, having simply fallen from the adjacent southern wall.

There is no doubt that the excavated walls in Cutting 1 form the south-west corner of what is shown on the 2015 geophysical data and Cochrane's 1910 plan (see below). Excavations confirmed that intact masonry feature survives sub-surface, with at least one wall now also definitely dated to the later twelfth or thirteenth century. Unfortunately, the phasing of the two walls was not apparent.

While previous identification of the walls as claustral is supported by Cochrane's plan, a recent publication on the geophysical survey noted that no ambulatory or arcade were evident in the data (Bhreathnach and Dowling 2021, 215). More importantly, the excavations revealed no finds or features that might have been associated with a cloister, such as fine sculpted stone or evidence of arcading. The only worked stone found was largely utilitarian in nature. It is possible that the site was effectively quarried for stone, but even from an extensively quarried structure it is unlikely that all finely cut stone, such as from a claustral arcade, would be removed. The excavations also revealed no evidence for any sort of metalled or cobbled surface consistent with an ambulatory or internal floor space, even in areas of the cutting that were not truncated by other features. This absence of evidence supports the suggestion, made elsewhere in this volume (ch. 6), that the cloister at St Mary's was not finished, at least not on every side as intended.

There was an almost complete absence of bone from Cutting 1, except for a human infant tooth from the ditch fills, a human adult tooth from a backfill layer, and a possible fragment of human bone from another backfill layer. This suggests that the cloister, or at least this area of it, was not used for burial.

Post-excavation analysis of Cutting 3 is on-going and so only a brief note on the excavation can be given here. The 2021 excavation clearly confirmed the existence of sub-surface walls at the south-west corner of the courtyard mapped by Cochrane, also revealing that these walls are likely to be structural and date from the twelfth to fourteenth century. It was suggested at the end of the 2021 dig (Shine et al. 2021) that the cloister was surrounded by *c.*5–7m-wide range of buildings that, with an internal claustral garth, would account for the 30m-wide geophysical anomaly surveyed in

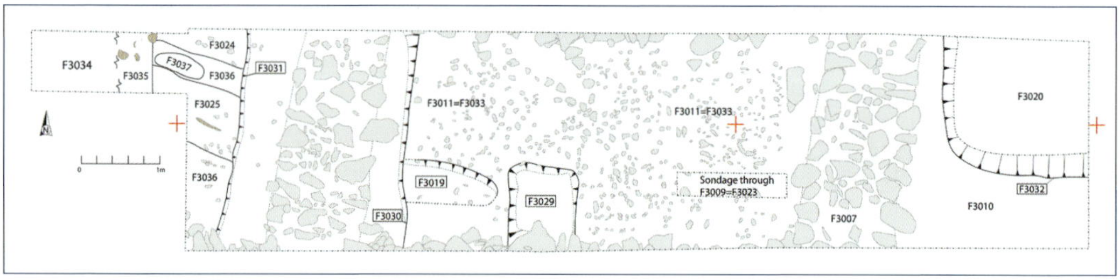

9.9 Ferns: post-excavation plan of Cutting 3 at the conclusion of excavations

9.10 Ferns: drone shot of Cutting 3, note the two east range walls, the westernmost (left) of which is contained in a foundation cut. The pit towards the top centre of the trench is a fire-pit/hearth

2015. To test this hypothesis, Cutting 3 was positioned to extend across the proposed east range, the area where DigVentures' GPR signal was strongest (Wilkins and Teale 2022) and where masonry at the 'courtyard's' eastern side had been recorded by Cochrane (1910; figs 9.9–9.11). Preliminary results indicate substantial intact masonry, most likely the remains of the eastern range, as well as a number of internal features, including a levelling clay, metalled surface, fire-pit and two raked-out burnt deposits (figs 9.9, 9.10). The fire-pit and burnt deposits are particularly interesting as they may point to a calefactory. Excavation of Cutting 3 clarified the range as being *c.*5m in internal width and defined by *c.*1.25m-wide walls on either side. Both walls

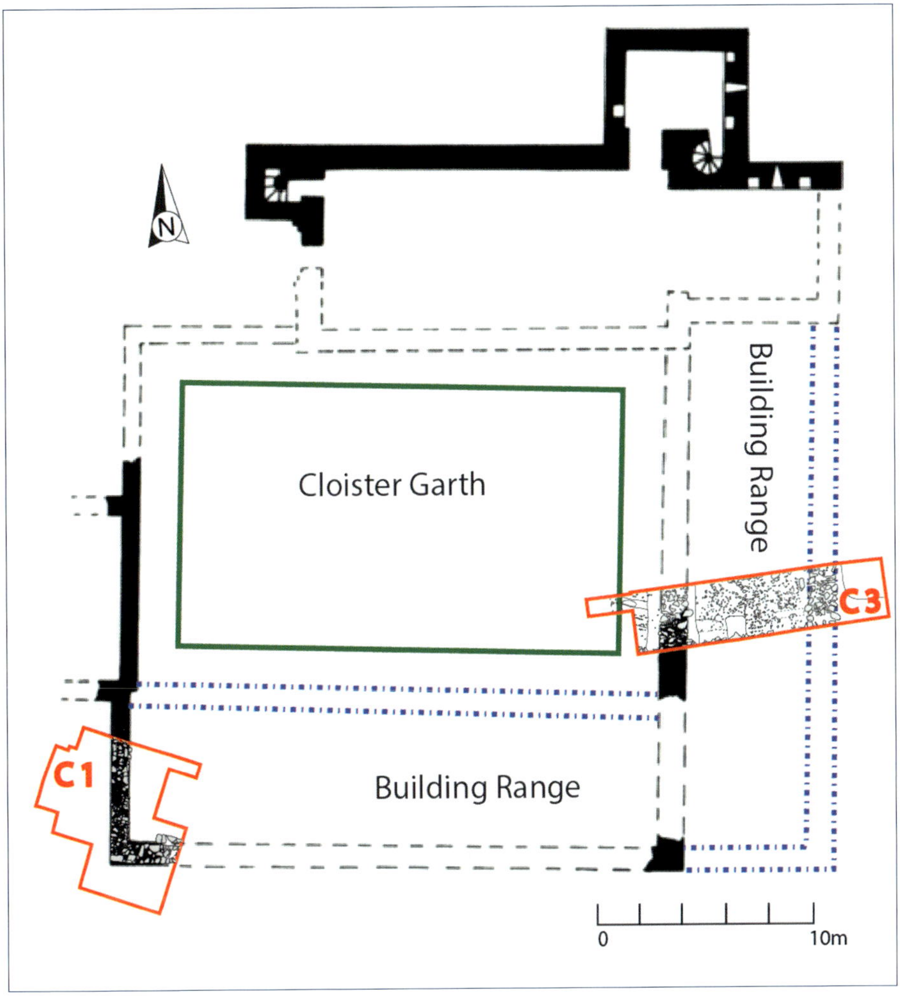

9.11 Ferns: schematic plan of Cochrane's 1910 drawing showing St Mary's Abbey and the adjacent rectangular structure, interpreted as a twelfth-century cloister by O'Keeffe (1997, fig. 11). The location of Cuttings 1 and 3 is shown, together with the planned walls and a re-interpretation of the possible layout of the cloister

generally consisted of a single foundation course of large local sub-rounded (*c.*30cm^3) 'field-stone', presumably collected from local glacial tills; these walls are similar in form to the southern wall excavated in Cutting 1 but markedly different to the western wall and the masonry extant in St Mary's Abbey church itself. The eastern east-range wall was constructed directly on a clay base, but the western wall was placed in a foundation cut, which contained two sherds of medieval pottery but also two post-medieval sherds. It is probable that the post-medieval finds are intrusive from an extensive overlying rubble/quarrying deposit, which has severely impacted the underlying medieval deposits in places. All other recovered pottery clearly infers a twelfth- to fourteenth-century date for the east range, especially for its internal features. The wall cut for the western east-range wall also disturbed a confirmed grave (containing a probable small adult female and accompanying juvenile/infant laid out east–west in Christian tradition) within the east range, as well as two possible grave cuts outside the range (in the area that would typically contain an ambulatory). This stratigraphic relationship points to burial pre-dating the east range and raises interesting questions regarding the date of the range buildings relative to the burials, and potentially St Mary's Abbey church itself. These intriguing questions will be explored in a future publication pending radiocarbon dates for the burials, which will also provide a *terminus post quem* for the western east-range wall and should clarify if the burials are associated with the early medieval or later medieval monastery. The excavations in Cutting 3 did not establish the presence or absence of a claustral walkway, partly due to the extremely limited excavation area. No claustral arcade, or finely work stone, was recovered. Three additional probable burials (which were left in situ), two of which were cut by the east-range western wall as outlined above, were observed as cut through a rough clay 'surface' in the area that would typically contain an ambulatory. Future research will assess this area further and explore in more detail the other features inside and outside the east range.

DISCUSSION: THE SIGNIFICANCE OF THE FERNS CLOISTER

While it is certain that the rectangular enclosure south of the abbey church was claustral, what little information is available about its form suggests that it was somewhat unusual. Although one cannot easily visualize their presence based on Cochrane's plan, future work may reveal that there was indeed a standard refectory (running west–east) on the courtyard's south side, opposite the church. Excavations have already confirmed the presence of an east range and it is possible, although at this time still entirely conjectural, that this had the conventional arrangement of a chapter house and other rooms at ground level and a dormitory overhead. Prior to excavation, the GPR anomalies, while not conclusive, had hinted at eastern and southern ranges, each about 7.5m wide, associated with a smaller central garth around 15m wide in each direction (fig. 9.11). The range's dimensions (5m wide internal space with two 1.25m-wide walls) are now confirmed, at least for the eastern range. However, the fact that the original twelfth-century church was not replaced or even updated, combined with the absence of a south-side entrance into it (such as one would expect in a church attached to a cloister), combined also with an absence of any finely carved stonework of post-Anglo-Norman invasion date, would suggest that the claustral area was never finished as intended. The apparent absence of evidence for a west range (indicated

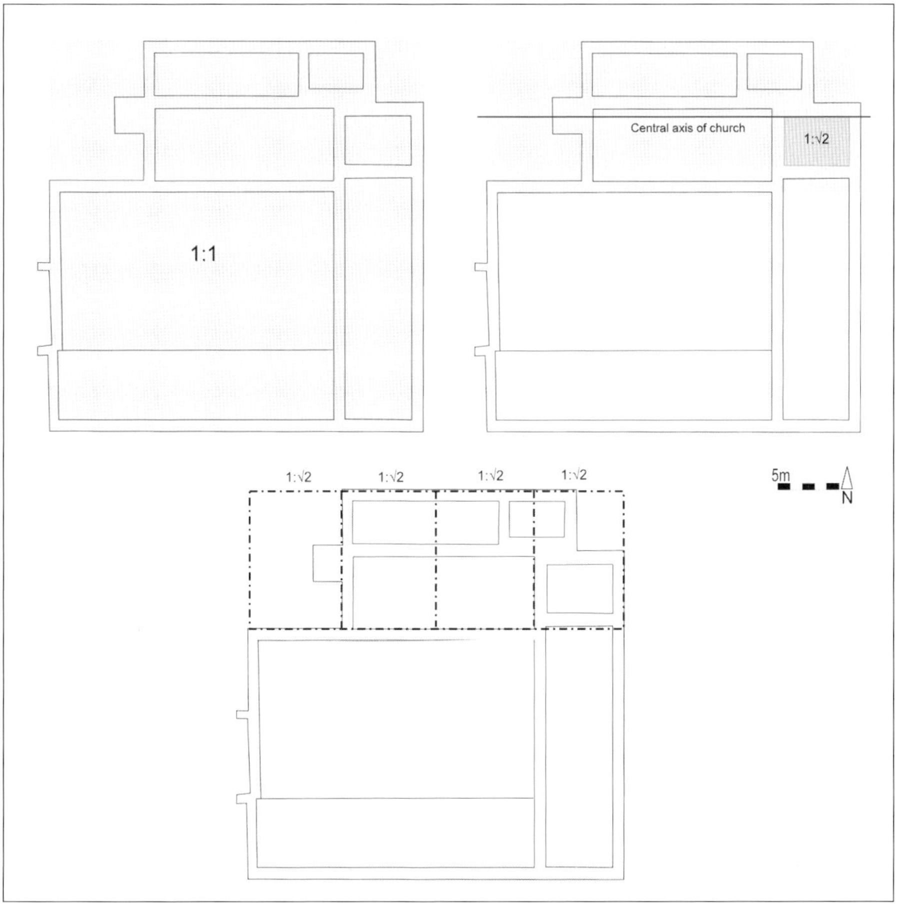

9.12 Ferns: metrological analysis of the site showing that the spatial arrangements of the abbey, both church and claustral court, were carefully worked out using standard medieval proportions

predominantly by the GPR survey, which identified no clear evidence for structural remains, either a building or rubble cast, in the area that would be occupied by a western range) is not a factor here for the western sides of cloisters did not always have buildings (O'Keeffe 1999).[2] An absence of a west range may also help explain the entirely different construction technique observed between both the western wall and the southern wall in Cutting 1, and between the western wall in Cutting 1 and both east-range walls in Cutting 3; at the very last these differences in masonry infer a different phasing and/or purpose.

Metrological analysis of the site (fig. 9.12) shows that the spatial arrangements of the abbey, both church and claustral court, were carefully worked out using standard

2 See, for example, the early thirteenth-century Augustinian priory of Bridgetown, Co. Cork (O'Keeffe 1999).

medieval proportions '1:1; 1:√2' (O'Keeffe 2015, 89–93), and that while space was reserved for a west range, it was seemingly never built, with the monastic arrangement similar to that presented above (fig. 9.11). None of this is to suggest that the claustral part of the abbey was left unfinished: evidence of an Augustinian community at Ferns through the Middle Ages tell us that the claustral area was probably occupied, but it could not have functioned as did other cloisters, because there was no direct access from the court to the church, and it is barely conceivable that its constituent buildings and features were completed as first intended, based on both the archaeological data and evidence from the ruins themselves. To date, geophysical prospection has not revealed clear evidence of a latrine-drain in its south-east corner. That is a feature that should be sought in excavation, for water-management was critical to how the refectory/kitchen and dormitory ranges functioned, and the absence of any such feature would have serious implications for how the Ferns enclosure is interpreted. Future excavation might also reveal more evidence that the cloister had a complex history as, in the limited excavation to date, it is apparent that the western wall is different to those toward the south and east of the cloister.

The available evidence indicates that building work on the cloister began after the church was built. The interval between the two acts is not known: the enclosure could have been laid out when the rule of St Augustine was introduced *c.*1160, or it could have been laid out as the first stage of a proposed – but ultimately abandoned – redevelopment of the abbey, which, based on current evidence, still occurred in the twelfth to fourteenth century. Whatever the case, the metrology of the church was extended into the claustral area so that the entire abbey, when completed (or redeveloped), would have conformed to a metrical scheme (fig. 9.12). That intention would lead one to think that the builders of the church, when the rule of St Augustine was introduced in the 1160s, also laid out the claustral enclosure, but one would wonder why, were that the case, the church was not suited to a claustral scheme. Perhaps the cloister was started after the invasion as the first step to develop the abbey, before being aborted. Perhaps further excavation will reveal that the claustral area was indeed laid out when the Anglo-Normans arrived in Ferns, but that its spatiality was determined by features built *before* the invasion. This might explain why the metrologies of the church and claustral enclosure are keyed into each other. Hopefully, continuing specialist analyses of the last two excavation seasons, together with an additional field season in 2023, will further resolve queries relating to both the phasing of the claustral area and the presence or absence of a claustral arcade and walk.

BIBLIOGRAPHY

Bhreathnach, E. and Dowling, G. 2021. 'Forming an episcopal see and an Augustinian foundation in medieval Ireland: the case of Ferns, Co. Wexford'. *Proceedings of the Royal Irish Academy*, 121C, 191–226.

Bronk Ramsey, C. 2009. 'Bayesian analysis of radiocarbon dates'. *Radiocarbon*, 51:1, 337–60.

Cochrane, R. 1910. 'Ferns, Co. Wexford'. In *78th Annual Report of the Commissioners of Public Works in Ireland*, 3–6, 16–17. Dublin.

Doyle, I. 2016. 'Telling the dancer from the dance: the archaeology of early medieval Wexford'. In Doyle, I. and Browne, B. (eds), *Medieval Wexford: essays in memory of Billy Colfer*, 35–61. Dublin.

Dowling, G. 2021. 'Geophysical survey report, Ferns, Co. Wexford (21R0297)'. Unpublished technical report prepared for the Irish Archaeology Field School and UoCD.

Dowling, G. 2015. 'Geophysical investigations at Ferns, Co. Wexford'. Unpublished technical report for the Discovery Programme.

Elliott, I. 2021. 'Report on archaeogeophysical survey (consent 19R0238) at Clone td, Co. Wexford'. Unpublished technical report prepared for the Irish Archaeology Field School.

Elliott, I. 2022. 'Report on archaeogeophysical survey (consent 21R0219) at Clone td, Co. Wexford'. Unpublished technical report prepared for the Irish Archaeology Field School.

Gwynn, A. and Hadcock, N. 1970. *Medieval religious houses: Ireland*. London.

Kavanagh, J. 2004. 'Preliminary excavation report: 04E0663'. Unpublished excavation report 04E0663.

Kavanagh, J. 2006. 'Archaeological test excavation report at Ferns Upper, Ferns, Co. Wexford'. Unpublished excavation report 06E0780.

Kavanagh, J. 2006b. 'Archaeological test excavation report at Castleland, Ferns, Co. Wexford'. Unpublished excavation report 06E0987.

McFall, T. 1957. *An account of the history of Ferns cathedral church*. Dublin.

McLoughlin, C. and Stafford, E. 2020. 'Medieval Ferns, Co. Wexford: from monastic centre to medieval town'. In Corlett, C. and Potterton, M. (eds), *The town in medieval Ireland in the light of recent archaeological excavations*, 85–100. Dublin.

McLoughlin, C. 2020. 'From early to late: uncovering medieval Ferns'. *Archaeology Ireland*, 34:2. 33–4.

O'Keeffe, T. 1997. 'Diarmait Mac Murchada and Romanesque Leinster: four twelfth-century churches in context'. *Journal of the Royal Society of Antiquaries of Ireland*, 127, 52–79.

O'Keeffe, T. 1999. *An Anglo-Norman monastery: Bridgetown Priory, Co. Cork, and the architecture of the Augustinian Canons Regular in Ireland*. Kinsale.

O'Keeffe, T. 2015. *Medieval Irish buildings, 1100–1600*. Dublin.

O'Keeffe, T. and Carey Bates, R. 2016. 'The abbey and cathedral of Ferns, 1111–1253'. In Doyle, I. and Browne, B. (eds), *Medieval Wexford: essays in memory of Billy Colfer*, 73–96. Dublin.

Reimer, P., Baillie, M., Bard, E., Bayliss, A., Beck, J., Blackwell, P., Bronk Ramsey, C., Buck, C., Burr, G., Edwards, R., Friedrich, M., Grootes, P., Guilderson, T., Hajdas, I., Heaton, T., Hogg, A., Hughen, K., Kaiser, K., Kromer, B., McCormac, F., Manning, S., Reimer, R.,

Richards, D., Southon, J., Talamo, S., Turney, C., van der Plicht, J. and Weyhenmeyer, C. 2009. 'IntCal09 and Marine09 radiocarbon age calibration curves, 0–50,000 years cal. BP'. *Radiocarbon*, 51, 1111–50.

Ryan, F. 1998. 'Archaeological findings from monitoring of Phase 1 of Ferns Sewage Scheme, Co. Wexford'. Unpublished excavation report 98E0132

Ryan, F. 2012. 'Excavation of a late Iron Age ring-ditch at Ferns Lower, Co. Wexford'. In Corlett, C. and Potterton, M. (eds), *Life and death in Iron Age Ireland in the light of recent archaeological excavations*, 273–90. Dublin.

Shine, D., Lacey, B. Corlett, C. Elliott, I. and Mandal, S. 2020. 'Clone, Ferns: a meadow of St Aidan?' *Archaeology Ireland*, 34:4, 24–9.

Shine, D. and Lacey, B. 2020. 'Clone community archaeological excavation report'. Unpublished technical report prepared for the National Monuments Service and Wexford County Council.

Shine, D. and Lacey, B. 2021. 'Clone Church archaeological excavation report'. Unpublished technical report prepared for the National Monuments Service and Wexford County Council.

Shine, D., Lynch, L., Mandal, S. and O'Meara, D. 2021. 'Discovering St Aidan's monastery: preliminary archaeological excavation report (December 2021)'. Unpublished technical report produced for the National Monuments Service.

Taylor, K. and Hurley, K. 2021. 'R772 Ferns Village Pavement Scheme Phase 2, Ferns, Co. Wexford'. Unpublished technical report for Wexford County Council.

White, N. (ed.). 1943. *Extents of Irish monastic possessions, 1540–1541*. Dublin.

Wilkins, B. and Teale, K. 2022. 'Rediscovering ancient connections, Wexford: archaeological geophysical survey report (licence nos 21R0196, 21R0197, 21R0198, 21R0199)'. Unpublished technical report for Rediscovering Ancient Connections Project Team and Pembrokeshire County Council.

CHAPTER TEN

Geophysical investigations at Ferns as part of the Ancient Connections Project

KIMBERLEY TEALE

INTRODUCTION AND PROJECT BACKGROUND

On 10 October 2021, DigVentures conducted a geophysical Ground-Penetrating Radar (GPR) survey (Licence 21R0196) in the grounds of St Mary's Abbey and field as part of a wider programme of geophysical prospection for the 'Rediscovering Ancient Connections' project (fig. 10.1). Originally planned as a community-focused investigation, the restrictions of Covid-19 led to the survey being carried out by a small professional team, disseminating the results through an online Storytelling Festival in March 2022 and an 'Introduction to Geophysics' workshop in April 2022.

'Rediscovering Ancient Connections: the Saints Project' is a cross-border arts and heritage project linking north Pembrokeshire in Wales and north Wexford in Ireland. The project is part of a work package called 'Exploring a Shared Past', which aims to revive the ancient links between communities in Pembrokeshire and Wexford using the shared heritage of St David and his pupil and protégé St Aidan. St David is the patron saint of Wales and is commemorated in the city of St David's where he spent much of his life, while St Aidan is closely associated with Wexford, in particular the town of Ferns.

Geophysical survey is a science that examines the earth's physical properties using non-invasive ground-survey techniques to reveal buried archaeological features, sites and landscapes (Gaffney and Gater 2003). The geophysical survey at Ferns was undertaken as part of a wider programme of prospection aimed at finding archaeological remains that could link the medieval history of Pembrokeshire and Wexford.

St Mary's field contains traces of an early ecclesiastical enclosure related to St Aidan's original monastic settlement at Ferns, with the later St Mary's Abbey at the core. The enclosure is in the civil parish of Ferns, townland of Ferns Lower in Co. Wexford. The field is directly east of St Edan's Cathedral, a nineteenth-century Church of Ireland structure built from the original core of the thirteenth-century cathedral (WX015-003003-), as well as an adjacent graveyard (WX015-003008-). The site is bounded by the N11 and Station Road on the north and south-west respectively, with a stream defining the field at its eastern extent (fig. 10.2). The remains of St Mary's Abbey

10.1 Ferns: the setting of St Mary's Abbey

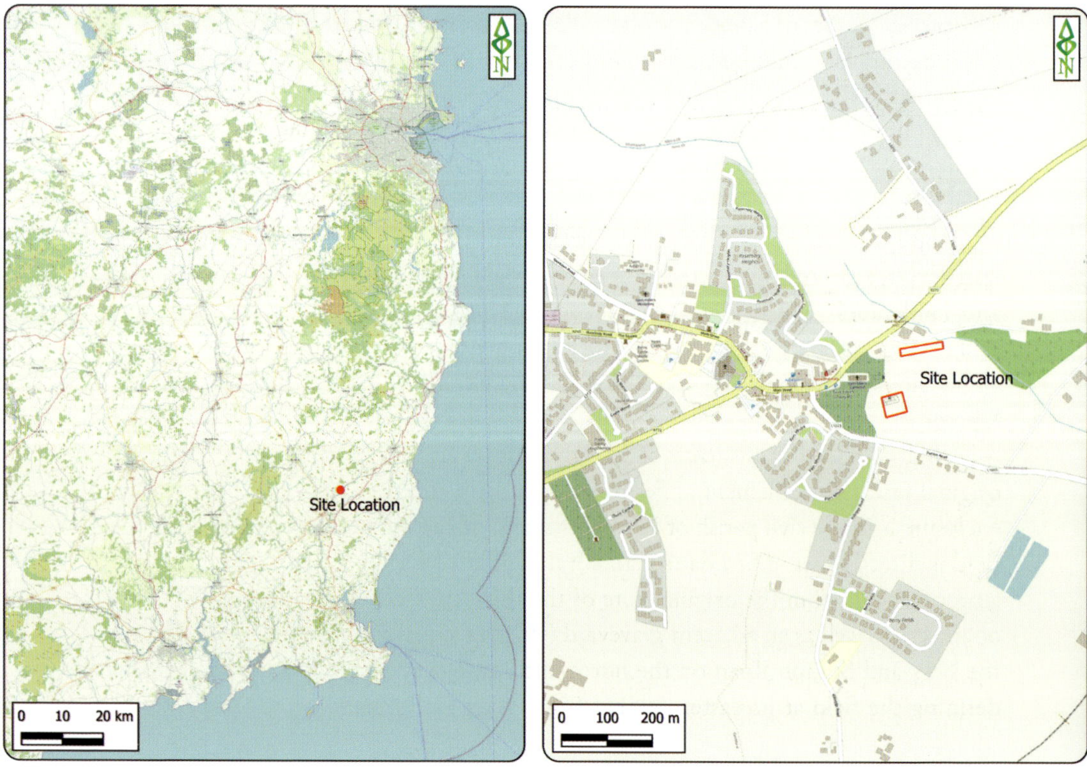

10.2 Ferns: map showing locations of survey

10.3 Ferns: plan of St Mary's showing the location of the survey grids

(RMP WX015-003004), a mid-twelfth-century Augustinian foundation, are located in the western portion of the field (Shine et al. 2021).

The site has been studied previously using the geophysical techniques of magnetometry and earth resistance, which measure changes in the ground's magnetic properties and soil moisture content respectively to help identify buried features such as walls, pits, ditches and areas of burning (Bhreathnach and Dowling 2020). Geophysical surveys undertaken in 2015 discovered significant evidence relating to an early monastic site, including the eastern limits of the monastic enclosure and anomalies suggestive of a structure. Archaeological excavations confirmed the presence of an inner and an outer enclosure as well as ironworking debris and charcoal. Excavations in the north-east of the field revealed the partial remains of a wooden watermill and stone mill as well as numerous finds indicative of early medieval occupancy. Based on the results of these surveys and investigations, DigVentures selected the technique of GPR to conduct their survey. This is a method favourable for discovering built foundations, structures, voids and graves, as well as providing depth information and stratigraphy for the site. The aim of the survey was to clarify some of these previously discovered monastic features as well as to better establish the remains of the mills in the north of the field.

The field is currently set in pasture grazed by cattle, with a gentle slope down towards the north-east from approximately 50m above Ordnance Datum (aOD) to 40m aOD. The bedrock geology of the site is recorded as Ordovician Felsic Volcanics of the Campile Formation, which are overlain by shale tills (Ordnance Survey Ireland, 2021; ch. 1).

The GPR survey focused on two areas within the grounds (fig. 10.3): an area immediately to the south and east of St Mary's Abbey (ITM 702218 649763) to further investigate anomalies identified during previous magnetometer surveys and an area in the north-east of the field (ITM 702272 649870) to further investigate the remains of watermills discovered during previous excavations.

HISTORICAL AND ARCHAEOLOGICAL BACKGROUND

This archaeological background and the details of previous excavations are taken from the 'Method Statement for Archaeological Excavations at St Aidan's Monastery, Ferns, Co. Wexford' generated on behalf of the Irish Archaeology Field School (IAFS) (Shine et al. 2021). Wexford has a rich early medieval tradition with sites that relate to saints such as Ibar, Abban and, particularly in north Wexford, Aidan, one of the most important figures in the story of early Christianity in south-eastern Ireland.

Although he was born and died during the sixth century, St David is known only through later texts and much of his actual life has become shrouded in myth and legend. While the earliest centre of his cult may have been focused in Ceredigion, by the ninth century he was closely associated with St David's (Pembrokeshire). Later, in the eleventh and twelfth centuries, it is clear that his cult took on a wider focus than St David alone. As with a number of early medieval saints, David became associated with a series of other ecclesiastical figures including Aidan, who played an important role in recording his journey from Pembrokeshire to Ireland in 'The Life', in which he founded his own religious houses and had particular associations with Clone and Ferns.

The monastic site of Ferns has an extensive history reflected in historical sources, built heritage and sub-surface archaeology (Corlett 2012; O'Keeffe and Bates 2016; Doyle 2016, 52; Ryan 2012, 283; Kavanagh 2007; Sheehan 2006). Ferns was founded sometime around the turn of the seventh century by St Aidan, also known as St Máedóc or St Mogue (d. 620–5), who was active in the sixth and seventh centuries, having originally derived from modern Cavan (Culleton 1999; ch. 2). The only above-ground evidence of the early monastery at Ferns is in the four high crosses in the large graveyard (Anon. 1909–10). A fifth granite cross, which might be a small high cross with an unpierced ringed head, and a granite cross-slab are in the chapter house at the east end of the cathedral (Harbison 1992 i, 89). The site was recorded historically, such as when it was raided by the Vikings in 835 and 839 (Culleton 1999). These raids, together with the high crosses around St Edan's Cathedral (WX015-003009-, WX015-

003010-, WX015-003011-and WX015-003012-), indicate the presence of a monastery of some importance.

From documentary sources, it is known that St Aidan's monastery was founded at the turn of the seventh century, possibly over a pre-existing prehistoric site (Shine et al. 2021). The density of prehistoric archaeology in the vicinity of the monastery indicates that archaeology pre-dating the early medieval period may be found at the site. Furthermore, it suggests the early monastic site was deliberately placed at this location due to an established pre-existing prehistoric significance – as has been observed at several other monastic sites throughout the county (O'Sullivan et al. 2018; Shine et al. 2021).

PREVIOUS ARCHAEOLOGICAL INVESTIGATIONS

Archaeological evidence of the site of St Aidan's is relatively limited and has been greatly enhanced by excavations conducted in recent years. Excavation in 2004 just 70m from the cathedral uncovered a Bronze Age flat cemetery, two parallel ditches interpreted as a possible ringfort and a 5m-wide V-shaped ditch (Kavanagh 2007). It was argued that this could represent an inner monastic vallum, meaning a circumference for the inner enclosure of *c.*200m (Doyle 2016, 55).

In May 2015 a programme of magnetic gradiometry and limited earth resistance survey was undertaken at the site as part of the Monastic Ireland Project, an IRC-funded research collaboration between the Discovery Programme, Trinity College Dublin and University College Cork, with funding secured by the Ferns Heritage Group (Shine et al. 2021). The survey revealed significant evidence relating to the early monastic site at Ferns including anomalies thought to represent two substantial ditches (WX015-003031-; WX015-003032) approximately 40m apart. These ditches were interpreted as the eastern limits of the monastic enclosure. The innermost ditch is positioned directly beneath the twelfth-century St Mary's Abbey (WX015-003004-).

Anomalies consistent with a structure (WX015-003033-) were also identified directly adjacent to and partly over the outer enclosure. Towards the west of the field the survey also identified anomalies interpreted as part of a field system (WX015-003034-) and a roadway (WX015-003035-) (Dowling 2015). Prior to this geophysical work, the circuit of the monastic enclosure had been contested for some time, although a ditch (now re-considered to be part of the outer enclosure) was found on Station Road (just opposite the junction with Clone Road) during the Ferns Sewerage Scheme in 1999–2000. The ditch contained ironworking debris and charcoal, a sample of which was dated to cal. AD331–557 (Ryan 2000, licence 98E0132; UCD0007 1620±50 BP, calibrated at 2-sigma level), meaning the feature could represent the very earliest enclosure of the site dating to the mid-sixth century. Based on this and other results, Doyle (2016) interpreted the route of the monastic enclosure as having an inner enclosure *c.*200m in diameter and an outer on *c.*300–350m in diameter.

Since the production of that paper a commercial excavation towards the centre of the town, directed by Catherine McLoughlin of Stafford McLoughlin Archaeology, revealed a V-shaped ditch, which is currently interpreted as the western limit of the monastic enclosure, meaning the monastic site is much larger than originally anticipated, with a diameter of >500m (Shine et al. 2021).

In 2019 TVAS (Ireland) Ltd conducted an archaeological excavation at the north-east corner of St Mary's field for Transport Infrastructure Ireland (TII) as part of a rehabilitation of the road pavement through Ferns Village (ch. 11). The excavations uncovered the partial remains of a wooden watermill and a later stone mill (built on the same site), as well as features excavated within the wayleave including portions of several ditches, at least one of which likely surrounded the monastery. Pottery sherds (early medieval), fragments of leather shoes, residue from smithing/smelting, a fragment of a worn turned alder bowl, a blue glass bead and a fragment of a stone bangle were retrieved during the works (Eoghan Greene pers. comm.; Keane 2020). Situated at the bottom of a gentle north-east-facing slope and *c.*120m north-east of the cathedral is the probable site of St Máedóc's early church (WX015-003002-). Archaeological testing (E004633) during 2019 and 2020 by Kate Taylor in advance of the installation of a west–east waste waterpipe from the R772 road (N11) to the north-west–south-east stream identified numerous archaeological features. There were seven phases of activity, none closely dated yet, but largely medieval. Towards the east end of the trench a mill was recorded and is preserved in situ (ch. 11).

GEOPHYSICAL SURVEY

The geophysical survey was undertaken with GPR, which uses electromagnetic (EM) waves to locate objects within the ground and determine their depth (fig. 10.4). The EM waves are emitted through a transmitter and travel down through the ground until they hit an object or interface (something with a different electromagnetic property). Some of the energy continues deeper into the ground, while some is reflected to the surface and is recorded by a receiver. The time the EM wave has taken to travel from the transmitter and be reflected to the receiver is used to determine the depth to the interface or feature. Using the depth information and the strength of the returning signal, a vertical section through the sub-surface can be generated called a 'radargram'. Low-amplitude features in the data are suggestive of cut features such as ditches and pits, whereas high-amplitude features are suggestive of structural remains such as walls, floors and voids.

The GPR survey was undertaken using a MALA GX450 Rough-Terrain Cart with a 400 to 500MHz mid-frequency antenna mounted on a skid. The survey was

10.4 Ferns: ground-penetrating radar survey in front of St Mary's Abbey and St Edan's Cathedral

conducted within a series of grids utilizing a 50cm traverse interval and a 2cm sample interval. Three 20m by 20m grids were surveyed immediately south and east of the remains of St Aidan's monastery and three 10m by 30m grids were surveyed in the north of the field, totalling an area of approximately 0.22ha.

The traverses of data (radargrams) were assembled using GPRSlice into a 3D block and processed for background noise with a gain adjust, before being 'sliced' at various depth- or time intervals. These time slices were combined with the GPS points and georeferenced in QGIS and are presented as greyscale data plots alongside their interpretations.

GPR SURVEY RESULTS

St Mary's Abbey

Three of the Depth Slices collected next to St Mary's Abbey revealed possible archaeological anomalies. In Depth Slice 3 (fig. 10.5), a rectangular high-amplitude

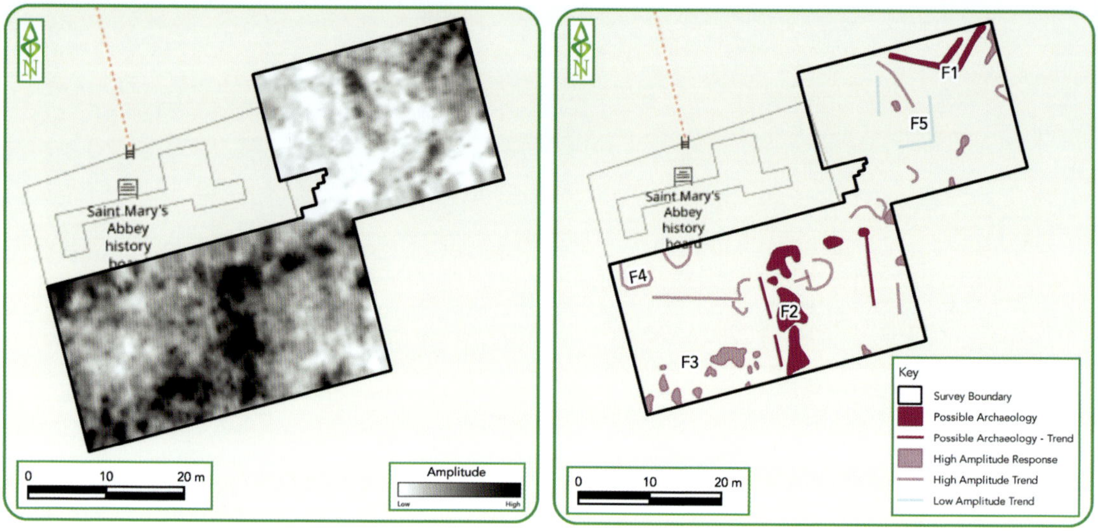

10.5 Ferns: results and interpretation of GPR survey at a depth of 0.49–0.74m (Slice 3)

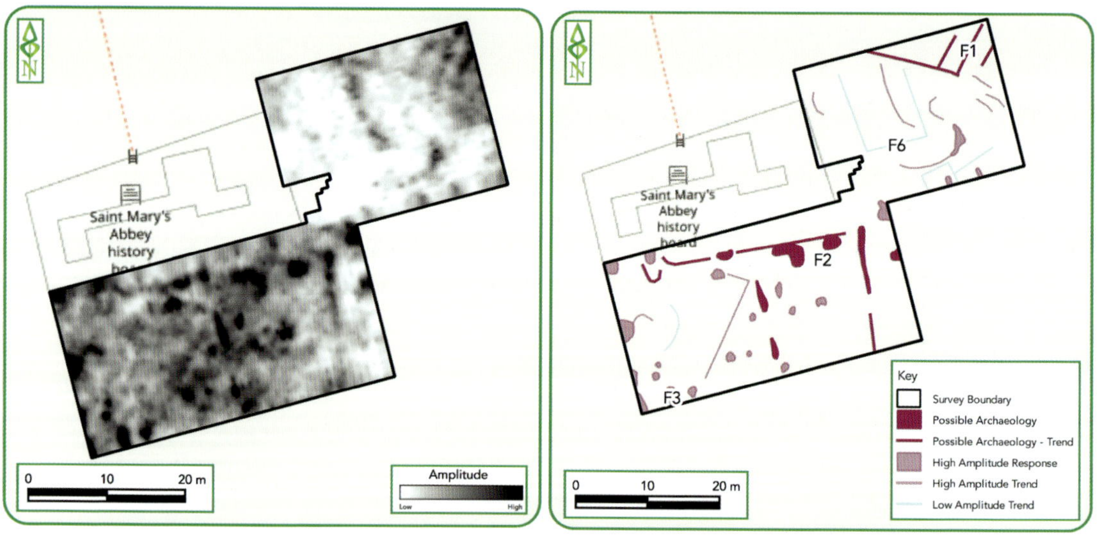

10.6 Ferns: results and interpretation of GPR survey at a depth of 0.74–0.98m (Slice 4)

anomaly has been identified in the north-east of the dataset [F1]. This could relate to the corner of a building or enclosure. The anomaly sits parallel to two other high-amplitude anomalies that could be related. A second rectilinear high-amplitude feature is visible to the south of St Mary's Abbey [F2]. This could also relate to possible building- or enclosure foundations. High-amplitude amorphous responses have been identified to the west of this [F3], but they do not form a discernible pattern and it is

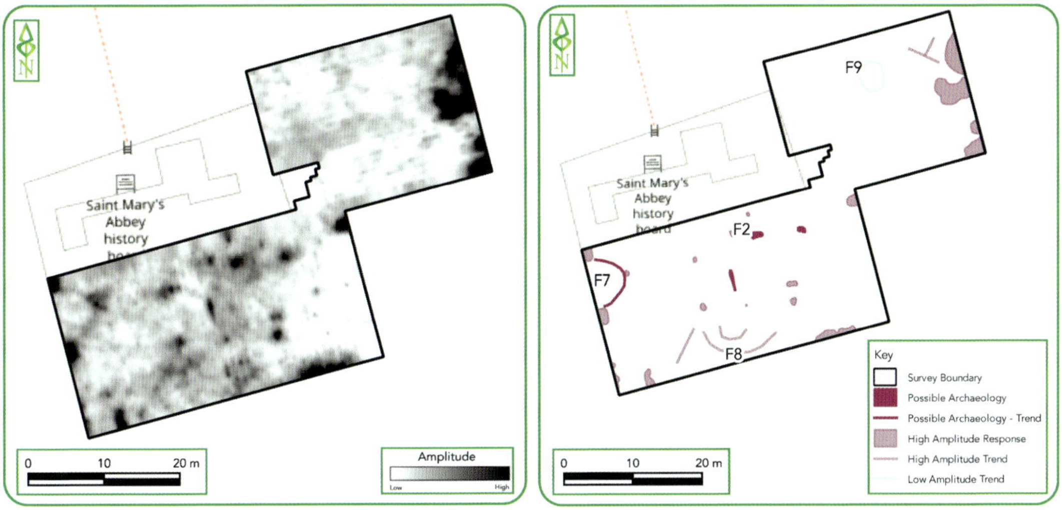

10.7 Ferns: results and interpretation of GPR survey at a depth of 1.24–1.48m (Slice 6)

not clear what they relate to. To the north, rectilinear and circular trends are visible [F4] immediately next to the abbey, which could also be archaeological. In the north-east of the dataset, a low-amplitude rectilinear trend has been identified that could be archaeological [F5].

In Depth Slice 4 (fig. 10.6) the possible enclosure [F1] is still visible in the north-east of the data. The rectilinear remains of the other possible enclosure [F2] to the south of St Mary's Abbey are also still visible, but the anomalies are much clearer and more pronounced. The feature measures *c.*14.7m wide and the northern boundary is seen to continue towards the west, curving towards the abbey at its western extent. Further linear high-amplitude trends adjacent to it are suggestive of additional archaeological remains. The amorphous high-amplitude trends [F3] in the south-west of the dataset are also still visible. In the north-east of the dataset, a rectilinear anomaly appears more pronounced and is suggestive of archaeological remains such as foundations, though its low-amplitude response suggests the foundations have been removed and the anomaly could represent robber trenches [F6].

In Depth Slice 6 (fig. 10.7), the remains of the possible enclosures [F1, F2] are just visible in the data but are of a much weaker amplitude. A circular high-amplitude anomaly measuring 6.6m in width is visible in the data immediately south of St Mary's Abbey, which likely has an archaeological origin [F7]. A weaker sub-circular anomaly has also been identified in the south of the dataset, and this could be archaeological [F8]. To the east of St Mary's Abbey, a small low-amplitude or corresponding broader high-amplitude circular feature has been identified [F9]. Measuring approximately 4m in diameter, the feature could relate to a small building or enclosure. The low-amplitude response is suggestive of robbed-out material, or perhaps a garden-type feature. To the east of this, a large high-amplitude amorphous anomaly is just visible at the edge of the dataset [F10] but it is not clear what it relates to.

St Mary's field

Several of the Depth Slices collected in the north of St Mary's field also revealed anomalies suggestive of the presence of archaeological remains. The western extents of Depth Slice 2 (fig. 10.8) revealed some shallow-depth high-amplitude linear and curvilinear responses that could relate to archaeological remains [F11]. Further high-amplitude amorphous responses are visible throughout the dataset, but it is not clear what they relate to.

The area of high-amplitude readings in the east of the dataset [F12] is more prevalent in Depth Slice 3 (fig. 10.9). This area is close to a stream and it could relate

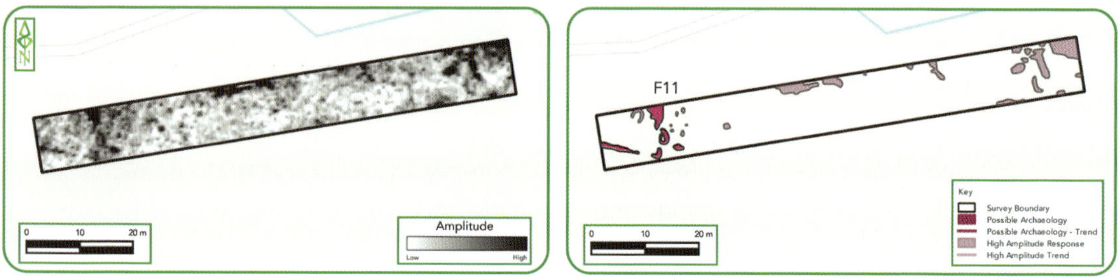

10.8 Ferns: results and interpretation of GPR survey at a depth of 0.25–0.50m (Slice 2)

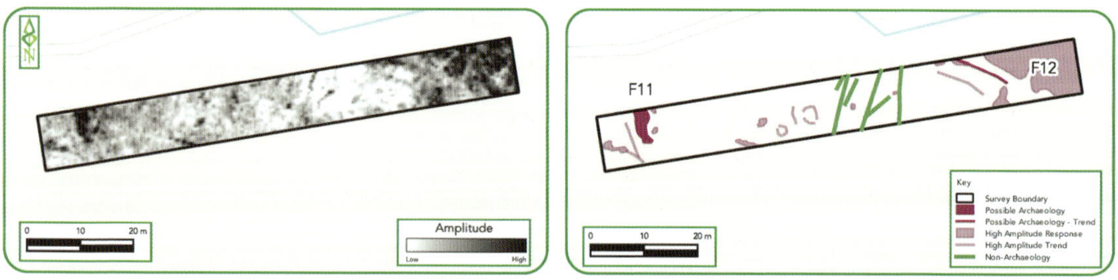

10.9 Ferns: results and interpretation of GPR survey at a depth of 0.50–0.75m (Slice 3)

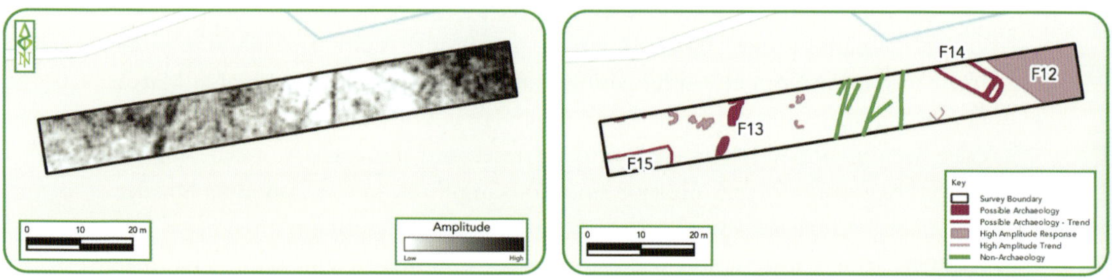

10.10 Ferns: results and interpretation of GPR survey at a depth of 0.75–1.00m (Slice 4)

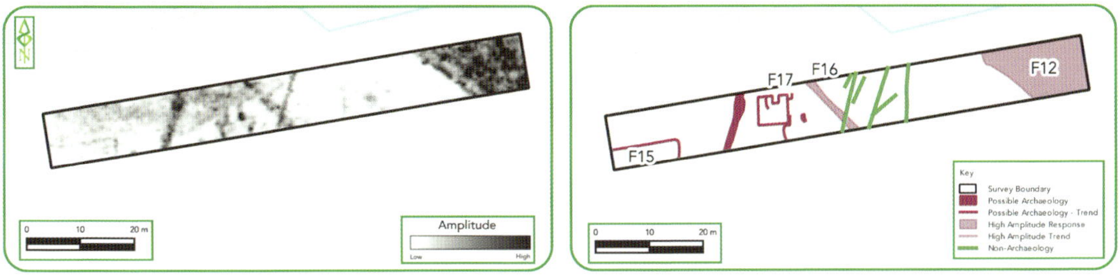

10.11 Ferns: results and interpretation of GPR survey at a depth of 1.00–1.26m (Slice 5)

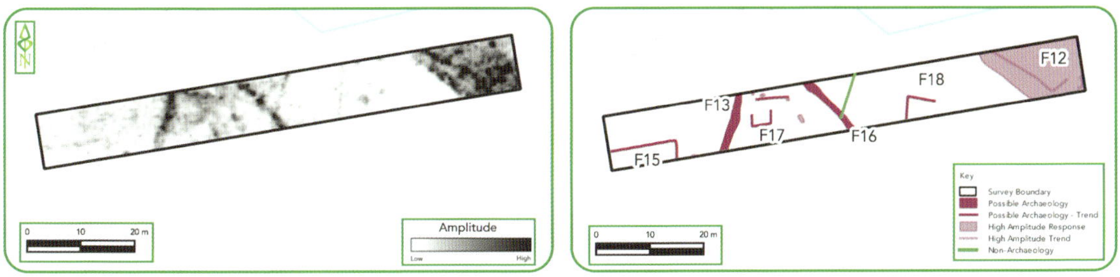

10.12 Ferns: results and interpretation of GPR survey at a depth of 1.25–1.50m (Slice 6)

to some geological variations or disturbance caused by sediments or flooding deposits. It could also relate to an archaeological feature situated next to the stream. Two parallel linear high-amplitude trends have been identified next to this running north-west–south-east, which could be archaeological in origin. Modern field drains run through the centre of the dataset from north-north-east–south-south-west. In the west of the data, the high-amplitude response [F11] is still visible adjacent to anomalies of a lesser magnitude.

In Depth Slice 4 (fig. 10.10), the two parallel linear trends are now visible as a rectilinear high-amplitude feature, which likely relates to archaeological remains such as building foundations [F14]. The feature measures approximately 4m wide and at least 11m long, however the northern extents run beyond the survey boundary. The southern extents of the feature appear to be split into a smaller room or enclosure. In the west of the dataset, a broad high-amplitude response runs north-east–south-west and could relate to a boundary or enclosure feature [F13]. To the west of this, a very weak rectilinear feature is visible just at the edge of the survey area [F15]. This is likely archaeological in origin, relating to a possible building or enclosure.

Depth Slice 5 (fig. 10.11) reveals that the rectilinear feature [F15] is still visible in the dataset, as is the aforementioned possible boundary feature [F13]. Immediately east of this, a square high-amplitude feature has been identified measuring approximately 5.5m in width [F17]. This anomaly is suggestive of building remains, but it is not clear if it relates to the reputed watermill or an early church building. A further broad high-amplitude response is seen to the east of this running north-west–

south-east [F16] and its trajectory suggests it forms a boundary or enclosure feature with the aforementioned possible boundary feature [F13].

Depth Slice 6 (fig. 10.12) reveals that rectilinear feature [F15] is still very much present. This likely relates to a building, associated with either the watermill or the wider ecclesiastical landscape. Similarly, the square feature [F17] is also still visible. Further ephemeral anomalies are visible throughout the Depth Slice, and these could be archaeological. In the east of the dataset, the high-amplitude area [F12] is also still prevalent, though some linear high-amplitude responses are visible within it, which suggests there are some archaeological remains among whatever the deposit is.

DISCUSSION

Ground-Penetrating Radar is an excellent methodology for identifying almost all below-ground remains, whereas magnetometry identifies only features with a magnetic property that can be detected by the sensors. By conducting surveys using different techniques, the datasets can complement each other and help to indicate features that other techniques might not have detected. GPR can help to identify features that have been missed in the magnetometry data and likewise magnetometry can help to identify features that might have been too ephemeral in the GPR data or may have been masked by ringing of the data against larger buried features.

In comparing the GPR data collected during this survey to the magnetometry and earth-resistance data collected in 2015 (Bhreathnach and Dowling 2020), there are correlations between the identified anomalies and features.

To the south of St Mary's Abbey, the rectangular GPR anomaly [F2] visible in Depth Slices 3, 4 and 6 correlates with the location of a positive rectilinear anomaly suggested by the authors to comprise the remains of a twelfth-century cloister. This was supported by an earth-resistance survey, confirming the presence of a high-resistance rectangular feature in an area of increased resistance, which was suggestive of buried stone features surrounded by building collapse and rubble. To the north-east of the abbey, another GPR anomaly [F1] seems to correlate with the location of a possible ditch, reflecting land divisions within the field.

In the north of the field, GPR features [F13, F16] visible in Depth Slices 4, 5 and 6 were suggested to relate to boundaries or enclosures. When compared to the magnetometer data (Bhreathnach and Dowling 2020), they correlate with the locations of a large broad ditch-type response and a large curvilinear ditch, which were suggested by the author to relate to field boundaries and the possible eastern boundary of an early church pre-dating St Mary's Abbey. Another GPR feature [F15] that could relate to a building or rectilinear enclosure, visible on Depth Slices 4, 5 and 6, is also visible in the magnetometry data as a positive linear response. The author suggests that the narrow, curvilinear ditch associated with this possible enclosure runs underneath and therefore pre-dates St Mary's Abbey. Subsequent investigations into this early medieval monastic enclosure placed the construction of the boundary at some time between the late seventh and ninth centuries and determined that the boundary was largely devoted to agricultural production and could have been as much as 590m by 430m in area (McLoughlin 2020).

The National Monuments Service of Ireland records suggested that situated at the bottom of a gentle north-east-facing slope and *c.*120m north-east of the cathedral is the probable site of the sixth-century St Máedóc's/St Mogue's Church, otherwise known as St Aidan's (WX015-003002-). It is quite possible that some of the features identified in the north-east of the field relate to this early church, such as the square high-amplitude feature [F17], or the rectilinear features [F15, F14].

The features identified in the GPR data in the north of the field also possibly correlate with features excavated by TVAS in 2020. These excavations revealed not only ditches consistent with the outer ecclesiastical enclosures possibly relating to St Aidan's, but also a medieval watermill with wooden remains including a wheel pit and a horizontal mill wheel (TVAS Ireland Ferns Excavations, YouTube).

CONCLUSIONS

The GPR survey at Ferns has achieved its aims and objectives, not only confirming and informing previous work and hypotheses, but also identifying previously unknown archaeological remains for investigation. The surveys have highlighted several potential features that would merit further investigation through a programme of targeted archaeological excavation, as well as providing a better understanding of the context and extent of the archaeological remains within the field surrounding St Mary's Abbey.

Possible ecclesiastical remains were discovered to the east and south of St Mary's Abbey, where rectilinear trends in the GPR confirm the reputed location of a cloister associated with the abbey. Possible smaller buildings or enclosures were also identified, which could relate to the abbey or earlier activity.

Potential ecclesiastical remains were also identified in the north of the field, where three anomalies suggestive of building remains were identified in the data, which could pinpoint the location of St Aidan's Church. One of the possible buildings could also relate to the watermill remains discovered during excavations in 2020, given their location close to a stream in the north of the field.

Linear trends suggestive of larger enclosures and boundaries were also identified in the north of the field, and these correlate with enclosure boundaries pre-dating St Mary's Abbey, confirming the presence of early ecclesiastical features such as boundary enclosures relating to an earlier church.

BIBLIOGRAPHY

Anon. 1895. 'Excursions in County Wexford'. *Proceedings of the Royal Society of Antiquaries of Ireland*, 5:4, 403–6.

Archaeological Survey Database: National Monuments Service: www.archaeology.ie/archaeological-survey-database, accessed 25 Feb. 2022.

Bhreathnach, E. and Dowling, G. 2021. 'Forming an episcopal see and an Augustinian foundation in medieval Ireland: the case of Ferns, Co. Wexford'. *Proceedings of the Royal Irish Academy*, 121C, 191–226.

CIFA, 2014. *Standard and guidance for archaeological geophysical survey*. Reading.

Corlett, C. 2012. 'Ferns, Co. Wexford'. *Archaeology Ireland*, Heritage Guide 59. Dublin.

Culleton, E. 1999. *Celtic and early Christian Wexford*. Dublin.

Dowling, G. 2015. 'Geophysical investigations at Ferns, Co. Wexford. Licence 15R042'. Unpublished report for the Discovery Programme.

Doyle, I. 2016. 'Telling the dancer from the dance: the archaeology of early medieval Wexford'. In Doyle, I. and Browne, B. (eds), *Medieval Wexford: essays in memory of Billy Colfer*, 35–61. Dublin.

Gaffney, C. and Gater, J.A. 2003. *Revealing the buried past: geophysics for archaeologists*. Stroud.

Harbison, P. 1992. *The high crosses of Ireland: an iconographical and photographic survey*. 3 vols. Bonn.

IAFS website: iafs.ie/ferns, accessed 25 Feb. 2022.

Kavanagh, J. 2007. 'Ferns Upper, Ferns. Multi-period'. In Bennett, I. (ed.), *Excavations 2004: summary accounts of archaeological excavations in Ireland*, 466–7, no. 1806. Dublin.

Keane, B. 2020. 'Ferns dig reveals window to our past'. *Wexford People*, 18 Aug. (https://bit.ly/3wytslh).

McLoughlin, C. 2020. 'From early to late: uncovering medieval Ferns'. *Archaeology Ireland*, 34:2, 30–4.

O'Keeffe, T. and Carey Bates, R. 2016. 'The abbey and cathedral of Ferns, 1111–1253'. In Doyle, I. and Browne, B. (eds), *Medieval Wexford: essays in memory of Billy Colfer*, 73–96. Dublin.

OSI GeoHive: https://osi.ie/services/geohive-2, 25 Feb. 2022.

Ryan, F. 2012. 'Excavation of a late Iron Age ring-ditch at Ferns Lower, Co. Wexford'. In Corlett, C. and Potterton, M. (eds), *Life and death in Iron Age Ireland in the light of recent archaeological excavations*, 273–90. Dublin.

Sheehan, C. 2006. 'Ferns Upper, Ferns: medieval'. In Bennett, I. (ed.), *Excavations 2003: summary accounts of archaeological excavations in Ireland*, 532, no. 2018. Dublin.

Shine, D., Lynch, L., Mandal, S. and O'Meara, D. 2021. 'Discovering St Aidan's monastery: preliminary archaeological excavation report (December 2021)'. Unpublished technical report produced for the National Monuments Service.

TVAS Ireland Ferns Excavations, YouTube: www.youtube.com/watch?v=1kpSQhYKFJY.

TVAS video: www.youtube.com/watch?v=1kpSQhYKFJY, 25 Feb. 2022.

Online Sources

Archaeological Survey Database: National Monuments Service – available at www.archaeology.ie/archaeological-survey-database last accessed 25.02.2022

Irish Archaeological Field School website – available at iafs.ie/ferns/ last accessed 25.02.2022

TVAS video – available at www.youtube.com/watch?v=1kpSQhYKFJY last accessed 25.02.2022

Ordnance Survey Ireland GeoHive – available at https://osi.ie/services/geohive-2/ last accessed 25.02.2022

CHAPTER ELEVEN

A timber watermill revealed in the ecclesiastical core of Ferns

KATE TAYLOR

INTRODUCTION AND PROJECT BACKGROUND

Archaeological test excavations carried out in 2019 in the footprint of proposed road pavement rehabilitation and pipelaying within Ferns village (WX015-003) revealed substantial evidence of early and later medieval occupation in several locations. Some archaeological material was found beneath the road surface, but the most significant remains were on the route of a proposed surface-water drain in a greenfield area at the eastern end of the village. Archaeological features that could not be preserved in situ at this location were excavated in 2020 (fig. 11.1).[1] Post-excavation analysis is ongoing and this chapter describes the preliminary results of the excavation, with a focus on the most significant features. The trenches excavated through the road surface contained possible early medieval ditches and later medieval occupation material, while the greenfield excavation revealed multi-phase activity including prehistoric artefacts, early medieval enclosure ditches potentially related to St Aidan's Church and part of a medieval watermill. Later medieval pits, ditches and dump layers and post-medieval features were also recorded. In consultation with the National Monuments Service and the National Museum of Ireland, the mill was preserved in situ with the route of the proposed drainage pipe redesigned to avoid direct impact.

LOCATION, TOPOGRAPHY, GEOLOGY

The works were located primarily within the existing road network along the R772 regional road (Main Street) and L1023 local road (Station Road) within Ferns village and within an agricultural field between the R772 and L1023, to the east of St Mogue's Cottage and north-east of St Edan's thirteenth-century cathedral (fig. 11.2). A stream flows in a south-easterly direction through this land, discharging into the River Bann less than a kilometre south-east of the village. The work took place in the

1 The work was carried out on behalf of Wexford County Council in advance of the proposed R772 Ferns Village Pavement Scheme Phase 2, centred on ITM 702078 649820. The fieldwork was directed by the author (for TVAS (Ireland) Ltd), under consent C000709 with registration number E004633 and detection number R000395 assigned to the archaeological work.

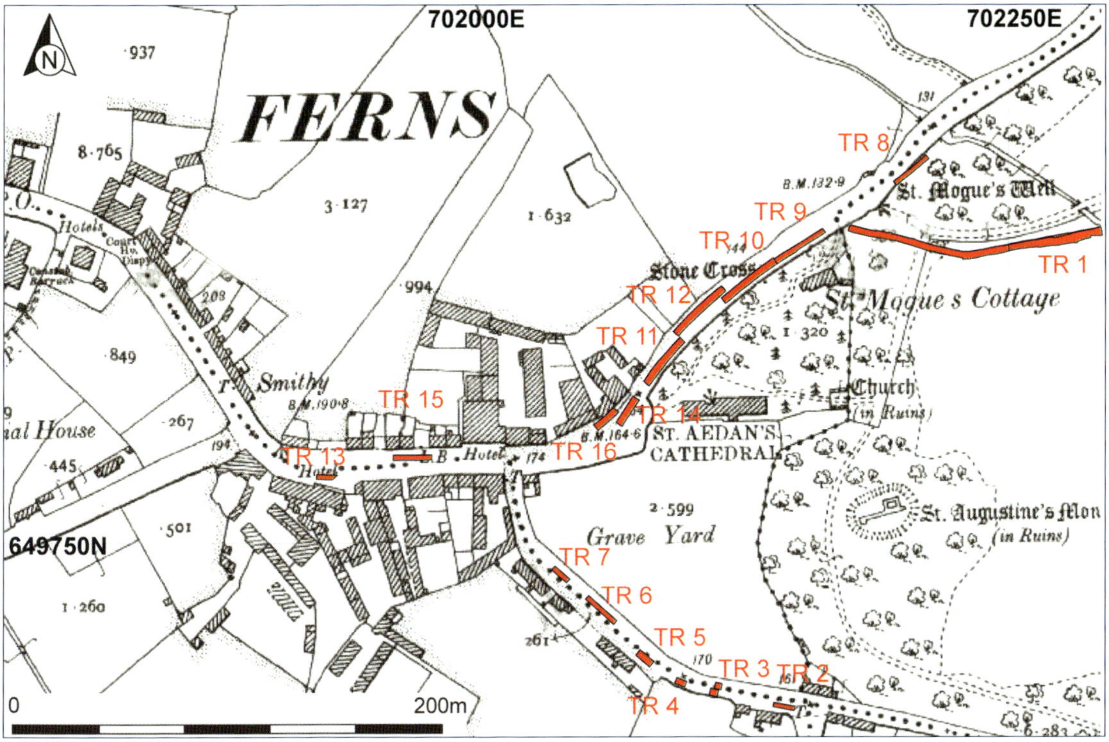

11.1 Ferns: trenches excavated as part of the Ferns Pavement Rehabilitation Scheme Phase 2, on Ordnance Survey map 1904. Grid ITM. Ordnance Survey 25-inch-to-1-mile map sheet WX015-07 (© Ordnance Survey Ireland/Government of Ireland copyright permit no. MP 000723)

townlands of Castleland, Ferns Upper and Ferns Demesne, in Ferns parish, Scarawalsh barony. The works lay between 50m and 60m above Ordnance Datum. A review of the geology and topography of the area is given in Chapter 1. Geological deposits encountered during testing and excavation are mixed glacial deposits, pale yellowy brown silt with shale inclusions, bright orange sandy silt, white chalky silt, pale greyish blue silty clay at greater depth by the stream and shale bedrock at greater depth elsewhere.

EXCAVATION BACKGROUND

The early medieval ecclesiastical foundation of Ferns and the history of the medieval development of the town are detailed elsewhere in this volume (chs 2, 3). The works took place in the eastern half of the historic village, close to the ecclesiastical core. Trenches were excavated in the roads north, south and west of the cathedral. The greenfield trench was situated at the northern edge of the field containing St Mary's

11.2 Ferns: aerial view of excavation Trench 1, with the ruins of the Augustinian abbey in the foreground. Looking north (TVAS)

Abbey. This large field was previously subject to a geophysical survey conducted as part of the Monastic Ireland project, an IRC-funded research collaboration between the Discovery Programme, Trinity College Dublin and University College Cork. Funding for the survey was secured by the Ferns Heritage Group through part funding from the Heritage Council, with the survey completed by Ger Dowling (fig. 11.3). The survey identified an extensive complex of potential archaeological features, including two lengths of concentric curving ditches likely to represent part of the eastern circuit of the ecclesiastical enclosure thought to be centred on the site of St Aidan's monastery, founded in the seventh century (Dowling 2015; Bhreathnach and Dowling 2021; see also ch. 9). The survey also revealed numerous other linear and curvilinear features in the field that appear to represent ditches, some of which clearly form enclosures or fields, and many smaller anomalies that are doubtless representative of negative features such as pits. Some stratigraphy is visible, in particular the abbey ruins clearly overlie the large curving enclosure ditches, suggesting that these buildings were constructed on top of the backfilled ditches (see also ch. 9).

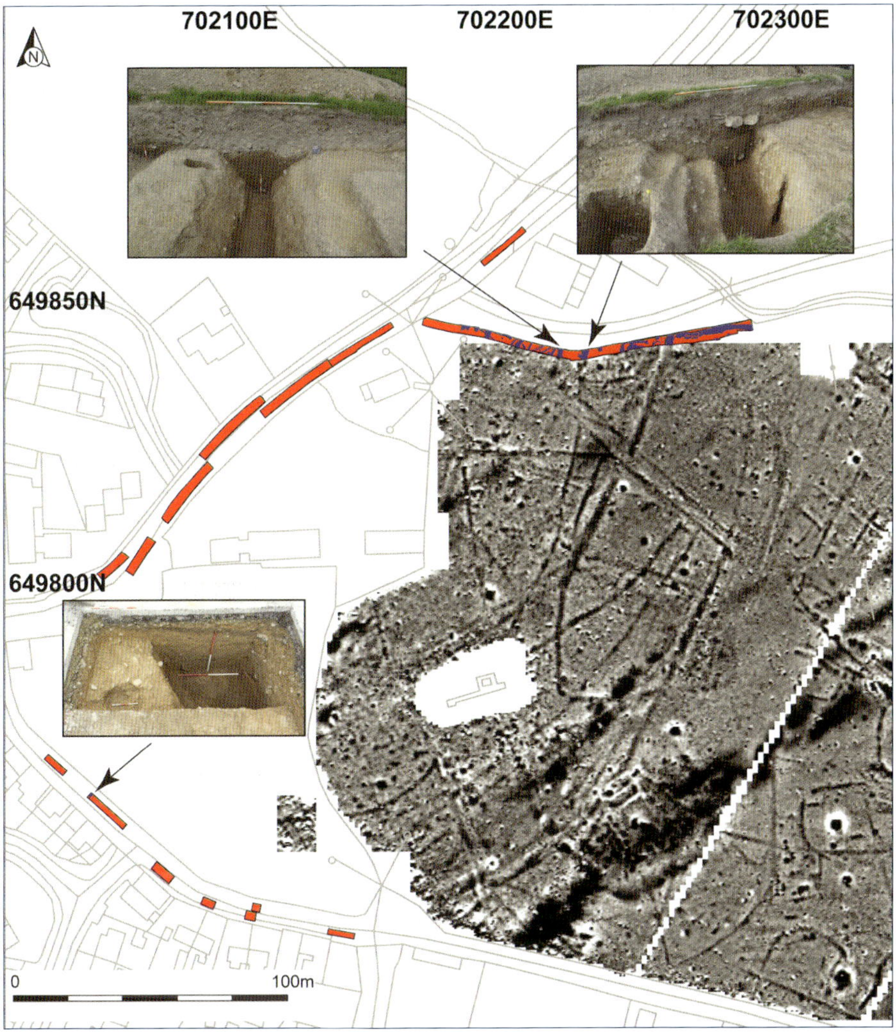

11.3 Ferns: greyscale image of gradiometry results with excavated trenches (red) and archaeological features (blue). The inner ecclesiastical enclosure ditch shown on the survey was encountered in two locations. Grid ITM. Based on Ordnance Survey Ireland digital mapping. Geophysical results from Dowling 2015 (© Ordnance Survey Ireland/Government of Ireland copyright permit no. MP 000723)

The northern limits of the 2015 geophysical survey are approximately on the line of the proposed greenfield surface-water outflow pipe. Therefore, it was anticipated that archaeological investigations of this strip of land might encounter some features identified in the survey. Indeed, some correlation between the geophysical results and the excavation results was observed and is described below. Of particular note are two large ditch-like anomalies that extend into the excavation area, one of which is one of the postulated ecclesiastical enclosure ditches that meets the trench at its centre.

Further east is a large linear anomaly that is considerably wider than the enclosure ditch feature. South of the excavated trench, on a north-west to south-east alignment is a pair of linear anomalies that may represent a trackway or droveway. These ditches appear to terminate at the north-west before reaching the trenched area, but it is possible that one of the ditches has a sharp right-angled turn and meets the trench just west of the centre.

TEST TRENCHING AND EXCAVATION AIMS AND METHODOLOGY

In 2019 test trenching was carried out on Main Street, Station Road and the greenfield route of the proposed drainage pipe. Sixteen trenches were excavated, fifteen in the road network and one in the greenfield area with the purpose of identifying and mitigating the impact of the pavement scheme on the village's archaeological resource (fig. 11.1). The trenching revealed a range of archaeological and potential archaeological features in both the greenfield area and under the existing roads. Those identified in the road trenches were recorded, covered and preserved in situ when the road was reinstated, with further archaeological work proposed to be carried out during the pavement works. The greenfield trench was reinstated and subsequently re-excavated. The testing results are described with the excavation results below.

In the hot summer of 2020, during tight Covid-19 restrictions, the team returned to excavate a single trench in the greenfield area on the line of the proposed drainage outflow pipe, essentially re-opening Trench 1 of the earlier test trenching. The pipe is to extend from Main Street north-east of St Mogue's Cottage, across the field to the east and drain into the small stream that flows eastwards at this point.

The pipe is designed to extend parallel to the field boundary and the trench was therefore not straight, taking the form of an obtuse angle. During the excavation the eastern end of the trench was widened beyond the limits of the original test trench to accommodate the preservation in situ of some specific archaeological materials. Therefore, the trench was 121.2m long, 2.8–4.8m wide and encompassed an area of 393m^2. The depth of the trench varied along its length depending on the thickness of topsoil and archaeological deposits, with a minimum depth of 25cm and maximum depth of 2.45m.

EXCAVATION RESULTS

The excavated features in Trench 1 consisted of a series of pits, postholes and stake-holes that might have a prehistoric or early medieval origin, as well as pits, gullies and ditches likely dating to the early medieval period, with later medieval pits, ditches and, most significantly, a watermill. Later features include a series of stone-lined drains. The archaeological features were overlain by 19–44cm of topsoil, while the natural subsoils are a mix of pale yellowy brown to blue clayey silt – concentrated at the western end of the trench – and pale greyish white silty clay, with blue hues with occasional rounded small-stone inclusions throughout.

The trenches on Station Road demonstrated that, despite the presence of numerous existing services, archaeological deposits survive in places beneath the modern road surface, particularly in the central section of the road. Testing along Main Street revealed fewer areas of potential, although deep excavation was more difficult. In summary, from west to east, Trenches 13 and 15 at the west did not contain any archaeological material, or earlier road surfaces. Trenches 14 and 16 revealed some early features beneath a sequence of road surfaces. Trenches 9, 10, 11 and 12 to the north-east did not reveal substantial archaeological remains, but did demonstrate that the road surface, as seen today, has been built up with imported clay that reaches depths of at least 1.2m, becoming increasingly deep to the north-east. Trench 8 at the north-east was positioned on the line of the former eastern edge of the road prior to its realignment and the previous road boundary wall was encountered at 80cm below the modern road.

Although no absolute dating is yet available for most of the site, stratigraphic relationships, some typological interpretation and determinations based on the presence or absence of medieval pottery can be used to provide a broad phasing for the excavated features.

A selection of the most significant features is described below, with details of some of the artefacts. The complete results of the excavation and analysis will be reported on in due course and a more detailed discussion and interpretation of the evidence will then be possible.

Early features

A number of the excavated features in Trench 1 are clearly stratigraphically earlier than the main phases of activity and it is possible that some are prehistoric. Specifically, a small number of features and deposits in the centre of the trench were sealed by upcast material related to probable early medieval ditches, although they are otherwise undated. Certainly, a number of pieces of struck flint from the site, including a retouched blade that is likely to be Neolithic, suggest at least a background scatter of prehistoric material.

As discussed in Chapter 1, previous investigations around Ferns village have revealed Bronze Age and Iron Age funerary sites and some evidence of domestic activity. In particular, prehistoric features were discovered during test trenching of the field on the opposite (western) side of Main Street to the current Trench 1 (Kavanagh 2006; 2009). This field overlooks the river valley in which Trench 1 is located. Excavations in the field to the south, now occupied by a housing estate, also revealed cremation burials and possible domestic features (Kavanagh 2007).

Towards the eastern end of the site, a cluster of unusual features, truncated by a medieval ditch, are clearly relatively early. A pit was found at the northern edge of the trench and to its south were two postholes partly enclosed by a gully. Immediately to the east was a double curvilinear row of stake-holes. The stake-holes, which were typically 9cm in diameter, were evenly spaced and formed regular pairs, with 80cm–1m between the two alignments. The western row would have held vertical upright stakes, while those on the east were inserted at an angle, so that the stakes would have leaned to the west, possibly positioned to brace against and support the upright western stakes.

Early medieval

Some of the features recorded during the excavation were almost certainly of early medieval date and likely relate to the monastic settlement established here in the seventh century. A number of the large linear features recorded in Trench 1 and within some of the road trenches may be from this phase of activity. The only readily identifiable early medieval artefact from the site is a fragment of a bangle of probable oil-shale, from a later gully in Trench 1.

Ecclesiastical enclosure

In the centre of Trench 1, immediately east of the bend in the trench, a large ditch corresponds with the inner ecclesiastical enclosure ditch as seen in the geophysical survey (fig. 11.3; Dowling 2015). The ditch, as it survived following a later recut, was 1.41m wide and 92cm deep, with a V-shaped profile (fig. 11.4) and there was some evidence of a bank on its eastern (external) side. Both the ditch and the recut were devoid of artefactual material, but medieval pottery was recovered from another large ditch that recut the top of both. The material evidence therefore suggests that the enclosure ditch had become entirely infilled before the late twelfth century, a supposition supported by the fact that the geophysical survey shows the ditch extending southwards beneath the Augustinian abbey, suggesting that it had been decommissioned by the time the abbey was built in the mid- to late twelfth century. It should be noted that excavations of this ditch much closer to the abbey in 2021 (ch. 9) indicate the ditch was placed out of use in this area in the twelfth century only, close to the time the abbey was constructed.

The same inner enclosure ditch may also have been encountered in trenches on Station Road. A large ditch was partially exposed at the north-western end of Trench 6 and another ditch was seen at the south-east end of neighbouring Trench 7. The geophysical survey (fig. 11.3) shows the inner ditch extending from the north, continuing beneath the upstanding ruins of the abbey and curving westwards where it is picked up in a small, targeted survey in the graveyard. Extrapolation of this alignment could meet with the ditches beneath the road surface. If the ditches in

11.4 Ferns: ecclesiastical enclosure ditch during recording (TVAS)

Trenches 6 and 7 are the same feature, it is approximately 3–6m wide and, where excavated, is over 90cm deep, with a very steep edge, suggestive of a large defensive ditch and possibly more substantial than as seen in Trench 1. Further extrapolation of the line of the ditch would follow the sharp curve in Station Road as it turns to meet Main Street, tantalizingly suggesting that the line of the original enclosure may be preserved in the modern road layout.

Other early medieval features

In the greenfield trench, another ditch, 7m to the west of the inner enclosure ditch, presented as 1.6–2m wide and 1.05m deep with a V-shaped profile. It is possible, looking at the greyscale gradiometry image (fig. 11.3), to identify a potential ditch in this location, a right-angled turn of the south-east to north-west aligned droveway that clearly crosses both outer and inner enclosure ditches south of the test trench, perhaps being part of the original enclosure layout.

Other smaller features in Trench 1, including pits, postholes and gullies both inside the enclosure delimited by the large ditch and outside it, may also date to this period. A small number of additional features beneath the road surface on Station Road could be early medieval and in the trenches on Main Street a number of undated features were identified beneath the road surface, and indeed beneath earlier iterations of the road. Some of these are doubtless medieval, but others, particularly two large features in Trench 16, could be earlier. This location, west of St Edan's Cathedral, which may sit on the site of the original St Aidan's monastery, would certainly have been within the inner circuit of the monastic enclosure and surviving features in this area could be of significance.

Later medieval

Ditches and pits: possible domestic activity

Several gullies, ditches, small pits and a hearth in the western half of Trench 1 contained later medieval pottery, broadly dating to the late twelfth to mid-fourteenth centuries. Some of these features were recuts of early medieval ditches or were cut through the upcast from the ecclesiastical enclosure ditches, providing some stratigraphic sequencing. These features have the appearance of small-scale domestic or agricultural activity, which may be expected on the outskirts of a small town such as Ferns.

In the centre of the trench, a thin occupation layer containing medieval pottery was spread over a wide area. However, at the east of the trench many of the layers that tipped down into the valley bottom also contained medieval pottery, along with occasional iron nails and pieces of slag. These large deposits, which were truncated by several cuts and recuts, may represent waste disposal, with material from elsewhere in the medieval town or the abbey being dumped here.

Medieval occupation was less easily identified within the road trenches. However, a spread of potential occupation material was recorded in Trenches 5 and 6 in Station Road, overlying the large probable early medieval ditch. This thin layer contained several sherds of medieval pottery and corresponds in both description and location with an occupation layer recorded during monitoring of the construction of the current sewer in 1998 (Ryan 1999; 2000). A gully in Trench 7, which was overlain by a hearth, also contained medieval pottery. This area along Station Road would have been within the medieval town.

No identifiable medieval features were seen in the trenches on Main Street, however some of the undated features beneath old road surfaces could prove to be medieval. It is also possible that some of the earlier road surfaces originate in this period.

Watermill

The most significant discoveries during the excavation were the remarkable remains of a medieval timber and stone structure, probably a watermill, in the low, wet area towards the eastern end of Trench 1, close to the stream that flows along the valley bottom. The waterlogged conditions were ideal for the preservation of structural

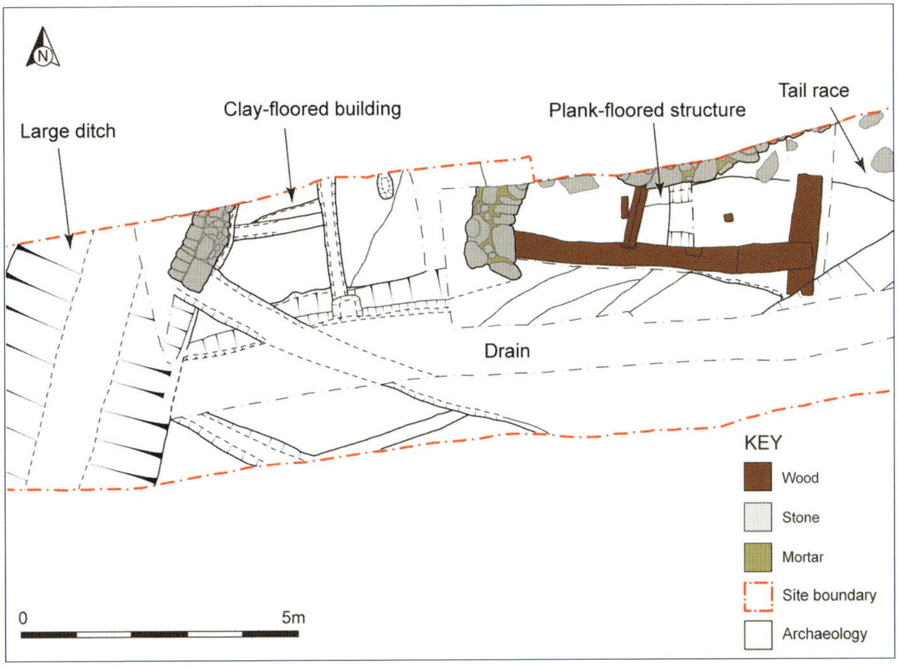

11.5 Ferns: plan of fourteenth-century watermill complex (TVAS)

11.6 Ferns: mill structures seen from the south (TVAS)

timbers and other organic items. The mill remains were found on the northern side of the trench and, unfortunately, the width of the pipe trench did not allow for their full extent to be revealed, with the majority of the remains probably lying outside the trench to the north. Given the archaeological and historical importance of the mill and the fact that it could not be fully excavated as it extends outside the excavation trench, the mill remains were preserved in situ.

Although it is not possible to fully interpret the partially exposed remains, the complex includes a large ditch at the west, a stone-walled and clay-floored building in the centre, a timber structure at the east and the tailrace extending eastwards from the mill (figs 11.5, 11.6). The timber elements were earlier than the stone walls, although whether they were all part of the same broad phase of construction or represent a timber mill later redesigned in stone is not clear.

Timber elements

The timber elements consist of three principal structural pieces, all laid horizontally: a large base-plate to the south, resting on a smaller, supporting timber to the east and a cross beam extending north from the large timber. Together, these timbers enclose a rectangular area measuring 2.1m east-to-west by at least 1.3m (to the trench edge) at the north.

Structurally, the support timber at the eastern end of the wheel pit was placed first. This large piece of wood, orientated approximately north to south, is 1.98m long, 42cm wide and at least 34cm thick. The eastern end of the large base-plate timber sits in a half-lap-joint close to the southern end of the support timber. Measuring at least 4.32m long, 35–38cm wide and 15cm thick, this large oak beam lies in an approximate east–west orientation, with the western extent continuing beneath the stone wall of the adjacent building. There are two half-lap-joints on the northern edge of the timber and one of these still holds the southern end of a cross beam; presumably the other had a similar function. The surviving cross beam, orientated north-to-south, measures at least 92cm by 18cm and 10cm thick and a rebate along its eastern edge would have held planks, presumably also supported on the other, now missing, cross beam.

Although the mill remains are sitting in a cut, there is very little depth below the timbers and so this enclosed area could clearly not have housed a vertical water wheel. It is therefore possible that the timbers represent the remains of the wheel pit for a horizontal wheel. The wheel itself was not present, although several wooden objects were recovered from the area in and around the possible wheel pit, including fragments of wooden planks and pegs, possibly structural elements, now degraded.

Dendrochronological dating of a fragment of the large oak beam gives a felling date for the tree from which it was cut of late AD1316 or early 1317 (Q12873) and, as this is a major structural element, this presumably provides an approximate date for the construction of the mill (table 11.1). Two loose plank fragments found in organic material above the structural timbers, assumed to be dislodged parts of the floor, were also dated by the same method. One gave a date of AD1312±9 years (Q12875) so was doubtless part of the original construction (table 11.1). The other plank produced a felling date of AD1350±9 years (Q12874) and must have been from a later repair to the structure (table 11.1).

Layers excavated over the box structure, represented by the timber elements, in common with the fills of the ditch and tailrace described below, are clearly post-abandonment deposits formed after the mill fell out of use and water was no longer flowing through its mechanical parts. A series of clay layers and humic silts contained sherds of medieval pottery, a copper-alloy spur buckle, possibly thirteenth century in date, a scrap of leather and several pieces of worked wood including fragments of a turned wooden bowl, a notched item and pieces of planks, the latter doubtless part of the mill mechanism. Overlying deposits included some large stones that could be parts of collapsed or demolished stone walls.

Table 11.1 Dendrochronological dates for mill timbers, supplied by Queen's University Belfast

QUB No.	Find/Sample	Rings	Start date	End date	Estimated felling date range
Q12873	Sample 80. Base-plate timber	91	AD1226	AD1316	AD1316/AD1317
Q12874	E004633:299:12. Plank fragment	150	AD1177	AD1326	AD1350±9 years
Q12875	E004633:299:14. Plank fragment	202	AD1091	AD1292	AD1312±9 years

Stone-walled building

West of the structural elements of the timber mill, a cluster of features on a level platform may indicate the location of a mill building. Two parallel stone walls aligned perpendicular to the large timber were positioned either side of and delimiting a hard clay surface or floor. Beam slots and postholes cut into this clay flooring represent the locations of internal timber structural elements. The eastern stone wall was built directly upon the western end of the main structural mill timber, either as part of the original construction or perhaps relating to a later redesign or conversion. The western wall was set into the edge of the clay floor and also in the side of a large ditch that was open directly to the west.

The floor surface of compact, pale whitish grey clay measured 2.8m by 1.5m within the trench. The floor was bounded by walls at the west and east and truncated by a later drain at the south, although there was no evidence that it had extended any further south and its edge was presumably in line with the ends of the two walls.

The two stone walls, which are 3.7m apart, extended no more than 1.4m south from the northern limit of the trench and both continue northwards. The walls were probably built to a much greater height in antiquity, with only the lower courses surviving, and were presumably part of the mill building with a clay floor.

The western wall was constructed in a foundation cut set into the eastern edge of the large ditch (see below). The wall survives to a height of 80cm, mostly in the side of the ditch, and is 40cm wide at the top with a slight batter, meaning it is slightly wider at the base. Roughly dressed shale and felsite (Stephen Mandal, pers. comm.) pieces are laid in irregular horizontal courses. Only the north-west face was visible during excavation, with up to eight courses observed; no bonding material was apparent.

The eastern wall was constructed on top of the western end of the large structural timber. With no visible cut, this wall appeared to have been freestanding, perhaps in the end of the cut containing the timbers. The 72cm-wide wall survives to a height of 35cm and is constructed of roughly dressed felsite pieces in three to four randomly placed horizontal courses. The wall is earth-bonded with a mid-brown gritty silt.

Western ditch

The ditch immediately to the west of the mill was the largest feature investigated during the excavation at 3m wide and 1.9m deep with a broad U-shaped profile, narrowing to approximately 1.4m wide at the base. The western mill wall is set into the eastern edge of the ditch. The lower fills were sterile and appear to have been deposited in flowing water in the ditch, while the later fills were more organic and would have formed in standing water. The ditch fills yielded the remains of at least two late twelfth- to thirteenth-century leather shoes, several sherds of late twelfth- to mid-fourteenth-century pottery, an iron nail and stone objects including a fragment of millstone. The ditch corresponds with a large linear anomaly identified as part of the geophysical survey, which extends in a straight line uphill to the south for 42m towards the ruins of St Mary's Abbey, stopping before it reaches the building. The function of this large ditch remains unclear, although its orientation corresponds with that of the mill building, so it appears that these features were designed to function together.

Tailrace

Part of the tailrace of the mill was also recorded. Extending eastwards from the wheel pit, this was essentially a meandering channel that carried water from the mill to the nearby stream, approximately 25m away. The channel deepens from 29cm at the west to 90cm at the east. In the section face on the northern edge of the excavated trench several large flat stones formed a rough layer tipping down over the mill wheel pit and perhaps into the tailrace. It is possible that these stones relate to the use or abandonment of the stone elements of the mill, with most of this phase of activity lying outside the excavated area to the north.

The lower fills of the tailrace were silty clay, with upper fills more organic. Finds include part of another late twelfth- to thirteenth-century leather shoe, several sherds of late twelfth- to mid-fourteenth-century pottery, iron nails, copper-alloy and lead pieces, a cut Henry III long-cross silver halfpenny dated 1247–72, iron slag, fragments of animal bone, millstone fragments and worked wood.

Initial discussion of the mill complex

The earliest evidence of Irish watermills dates to the early medieval period when sophisticated canal systems, mill dams and mill ponds were constructed to feed both horizontally and vertically wheeled mills (Rynne 1989). Water was channelled from a natural river or stream, via a mill race or leat, and the flow was carefully controlled. The water was then directed into a hollowed-out wooden chute or flume, which narrowed towards the wheel, thus producing a concentrated jet of water to push the paddles of the wheel. In a horizontal mill, the rotation of the wheel then turned the millstones above, within the mill building. Vertical mill wheels turned on a horizontal axis and gearing mechanisms converted the power to rotate millstones in a mill building to the side of the wheel. In both cases, on flowing out of the mill itself the water was directed back to the watercourse via the tailrace (Rynne 2006).

As watermill design was relatively stable over many centuries, it is not possible to suggest a date for any structure based on its type. The choice between horizontal and vertical wheels may have been based on local circumstances and the nature of the water supply rather than on date (Rynne 2006, 31–2).

The Ferns mill was only partially exposed, and its mechanism of use is not entirely clear. The timber elements essentially formed three sides of a box that could represent the wheel pit of a horizontal mill; certainly, a vertical wheel could not have been accommodated in this location. Were this to be the case, then the most substantial beam exposed would have been a base plate that supported upright timbers for the mill building itself; a vertical tower over the wheel in which the millstones would have operated. Having said that, although supporting beams for a plank floor were evident, there were no mortise holes in the large base beam to hold large timber uprights and it is possible that this was a plank-floored structure with a different function in the mill complex.

To the west of the timbers were stone walls and a clay floor that appear to represent a building. This could be a mill building related to a vertical mill, where the wheel rotates on a horizontal axis and the millstones are to the side of, rather than above, the wheel. No wheel or gear pit for a vertical wheel were identified, but as so much of the structure was not exposed it is possible that both were present on the north side of the mill building.

Whatever the mechanical arrangement of the mill, it is clear that the tailrace at the east would have taken the water after it had turned the wheel and channelled it back into the stream, re-joining it at a bend immediately beyond the end of the trench.

Dendrochronological dating results demonstrate that the mill was not built before the early fourteenth century and at least one plank, presumably a repair, was laid in the mid-fourteenth century (table 11.1). Artefacts from the infilled western ditch and tailrace, as well as overlying the mill timbers, are broadly thirteenth-century, with some of the pottery potentially fourteenth-century. The lack of later material in these post-abandonment deposits suggests that the mill was not in use for a particularly long period.

It is hoped that a more detailed interpretation of the mechanics of the mill will be possible following further analysis of the timbers themselves and the many samples and artefacts collected from this part of the site during the excavation.

11.7 Ferns: medieval leather shoes (left: E004633:297:1 and right: E004633:297:2) from the large ditch next to the mill (John Nicholl)

Medieval artefactual assemblage

Analysis of the artefacts from the site is not complete, but there is an extensive assemblage of medieval material, mostly from the main excavation in Trench 1. Pottery is largely Irish, including Leinster Cooking Ware and various locally produced Wexford-Type Ware, with occasional imports of English Ham Green B and Redcliffe wares and French Saintonge. Metal items include thirteenth-century coins, a spur buckle, a barrel padlock, knife blades and part of a copper-alloy vessel. Personal items include a pair of heavily worn late twelfth- or thirteenth-century decorated shoes, beautifully preserved in the waterlogged deposits around the mill (fig. 11.7). Industrial waste includes iron slag from smithing and smelting as well as a fragment of crucible used to melt bronze.

Post-medieval and early modern

Despite being in a continuously occupied village centre, the excavation revealed relatively little in the way of post-medieval disturbance. A description of the abbey in the sixteenth century refers to a church and belfry, dormitory, chapter-house, hall and other buildings along with six hundred acres (Gwynn and Hadcock 1970, 175–6) and the field containing Trench 1 was doubtless part of the curtilage of the abbey. A small amount of seventeenth-century pottery was recovered from the trench and there may be one or two pits of this date. Additionally, at the very western end of the trench was a large early modern refuse pit. Historic maps from the nineteenth century show the field as fairly empty other than the ruins of St Mary's Abbey and some wooded areas. A footpath that circles the west side of the ruins extends northwards across the line of the excavated trench and some of the gullies recorded in this area could mark the edges of the track, although they contained only earlier material.

The trenches in Station Road revealed little evidence of post-medieval activity other than water and sewer pipes, along with small sections of previous road surfaces. Investigations on Main Street exposed a complex sequence of previous road surfaces, however, including at least two phases of cobbles separated by a deliberate infill layer. Although the upper of these surfaces had late pottery on it, the lower road is undated.

CONCLUSIONS

The testing and subsequent excavation related to the pavement and drainage works in Ferns have, despite the small areas investigated, revealed an impressive array of archaeological features, largely dating to the medieval period. Most unexpected was the discovery of part of an early fourteenth-century probable watermill, likely to have been constructed in AD1316 or 1317. This important structure has been preserved in situ and its secrets remain to be discovered.

Further research will hopefully allow better understanding of the functional mechanism of the mill complex and, perhaps more importantly, the historical setting of its ownership and use. The history of Ferns in the thirteenth and fourteenth centuries, including the complex political relationships between the church, the landlords and the crown, is murky and contested. The land on which the mill was situated was doubtless part of the episcopal manor and was probably one of several mills owned and controlled by the church. There are numerous references to income from mills during this period (Hore 1911, 187–97), however it is nearly impossible to establish the exact location of any particular building mentioned in the documents. It is noteworthy that large parts of Ferns were destroyed around the time of the Bruce wars in the early fourteenth century, including the castle and several church buildings, with the abbey itself being burnt in 1317. At least one mill suffered the same fate, as recorded in an inquisition of 1324 of the manor of Ferns that included the castle (therefore not the episcopal manor). That document notes that a watermill, previously listed in 1307 as generating valuable income, was no longer of any value as it had been 'thrown down and destroyed' (Hore 1911, 9). Should church-owned mills similarly have been destroyed, it is easy to imagine that new buildings would have been hastily erected to replace them but that perhaps the devastated economy could not support their ongoing use, leading them to fall into disrepair after a few short years.

BIBLIOGRAPHY

Bhreathnach, E. and Dowling, G. 2021. 'Forming an episcopal see and an Augustinian foundation in medieval Ireland: the case of Ferns, Co. Wexford'. *Proceedings of the Royal Irish Academy*, 121C, 191–226.

Dowling, G. 2015. 'Geophysical investigations at Ferns, Co. Wexford, 15R042'. Unpublished Discovery Programme report.

Gwynn, A. and Hadcock, R.N. 1970. *Medieval religious houses: Ireland*. Dublin.

Hore, P.H. 1911. *History of the town and county of Wexford, vol. 6*. London.

Kavanagh, J. 2006. 'Archaeological test excavation report for Ferns Upper, Ferns, Co. Wexford, 06E0780'. Unpublished Icon Archaeology Ltd report.

Kavanagh, J. 2007. 'Ferns Upper, Ferns. Multi-period'. In Bennett, I. (ed.), *Excavations 2004: summary accounts of archaeological excavations in Ireland*, 466–7, no. 1806. Dublin.

Kavanagh, J. 2009. 'Ferns Upper, Ferns, Wexford, 06E0780'. In Bennett, I. (ed.), *Excavations 2006: summary accounts of archaeological excavations in Ireland*, Dublin (www.archaeology.ie entry 2006:2104).

Ryan, F. 1999. 'Preliminary report of monitoring of sewerage scheme at Ferns, Co. Wexford 98E0132'. Unpublished Frank Ryan report.

Ryan, F. 2000. 'Archaeological findings from monitoring of Phase 1 of Ferns Sewerage Scheme, Co. Wexford, 98E0132'. Unpublished Mary Henry Archaeological Services report.

Rynne, C. 2006. *Industrial Ireland, 1750–1930: an archaeology*. Cork.

CHAPTER TWELVE

Clone, Ferns: church, community and continuity

DENIS SHINE, IAN ELLIOTT, BARRY LACEY, LAUREN GOODALL-BYRNE & STEPHEN MANDAL

INTRODUCTION

Clone is a beautiful medieval church located approximately 2.25km south of Ferns town, in the ancient territory of Uí Chennselaig (townland of Clone; barony of Scarawalsh). According to tradition, the church was dedicated to St Aidan, also known as St Máedóc (d. *c.*625), who is also associated with the larger nearby ecclesiastical site at Ferns. The church at Clone is situated on a slightly east-facing slope, overlooking a small well-defined valley to the north-east and east. This valley contains a small stream that is a tributary of the River Bann (itself a tributary of the River Slaney), which forms the western boundary of the present townland of Clone.

The remains of Clone Church consist of a church (WX015-023001-) (fig. 12.1) and graveyard (WX015-023001-), as well as three cross-slabs, a sundial, two bullaun stones and a recently discovered piece of passage-tomb rock art. The church itself is poorly preserved, but retains a Romanesque doorway (and a series of carved stone heads) at the west end, dating from approximately the twelfth century (Cosgrave 2016, 7; ch. 5).

Recent geophysical surveys and excavations at the site by the Irish Archaeology Field School (IAFS) and Clone Church Conservation Project (CCCP, an initiative of the Ferns Heritage Archive Group) have revealed several features that confirm this ecclesiastical site significantly pre-dates the twelfth century, as indicated by the early medieval monuments it contains. This research was prompted by a request by the CCCP to the IAFS to conduct research at the site after a drone survey during a drought in 2018 identified a probable monastic enclosure (WX015-023013-) surrounding the church and graveyard.

Geophysical surveys at the site, by Ian Elliott of Irish Geophysical and Archaeological Services (IGAS), were initially completed in August and October 2019 (Licence 19R0238; Elliott 2019) followed by more extensive surveys undertaken in October and December 2021 (Licence 21R0219; Elliott 2022). Two seasons of community-focused archaeological excavation were undertaken at the site in December 2019 and August 2021 (Shine and Lacey 2020, 2021). This chapter describes the results of these investigations at the site (see also Shine et al. 2020). A

12.1 Clone Church prior to ongoing conservation works on site (image courtesy of Christiaan Corlett)

brief historical summary and description of the site's built heritage is also included, to provide context to the archaeological excavations.

HISTORY

Clone Church functioned as a parish church in the early thirteenth century and was a valuable prebend and canonry (Cosgrave 2016, 9). W.H. Grattan Flood records a person being confirmed in the canonry and prebend of Clone in 1352, while rectors were appointed to the parish and church until the end of the sixteenth century. Post-Reformation Protestant rectors continued to be appointed although the church started to fall into ruin, possibly being 'unroofed' from the mid-seventeenth century (Cosgrave 2016, 10). The building is recorded as being in poor condition in the Ordnance Survey letters by John O'Donovan in 1840 (100–1) while George Kinahan, writing in the later nineteenth century, stated that the church had been partially pulled down to provide stone to build the present graveyard wall (Kinahan 1889, 9).

Associations with St Aidan and the early medieval period have regularly been

12.2 Aerial photograph of crop-marks at Clone Church. Note the two concentric curvilinear features (backfilled ditches) around the church, joining the curved field boundary. These features represent a monastic enclosure

suggested, including by Grattan Flood (1916, 39), who recorded that 'Clone was one of the oldest foundations in the diocese of Ferns, and is rightly ascribed to St Aedan'. Renowned Wexford antiquarian Philip Hore (1911, 157) also associated the site with St Aidan, stating 'it was probably during his rule that the abbey of Clone – now represented by the most ancient church in the district, the ruins of which display peculiarities both of construction and ornamentation – was founded'. The toponymy of Clone may also suggest an early medieval origin, with the Irish name *Cluaín* generally referring to a meadow or pasture that is frequently documented in association with ecclesiastical sites (Ó Crualaoich 2016, 660).

More indicative of Clone's early medieval antecedents are the cross-slabs and bullaun stones from the site (e.g., Mulligan 2016, 10; O'Sullivan et al. 2018; ch. 5). The cross-slabs include two examples with a Maltese cross in false relief, likely dating from the eighth to tenth centuries, as well as another incised example, dating from the sixth to eighth century (Colbert 2019). George Victor du Noyer (1864–6) also describes a stone 'font' at the site, which could be a socket for a high cross or have housed the medieval sundial that originated from the site (see below). Clone's early medieval origins, as suggested by both these monuments and various historical references, seemed confirmed in 2018 when a series of crop-marks revealed a monastic enclosure (WX015-023013-) (fig. 12.2).

BUILT HERITAGE

The built heritage from Clone clearly also indicates a multi-period site, containing both early and high medieval monuments (Shine et al. 2020). Considering the importance of these monuments to understanding the site's origins, a summary is presented here.

The surviving church consists of a unicameral rectangular building, 14.7m long and 5.7m wide. The eastern end of the church was entirely rebuilt in 1956 by Wexford County Council (WCC) during conservation works coordinated by Fr Ranson, a Wexford historian and founder of the Castle Museum in Enniscorthy (Ranson 1957). With no evidence for the former east window, it had been suggested that the Romanesque window at St Peter's Church in Ferns had been rescued from Clone; however, probable window fragments (WX015-023008-) have been uncovered recently at Clone itself (Shine et al. 2021; ch. 5). The most interesting feature of the church is the west doorway, which originally consisted of a Romanesque arch surrounded by a series of carved stone heads (WX015-023011-) (see ch. 5 for a detailed description). These heads were rearranged, and the doorway reconstructed, during the 1956 reconstruction works. In the mid-nineteenth century a carved head from the doorway was also brought to Ferns and used in the construction of the building over St Mogue's Well (Shine et al. 2021). In 1996 the church was taken into state care; partial collapse of the building in 2016 prompted conservation works by the National Monuments Service (NMS) of the Office of Public Works (OPW), which remain ongoing.

One of Clone's most unusual features is the sundial (WX015-023004-), which is currently on display at the OPW visitor centre beside Ferns Castle. It consists of a stone pillar measuring 1.63m tall topped by a semi-circular head (Shine et al. 2020, 25–6) (fig. 12.3). When Du Noyer visited the site in 1862 he described the ancient sundial as having been situated close to the stream, approximately 60m from the church (on notes accompanying a painting of the sundial held in the Royal Society of Antiquaries of Ireland). The sundial may also be associated with a 'stone font' recorded by Du Noyer, which was located in the graveyard, but has since gone missing; this 'font' could be a socket for the sundial, or perhaps a high-cross base, with the cross now also missing.

Three cross-slabs are also recorded from the site. The original location of two of them is not known, though one (WX015-024- - - -) was known to have been located *c.*80m south-east of the church (Shine et al. 2020, 26). This slab has an incised Maltese cross within a circle; it was moved into the graveyard but has since been removed for

12.3 Sundial from Clone (image courtesy of Christiaan Corlett)

safe keeping. A second slab, displaying a Maltese cross in false relief with a central boss and cup, was also removed (WX015-023006-). The final cross-slab remains on-site, although not in its original location, beside the church doorway; it features a Maltese cross in false relief, with a central cup (WX015-023003-) (fig. 12.4). Two bullaun stones (WX015-023005; WX015-023007) are also located in the graveyard.

The most intriguing carved stone from Clone (first recorded in 2018) is a grave marker located *c.*5m west of the church door that is decorated with megalithic rock art (WX015–023014) (fig. 12.5). The stone is decorated with at least four pecked arcs of closely spaced lines in an oval pattern. Parallels have been drawn between this art piece and megalithic motifs at Knockroe, Co. Kilkenny (Shine et al. 2020). The stone at Clone is the only example of passage-tomb art known from Co. Wexford.

The collection of sculpted stones at Clone represents an intriguing mix of monuments, possibly from several time periods. Some of the stones may have served a 'common' purpose, however, as there are suggestions that they were linked with pilgrimage. Peter Harbison (1991, 191–5) associated the 'cross-of-arcs' symbol, as depicted in Clone's cross-slabs, with pilgrimage, noting its location at several known pilgrim sites, including along the Saints' Road on the Dingle Peninsula in Co. Kerry. In mapping the countrywide occurrence of this design, Harbison (1991, 193) recorded

12.4 The final cross slab remaining at Clone (image courtesy of Christiaan Corlett)

12.5 Megalithic art from Clone (image courtesy of Christiaan Corlett)

three examples in Wexford, namely at Begerin, Bulgan and Clone. Harbison (1991, 211–15) further argued for a pilgrimage association for sundials, citing an example also on the Saint's Road at Kilmalkedar, Co. Kerry, where the sundial also displays a cross-of-arcs. Sundials are also located in other high-status monastic sites such as Monasterboice, Co. Louth, where a founder's relic was preserved until the sixteenth century. For sites containing sundials where pilgrimage was possibly practised, but is not documented historically, Clone together with Toureen Peakaun in Co. Tipperary are noted as also containing both a Romanesque church and a cross-of-arcs (Harbison 1991).

A link to pilgrimage for the cross-of-arcs and sundial at Clone suggests it acted as a pilgrim site during the medieval period, considering both the understood chronology of sundials and the continuation of pilgrimage for several centuries at comparable sites. One such site is Begerin Island in the Wexford slobs, which also contains a 'cross-of-arcs'. Like Clone, Begerin has a monastic origin (being founded by St Ibar in the later

12.6 The bird motif on the pillar at Clone

sixth century) while also remaining a church site following the Anglo-Norman arrival (Culleton 1999, 143–4). Crucially at Begerin a small wooden chapel was recorded in 1682 at which a statue of 'St Ibernion' was still venerated and used for taking oaths (Culleton 1999, 144). Whether this veneration is a continuation of much earlier practices is unknown, but it is tempting to suggest a similar pattern at Clone, whereby a longstanding pilgrimage may have been established around the cult of St Aidan. The original placement of some of the monuments, where they are known, also suggests a *Turas* at Clone, with the sundial and one cross-slab originally located 60m and 80m from the twelfth-century church respectively. The church is situated near the centre of the early monastery, with the placement of monuments around it suggestive of a *deiseal* or clockwise movement to various stations around the monastery core.

A final carved stone in a gate pier, *c.*350m from Clone Church, also merits mention here. This stone displays an incised bird-like image, which could be a peacock, and is likely to have originated from Clone Church (fig. 12.6). Bird carvings have been found at other early medieval monastic sites, for example at Caherlehillan, Co. Kerry, where peacocks are displayed on three sixth- or seventh-century cross-slabs (Sheehan 2009, 200–2). Peacock motifs have been used in 'the Mediterranean world as a symbol of the Christian theme of immortality, and [were] promoted as such in the teachings of

Augustine' (Sheehan 2009, 200). The later medieval abbey of St Mary's in Ferns was Augustinian.

ARCHAEOLOGICAL SURVEYS

Further evidence for a monastic foundation at Clone first came to light during the summer of 2018 when crop-marks revealed a possible monastic enclosure (WX015-02313). These crop-marks indicated two enclosing elements, an outer double-ditched enclosure as well as an inner ditch, possibly defining an outer and inner core of a monastery, as is typically observed on similar sites (Edwards 1998, 106). Targeted geophysical surveys of the crop-marks commenced in October and December 2019, followed by a second survey season in August and October 2021 (consents 19R0238 and 21R0219 respectively; Elliott 2019 and 2022); these surveys collectively revealed a density of archaeological features, which are likely to span several centuries of activity (fig. 12.7).

The first surveys in 2019 (Areas A and B on fig. 12.7) revealed part of a pair of broadly concentric enclosures. The outer enclosure was clearly bivallate, with a pair of broad fosses (*c.*3m wide) separated by what was presumed to be a bank (*c.*6m wide). Approximately 25m inside the outer enclosure is an inner enclosure, which is also possibly partially bivallate and characterized by quite a sharp angle at its south-western extremity. During survey the inner ditch appeared *c.*1–1.5m in width, with clearly defined edges. The outer element appeared broader, but also sharply cut. A further fosse projecting directly from the western end of the present church enclosure was also recorded.

This fosse and the archaeological complex surrounding Clone Church in general were further surveyed in August and October 2021 (Areas C and D on fig. 12.7). This extension to the 2019 surveys placed the earlier results in a much broader context and demonstrated that the enclosure elements identified in 2019 continue well to the south, as suggested by the 2018 photographed crop-marks.

Preliminary results from the survey of Area D show that the core of the monastic complex, lying within the outer bivallate enclosure, was fully revealed in the earlier survey, although at least one contiguous ditch arcs for some distance away from the south-west corner. Otherwise, most of the anomalies point to the existence of remnant radial and linear field boundaries, the latter being of varying orientation. All these are set against a background of strong linear anomalies, oriented south-west–north-east, that are believed to originate from the underlying solid geology of this region, which comprises intermediate volcanic rocks of Ordovician age. Whereas these extrusions will have a marked magnetic signature affecting the fluxgate gradiometer data, and therefore may mask some of the weaker 'overlying' archaeological anomalies, they should have negligible influence on soil-moisture content, which is what generates the

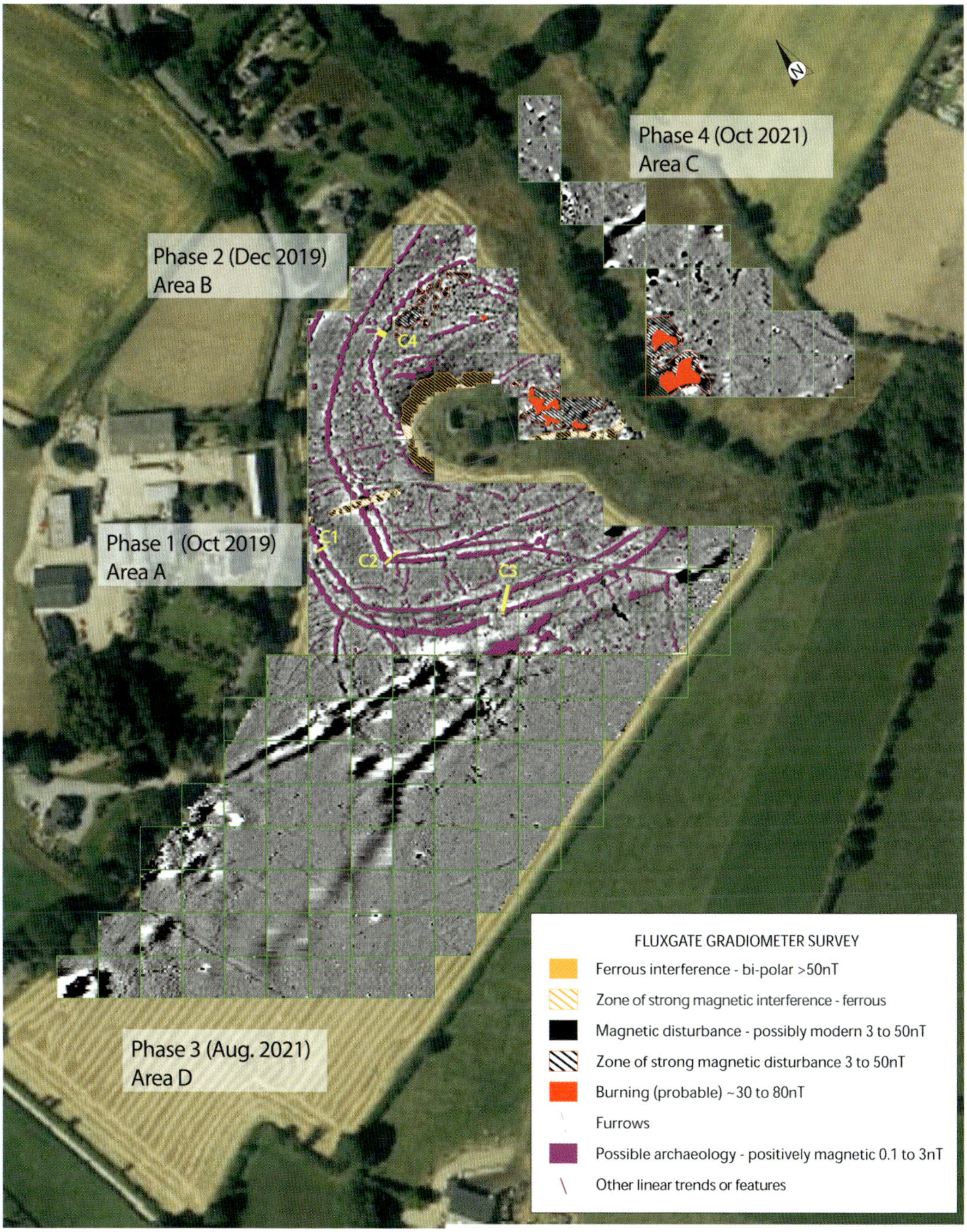

12.7 Geophysical survey (from IGAS) showing multiple seasons of surveys. Locations of the archaeological cuttings (in yellow) are shown overlaying the enclosures and geophysical features (in purple), with areas of high magnetic response/industrial areas shown in red

crop-marks. It is clear, also, that some previous anomalies tentatively identified in 2019 as 'archaeological' were in fact associated with this peculiar geology.

A similar strong, broad linear 'geological' anomaly is present in the data from the northern part of Area C, which, when set within the context of the other survey datasets, is clearly analogous to the 'natural' dykes encountered in Area D. Numerous weak linear anomalies exist, particularly on the elevated ground in the eastern portion of the area – some, but by no means all, of these may relate to the programme of test trenching conducted by Catherine McLoughlin in 2006, which revealed a number of gullies and burnt features (WX015-023010-; Mcloughlin 2006; see below). A broad area of strong magnetic disturbance indicated by the bi-polar anomalous data at the south-western corner of the survey is suggestive of the presence of an extensive area of burnt material, ash or metalworking slag on the low ground close to the stream. This is consistent with the results of the 2006 testing in this area (McLoughlin 2006), which also revealed a burnt spread of stone, charcoal and slag in this field (WX015-023009-). While it is understood that some filling material (clay) was deposited in recent times by the landowner to counter waterlogging of the lower-lying areas of the field, it is unlikely that this material is the cause of such a distinctive anomaly.

It is not clear that the archaeological complex continues across the stream; certainly, there is no indication of an enclosure in the geophysical data to the east of the stream but evidence for burning/industrial activity in this area strongly suggests that at least some early medieval activity extends into this field. If this activity across the stream were enclosed, it is tempting to suggest that a D-form enclosure would be neatly formed by the pre-cursor of the north-west–south-east-oriented field boundary standing on the high ground some 75m to the north-east of the stream. This may also explain why no eastern boundary has yet been traversed by a survey. The overall enclosure thus formed would contain *c.*4.75ha. Alternatively, and probably more likely, the eastern boundary of the monastery was formed by the current stream – with some industrial activities placed outside the monastery limits; in this instance the size of the monastery is *c.*3.5ha.

The surveys from 2019 and 2021 add significance to the results of archaeological test trenching at and adjacent to the site by McLoughlin in 2006 (Licence 06E0287). At that time, sixteen test trenches were excavated – six in the field containing Clone Church and ten in the field to the east – in advance of a proposed private development. This testing revealed multiple archaeological features. In the field containing the church a portion of a wide ditch was encountered, which now appears to be part of the northern outermost monastic ditch, as indicated by geophysics and drone survey; a second ditch was also encountered in this portion of the field. In the field east of the river, a series of charcoal spreads and discrete features containing charcoal, slag and burnt bone were recorded; these were interpreted as industrial in nature and associated with a monastery at Clone (Mcloughlin 2006, 9). They were noticeably concentrated in the south-west of the field, where geophysics has also indicated the presence of an industrial area. None of the features was dated but industrial activity such as metalworking, inferred by the recovery of slag, is common on most monastic sites (Swan 1991, 138; Edwards 1996, 68; O'Sullivan et al. 2008, 215–16).

Collectively, the geophysical surveys pointed to a substantial early medieval site at Clone. Archaeological evidence indicates most early medieval monasteries date to between the late sixth and early eighth centuries (O'Sullivan and McCormick 2017, 112). Correspondingly, documentary evidence demonstrates that many ecclesiastical sites were founded from the middle of the sixth century with no saints founding sites after about AD800 (O'Sullivan and McCormick 2017). While the available evidence from Clone, even in advance of archaeological excavation, clearly pointed to a substantial early medieval monastery, excavation was still required to clarify the age of the site, and whether it was consistent in date to most other early medieval monasteries.

RECENT COMMUNITY ARCHAEOLOGICAL EXCAVATIONS

To assess the site's antiquity and form, two excavation seasons were undertaken by the IAFS and community volunteers, a weeklong dig in December 2019 and a two-week one in August 2021 (fig. 12.8). The aim of these excavations was to investigate some of the surveyed geophysical anomalies, clarifying the nature and age of the enclosures surrounding the site. An ancillary objective of the project was to engage the local community from Ferns and surrounds in a community excavation, bringing the site of Clone to the centre of local public consciousness.

In total, during both excavation seasons, four archaeological cuttings were opened, dug, assessed and backfilled. All cuttings were found to contain multiple archaeological features amounting to twenty-one discrete features and seventy-three individual contexts. The features within the cuttings can be summarized as follows:

- Cutting 1: a ditch (and associated fills), representing the inner ditch of the outer monastic enclosure, in addition to two furrows and an area of burning.
- Cutting 2: a ditch (and associated fills), interpreted as the inner monastic enclosure, in addition to two further 'ditch' features, as well as a single furrow.
- Cutting 3: both ditches (and associated fills) of the outer monastic enclosure, with the outer ditch containing a drystone wall. A small linear feature of indeterminate function, two pits/post-holes, two hearths/pits, a single stake-hole and a burnt deposit, as well as a later furrow and French drain.
- Cutting 4: a smaller rock-cut ditch, marking the line of an internal oval enclosure, as was a linear feature/gully of uncertain function.

12.8 Community volunteers and IAFS staff at Clone in 2021 in Cutting 3

Archaeological features in Cuttings 1, 2 and 4 were found to be devoid of artefacts, despite a metal-detection survey (Licence 19R0274) and a rigorous sieving programme to boost the retrieval of artefacts; this meticulous approach to finds retrieval did assist in the recovery of a body sherd of later medieval Leinster Cooking Ware (LCW) and a broken roof slate from topsoil in Cutting 2, as well as a worked flint from topsoil in Cutting 4. Thirty-five finds were recovered from Cutting 3, including a range of medieval pottery (N=28: 27 LCW and a sherd of Wexford-Type Cooking Ware) a 'worked stone', two struck flints and four medieval nails. These finds were almost exclusively recovered from the tertiary fills of the outer ditch of the outer monastic enclosure. For ease of description, the archaeology is discussed initially by cutting.

Cutting 1: the outer enclosure inner ditch

Cutting 1 measured approximately 6.1m by 1.3m and was excavated to a depth of 1.5m along a broadly east-to-west axis. Two furrows were located toward the eastern end of the cutting, one of which cut through the upper fills of a ditch representing the inner circuit of the bivallate outer monastic enclosure (figs 12.9, 12.10). The ditch contained five distinct fills, of which the basal fill was noticeably different from the others, consisting of subsoil-like clay containing frequent large stones (20–30cm^3), which was not noted in the other fills. Subsequent radiometric dating of charcoal from

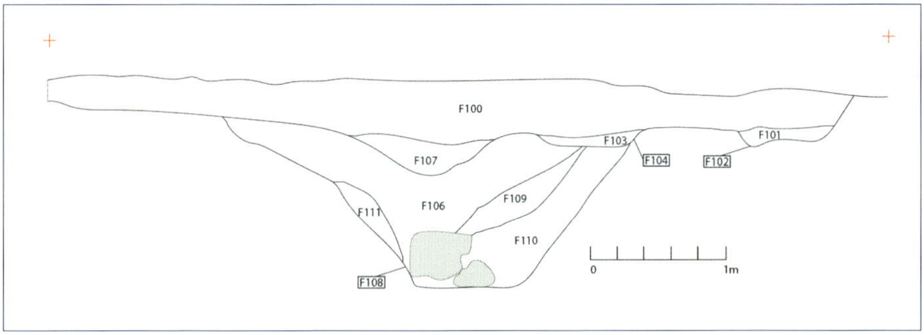

12.9 Section drawing of the inner ditch of the outer monastic enclosure in Cutting 1

12.10 Post-excavation section of the inner ditch of the outer monastic enclosure in Cutting 1: note the large stone in the basal fill

this basal fill returned an age of 3716–3954 cal. BC – an intriguing Neolithic date (table 12.1). While additional excavation and radiometric dating is required before reaching any definitive conclusions, it is tantalizing to consider that the stone in the basal fills could derive from a Neolithic monument that was 'razed' during the establishment (or destruction) of the early medieval monastery. Such a suggestion may also explain the presence of passage-tomb art on the site and the pieces of flint mentioned above, which consist of a simple modified flake, a decortical flake and an

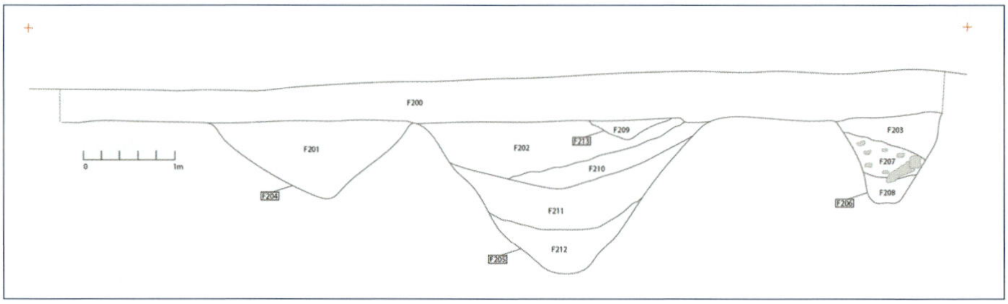

12.11 Section drawing of the ditches of the inner monastic enclosure in Cutting 2

12.12 Post-excavation section of the ditches of the inner monastic enclosure in Cutting 2

irregular core. Although, all were found in secondary contexts, they hint at activity nearby in the Neolithic.

A slip of bank-like material was also recorded along the cut's western edge, possibly deriving from a bank between the inner and outer ditch of the outer monastic enclosure; while the outer ditch was not stripped or assessed in 2019 it was excavated in 2021, when more bank-like fills were observed. Of note, one of the ditch-fills in Cutting 1 also consisted of ex-situ burnt material, containing much charcoal, which may have been thrown into the ditch after it had been mostly backfilled. This fill was located only 2.2m east of a patch of oxidized clay representing in-situ burning outside the ditch, with the two features possibly related.

Table 12.1 Radiocarbon dates for Clone. Calibration after OxCal. 4.1 (Bronk Ramsay 2009) using the IntCal09 dataset (Reimer et al. 2009)

Lab. code	Charcoal	Sample no.	14C age (BP)	Calibrated age (95.4% prob. (cal. BC/AD)
UBA-43373	*Maloideae*	105	5047±30	3716–3954BC
UBA-43373	hazel	204	1271±26	AD667–821
UBA-47034	apple	321	1289±27	AD664–774
UBA-47035	hazel	404	1575±29	AD424–529
UBA-47036	hazel	319	964±23	AD1026–1157

Cutting 2: the inner enclosure

Cutting 2 measured approximately 10.7m by 1.3m and was excavated to a maximum depth of 2.1m along a broadly north-east–south-west axis. A single furrow was recorded centrally in the cutting, cut through the uppermost fill of a ditch that marks the location of the inner monastic enclosure, as recorded in the geophysical survey (figs 12.11, 12.12). Radiometric dating of charcoal from the upper fill of this ditch returned an age of cal. AD667–821 (table 12.1), confirming the ditch was backfilled in the early medieval period. In total, the ditch contained four distinct fills, with the lower fill being consistent with natural subsoil, and again probably deriving from a bank originally associated with the ditch. Of note, a lower/secondary fill of the ditch was almost identical in composition to the singular fill of a much smaller ditch positioned to the east of the inner enclosure. This may indicate both are broadly contemporary, or at least were backfilled at the same time. The smaller ditch may also mark the line of the inner internal monastic enclosure, although it should be noted that it does not form a continuous bivallate circuit in the geophysical survey. A third ditch, containing three fills, is also recorded to the west of the monastic enclosure.

Cutting 3: the outer enclosure/entrance

Cutting 3 measured approximately 16m by 4.4m in maximum dimensions and was excavated to a maximum depth of 2m along a broadly north-to-south axis. A furrow and a French drain were located towards the central portion of the cutting, with the latter also cutting a narrow linear feature, which was of indeterminate function. Two major clusters of archaeological features were concentrated towards the northern and southern ends of the cutting where the inner and outer ditches of the outer monastic enclosure were located (fig. 12.13).

The inner ditch, which was again clearly recorded on geophysics, contained four distinct fills. The lower fills, like those recorded in Cutting 1, included re-deposited natural subsoil or natural/relict topsoil mixes, likely deriving from a 'pushed-in' bank. The basal fill did not contain any large stone, however, unlike in Cutting 1 (figs 12.14, 12.17).

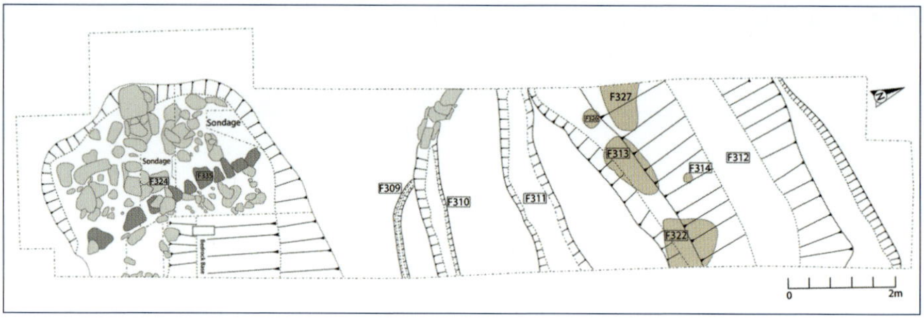

12.13 Plan of Cutting 3. Note the solid brown features were overlying the inner ditch of the outer monastic enclosure and were resolved in advance of excavating the ditch itself

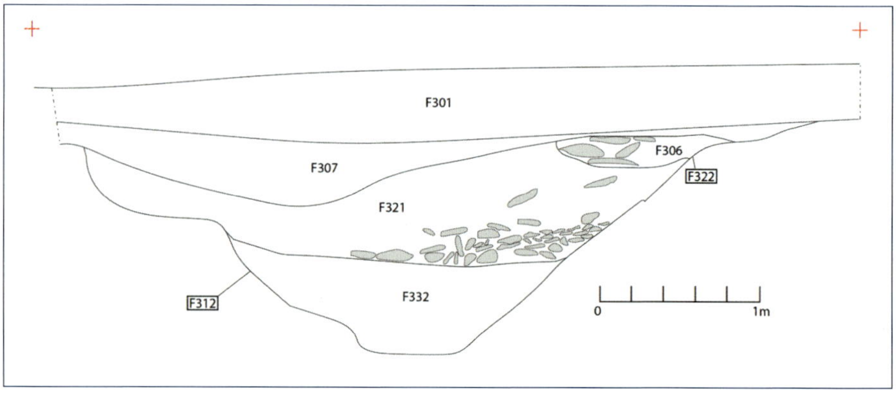

12.14 Section drawing of the inner ditch of the outer monastic enclosure in Cutting 3

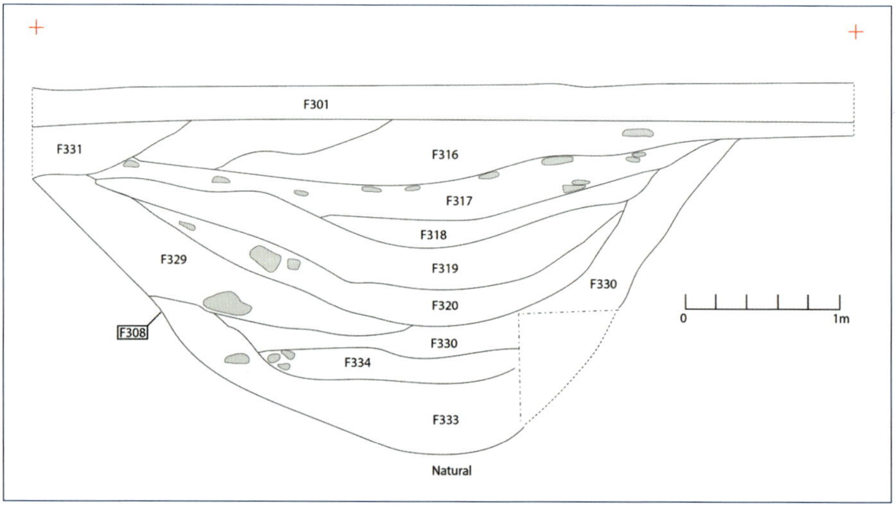

12.15 Section drawing of the outer ditch of the outer monastic enclosure in Cutting 3

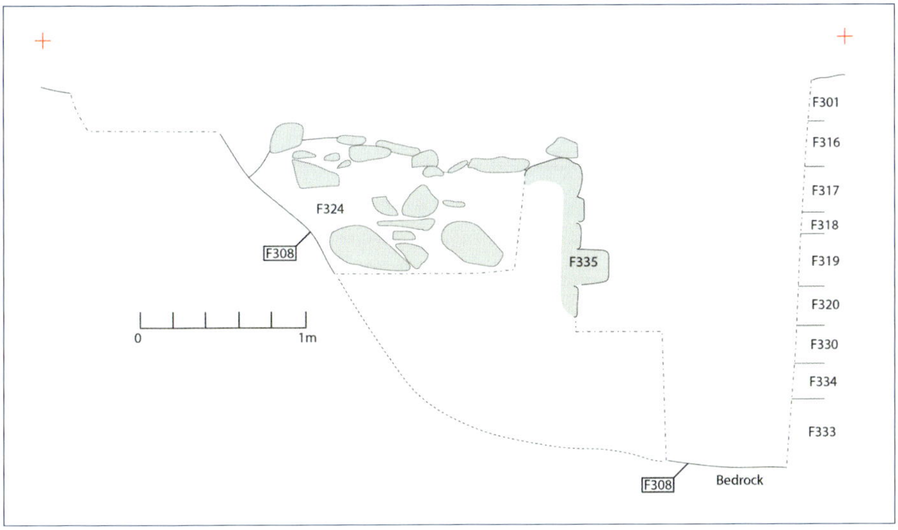

12.16 Section drawing/profile of the outer ditch of the outer monastic enclosure in Cutting 3, showing the drystone wall

12.17 Post-excavation section of the inner ditch of the outer monastic enclosure in Cutting 3

12.18 Post-excavation section of the outer ditch of the outer monastic enclosure in Cutting 3

12.19 Mid-excavation image of the drystone wall in Cutting 3

A pit was cut through the ditch's upper fills, the base of which was heavily oxidized indicating repeated burning at high temperatures. It was one of several features cut through the upper fills of the ditch, with a second pit/hearth and two postholes/small pits also cut through the ditch's tertiary fill. These features collectively are likely to represent light industrial activity, which geophysical survey results indicate is quite dense to the north-west of the cutting. Charcoal from a secondary fill of the ditch was dated to cal. AD664–774 (table 12.1), indicating when the ditch passed out of use, and confirming an early medieval date for the outer enclosure.

The southern cluster of features was concentrated around the outermost monastic ditch, which contained ten fills (figs 12.15, 12.18). A possible stake-hole was recorded at the north-west edge of the ditch. The ditch was initially identified by geophysical survey, which indicated a terminus/entrance at the point Cutting 3 was excavated, a finding confirmed by the excavation.

The ditch's two lower fills appear to be accumulations of silty clays that collected after the ditch went out of use. These were sealed by a natural-like fill, which may derive from a slipped or pushed-in bank at the ditch's edge. Intriguingly, directly above this natural fill a drystone wall was constructed, *c.*2.4m west of the existing terminus of the ditch. This wall consisted of six random courses, with a clear external or east-facing front (fig. 12.19). This wall represents a stratigraphic break in the chronology of the backfilling of the outermost monastic enclosure (fig. 12.16). To the west of the wall, the 2.4m area between the wall and the ditch terminus was backfilled with a sandy silt and rubble infill (which also contained the only recovered piece of crudely worked stone, a possible aborted attempt at a chamfered windowsill). To the east of the wall, and post-dating its construction, were seven upper ditch fills, consisting of a series of silts and sands; several of these contained twelfth- to fourteenth-century pottery, namely twenty-seven sherds of Leinster Cooking Ware (LCW) and a single sherd of Wexford-Type Cooking Ware. These artefacts were concentrated in the first fill immediately post-dating the drystone wall, which contained eighteen sherds of medieval pottery. As least eight of these derived from the same vessel, a shallow dish of LCW with a straight-sided rim, and an unusual inside curve.

LCW is one of the more common medieval pottery types in eastern Ireland and dates from the late twelfth to mid-fourteenth centuries. Its presence in several of the upper fills indicates that the ditch was backfilled and put out of use at this time. This is broadly confirmed by a radiocarbon date of cal. AD1026–1157 from charcoal in a secondary ditch fill (table 12.1). Prior to this backfilling the outer monastic enclosure was not being regularly maintained, with silts accumulating at its base, and a bank or banks having already been pushed back into both the outer ditches. While the outermost ditch remained partially open the wall was constructed close to the ditch terminus, possibly to formalize an entrance to the site. Finally, at some point in the twelfth century the outermost ditch was entirely backfilled, probably at the same time the upstanding church was being constructed as part of a general later medieval re-ordering of the site.

Cutting 4: a secondary inner enclosure

Cutting 4 measured approximately 6.6m by 2.2m and was excavated to a depth of 1.1m along a broadly east to west axis. A single linear feature/gully was located towards the western end of the cutting, which matches perfectly with the location of a small 'spur' that is shown as jutting from a smaller oval enclosure on the geophysics. A similar spur is recorded in the geophysical survey on the inner monastic enclosure, west of Cutting 4, indicating they could be contemporary. The cutting also contained a rock-cut ditch, which forms part of an arching/oval enclosure >45m across from its northern edge to where it can no longer be traced as it joins the current graveyard. The ditch contained four fills, with the basal fill (a stone/sand mix) appearing to have accumulated in the ditch after it passed out of use (figs 12.20, 12.21). A secondary fill of charcoal was placed in the ditch when it had been mostly backfilled. Charcoal from a lower fill was dated to cal. AD424–529 (table 12.1), the earliest early medieval date from the site, soon after the arrival of Christianity in Ireland. The function of the ditch is not clear, but as it is cut through a bedrock its original excavation represented a considerable investment of labour.

DISCUSSION

Prior to the commencement of excavation, several strands of evidence including the cross-slabs, bullaun stone, association with St Aidan and, not least, the drone survey in 2018 all pointed to the likelihood of an early medieval foundation pre-dating the extant twelfth-century church. Geophysical surveys in 2019 and 2021 confirmed the existence, and crucially the location and form, of these enclosures as well as several other radial elements, including a smaller oval enclosure, which is now also confirmed as early medieval.

The 2019 and 2021 excavations broadly matched the results of the geophysics, revealing three sets of enclosing ditches, as well as 'lesser' features such as furrows, postholes, hearths and pits. The burnt features are an addition to several 'burnt features' noted in earlier archaeological testing at Clone (McLoughlin 2006), as well as geophysical evidence of industrial areas, notably west and east of the river.

The monastic ditches are undoubtedly the features of greatest archaeological interest, with three enclosing elements now confirmed, including an outer bivallate enclosure and an inner enclosure (also potentially bivallate) that surround a small oval ditch; these enclosures measure respectively *c.*200m, 130m and >45m in diameter. At least one of these features, the outermost ditch, continued in use from the early to later medieval period, with the available dating evidence (from pottery and radiocarbon

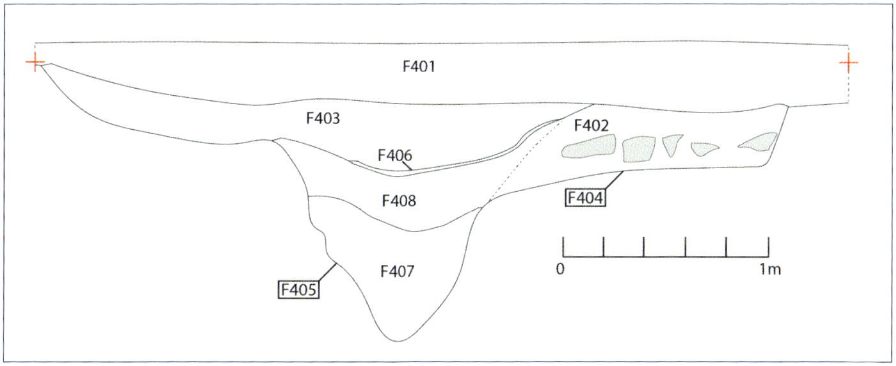

12.20 Section drawing of the rock-cut ditch in Cutting 4

12.21 Post-excavation section of the rock-cut ditch in Cutting 4

dating) indicating it was finally backfilled in the twelfth century. This differs to dates returned from both the inner ditch of the outer enclosure and the inner enclosure itself, which were backfilled much earlier, sometime between the seventh and ninth centuries. The smallest oval enclosure appears to be earlier yet, having been backfilled in the fifth to sixth century. An intriguing Neolithic date was also obtained on the inner ditch of the outer monastic enclosure and, while anachronistic for the ditch, it is tempting to link this date to a razed Neolithic monument on the site, possibly related to Clone's passage-tomb art.

Possibly the feature of greatest intrigue is the drystone wall. This was built in the partially backfilled outermost monastic enclosure only 2.4m east of a terminus in this ditch and may represent a formalizing and restructuring of the original early medieval entrance. After the construction of the wall, several fills were placed into the ditch in the twelfth to fourteenth centuries, which put the outer enclosure out of use. This final backfilling of the ditches is likely to be representative of a wider re-purposing of space, which included the construction of the upstanding medieval church. A similar programme of backfilling has been observed at nearby Ferns (and other early medieval sites), where the inner monastic enclosure was backfilled broadly at the same time as the construction of the twelfth-century Augustinian priory of St Mary's (Shine et al. 2021; ch. 9).

The exact foundation date for Clone is unknown, but it appears (based on the smaller oval enclosure) to date to the early stages of Christianity in Ireland sometime in the fifth and/or sixth centuries. This date raises intriguing questions about Clone's antiquity and its relationship with St Aidan's primary monastery in Ferns, which is known to have been founded sometime around the turn of the seventh century (Culleton 1999). Available dates from excavations of Ferns' early medieval enclosures are predominantly later than Clone's oval enclosure, but broadly contemporary with the backfilling of its main enclosures; for example, excavations in Castleland have produced dates of cal. AD659–851 and 727–940 (McLoughlin and Stafford 2020, 91; ch. 8), while a date of cal. AD655–773 was returned for a sample from excavations in Ferns Demesne (close to St Mary's Abbey) (Shine et al. 2021; ch. 9). Admittedly, an earlier outlying date for Ferns of cal. AD384–535 was obtained from excavations by Frank Ryan on Station Road (Ryan 1998; ch. 8). Ryan originally believed his ditch was an Iron Age feature, but Ian Doyle (2016, 55) has since suggested that it forms part of an early sixth-century monastic enclosure at Ferns. This is the only 'early' date for Ferns, with all others indicating that Clone's oval enclosure pre-dates Aidan's primary monastery at Ferns.

While it is possible that Clone pre-dates Ferns, the latter remains undoubtedly the larger of the two sites, with Ferns potentially being *c.*350m to possibly >500m in diameter (Doyle 2016, 53; McLoughlin 2020; McLoughlin and Stafford 2020; ch. 8) and Clone measuring only approximately half that at *c.*200m across. This undoubtedly speaks to Ferns' higher status as a site around which the cult of St Aidan was established (see, for example, Bhreathnach and Dowling 2021). Excluding Clone's oval enclosure, all the other enclosures at both sites appear broadly contemporary, so the sites surely interacted. As the 'lesser' monastery, the role played by Clone in relation to Ferns is difficult to assess archaeologically. It is tempting to think Clone served a pilgrimage function to Ferns, considering its finer decorative elements such as the carved bird, 'cross-of-arcs' stone and sundial – which have all been ascribed a pilgrimage association. The original placement of several of these monumental elements may also be suggestive of a *Turas*, possibly in a localized clockwise (*deiseal*) movement, as has been observed at other early medieval monasteries (e.g., O'Sullivan et al. 2018). Alternatively, perhaps Clone acted as a pilgrimage site en route to Ferns, being near the valley of the River Bann, a natural routeway leading to Ferns and the River Slaney. Such conjectures, of course, require further investigation but offer a tantalizing glimpse of where future research avenues might lead for this enigmatic site.

BIBLIOGRAPHY

Bhreathnach, E. and Dowling, G. 2021. 'Forming an episcopal see and an Augustinian foundation in medieval Ireland: the case of Ferns, Co. Wexford'. *Proceedings of the Royal Irish Academy*, 121C, 191–226.

Bronk Ramsey, C. 2009. 'Bayesian analysis of radiocarbon dates'. *Radiocarbon*, 51:1, 337–60.

Colbert, K. 2019. 'Early medieval sculpture in south-east Ireland: identities, landscape and memory'. PhD, UCC.

Cosgrave, W. 2016. 'Twelfth-century church at Clone, Ferns'. *The Past: The Organ of the Uí Cinsealaigh Historical Society*, 32, 5–13.

Culleton, E. 1999. *Celtic and early Christian Wexford, AD400 to 1166*. Dublin.

Doyle, I. 2016. 'Telling the dancer from the dance: the archaeology of early medieval Wexford'. In Doyle, I. and Browne, B. (eds), *Medieval Wexford: essays in memory of Billy Colfer*, 35–61. Dublin.

Du Noyer, G.V. 1864–6. 'Early Irish and pre-Norman antiquities'. *Proceedings of the Royal Irish Academy*, 9, 423–44.

Edwards, N. 1996. *The archaeology of early medieval Ireland*. London.

Elliott, I. 2019. 'Report on archaeogeophysical survey (consent 19R0238) at Clone td, Co. Wexford'. Unpublished technical report prepared for the Irish Archaeology Field School.

Elliott, I. 2022. 'Report on archaeogeophysical survey (consent 21R0219) at Clone td, Co. Wexford'. Unpublished technical report prepared for the Irish Archaeology Field School.

Grattan Flood, W.H. 1916. *History of the diocese of Ferns*. Waterford.

Hore, H.P. 1911. *History of the town and county of Wexford*, vol. 6. London.

Harbison, P. 1991. *Pilgrimage in Ireland: the monuments and the people*. New York.

Kinahan, G.H. 1889. 'Proceedings'. *Journal of the Royal Society of Antiquaries of Ireland*, 9:78, 3–18.

McLoughlin, C. 2006. 'Archaeological testing report, Clone, Ferns, Co. Wexford (06E0287)'. Unpublished excavation report for the National Monument Service.

McLoughlin, C. 2020. 'From early to late: uncovering medieval Ferns'. *Archaeology Ireland*, 34:2, 30–4.

McLoughlin, C. and Stafford, E. 2020. 'Medieval Ferns: from monastic centre to medieval town'. In Corlett, C. and Potterton, M. (eds), *The town in medieval Ireland in the light of recent archaeological excavations*, 85–100. Dublin.

Mulligan, P. 2016. *A short guide to Irish antiquities*. Dublin.

National Monuments Service, Historic Environment viewer database and mapping service. 2020. www.archaeology.ie, accessed 10 Jan. 2020.

Ó Crualaoich, C. and Mac Giolla Chomhghaill. 2016. *Townland names of Co. Wexford*. Dublin.

O'Donovan, J., O'Keeffe, P. and O'Connor, T. 1840. *Ordnance Survey letters: Wexford, vol. 2*. Dublin.

O'Sullivan, A., McCormick, F., Kerr, T. and Harney, L. 2008. *Early medieval Ireland: archaeological excavations, 1930–2004*. Dublin.

O'Sullivan, A. and McCormick, F. 2017. 'Early medieval Ireland: investigating social, economic and settlement change, AD400–1100'. In Stanley, M., Swan, R. and O'Sullivan, A. (eds), *Stories of Ireland's past: knowledge gained from NRA roads archaeology*, 101–32. Dublin.

O'Sullivan, M., Rodgers, M., Shine, D. and Mandal, S. 2018. 'Seir Kieran: place, pilgrimage and tradition in the monastic midlands'. *Offaly Heritage*, 10, 21–42.

Ranson, J. 1957. 'Restoration of twelfth-century church at Clone'. *Enniscorthy Echo*.

Reimer, P., Baillie, M., Bard, E., Bayliss, A., Beck, J., Blackwell, P., Bronk Ramsey, C., Buck, C., Burr, G., Edwards, R., Friedrich, M., Grootes, P., Guilderson, T., Hajdas, I., Heaton, T., Hogg, A., Hughen, K., Kaiser, K., Kromer, B., McCormac, F., Manning, S., Reimer, R., Richards, D., Southon, J., Talamo, S., Turney, C., van der Plicht, J. and Weyhenmeyer, C. 2009. 'IntCal09 and Marine09 radiocarbon age calibration curves, 0–50,000 years cal. BP'. *Radiocarbon*, 51, 1111–50.

Ryan, F. 1998. 'Archaeological findings from monitoring of Phase 1 of Ferns Sewage Scheme, Co. Wexford'. Unpublished excavation report 98E0132.

Sheehan, J. 2009. 'A peacock's tale: excavations at Caherlehillan, Iveragh, Ireland'. In Edwards, N. (ed.), *The archaeology of the early medieval Celtic churches*, 192–204. Leeds.

Shine, D. and Lacey, B. 2020. 'Clone community archaeological excavation report'. Unpublished technical report prepared for the National Monuments Service and Wexford County Council.

Shine, D. and Lacey, B. 2021. 'Clone Church archaeological excavation report'. Unpublished technical report prepared for the National Monuments Service and Wexford County Council.

Shine, D., Lacey, B., Corlett, C., Elliott, I. and Mandal, S. 2020. 'Clone, Ferns: a meadow of St Aidan?' *Archaeology Ireland*, 34:4, 24–9.

Shine, D., Lynch, L., Mandal, S. and O'Meara D. 2021. 'Discovering St Aidan's monastery: preliminary archaeological excavation report (December 2021)'. Unpublished technical report produced for the National Monuments Service.

Swan, D.L. 1991. 'Early monastic sites'. In Ryan, M. (ed.). *The illustrated archaeology of Ireland*, 137–9. Dublin.

CHAPTER THIRTEEN

A glimpse of light in Wexford: late medieval rushlight holders

CLARE McCUTCHEON

> The question is, are we, as archaeologists, anxious to penetrate into the life of the past, to scan the household arrangements of the humble as well as the wealthy, to become familiar, as far as the remnants of antiquity will permit, with the means and fashions of every grade of society? For, if this be our aim and province, then scorn not the matters here presented, and turn not away with contempt from the smallest item, the merest trifle, which affords a glimpse of the social aspect of bygone times (Jones 1890, 293).

During excavations at Ferns Castle in 1972–5, David Sweetman recovered an oddly shaped item, 'found in the middle layers of the south fosse, east section, under the charcoal layer' (Sweetman 1979). The object was subsequently published as 'a possible candlestick'. Raghnall Ó Floinn (1988, 331) referred both to this and to others in his defining work on Leinster Cooking Ware, 'Candle-holders occurred at Ferns and at the moated site at Barmoney, Co. Wexford'. Now, fifty years later, over two dozen of these items have been recovered, principally but not exclusively in Co. Wexford (fig. 13.1). For this reason, it seems timely to discuss this ceramic form, which has been suggested as candlestick, candle holder and lamp before returning full circle to being a candle and a rushlight holder.

While the pieces may not be the most attractive of artefacts, undecorated and simple in design, they are very interesting and odd items that highlight the development of lighting during the second stage of Anglo-Norman settlement in Ireland. Based on just a few at the time, Ó Floinn's description still holds well 'these are cylindrical in form with concave sides flaring outwards at rim and base and are provided with a central socket. These may be derived from stone lamps of similar shape which are very common in Carlow, Wexford and Waterford and are dated to the tenth to twelfth centuries AD' (Ó Floinn 1988, 331).

The first time these pieces were fully discussed, drawn and published was in relation to the city-centre excavations in Waterford (Moore 1997). Various curious items were being allocated for specialist treatment and it was decided to bundle the pottery lamps in with the stone lamps in line with the layout of the Winchester example (Barclay and

13.1 Finds spots of Leinster Cooking Ware rushlight holders from Wexford and Waterford (red) as referred to in the text

Biddle 1990) and to avoid unnecessary cross-referencing (Moore 1997). The two lumps of Leinster Cooking Ware made it onto the page of rather more classic double-shelled English lamps in the form of squat pedestal bowls; a classic spiked lamp from Normandy and a very strange stem piece: 'the identification of this piece in English ware as a cresset lamp is questionable' (Moore 1997, 435, fig. 14:17.6). The latter was subsequently shown to be an oil lamp from Rouen, with a cup or reservoir above and a saucer below over a stem and a base plate, as the saucer from an identical piece was recovered at Wood Quay, Dublin (McCutcheon 2006, 90–1, fig. 39.3). This emphasizes the difficulty in identifying the true form of what may appear to be unpromising 'lumps' of fired clay.

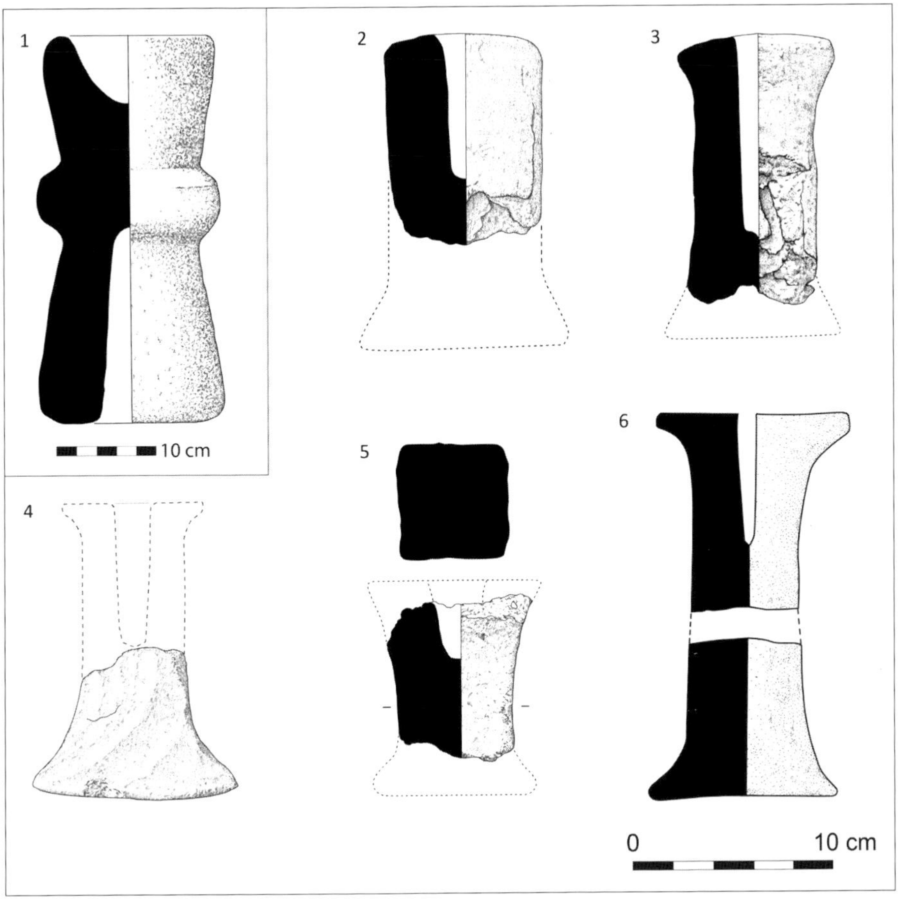

13.2 Stone lamp and Leinster Cooking Ware rushlight holders: 1. Stone cresset lamp, Waterford; 2. Killann; 3. Bridgetown; 4. Deanery Gardens, Waterford; 5. 62–68 North Main Street, Wexford; 6. Arundel Square, Waterford

While the stone cresset lamp from Waterford (fig. 13.2:1) has been taken as the template for the Leinster Cooking Ware 'lamps', it now seems more likely that this lamp is itself more of a transitional form. There would be no reason to hollow out a funnel shape in stone unless it had a specific function, and this piece may be seen as dual-purpose oil lamp on one end with the hollowed-out cup for oil and wick and a rushlight or candleholder on the other end in the hollowed-out funnel. Whichever way this transitional lamp was placed, the distinctive central collar, both decorative and functional, and the splayed ends allowed for both a secure carrying mechanism and placement on a flat surface. These pieces in Leinster Cooking Ware can no longer be described as lamps, as the anticipated cup or reservoir for the liquid fuel has been shown to be absent and, instead, the piece has a funnel-shaped hollow (Moore 1997, fig. 17:4:4). As both pieces from Waterford had the classic sand-gritted finish on the flared surface, these were taken as bases for two lamps and the hollowing was thought to have been for the purpose of reducing the thickness of the stem to assist in the firing. This suggestion was carried through to the various reports, published and unpublished, on these pieces since 1997 (cf. McCutcheon 2009; Moriarty 2021c). As more have been found in the years since, however, it has become clear that these are not oil lamps, as no cup or semblance of a cup has been found. In addition, the solid flat surface has often been smoothed and it is evident that there is a consistent use of a funnel or cone-shaped hollowing in many of the pieces. The Leinster Cooking Ware lighting is only in use at one end and is not to be turned over and so the decorative collar seen on the stone cresset lamp is not required, indicating that they are the next step from the single stone cresset lamp from Waterford, as they have lost the dual function of oil lamps and candleholders. They are without cups, and the funnel, thought to have assisted in better firing, in fact functions solely as a rushlight/ candleholder (fig. 13.2:6). Among these pottery candleholders, the only consistency is the hollowed funnel as they display various degrees of splay at the ends (figs 13.2:3, 4, 6).

The evidence then points to generally a solid round rod, flared at the base for balance, flared at the top and containing a funnel hollowed out to a depth of about half the height. Naturally there are exceptions to this general rule, as with the top from the Killann example, which is a cylinder and only slightly flared (fig. 13.2:3), and the stem fragment from North Main Street, Wexford, which is square in section (fig. 13.2:5; Sheehan 2004). The funnel is what distinguishes these items as candle or rushlight holders rather than as lamps. The first outlier was 'the Waterford Two' recovered in Waterford city excavations (Moore 1997), the first to be fully examined, described and published, while a second was found during works at the undercroft in the Deanery Gardens in 2010 (Scully 2010). This latter is particularly interesting as the fine illustration by Sara Nylund highlights the swirling marks, possibly made by the left thumb of the potter while holding the item in his/her right hand (fig. 13.2:4). In addition to the two in Waterford, two others were found in south Co. Dublin, at Carrickmines Great (McCutcheon forthcoming) and at the manor of Merrion Castle (McCutcheon 2004). Other than these four, the candle or rushlight holders are confined to Co. Wexford despite the widespread recovery of Leinster Cooking Ware from Dungarvan to Dundalk. With one lamp from Ferns Castle (Sweetman 1979), four from Castleland, Ferns (McLoughlin 2019) and another recent find from near Ferns Cathedral (Shine et al. 2021), this curious item provides six varied remains as a cluster in the town of Ferns.

It appears that all are associated with primarily Anglo-Norman settlements – castle, urban, motte-and-bailey, moated sites. Those in the countryside have generally come to light because of archaeological investigations in advance of roadworks – especially those that uncovered moated sites, and so the dating of the holders appears to be upwards of a century later than previously thought.

The fabric is the typical quartz- and mica-rich clay. Seven sherds were thin-sectioned from the Dublin Castle excavations:

> All are very similar in that they are coarse grained (inclusions up to 4mm) and contain a high percentage of granitic rock (fragments up to 50%) with smaller quantities of quartz (20%), feldspar (up to 40%) and mica (up to 30%). The clay matrix of the sherds is very variable in terms of the naturally occurring 'background' inclusions, tiny grains of the order of .01mm in size (Sandes forthcoming).

As the rod is so thick and Leinster Cooking Ware was fired in a bonfire or clamp kiln, the holders are very often poorly fired and can crumble. One such example, from Coolamurry near Enniscorthy, consists of forty-five fragments with only a couple of sherds having the characteristic smoothed exterior surface.

Given that these items can be identified as rushlight or candle holders, then the question is how the rushlights were made. Ffrench (1891, 627) suggested the earliest-known recorded preparation of rushes for lighting in Ireland dates to the early third century, with the woman in question stating 'that it was the work of the women to cut and peel the rushes, as women are the light of the house'. Ffrench went on to say that 'the preparing and peeling of rushes was part of the work of every farmer's wife, almost to our own time; and the preparing and selling of bundles of rushes to old bachelors, and other unfortunates who had no women in their families to do the work, was a regular industry among the poor' (ibid.). Naturalist Revd Gilbert White is quoted as writing that 'decayed labourers, women and children make it their business to procure and prepare them ... and we have seen an old woman, stone blind, performing this business with great despatch, and seldom failing to strip them with the nicest regularity' (Jones 1890, 297). It seems that the Irish and Welsh rushlights had much in common, as 'the Welsh rushlight is a taper about 2 feet long, made from the common rush or sedge; the out skin is peeled off with the exception of a narrow strip left for strength, and the pith is drawn through fat melted in a frying pan or any other suitable vessel' (Le Neve Foster 1886, 142).

> The Romans are thought to have invented the dipped candle. In the medieval period, beeswax candles could only really be found in churches and richer households. Poorer people would make do with firelight, rushlights or tallow. Homemade rushlights were made by rolling the dried pith of rushes in fat to make a rough and ready lamp, with the pith as the wick. They burned quickly – one 40cm long would burn for about half an hour. Tallow candles were another cheap option, and they burned for longer than rushlights. Made of a kind of rendered animal fat, they were a nasty brown colour and could give off an even nastier smell (Moriarty 2017).

Although the blog above from English Heritage refers to 'a nasty brown colour' and an 'even nastier smell', in fact the choice of animal fat was important and the use of the white clean fat around the kidney was especially prized. I saw my late mother rendering kidney fat in 1958 to use in making homemade soap, resulting in yellowish, smell-free long bars of soap, perfect for use on a washboard.

From the Schools' Collection (1937–9) comes a memory of rush and candle making passed down to Diarmuid Ó Cróinín from his father Mícheál, near Castletownbere, Co. Cork:

> Long ago the people used rushes as candles. They used to gather the strong rushes and peel them. They used to leave one little strip on it and leave them dry. Then they used to melt tallow in a box and rub the rush along the melted tallow, and leave it there until it dry. They used to put the rush into a piece of timber used as a candle stick. They used to make candles out of tallow also. They had a mound or *sligire* for making them. They used to melt tallow and they used to double a string and put it into the mould. They used to put a nail in the end of the string in order that they would pull the candle out of the mould. When the tallow would be melted they used to put it into the mould, and leave it there until it gets hard. Then they used to put it to the fire until it soften a little. Then they would catch the nail and pull out the candle (Schools' Collection, vol. 0275, 147).

Finally, the Wexford area has another curious twist in the pottery tale as both there and in Dublin, another vessel, known as an incurved or West Country dish, is found that may have been associated with the making of rushlights or candle wax. The two vessels do not appear to be exactly contemporary, with the incurved dish dating to the later twelfth and early thirteenth centuries, and the rushlight holders possibly dating to the later thirteenth to early fourteenth centuries. Needing further detailed investigation, however, is the recovery of a semi-complete incurved dish and some fourteen sherds of rushlight holders from the 1986–7 excavations at Ferrycarrig. While not yet proven conclusively, the lipid analysis from sherds from several incurved dishes in Dublin 'plot firmly within the ruminant carcass range' (Dunne 2018) and may indicate that they were used for rendering fat for both candles and soap. The shape of the incurved dish is a shallow, flat-bottomed, up to 34cm in diameter. A small hole in the side, closed with a wooden plug, might allow any juice to be drained off after the fat was rendered and rose to the top of the vessel to harden.

To echo the words of Syer Cuming, quoted at the beginning, this note has attempted to examine this 'smallest item, the merest trifle, which affords a glimpse of the social aspect of bygone times' (quoted in Jones 1890, 292).

BIBLIOGRAPHY

Barclay, K. and Biddle, M. 1990. 'Stone and pottery lamps'. In Biddle, M., *Object and economy in medieval Winchester*, 988–1000. Oxford.

Dehaene, G. 2009. 'Medieval rural settlement beside Duncormick motte, Co. Wexford'. In Corlett, C. and Potterton, M. (eds), *Rural settlement in medieval Ireland in the light of recent archaeological excavations*, 59–65. Dublin.

Doyle, N. 2009. 'Medieval and post-medieval pottery from Carrowreagh'. In Tierney, J., 'Archaeological excavation report E0471 Carrowreagh, Co. Wexford, medieval moated site and pottery kiln'. *Eachtra Journal*, 4, 49–71: www.slideshare.net/eachtra/archaeological-excavation-report-e0471-carrowreagh-co-wexford-ireland-eap-journal.

Dunne, J. 2018. 'Dean Street, Dublin: organic residues results'. Unpublished report for ACAS Ltd.

Eogan, J. and Kelly, B. 2016. 'New roads to medieval Wexford'. In Doyle, I. and Browne, B. (eds), *Medieval Wexford: essays in memory of Billy Colfer*, 211–20. Dublin.

Fegan, G. 2009. 'Discovery and excavation of a medieval moated site at Coolamurry, Co. Wexford'. In Corlett, C. and Potterton, M. (eds), *Rural settlement in medieval Ireland in the light of recent archaeological excavations*, 91–108. Dublin.

Ffrench, J.F.M. 1891. 'On a manner of lighting houses in old times, illustrated by rush-light candlesticks'. *Proceedings of the Royal Irish Academy*, 1:5, 626–30.

Freeman, M. 1979. *Farming people*, 2 Mar. 1979

Hackett, L. 2009. 'Bridgetown South'. In Bennett, I. (ed.), *Excavations 2006: summary accounts of archaeological excavations in Ireland*, 552, no. 2092. Dublin.

Hession, J. 2012. 'Landscape 2 (E4108): final excavation report'. Unpublished Rubicon Heritage Services Ltd report for Wexford County Council.

Jones, M.C. 1890. 'Notes upon some archaic domestic appliances in the Powys-Land Museum'. *Archaeologia Cambrensis*, 7:28, 293–304.

Le Neve Foster, C. 1886. 'The rush-light in north Wales'. *Journal of the Royal Institution of Cornwall*, 8, 142–3.

McCutcheon, C. 2006. *Medieval pottery from Wood Quay, Dublin*. Dublin.

McCutcheon, C. 2008. 'The medieval pottery'. In Baker, C., 'Excavations within the manor of Merrion Castle, Dublin'. In Duffy, S. (ed.), *Medieval Dublin VIII: Proceedings of the Friends of Medieval Dublin Symposium 2006*, 251–9. Dublin.

McCutcheon, C. 2009. 'The medieval pottery'. In Fegan, G., 'Discovery and excavation of a medieval moated site at Coolamurry, Co. Wexford'. In Corlett, C. and Potterton, M. (eds), *Rural settlement in medieval Ireland in the light of recent archaeological excavations*, 102–7. Dublin.

McCutcheon, C. Forthcoming. 'The medieval pottery'. In Breen, T., 'South-Eastern Motorway Scheme: archaeological resolution. Final report: 00E0525, 02E1532 – Carrickmines Great, County Dublin'.

McLoughlin, C. 2020. 'From early to late: uncovering medieval Ferns'. *Archaeology Ireland*, 34:2, 30–4.

Moore, M.J. 1997. 'The stone and pottery lamps'. In Hurley, M.F. and Scully, O.M.B., *Late Viking Age and medieval Waterford*, 432–6. Waterford.

Moriarty, C. 2020. 'The ceramic lamp report for Castleland, Ferns'. Unpublished report for Stafford McLoughlin Archaeology.

Moriarty, C. 2021a. 'The ceramic lamp report for High Hill, New Ross'. Unpublished report for Stafford McLoughlin Archaeology.

Moriarty, C. 2021b. 'The ceramic lamp report for Killann, Co. Wexford (21E0660)'. Unpublished report for De Faoite Archaeology.

Moriarty, C. 2021c. 'Medieval ceramic lamps from Co. Wexford': www.irisharchaeology.ie/2021/12/medieval-ceramic-lamps-from-co-wexford, accessed 12 Feb. 2023.

Moriarty, T. 2017. 'The illuminating history of lighting': www.english-heritage.org.uk/visit/inspire-me/blog/blog-posts/history-of-lighting.

Noonan, D. 2002. 'Bricketstown: corn-drying kiln and field system'. In Bennett, I. (ed.), *Excavations 2000: summary accounts of archaeological excavations in Ireland*, 350, no. 1041. Bray.

Ó Floinn, R. 1988. 'Handmade medieval pottery in S.E. Ireland: "Leinster Cooking Ware"'. In Mac Niocaill, G. and Wallace, P.F. (eds), *Keimelia: studies in medieval archaeology and history in memory of Tom Delaney*, 325–49. Galway.

Papazian, C. Forthcoming. 'The pottery'. In Cotter, C., 'Excavations at Ferrycarrig, Co. Wexford (E352)'.

Sandes, C. with McCutcheon, C. Forthcoming. 'The medieval pottery'. In Lynch, A. and Manning, C., *Excavations at Dublin Castle*, III.

Schools' Collection (Dúchas): Folklore (www.ucd.ie).

Scully, Ó. 2010. 'Excavations at Deanery Gardens, Cathedral Square, Waterford (licence E4077; excavation 2010:655)'. Unpublished excavation report: www.excavations.ie/report/2010/Waterford/0021865.

Sheehan, C. 2004. 'Shaw's, 62–68 Main St. North, Wexford'. In Bennett, I. (ed.), *Excavations 2002: summary accounts of archaeological excavations in Ireland*, 523, no. 1934. Bray.

Shine, D., Lynch, L., Mandal, S. and O'Meara, D. 2021. 'Discovering St Aidan's monastery: preliminary archaeological excavation report (December 2021)'. Unpublished technical report produced for the National Monuments Service.

Sweetman, P.D. 1979. 'Excavations at Ferns Castle, Co. Wexford'. *Proceedings of the Royal Irish Academy*, 79C, 217–45.

Wren, J. 2002. 'Cornmarket, Wexford'. In Bennett, I. (ed.), *Excavations 2000: summary accounts of archaeological excavations in Ireland*, 358–9, no. 1070. Bray.

APPENDIX 13.1

Catalogue of rushlight holders

The catalogue is laid out as follows: Date of recovery; Name of site; National Monuments site number; Site type; National Museum find number; Dimensions. In a number of cases the material has not been available for examination and so the information is sometimes incomplete. Further, in reports carried out by the author, measurements were also not taken so the information is as appears in unpublished reports.

1. **1972–5: Ferns Castle**; Castleland: WX015-003001-; Anglo-Norman masonry-castle fosse: E107:702: Top: extant H. 100mm; D. 850mm; Depth of funnel 80mm (Sweetman 1979, 232, fig. 6:5).

2. **1978: Barmoney**: WX031-036-; Moated site: 1978:132:1-3; 133: Following the recovery of a sword at 'a square Rath', 'the news of the find prompted ... Ned Roche to rummage through the clay at the same site and to discover what archaeologists now believe to be pottery lamps made from burnt clay in the 11th or 12th century' (Michael Freeman, *Farming People*, 2 Mar. 1979). 132:1: Top: extant H. 84.45mm; D. 105.32 x 95.5mm tapering to 76.9mm; Depth of funnel 68mm; Max. D. funnel 30.50mm. 132:2: Base: extant H. 112.91mm; D. base: 109.51mm; D. shaft 81.20mm; 132:3: Base: extant H. 67.75mm; Base D. 99.61mm D. shaft 79.47mm. 133: Ten clay fragments (NMI files).

3. **1986–7: Ferrycarrig**: WX037-028002-: Ringwork: E352:261: Fourteen sherds noted on a rapid examination including one with a small perforation (no. 261). Lamp: 215 base of lamp with inner perf. 238, 293x6; 346, 382x4, 386, 402(B) (Papazian forthcoming).

4. **1990: Arundel Square, Waterford**: WA009-005003-: Urban medieval: Organic layer IN2:L13: early to mid-thirteenth century: E527:614:2: Base: D. 97mm; 614:3: Top: D. 101mm; Depth of funnel 70mm, overall H. >182mm: (Moore 1997, 436, fig. 14:17:4, 5).

5. **2000: Camaross**: WX036-079001-5: Moated site, corn-drying kiln and field system: 00E0471: Measurements and complete number of tops and bases unavailable. Minimum vessels represented 8 (Doyle 2009; Ian Doyle pers. comm.).

6. **2000: Bricketstown, Taghmon**: WX036-083-: Corn-drying kiln: 00E0476:48:9. Body sherd. A sample from the kiln fill produced a radiocarbon date of cal. AD1450–1650 (Noonan 2002).

7. **2000: Carrickmines Castle, Co. Dublin**: DU026-005001-: Castle, unclassified: 00E0525:346:5–7 and 1531:172). Two fragments were recovered on the site (346 and 1531). Both are very friable internally with an external smoothed surface and the larger, reassembled fragment (F346:5+6+7) has evidence of the edge of a sand-gritted base (McCutcheon forthcoming).

8. **2000: The Cornmarket, Wexford**: WX037-032041-: Urban medieval: 00E0713:78:87: A thick stem partially hollowed out. Layers of medieval material dating from the 12th to the 14th centuries. No measurements taken (Wren 2002).

9. **2002: 62–68 North Main Street, Wexford**: WX037-032021-: Urban medieval: 02E0048:38:21. The most unusual item is a large piece, square in section (W. *c.*52mm) and broken at both ends. The remaining length is *c.*74mm with a hollow (*c.*30mm deep) in one end. 12th-century land reclamation led to 13th-century stone-built house or warehouse (Sheehan 2004).

10. **2003: Barmoney**: WX031-039: 'Near Dolmen': 2003:24: Base: extant H. 70.10mm; D. 107.42mm at base; D. 61.50mm at top (NMI files).

11. **2004: Merrion Castle, Co. Dublin**: DU023-001-: Manor environs: 04E0272: 'Fragments of a lamp were recovered in features 61 and 62 and from topsoil in Grids 1 and 18. In addition, a sherd from a lamp was modified as a face, with two eyes stabbed into the clay (15:11) (McCutcheon 2008). 15:11; 61:58; 62:24; Grid 1:122; Grid 18:1511.

12. **2004: Coolamurry, Enniscorthy**: WX025-053-: Moated site: 04E0326: 45 fragments, 2 lamps, one hollow? The oak timbers of a wooden bridge that probably had an associated wooden gatehouse were found towards the west end of the north moat and the outer edges of one produced a calibrated radiocarbon date of AD1257–1386 (Eogan and Kelly 2016, 214–15).

13. **2006: Bridgetown South**: WX047-026-: Moated enclosure: 06E0014: A semi-complete rushlight holder was recovered as a surface find from the initial monitoring on the site. The extant height is *c.*130mm. The stem has a diameter of *c.*59mm flaring to *c.*80mm at the end. Funnel depth *c.*100mm with a diameter of *c.*19.5mm at the top and *c.*7mm where the voiding is broken (Hackett 2009).

14. **2006: Duncormick**: WX WX046-035001-: Castle, motte and bailey: 06E0929:54:16: Shaft with smoothed exterior surface, slightly flared, hollowed top (D. 68.14mm) narrowing just below the top (D. 55.09mm); funnel D. 15.60mm; relatively well-fired with a reduced grey centre, not as low-fired and crumbly as many of the lamps recovered (McCutcheon 2006; Dehaene 2009).

15. **2009: Landscape 2, New Ross**: WX034-086-: Defined but not defended rural space. E4108:37:3; 75:134; 250:1: Two large end fragments both sand-gritted and a small third 'base' fragment represent two lamps, one piece hollowed out (McCutcheon forthcoming). Two calibrated radiocarbon dates of 1270–1400 and 1260–1390 are recorded from the house (Hession 2012, 34–43; 2013; Eogan and Kelly 2016, 224–6, Building 2).

16. **2010: Deanery Gardens, Waterford**: WA009-005040: Urban medieval: E4077. Base: extant H. 76.75mm; Base D. 90.85; Shaft D. 50mm (Scully 2010).

17. **2019: Castleland, Ferns**: 2019: 22 pieces from a deserted medieval village at Castleland, Ferns ... void is visible (Moriarty 2020). Four complete and one fragmentary bases have been seen by this author but no measurements are available.

18. **2020: High Hill, New Ross**: WX029-013079-: Urban medieval: 19E0256: 'void is visible' (Moriarty 2021a).

19. **2021: Ferns: St Aidan's monastery**: WX015-0030-; E5108:1016:22: Extant H. 58mm, shaft D. 23mm; Base D. 77mm, Top D. 66mm; Funnel D. 21mm (Shine et al. 2021).

20. **2021: Killann**: Medieval pit fill: 21E0660:15:1 (top) and 2 (fragment): Top: extant H. 100mm, D. 70mm; depth of funnel, not recorded; Fragment: L. 40mm x W. 20mm x Th. 14mm (Moriarty 2021b).

CHAPTER FOURTEEN

Captured: a digital approach to representing medieval Ferns

MICHAEL 'BODHI' ROGERS & SAMUEL S. CHEN

INTRODUCTION

The modern village of Ferns covers an area of approximately 600ha with a gentle uphill walk from the ruins of St Mary's Abbey to those of Ferns Castle. Walking through the village one can see how the modern built environment is intertwined with the medieval history of the place. This interwoven streetscape can be examined using 3D laser scanning to document the built environment in fabulous detail to digitally preserve the standing architecture and look at connections across the landscape.

The castle seen by today's visitors was built in the thirteenth century. It is of a type referred to as a 'towered keep' by Harold Leask (1951, 47–51; see also Colfer 2008, 75–9; 2013, 62–4; O'Keeffe 2015, 232–4; Toy 1939, 126) and was built in the same location as earlier fortifications (Sweetman 1999). The south-east tower has a striking chapel with rib vaulting not commonly seen in Ireland at that time (McNeill 1977). There are four towered keeps, located at Ferns, Carlow, Lea (Co. Laois) and Terryglass (Co. Tipperary), with a fifth and sixth that may have been at Wexford and Enniscorthy respectively. These types of castles are rectangular with thick walls and a tower at each corner. David Sweetman conducted archaeological excavations at Ferns Castle in the mid-1970s and discovered a moat that was 5m wide at the top and 3.5m wide at the bottom, and which can be seen by today's visitors (Corlett 2012). For a more detailed history of the castle, see Chapter 2.

In the summer of 2019 an Ithaca College (Ithaca, New York, US) team of four third-level students and Rogers partnered with the Irish Archaeology Field School to commence a programme of 3D laser scanning of the upstanding remains of the medieval landscape of Ferns, including the castle, the cathedral and St Mary's Abbey. Using two 3D scanners manufactured by Leica Inc. (fig. 14.1), the team established ninety-five scan locations around Ferns and inside some of the standing architecture (fig. 14.2). Laser scanning creates a truly three-dimensional picture, called a point cloud, that one can zoom in to and out of, rotate up and down and left and right, and even move through walls to see inside rooms (O'Sullivan et al. 2018; Rogers et al. 2018).

14.1 Ferns: Leica C-10 3D laser scanning the castle

Data gathered for digital conservation are recorded every 5mm, resulting in a high-fidelity digital version of the standing architecture. This point cloud creates a conservation record allowing for the creation of architectural renderings, site monitoring for structural stability, to guide required construction works, and to guide reconstruction in the case of unexpected future damage. For example, the 2019 fire at Notre Dame Cathedral in Paris is a conservationist's worst-case scenario. Fortunately, in 2010 Andrew Tallon, an art and architectural historian, embarked upon a programme of 3D laser scanning the cathedral. The resulting point cloud may aid in reconstruction efforts by providing detailed and measurable documentation of architectural elements destroyed by the fire (Dollard 2019; Kenney 2019).

Due to the very large files associated with conservation-grade data (the raw data from Ferns totals 130 gigabytes) they must be reduced prior to other uses such as outreach, education and remote touring. The improvement in performance of virtual and augmented reality viewing devices can allow someone, with the proper equipment,

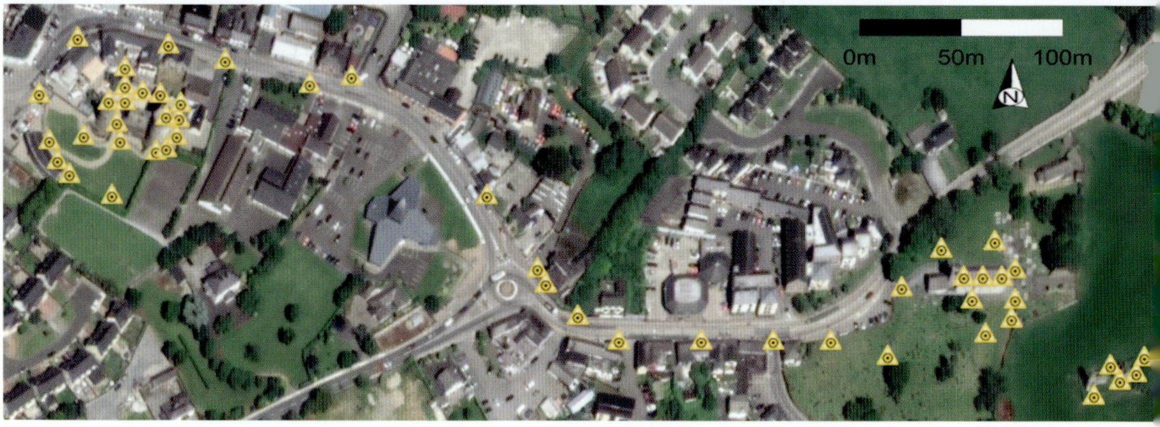

14.2 Ferns: map showing scanner locations within the village

14.3 Ferns: image of the castle point cloud. This image is created by individual points spaced 5mm apart

to visit Ferns Castle in three dimensions without leaving their sitting room. Erik Champion's 2014 chapter 'History and cultural heritage in virtual environments' gives a nice overview of the history and challenges surrounding virtual tourism and virtual heritage (Champion 2014, 269–83). Most publications point towards the 1994 3D reconstruction of Dudley Castle, West Midlands, England, as the first example of virtual heritage, but they had minimal interactivity for their 'Virtual Tour' (Baik 2021; Di Mascio et al. 2016; Messemer 2016; Ramsey 2017; Wei et al. 2018). The digital reconstructions of the Villages of Shirakawa-go facilitated bringing virtual tourism to a UNESCO-designated region that are private residences (Hirayu et al. 2000, 61–4). MIRALab's research into placing virtual actors at Pompeii explored a new aspect of augmented heritage (Papagiannakis and Magnenat-Thalmann 2007, 395–415). Since these early efforts there are now more opportunities to take virtual tours. Goodrich Castle (English Heritage 2021), TimeRef (Needham 2021), RomeReborn (Flyover Zone 2020) and Virtual Visit Tours of Castles in Ireland (Virtual Visit Tours 2021) provide different experiences using photographs, artistic renderings and digital reconstructions. The Anne Frank House in Virtual Reality is an excellent example of virtual tourism that takes the viewer on a partially interactive guided tour (Anne Frank House 2021). Most of these virtual tours use photographs, video and digital constructions with only a few emerging projects such as 'Florence As It Was' relying on laser-scanning data (Bent 2021). The advantages to laser scanning are higher resolution and a truly 3D experience with reduced visual distortion. An additional experience for a visitor on a virtual tour using laser-scanning data is knowing that one is looking at the actual object or architecture instead of an artistic rendering.

HOW LASER SCANNING WORKS

The 3D laser scanners used to document Ferns calculate the distance between the scanner and the point on the object by using the time it takes for a laser pulse to leave the scanner, reflect from an object's surface and return to the scanner. Extremely sensitive angle measuring devices on the scanner also record the up-down and left-right position of the scanner to determine the X, Y and Z location of the point that was just scanned. The scanners used at Ferns can reach out to 270m and record a million points per second. The laser pulses do not penetrate the objects, but rather reflect off them. Similar to how sunlight reflects from surfaces, the laser-scanning process also results in shadows. Objects in the foreground block the laser light from interacting with objects hidden behind the closer objects. To remove these shadows the scanner is moved to a new location where it can 'see' the areas that were previously hidden. A local grid system is employed to ensure that the points from different scanner locations are aligned. The scanners also have photographic cameras used to take digital photographs from the scanner location. These colour photographs are then used to assign a colour value to each of the scanned points, giving the point cloud photorealistic colour. Figure 14.3 is a black-and-white image of the Ferns Castle point cloud, and Figure 14.4 is a colour image of inside Ferns Cathedral. Note that both figures are point clouds composed of millions of individual points spaced 5mm apart.

After acquiring data in the field, the point cloud is made ready for presenting by removing unwanted scanned objects such as partial scans of buildings in the far distance, birds, people, pets and cars (Rogers et al. 2019). The photographs also need

14.4 Ferns: point cloud of the altar inside the cathedral

14.5 Ferns: black-and-white image of the St Mary's Abbey point cloud with the cathedral in the background

to be examined for proper exposure, saturation and tint before applying the colours to the points. Figure 14.5 is the processed point cloud for St Mary's Abbey with Ferns Cathedral in the background, where a tree in the lower right of the image was removed in the point cloud to facilitate seeing the standing architecture. It is also possible to display the point cloud in thin slices to see floor plans and room layouts more easily (Rogers 2014; Rogers and Stull 2015).

VISUALIZING MEDIEVAL FERNS

Beyond the creation of a conservation record and an academic resource, the point cloud provides opportunities to visualize Ferns in new ways. Visitors to Ferns Castle get to see the remaining architecture and even tour the inside of the south-east tower. For visitors with mobility limits or those just nervous about walking up narrow spiral staircases, touring the south-east tower is not an option. Many historic sites provide scale models and photographs to give visitors some experience in these more difficult-to-access parts of the site. A point cloud can provide additional experience through a web-viewer where a visitor can use the computer mouse or keys to move around the inaccessible spaces. Virtual Reality devices such as an Oculus Quest 2 take that experience even further by providing a fully 3D image of the point cloud in which one can look around by turning one's head. The environment is truly three-dimensional where one can even walk up to and around objects that are in a room. This immersive experience can be unsettling and disorienting for some people, so augmented reality devices such as the HoloLens 2 can blend the point-cloud environment with the actual space. This is a compromise between feeling fully in the room using the Oculus and the two-dimensional feel of the web-viewer.

We are currently researching methods and pathways for converting the research-grade data into formats that preserve details of the scanned object and can be managed by web browsers, phones, tablets and other visualization devices. Much work remains to be done to make the user experience a polished one and our early-stage efforts can be viewed online.[1] Following the link to 3D Laser Scanning will give an option to open our web-viewer for Ferns Castle. Inside the web-viewer the menu will allow the user to select different floors of the south-east tower and different views around the standing architecture. Using a device that supports WebXR, one can enter virtual or augmented reality modes for a more immersive experience.[2]

The point cloud can be converted into a model that can then be 3D-printed (fig. 14.6), and this can be used for education, outreach or conservation. We have not yet embarked upon any conservation efforts at Ferns. An example of using 3D printing as part of conservation is a partnership with the New York State Parks, Recreation and Historic Preservation, where hand-held laser scanning was used to document papier mâché decorative ceiling elements at Philipse Manor Hall in Yonkers, New York. After digitizing fifty-three individual design elements of the 1750s Rococo ceiling, 3D moulds were printed to facilitate the creation of new papier mâché decorative elements that were installed in Schuyler Mansion in Albany, New York (Moroney 2019).

Our plan is to continue researching and creating pathways to go from conservation-grade data to models that retain architectural details that can be quickly loaded and displayed on any phone, tablet or computer. Work remains to develop intuitive user interfaces and controls that allow one to move through and around these models. As we develop a suite of tools to visualize not only medieval Ferns, but any historic site we need to identify what tools are appropriate for each place. The suite of tools might

1 https://clas.ucdenver.edu/rogers-lab/. 2 Support information for WebXR available at https://immersiveweb.dev/#supporttable.

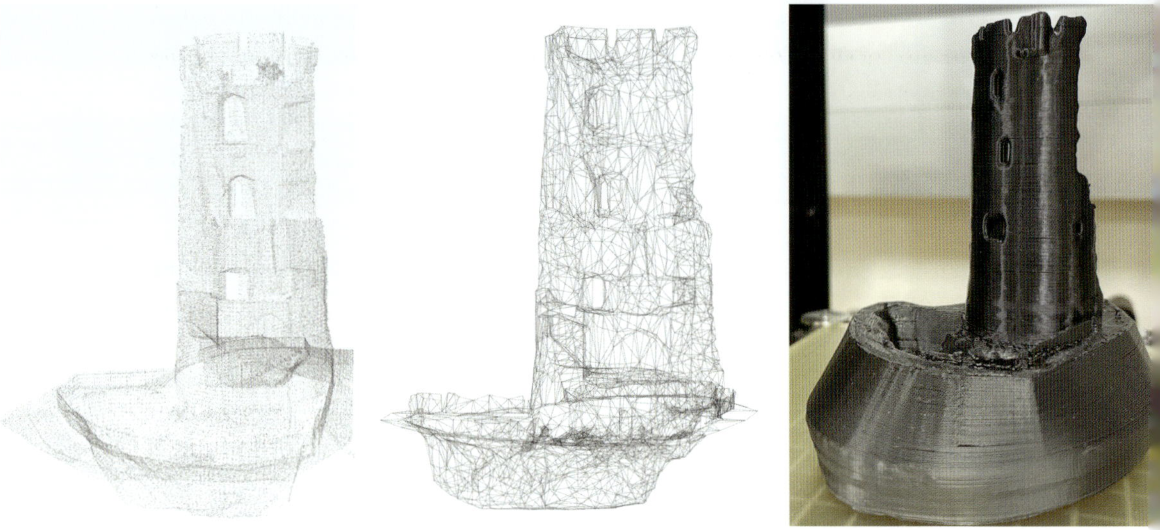

14.6 Ferns: stages of processing from a point cloud (a) to a wire frame mesh (b) and to a 3D-printed model (c)

14.7 Ferns: wearing a virtual reality device to look at the castle chapel

contain a large computer display in the visitors' centre and included in the medieval Ferns Experience, which already comprises virtual-reality tour experiences at the Ferns Community Centre (Ferns Village 2022), where visitors can tour the site using our web-viewer to include inaccessible areas or sections that are otherwise off-limits to the public. Visitors might be able to check-out a tablet for an enhanced walk around the site grounds or use their own devices. They might also check out augmented- or virtual-reality devices (fig. 14.7) like the National Museum of Natural History (Smithsonian Institution, Washington DC) Critical Distance exhibit that uses HoloLens 2 to visualize a holographic orca pod to educate visitors about this endangered species (Smithsonian 2021; Strange 2021). People unable or who cannot afford to visit these historic sites in person might access these various ways of visualizing the site from home.

Artistic and architectural renderings can also be blended with the laser-scanning data and standing architecture. Visiting Ferns Castle with a tablet or phone with a still-in-development app will allow visitors to see the current state of the castle, but also to fill in the missing architecture and details. We envision having a way for visitors to choose various time periods for the exploration of medieval Ferns. Using a combination of laser scanning and artistic renderings to create virtual and augmented reality experiences for sites like medieval Ferns has the potential to transform the visitor experience. Our aspiration is not only for an enhanced experience while visiting Ferns, but also bringing the excitement of medieval Ferns to distant visitors who may then be inspired to make the journey to experience Ferns in person.

BIBLIOGRAPHY

Anne Frank House. 2021. The Anne Frank House in virtual reality: www.annefrank.org/en/about-us/what-we-do/publications/anne-frank-house-virtual-reality, accessed 9 Jan. 2022.

Baik, A. 2021. 'The use of interactive virtual BIM to boost virtual tourism in heritage sites, historic Jeddah'. *ISPRS International Journal of Geo-Information*, 10:9, 1–18.

Bent, G. 2021. 'Florence as it was: the digital reconstruction of a medieval city': https://florenceasitwas.wlu.edu, accessed 9 Jan. 2022.

Champion, E. 2014. 'History and cultural heritage in virtual environments'. In Grimshaw, M. (ed.), *The Oxford handbook of virtuality*, 269–83. Oxford.

Colfer, B. 2008. *Wexford: a town and its landscape.* Cork.

Colfer, B. 2013. *Wexford castles.* Cork.

Corlett, C. 2012. 'Ferns, Co. Wexford'. *Archaeology Ireland*, Heritage Guide 59. Dublin.

Di Mascio, D., Chiuini, M., Fillwalk, J. and Pauwels, P. 2016. *3D digital reconstructions of lost buildings: a first critical framing*, 511–20.

Dollard, C. 2019. 'Precision laser scans of Notre Dame Cathedral can help to preserve, restore and rebuild': https://shop.leica-geosystems.com/blog/precision-laser-scans-notre-dame-cathedral-can-help-preserve-restore-and-rebuild, accessed 9 Jan. 2022.

English Heritage. 2021. 'Virtual tour of Goodrich Castle': www.english-heritage.org.uk/visit/places/goodrich-castle/history-and-stories/virtual-tour, accessed 6 Jan. 2022.

Ferns Village, 2022. 'Medieval Ferns Experience': https://fernsvillage.ie/medieval-ferns-experience, accessed 24 May 2022.

Flyover Zone, 2020. 'Rome reborn': www.romereborn.org, accessed 9 Jan. 2022.

Hirayu, H., Ojika, T. and Kijima, R. 2000. 'Constructing the historic villages of Shirakawa-go in virtual reality'. *IEEE MultiMedia*, 7:2, 61–4.

Kenney, N. 2019. 'Laser scan may one day aid Notre Dame's restorers'. *The Art Newspaper*: www.theartnewspaper.com/2019/09/16/laser-scan-may-one-day-aid-notre-dames-restorers, accessed 9 Jan. 2022.

Leask, H. 1951. *Irish castles and castellated houses*. Dundalk.

Messemer, H. 2016. 'The beginnings of digital visualization of historical architecture in the academic field'. *Virtual Palaces, Part II. Lost Palaces and their Afterlife. Virtual Reconstruction between Science and the Media*, 21–54.

Moroney, E. 2019. '21st-century technology recreates 18th century luxury'. *NY State Parks Blog*: https://nystateparks.blog/tag/papier-mache, accessed 9 Jan. 2022.

Needham, M. 2021. 'TimeRef: 3D virtual reconstructions': www.timeref.com/3dindex.htm, accessed 9 Jan. 2022.

O'Keeffe, T. 2015. *Medieval Irish buildings, 1100–1600*. Dublin.

O'Sullivan, M., Rogers, M., Shine, D. and Mandal, S. 2018. 'Seir Kieran. place, pilgrimage and tradition in the monastic midlands'. *Offaly Heritage*, 10, 21–42.

Papagiannakis, G. and Magnenat-Thalmann, N. 2007. 'Mobile augmented heritage: enabling human life in ancient Pompeii'. *International Journal of Architectural Computing*, 5:2, 395–415.

Ramsey, E. 2017. 'Virtual Wolverhampton: recreating the historic city in virtual reality'. *ArchNet-IJAR: International Journal of Architectural Research*, 11:3, 42–57.

Rogers, M. 2014. 'Visualizing an integrated landscape using archaeogeophysical and 3D laser surveying'. *From west to east: current approaches in medieval archaeology*, 6–19. Cambridge.

Rogers, M. and Stull, S. 2015. 'Visualizing an integrated landscape through ground-based LiDAR, geophysical archaeology and archaeological excavation'. *Archaeologia Polona*, 53, 496–8.

Rogers, M., Bouricius, R., Shine, D. and Mandal, S. 2019. 'Capturing Carrick: a digital approach to constructing and deconstructing the modern and relict landscape'. In Shine, D., Potterton, M., Mandal, S. and McLoughlin, C. 2019 (eds), *Carrick, County Wexford: Ireland's first Anglo-Norman stronghold*, 163–73. Dublin.

Rogers, M.B., Bouricius, R., Shine, D., Mandal, S. and Stull, S. 2018. 'Laser-scanning Trim Castle'. *Archaeology Ireland*, 32:3, 34–9.

Smithsonian. 2021. 'Critical distance': https://naturalhistory.si.edu/exhibits/critical-distance, accessed 9 Jan. 2022.

Strange, A. 2021. 'Microsoft HoloLens 2 & Unity used to highlight the threat to endangered whales at the Smithsonian'. *Next Reality News*: https://hololens.reality.news/news/microsoft-hololens-2-unity-used-highlight-threat-endangered-whales-smithsonian-0384877, accessed 9 Jan. 2022.

Sweetman, D. 1999. *Medieval castles of Ireland*. Cork.

Toy, S. 1939. *Castles: their construction and history*. London.

Virtual Visit Tours. 2021. 'Castles Ireland': www.virtualvisittours.com/category/castles-ireland, accessed 9 Jan. 2022.

Wei, C.C., Chen, F., Chen, C.H. and Lin, Y.C. 2018. 'Virtual and augmented reality to historical site reconstruction: A pilot study of east Taiwan Old Railway Station'. In *Proceedings of the 2018 International Conference on Artificial Intelligence and Virtual Reality*, 42–6. New York.

CHAPTER FIFTEEN

'Sheep in the abbey': the community of Ferns engaging with its medieval heritage

CATHERINE MACPARTLIN

Known as the 'Ancient Capital' of Leinster, Ferns is recognized by many as being central to Wexford's medieval story. Its significance in the medieval period – from an ecclesiastical settlement in the seventh century to its dominance as the seat of power of the kings of Leinster in the tenth to twelfth century – is the stuff of legend. But what of the local people – the Ferns community? A community that has lived side by side with monuments of national importance, some of whom played on the stairs of a castle once climbed by Anglo-Norman knights, whose sheep climbed an abbey founded by Diarmait Mac Murchada (generally spelled MacMurrough locally), king of Leinster, whose warts were cured with the waters of a well brought magically into being by a saint. These are tangible connections and they run deep in the local psyche.

This chapter will look at how the community has engaged with its medieval heritage over the years, its perception of what stands above and lies below ground, how it has changed through time and what influenced that change. This is a conversation; a conversation with different people in our community, from different backgrounds and with different perspectives. Some are young, some are elderly. Some have roots here that go back generations. Some are more recent arrivals.

I spoke to Aaron Sharlott and Leah Sweeney who are sixth-class pupils in Scoil Naomh Maodhóg, which sits in the shadow of Ferns Castle. I was interested to hear what they made of the complex narrative that is Mac Murchada, so often presented as a simple story of ambition, greed for power and betrayal. It is seen as an important part of Irish history and covered on the fifth-class curriculum in Irish national schools. The children learn about Mac Murchada's battles with other Irish kings, his fraught relationship with Tigernán Ua Ruairc resulting in him being ousted from his Kingdom and seeking help from Henry II, all of which ended in the Anglo-Normans arriving in Ireland. I asked why they thought Mac Murchada went to Henry for help, and they both agreed that Mac Murchada's army was too weak and that Strongbow brought it strength. Leah felt 'he didn't like to give up easily' and Aaron said 'he was kind of strong, as in powerful, but I wouldn't say he was strong in a physical way. Some feared him, others liked him and that's why they joined his army'. Leah reckoned that he was liked because he protected his people from attackers. They agreed that the reason he asked for assistance was simple: his castle was being attacked! We talked of St Aidan and other characters of the medieval period and I asked, if they had a choice, which one they would like to be. Aaron said St Aidan because 'in the stories, he never really gets told what to do and he's like the bishop of Ferns. There's so many stories about him and he seemed so famous in Ferns'. Leah chose Isabel, daughter of Aífe and Strongbow and grand-daughter of Mac Murchada. She married William Marshal and they became a powerful and influential couple. Leah chose Isabel 'because both her parents were kinda powerful so I'd feel safer and more protected'. Asked how they felt about Ferns and its history, Leah said

> it makes me feel that it's like more than just a small village – it played an important role in medieval times. I feel most of the time I do take things for granted and when you think about it, in America and places, there wouldn't be a castle outside their school.

Aaron remarked that 'Ferns is one of those places that should be talked about, but most people forget about and think it's just a small village in Wexford'. In school, students are encouraged to talk to their parents and grandparents about their heritage. Leah said her Granny Peggy told her that 'people would go to Mogue's Well when they had blisters or anything; they would go to the well for holy water to get healed'. Aaron added that his grandad told him that as well and that 'Strongbow would only come over if he got something from Diarmait – he got to marry Diarmait's daughter Aoife and he got some of Diarmait's land and I just found that story interesting – it wouldn't happen now'.

From children appreciating learning and playing in the shadow of the castle, I moved on to speak to Bartie Kehoe, a local stonemason who remembers working on the castle at the time of its restoration in the 1970s. The preservation and restoration work done at that time meant that the east tower was made accessible for tours with Office of Public Works (OPW) guides. Bartie left school after his Leaving Certificate and worked in the general building trade. He knew a man called Dan Sheehan who was working as a mason on the castle and when Dan died Bartie applied to the OPW for the job and got it. Bartie worked on the castle from top to bottom and remembers particularly working on the fireplace on the second floor, which contains a beautiful chapel, as well as the parapet around the top. He is very proud of his work on the castle and recalls fondly working under Richie Grace, the foreman from Kilkenny who travelled to Ferns every day. Bartie spent twelve years working with the OPW including five years training with Richie who, he said, was 'the best stonemason in Ireland' and the time spent with him the 'best five years I ever spent'. Bartie's love of all things stone is evident in how he speaks of it; 'everything about stone, I loved it, had a passion for it … you have passion and it would drive you stone mad if you didn't have it!' Every job he does in stone is a once-off. He loves it all. 'When you do a wall for a house, it's very seldom you'll have two the same'. When you talk to Bartie, you can't help but think that each stone has its own character – its shape and size dictating where it's to be placed and what sits beside it. His work on the restoration of the castle makes Bartie think of the stonemasons who worked there in the thirteenth century. He says it is

> unbelievable how they did it; there were no teleporters then … time didn't make any difference, there were no labour costs – they were great men! The detail on some of the fireplaces, they should have been so proud. They say it took forty years and four hundred men to do the castle, and if somebody died they got another.

To get a sense of what Bartie and his fellow craftsmen over the centuries have achieved, you need to visit the castle and take a tour of its intact tower, looking closely at the detail on the fireplaces, doorways, stairs and the chapel on the second floor.

One of the most valuable artefacts of modern times is featured in the castle visitor centre. The *Ferns Tapestry* is a series of twenty-five panels of crewel embroidery created by a group of local women. It depicts the story of Ferns from the Bronze Age through the Iron Age, the arrival of St Aidan in the sixth century and the coming of the Anglo-Normans in the twelfth. May McClean is one of the Ferns Tapestry group and she told me how the tapestry came into being: a couple of members attended a heritage course in Enniscorthy and, as part of the course, they visited the Fishguard tapestry and St David's in Wales, where they were inspired by what they saw, and on their return contacted others with a view to creating a tapestry focusing on key events in the history of Ferns. An enthusiastic group was formed, including Betty Byrne who was an expert in stitching, Stephanie Breen who looked after the artistic side of things and Kristine Byrne who took care of the colour work. Betty taught the members how to stitch in crewel embroidery, a traditional style that goes back centuries. They worked for over four years on the actual stitching, starting in 1998 and working through the Millennium. May said they really enjoyed the process, particularly

> the joy we got out of the skill – the in and out of the needle was so therapeutic. We enjoyed the togetherness and just being involved with the group. It was great to be going in every Thursday night but then you'd go home with homework.

In fact, May said that when Betty started, she thought it was only going to be one panel but wasn't turned off when she learned it was to be twenty-five! She was a true champion of the tapestry group. When she heard there were plans for a visitor centre at the castle, Betty met with the architect and suggested the tapestry panels be located in the centre. She was a persuasive lady: the plans for the centre were altered to accommodate what is a true treasure and a valuable legacy enjoyed by locals and visitors. The visitor centre and tapestries were officially opened to the public by President Mary McAleese in 2004. The tapestry group was proud and delighted to have the panels housed in such a prominent and accessible location; however the castle and visitor centre are only open from May to September and May thinks 'it's a pity that they're not accessible all year round'. Having grown up in Ferns with pride in her heritage, May would love the tapestries to be shared with everyone who comes to Ferns at any time of the year.

The castle played a central role in the lives of many who lived in and around Ferns – it was the base for daredevil feats of climbing and play. Alan Owens, a longstanding chronicler of Ferns and its history and events over the decades, can remember playing in the castle as a child:

> The castle green was the centre of Ferns. People met on the green, circuses came and performed, and horseshoes, handball and hurling were played – everything happened on the castle green. It was a regular playground and very different to what it is today. Before its renovation by the OPW, it was open to all; no key was needed to get in. Kids climbed up, got in through a hole in the wall and entered on the second floor – they climbed walls and shimmied up chimneys, up to the very top with its panoramic views.

Before its restoration, there was no floor in the chapel but a stone pillar ran from one side to the other, which you could walk across. Alan remembers an incident when, after a procession, a young girl was walking along the pillar and fell to the ground two floors below. Fortunately, she wasn't seriously injured but it goes to show how the castle was an intrinsic part of growing up in Ferns.

Because Alan spent a lot of time in the castle as a child it is one of his favourite buildings in Ferns, although St Mogue's Well also holds special memories for him. He said it was a great place for curing warts; people went to the well, washed their hands in the waters and their warts disappeared. At that time everybody believed in the powers of the water and some still do. There is some evidence that these wells and other traditional cures do work for warts, particularly for children – much of which is down to the power of suggestion (Logan 1981)!

Alan remembers the excavations at the castle in the 1970s and the fact that people expressed an interest in what might be found in the moat. Alan says

> There was a lot of talk of possibly finding swords and cannonballs and there were all sorts of stories of tunnels but nothing was ever found. When work on reconstructing sections of the castle was underway, they used the original stone from the castle which was found miles away. It was drawn far and wide from farm buildings and all sorts but they recovered a lot of it.

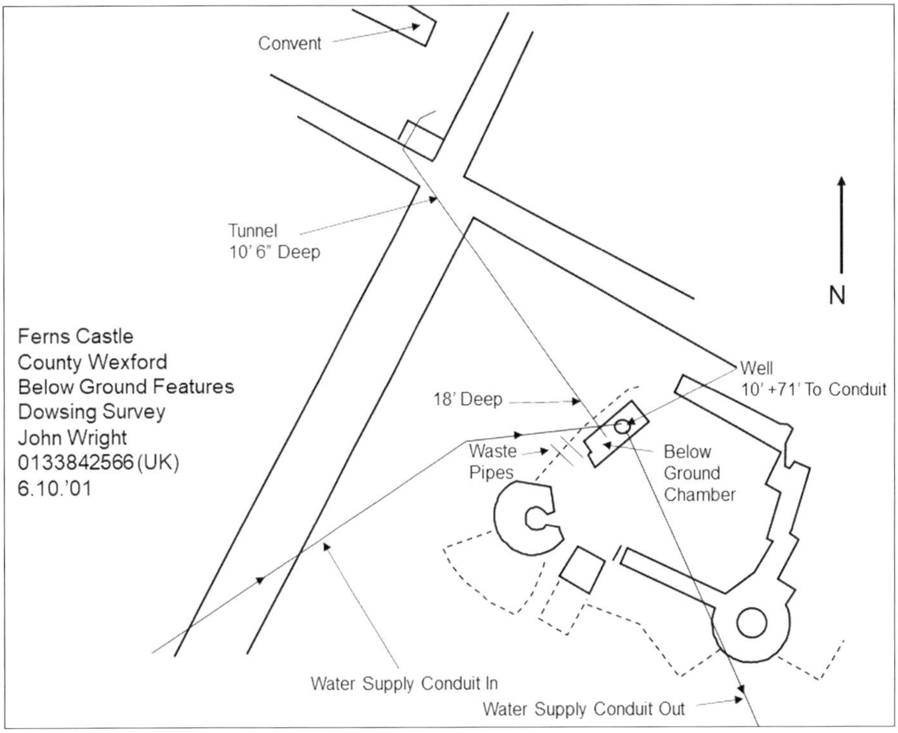

15.1 Ferns: map of possible tunnels courtesy of Alan Owens

Alan actually has a map drawn by a water diviner in 2001 which indicates a tunnel from the castle (fig. 15.1). Recent digs conducted by the Irish Archaeological Field School (IAFS) with support from the Ancient Connections project have confirmed what Alan and many knew – that there were significant underground structures linking to our medieval past. Alan shares the views of many, that these underground walls, which have since been covered over, could be on permanent display. People could come and see the impressive boundary walls from the twelfth and earlier centuries and this would be a powerful way of connecting to our past. The approach taken at contemporary excavations at Ferrycarrig where above-surface walls have been reconstructed following the line of the real walls underneath (now covered back in), might be an option.

Another story Alan remembers hearing involves Oliver Cromwell and his soldiers attacking Ferns. They tried to remove a stone statue of St Aidan from St Edan's Cathedral. In the attempt, a chip came off the nose and blinded one of the soldiers and the statue was left untouched after that. It is interesting how this story resurfaces in different guises – but all go to explain the chip on the nose of the effigy, said to be of Bishop John St John, lying in the nave of the cathedral to this day. Like many stories, it ties key events in our history to unexplained phenomena. It shows how carefully people observe their heritage, noticing the little things like the chip off the nose, and develop stories to explain them.

When Alan was young there was no television, and conversations around the fire were a great way of passing on stories, folklore and tall tales – stories which at the time he believed, but looking back he thinks many were more in the realm of fairy tale. One such tale involved a girl who didn't go to mass and instead climbed the abbey. Alan wasn't sure whether she fell or was pushed but in any event she died and left a mark on the ground where grass never grew afterwards – he remembers seeing the mark but says it's not there today. You can imagine how that story would have left an imprint on a young child's mind. The story is a common enough one in folklore but what is interesting here is how it has been applied to part of our village's medieval heritage and what happens to those who don't respect it or its traditions.

Over the years people's interaction with their medieval past has either stayed constant or changed because of health-and-safety concerns or reasons of preservation of valuable monuments. This is the case particularly with the castle, which, since its conservation, has been managed and maintained by the OPW and access is permitted by guided tour only. The waters of St Mogue's Well are a constant, however, still running clear and continuing to offer great comfort to those faithful to the well's origins. One such person is Enda Killeen, who has been drinking water from Mogue's Well since he was a child and bringing it home to make tea or whatever for many years. Enda's mother was a Ferns woman and Mogue's Well was always talked about at home. He says people 'didn't just go down to the well to bring water home, they'd go down and drink the water and put their feet in. People went if they had a pain or whatever – they'd go down and bless themselves and say prayers'. He remembers going to the well as a kid: 'you could go down the steps and under the tunnel – the water was so cold and clear, it never needed anything done to it – it's so pure. I've done it for a lifetime and have no reason to give it up'. His daily visits to the well have ceased in recent weeks due to ill health but his daughter now goes down and gets a few cans as he doesn't use water out of a tap for tea, coffee or anything – he just uses water from the well.

Enda spoke of seeing visitors coming to the well because they'd heard of its curative powers. At one stage a bus-load of people arrived (he thinks they were on a tour from Germany) and he watched as they drank the water, shaking it on their heads, and dipping their feet. He says his use of the water was not because of any religious reason and he believes the water has no particular 'medical' value – it's just pure, fresh, running water. He drinks it on the basis that

> the well is doing me good, always did me good, always felt that way, when I got the water, it was pure – no chemicals in it. If you go out to a water supply, you don't know where its coming from, there's always something put in it. If I wasn't in good form, I'd go down and it would help me; that's the way I felt about it.

Enda says he isn't conscious of St Aidan's miracles: 'the only thing is myself, the feeling I have about it, I always drink it, make tea and get a couple of cans of water the whole time'. His thinking is that the water was blessed:

> What happened with these saints, they'd never be able to go to a place without flowing water being there and they'd bless the water then. St Aidan was in Ferns in the first place because of the water – it was blessed by St Aidan and I'm happy with that. I've a feeling it's doing me good and it's up to others what they think, but that's the way I think'.

Enda remembers playing in the castle and the abbey as a child, particularly around the abbey and the old graveyard. Back then there was no evidence of underground structures in the abbey area, which in recent years have drawn huge attention. Geophysical studies conducted in 2015 (Bhreathnach and Dowling 2020) indicated significant underground boundary walls and last year's community dig (ch. 9) revealed the most beautiful stone walls, possibly linking two medieval periods. The data is being evaluated and we are looking forward to what the results bring to light.

One of the most valuable finds to take place in recent years was the discovery of the 'Knight on the Tile'. The floor tile was found in the cathedral graveyard in 2016 by Joey Carr (Corlett 2018). Joey is a gravedigger in Ferns and gladly handed over the tile to the National Museum of Ireland. Well-deserved praise has been heaped on Joey for his actions, which have meant that the tile, depicting a knight on horseback, holding a sword and wearing a helmet, is now in safe keeping. Joey has dug graves in Ferns for years, initially as a helper to his father and then on his own after his father retired. For years he dug graves, generally without incident – his biggest challenge was the possibility of the grave caving in because it was old. On the day of the discovery, he thought it was a new grave he was digging – he approached the dig as he normally would by putting in a test bar to see if the grave had been disturbed before and he found that, yes, there had been a burial there – centuries before. His reaction when he found the tile? 'I knew well it was something when I saw white marking on it. I took it up, wiped soil off and put it in the van'. If Joey had not declared the tile and sought instead to gain personally from it, this beautiful and valuable tile might have been sold off to the highest bidder and lost to us. We hope at some stage to get it back to Ferns to be displayed for all to see. It is a beautiful artefact – a tangible link to a time when Anglo-Norman knights rode on horseback through the streets of Ferns.

The abbey itself was built by Mac Murchada in about 1160 'for the health of my soul and my ancestors and successors' (chs 2, 3). It is where Mac Murchada waited, in the winter of 1168, for the arrival of the Anglo-Normans to help him regain his kingdom. It is also possibly where he is buried, although the stem of a high cross in the adjacent graveyard is traditionally held to mark his grave (ch. 2). The field around the abbey has been the focus of much investigation over the years and has yielded some remarkable material. Recent works by TVAS Ireland, in preparation for waterworks in the area, unearthed a horizontal mill, possibly medieval – another piece of the jigsaw (ch. 11). It is such a privilege to see these treasures in situ and credit is due to those working on the site who welcomed local people keen to get sight of such an amazing find. This approach has many benefits, including sharing the knowledge gained in such digs, enabling local people to take pride in their home place and raise awareness of the treasures that lie beneath. The insights and evidence gained from recent digs will add another layer of colour to our story and will feature in our guided tours.

There is a lot of history in this field and over the years many surveys have been conducted and many visitors have walked through to visit the abbey – all with the permission of Pat Cousins, the landowner. Without landowner permission to access our built heritage, many pieces of the jigsaw would remain lost to us – and that goes for our natural heritage too. How many beautiful walks have been developed over recent years thanks to the permission of landowners? Pat lives in what was the farmyard of the bishop's palace. When he came to Ferns years ago, he was not aware of its history but would have heard stories by listening to people talking about tunnels from the abbey to the palace. Talk of tunnels features regularly in conversations with people in Ferns, however none have been found to date. Pat remembers kids regularly playing in the abbey and

> people would ring from the village and say you'll need to go up and get the sheep down from the abbey – they used to go up every now and then, they were able to climb to the top but couldn't get down and I'd have to go and get them down.

At that time, the abbey tower was open to all. It is intriguing because it has a square base and a cylindrical barrel on top, which is unusual (ch. 6). It is possibly linked to the round towers found on other early church sites, but we have no definitive answer to this conundrum. There are some beautiful architectural features in the abbey: the sacristy, the chancel and the round-headed doors and windows and sconces. On guided tours, as we go from the graveyard to the abbey, we walk through the ruins of what was once probably a chapter house at the back of the cathedral – we point out the Gothic lancet windows to our visitors, evidence of thirteenth-century Anglo-Norman architecture and then on to the abbey with its rounded Romanesque windows of the twelfth century. As you stand at the abbey, looking east, you get a great sense of the landscape in which it sits and can try to imagine what it was like when monks walked in thoughtful prayer or tended to the people of the locality. The tower is no longer accessible for health-and-safety reasons. As a National Monument, it is managed by the OPW. Realistically it is unlikely to be fully restored, however it would be wonderful to see some work being done on it, to ensure preservation and ease of access. It is such an important site and a gateway to the past, linking the monastic to the Gaelic kingship periods – it would benefit from some interpretation of what it was like in its heyday. In a few years when the data from the various digs and studies are fully published and digested, we could look to creating something that would do justice to this significant site.

As a community meeting challenges of sustainability, we looked to develop our tourism potential because of our unique medieval heritage with a fascinating story to tell. Traditionally a very competitive industry, and one we had no experience of, we are fortunate that the landscape of tourism in Wexford has changed over the years. Now a more collaborative approach rather than a competitive one is the order of the day. This is in no small way influenced by the development of the Wexford Trails network, a county-wide series of tourism trails with over one hundred members. Several workshops and programmes organized by Wexford Local Development and Wexford County Council were of particular benefit to community groups and tourism attractions. Involvement with tourism bodies such as Visit Wexford and North Wexford Tourism Group and engagement with our local authority gave an insight into how things worked and a recognition that we needed to be proactive and to develop a strategy to achieve identified goals.

It became increasingly obvious that Ferns needed to expand its tourism offering, developing a year-round package. Looking at the variety of tourism options throughout the county, one could see how tourism was changing. While word of mouth was still a valuable tool, social media was key to reaching a wider audience. A level of professionalism was necessary; access to information and upskilling were more important than ever. A focus on developing activities and events during the shoulder season was also encouraged. It was not enough to open for the high season – June to September – tourism operators needed to provide alternative options to attract both domestic and international tourists. Fáilte Ireland's regular communications on tourism markets, customer expectation and standards were very useful tools in identifying direction and operation. Because of the limited opening times of the castle, their very popular guided tours were not available for seven months of the year. Outside that time, guided tours were offered by Colm Morris, caretaker of the castle in the closed period, who is passionate about Ferns and its history through the ages, from the prehistoric to the medieval and the modern. Colm offered tours on a voluntary basis to those he met, sometimes randomly, and to those who booked a tour, having heard of his knowledgeable and entertaining tours. Colm still loves to share his passion.

As an ancient capital of Leinster, Ferns' story of Gaelic kingship, so-called invasion, kidnapping, hostage-taking, tyranny and betrayal, was the stuff of legend – a real-life *Game of Thrones*! Add to that the stories of saints, miracles, monks, holy wells and high crosses – as a monastic settlement from the seventh century, Ferns was a significant

15.2 Ferns: Medieval Gathering Parade, 2013

player in the medieval period, worthy of showcasing its complex history. It had all the ingredients for the development of a significant tourism attraction.

As a community, we have always relied on Ferns Castle as our iconic tourism attraction – a thirteenth-century Anglo-Norman castle run by the OPW. Over the years there have been community-led events including battle re-enactments and the Ferns Medieval Gathering in the 2013 (fig. 15.2). However, to grow our tourism offering, a more focused approach was needed and so in 2015 the Ferns Heritage Project (FHP) was set up as a sub-group of the Ferns Community Development Association (FCDA). The group had a simple vision – to develop and promote Ferns' medieval story. At the top of our wish-list was the creation of a visitor attraction to showcase our early medieval, Gaelic kingship and Anglo-Norman heritage and we knew this would take time and money. At county level there was a focus on developing the Anglo-Norman side of Wexford's medieval story by creating a phased Anglo-Norman trail starting in the New Ross area, which would, in time, come to Ferns. The FHP set down a route map to achieve our goals, the first of which was putting on an annual Ferns Medieval Conference. It was designed with two objectives in mind – to

15.3 Ferns Conference, 2019 (photograph courtesy of Michael Freeman)

explore the many layers of our medieval past and to influence decision makers. We needed funding to develop an attraction and we needed to convince the decision makers at county level and beyond that we had what it takes, in terms of resources and the ability to deliver. For the conference we wanted to attract speakers who were prominent in their field of expertise, from local, to national and international.

Our first step was to talk to Ronan O'Flaherty, a well-respected tourism and heritage consultant with a background in archaeology. Ronan was a consultant on the setting up of the Wexford Heritage Trail and had been extremely helpful and supportive. Running our ideas on the conference by him and getting advice on topics and speakers was hugely helpful and gave us confidence that we were going in the right direction. The first conference was held in 2016 and the series continued each year until Covid-19 hit. Ronan has been a key part of each one – all on a voluntary basis.

Each conference had a theme, the first of which was 'Gaelic capital and Norman stronghold: Ferns and the transformation of Ireland'. Over the years our understanding of our ecclesiastical history, Gaelic kingship and Anglo-Norman heritage has grown. The symbiotic relationship between church and kings remained constant and intriguing. Our understanding evolved so that the Anglo-Normans changed from being branded as 'invaders' to being viewed as more complex and multi-layered.

15.4 Ferns: the MacMurrough Inquiry, 2019

The most successful and memorable conference was our last one in 2019 – before the pandemic (fig. 15.3). The *MacMurrough Inquiry* used the model of a judicial inquiry to investigate the actions and motives of Mac Murchada and his responsibility or otherwise for the Anglo-Norman 'invasion' (fig. 15.4). It was a community-led event that took a unique approach to exploring this iconic story. Local people collaborated with legal professionals, academics and historians to explore the fascinating tale of power and intrigue in the medieval period, using a mix of legal sources, history and costume drama. It was held in St Edan's Cathedral, as were all but the first conference, which took place in the Ferns Castle Visitor Centre.

One of the most revealing sessions was a 'reading-the-building' session that unveiled some fascinating insights into the cathedral – internal and external. The original footprint of the cathedral was shown to be cruciform and the location of the medieval piscina indicated the location of the original altar. At that session, what looked like consecration-crosses were discovered on pillars in the cathedral. These crosses are normally marked at intervals around a church by the bishop when it is being initially consecrated and are then carved as a permanent record of the act. If these are indeed

15.5 Ferns: ask the locals at Diarmait Mac Murchada's grave

consecration crosses, then they may have been marked by Bishop John St John himself. At another session, we learned that what we used to call the 'ruins of the original cathedral' were not in fact part of the cathedral at all, new or old. The building in question may have been a chapter house, or a Lady Chapel or even a funeral chapel for the Marshal family. One thing we do know is that because of its architectural style, it was built after the arrival of the Anglo-Normans and is of similar date to the cathedral. Its origins remain a mystery and it would benefit from further exploration.

Conference participants included a mix of locals and people from neighbouring counties in the main. The coffee and lunch breaks were abuzz with convivial conversation, much of it relating to what we had heard on the day. As one walked around, snatches of conversation would range from the torments of the afterlife in the medieval period, to the use of relics to exert power and control in the early Irish church and society.

The FHP likes to take an innovative approach to exploring medieval history. A medieval feast demonstration and talk by author, lecturer and food historian Regina Sexton gave participants a taste of the past. One of the key things we discovered was the availability long ago of exotic spices such as ginger and almond milk, pointing to the trade links established in the medieval period. We were not the island nation cut off from external influence and trade that many of us thought.

15.6 Ferns: tour-guide training, 2018

One of the more innovative initiatives undertaken by the FHP and one that stands out as something special in terms of community engagement is the 'Ask the Locals' campaign (fig. 15.5). It was sponsored by the Wexford Trails network and piloted in Ferns. It was intended to give visitors a truly 'local' insight into what to see and do. Workshops were organized and attended by the businesses on Main Street that were most likely to meet visitors. An information pack was developed which answered questions visitors were likely to ask and included recommendations on what to visit in Ferns, its hinterland and countywide. These packs were distributed to local businesses and accommodation providers. Participating locations were clearly identified with the Ask the Locals window stickers. A feedback questionnaire was distributed after the pilot finished and the response was very positive. It indicated that there was a high awareness of the campaign, all were eager to participate again, and most participants knew more about Ferns than they did before the campaign. Concurrent with the Ask the Locals programme, tour-guide training was organized by the FHP. Participants were volunteers who undertook training in giving one-hour tours of medieval sites in Ferns. They were a great success and were rolled out in 2019 (fig. 15.6). The following two years saw a huge decrease in demand because of Covid-19 restrictions. We now have two tour options in Ferns; the first is the one-hour medieval tour, which is available through the 'Medieval Ferns Experience' (MFE) and the second is a longer tour that covers Ferns through all its historic periods to the present day. We are really looking forward to sharing our fascinating story with our visitors in the current year and beyond.

In 2017 the FHP sourced Heritage Council funding for a geophysical study of the double-aisled building discovered close to St Mary's Abbey during the 2015 fieldwork campaign. The survey was conducted by Ger Dowling and, the following year, a talk and site visit were led by Edel Bhreathnach, then CEO of the Discovery Programme, who outlined the findings of recent surveys, monasticism in Ireland and a general overview of Ferns as an early church site and as a royal site. It was a very well-attended event with an energetic presentation and engagement from those in attendance.

Barry Lacey is a local archaeologist and member of the FHP. He has worked on several excavations in Ferns in recent years, as well as providing archaeological supervision for the upgrade of waterworks on Main Street and Station Road. He is in a strong position of working as an archaeologist in his own backyard and can engage with people as they pass by. He said a lot of people approached him on the street and said they 'see archaeologists coming in but nothing coming back'. Barry would like to see the results of archaeological works being published so the public can get access. The results of so much commercial archaeology end up in a report and get filed away or get circulated only in an academic volume. Publication of material on more accessible platforms would make it easier for anyone interested (and there are many) to keep up-to-date on findings in their area. For communities in which surveys and digs take place, efforts should be made to present the information to local communities, keeping them appraised of findings and their significance. And on the question of tunnels in Ferns? No, Barry says there were no tunnels found during current works. We see the interest in our local heritage and archaeology, people will continue to want to know 'what's in there?', 'was anything found?', 'what's that?' To satisfy the continued interest, funding should be ring-fenced, particularly in commercial archaeology, to ensure that the results are easily accessed and understood, especially by the local community in which the work is undertaken – a sort of 'archaeology-for-all' ethos.

Covid-19 meant that some activities such as the annual conference have been put on hold. It also impacted on a planned concert and re-enactment of a medieval joust that were to take place in 2020. Funding for these events was provided by the Ancient Connections project and included the commissioning of a suite of music inspired by St Aidan and St David – phase 1 of which will be performed soon. They will form part of a weekend of events to mark the launch of the Creative Camino as part of the Ancient Connections project.

In 2018, with a lot of work done and information gathered, the FHP was ready to take another step forward. A call-out for applications under the 2018 'Town and Village Renewal Scheme' focused attention. With a short lead-in time, projects needed to be shovel ready. Under the FCDA, funding for several projects was sought including

15.7 Ferns: Medieval Ferns Experience

15.8 Ferns: Inauguration Stone Challenge in Medieval Ferns Experience, 2021

a tourism attraction with a medieval theme which became known as the 'Medieval Ferns Experience' (MFE). Through Covid-19 lockdowns and restrictions, it is testament to the commitment of community and volunteerism that these projects were delivered at all, let alone to such a high standard (figs 15.7, 15.8).

The MFE opened in August 2021 – we called it a soft opening because tourism was still under the restrictions associated with Covid-19. Even now, international tourism is almost non-existent, and the domestic market is difficult because of people's reluctance to gather indoors. At the time of writing, we are on our fourth wave and counting, hoping that each wave will weaken its effects and that soon it will be viewed as we would a common cold.

While numbers are understandably low, we have had a tremendous response from those who have visited the 'Experience'. Many are impressed by how professionally it is presented and enjoy the interactive and entertaining aspects. The audio-visual, inauguration-stone challenge and virtual-reality headsets stand out as highlights. A common response by visitors is surprise at what they see, especially locals who learn something new and leave with a renewed sense of pride of place.

On a visit to the MFE, Pat Durack, owner of Centra supermarket in Ferns, was really impressed by what he saw. When Pat came to Ferns in 2016, he was not aware of its terrific history. He was attracted to Ferns because he thought it provided a good business opportunity. At an early stage he did a tour of the castle and was fascinated. It saddens Pat to see 'run-down buildings' and he would love to see an improved streetscape in keeping with a village of such renown. He has plans to start renovations on his own business very soon: 'I really like the history of Ferns and want to build something in keeping with its history'. Commenting on his visit to the 'Experience', he said he loved the history of Mac Murchada:

> there's stuff there I didn't know – I had a brief bit of the history, about what he did but I didn't know how it began. I'd heard how he started off with kidnapping someone's wife, but I didn't know how it came about. I didn't realize her family had anything to do with it. It kind of humanizes him a bit because I had him down as some kind of evil king but now I think 'maybe he wasn't so bad'.

Pat suggested that if people were visiting Ferns for the historic side of things, they should start at the MFE,

> because you get the film which is really very good, it brings you back in time and you start thinking about the history … and coming into the inauguration stone, I think that's great, a bit of craic, a bit of fun and I think the guy from the Brehon Law is very official looking and good as well. The virtual-reality headset

> – amazing. To look at that first and then to go and look at the castle, the abbey and the other sites – it's the way to do it. To do it the other way around I think you'd be lost.

On developing tourism in Ferns, Pat would love to see music on the streets, maybe medieval, and he'd like to see the castle rebuilt to what it would have looked like when it was constructed in the thirteenth century. Now that's some ambition!

Elena Potosca arrived in Ferns in 2012. Originally from Romania, Elena came for love and is now working on the community employment scheme as part of the MFE team. She knew nothing of Ferns' history before she came but was delighted to hear it was an ancient capital of Leinster because she had grown up in the old capital of Romania, which was also known as the sunny south-east. Now *there's* a coincidence! Last year she volunteered to help prepare for the opening of the MFE. Since coming to Ferns Elena developed an interest in art and craft-making and she brought her innovative skills to great effect at Halloween (figs 15.9, 15.10). She worked with the team in making flying bats, creepy spiders and arrangements resulting in a spooky atmosphere admired by those who visited. One of the aims of the project was to use recycled items when possible. So, apart from the fun we had, it was also a low-cost exercise and we learned so much about repurposing simple household items into quirky, fun, Halloween decorations – lessons we will bring with us to future projects. Working side by side on projects such as this benefited everybody involved, each bringing their own skills to the project – a great team-building exercise.

Elena also volunteered at the community dig conducted by the IAFS in July/August 2020 and, while it was tough work at times, she was thrilled to be part of it:

> Getting to know the American students was a bonus – each learning from the other. In the beginning I found it difficult to get to know the terminology used but I soon got used to it and was excited every day at the prospect of finding something. Every day I wondered what I was going to find that day – you never knew what you might find … I found a very heavy rock that wasn't a rock, it was a piece of metal that got smoother over the years. Another piece looked like a pendant with red and black lines on it, like a necklace – I'm waiting to find out what exactly they are.

When Elena joined the MFE team she was not sure at first because she felt 'that I might be asked questions I wouldn't know the answers to. I thought, what am I taking on, there's a lot of history back there and I know so little and don't want to get it wrong'. Elena has settled in now and is delighted to be part of the team, all of whom shared her concerns about being asked questions and getting the answers wrong. 'I have people round me to help me to learn the steps needed and I actually enjoy

15.9 Ferns: Halloween event at Medieval Ferns Experience

15.10 Ferns: witch's apprentice at Halloween event at Medieval Ferns Experience, 2021

learning about the history here more than anywhere else'. Before she started, she was nervous because she'd never done anything like it before, but

> now I'm more confident, every day I learn something new, I know more of the story and I'm building up what I know. When customers come in now we have worked out a way of greeting them and showing them around, telling them what to expect and helping them enjoy their experience.

The MFE is a social enterprise that relies totally on volunteerism and community employment schemes and aspires to creating fulltime employment opportunities. Our wish-list for the future is as follows

- Space and facilities to allow artefacts found locally and currently stored in the National Museum of Ireland to come back 'home' for display and to be enjoyed by the local community and visitors;
- A digital representation showing the evolution of Ferns from early monastic settlement to its heyday in the tenth to twelfth centuries – this would transform visitors' experience of the various sites;

- A mechanism for explaining to the local community in a simple and engaging way the significance of the many exciting archaeological findings now being made (online and print media please!);
- Presenting the walls that were found during the recent digs to the public – either by conserving them so they can remain on view rather than being backfilled, or if it must be backfilled for protection, for the line of the wall to be reconstructed above ground in some way, as was undertaken at Ferrycarrig in the Irish National Heritage Park by the IAFS;
- That Ferns becomes a hub for interpretation of the interweave of Christian, Gaelic kingship and Anglo-Norman story;
- Access to the castle green for events – develop a system/template where discussions and permissions can be processed more quickly;
- Tapestries viewable all year round;
- Original 'footprint' of the cathedral interpreted in some way on-site;
- Continued support for our annual Ferns Medieval Conference from Wexford County Council;
- MFE expands and becomes a must-visit tourist attraction – an ideal introduction to understanding Wexford's medieval story.

We look to the future with optimism!

BIBLIOGRAPHY

Bhreathnach, E. and Dowling, G. 2021. 'Forming an episcopal see and an Augustinian foundation in medieval Ireland: the case of Ferns, Co. Wexford'. *Proceedings of the Royal Irish Academy*, 121C, 191–226.

Corlett, C. 2018. 'A knight on the tile'. *Archaeology Ireland*, 32:4, 23–4.

Logan, P. 1981. *Irish country cures*. Belfast.

Index

Compiled by Michael Ann Bevivino